Averting a Great Divergence

Averting a Great Divergence

State and Economy in Japan, 1868–1937

Peer Vries

BLOOMSBURY ACADEMIC
LONDON • NEW YORK • OXFORD • NEW DELHI • SYDNEY

BLOOMSBURY ACADEMIC
Bloomsbury Publishing Plc
50 Bedford Square, London, WC1B 3DP, UK
1385 Broadway, New York, NY 10018, USA
29 Earlsfort Terrace, Dublin 2, Ireland

BLOOMSBURY, BLOOMSBURY ACADEMIC and the Diana logo are
trademarks of Bloomsbury Publishing Plc

First published in Great Britain 2020
This paperback edition published in 2021

A catalogue record for this book is available from the British Library.

A catalog record for this book is available from the Library of Congress.

ISBN: HB: 978-1-3501-2167-6
       PB: 978-1-3501-9617-9
       ePDF: 978-1-3501-2168-3
       eBook: 978-1-3501-2169-0

Typeset by RefineCatch Limited, Bungay, Suffolk

To find out more about our authors and books visit www.bloomsbury.com
and sign up for our newsletters.

Contents

Introduction

Wildly differing opinions

It is now some twenty-five years that I have been studying the Great Divergence, particularly the role the state has played in it. This debate on the emerging of this huge global gap in wealth, development and growth, and thus on the origins of modern economic growth, has long focused on comparing China and North-western Europe, in particular Great Britain, in the early modern era. That is striking because, as has become increasingly clear, the differences between these two societies were actually so numerous and big, that comparing them is not very informative when it comes to explaining what caused one of them to industrialize whereas the other did not. The world of 'surprising resemblances', in the famous expression by Kenneth Pomeranz, actually has proved to be a world of fundamental differences. That makes it a fruitless endeavour to try and isolate causally relevant factors via comparison of these regions.[1] Fortunately, in recent research other world regions and countries have also been taken on board.[2] Although it would be an exaggeration to claim that the case of Japan has been and is still being ignored, it is fair to say that it is much less present in the debate than one would expect.[3] After all, it was the first country outside the West that went through a process of industrialization, commencing in the nineteenth century. A student of the origins of modern economic growth can only profit from analysing this case of a major, non-Western country that managed not to fall further behind in the nineteenth century.

The Japanese case is even more interesting, for me at least, as it provides an excellent testing ground for all sorts of claims about the role of the state in fostering or hampering the emergence of modern economic growth. That is a highly debated issue, not just in general but also, as we will see, in the case of Japan's history since at least the Meiji Restoration. As in all my work, I will focus on the period of 'transition', in this case the period when Japan's economy 'took off' and 'modern economic growth' emerged. More concretely, that boils down to studying the period when the country's 'industrialization' took place.[4] Traditionally that has always been the Meiji era, 1868–1912. That seems justified. Indeed, there can be no discussion that the Meiji Restoration was a period in the economic history of Japan when economic growth accelerated sharply and all the features associated with industrialization became prominent. Any study of the origins of modern economic growth in Japan will have to give a very prominent position to the Meiji era.

A growing group of scholars, however, holds the view that the Meiji Restoration was less of a break for Japan's economy than has long been claimed and that the economic spurt after 1868 would have been inconceivable without developments that had already taken place in the Tokugawa era, 1603–1868. The picture of Tokugawa Japan, that has long been rather bleak, has changed substantially and many scholars now claim that Japan's take-off under Meiji rule cannot be understood without studying 'the Tokugawa legacy'. Although, as will be apparent in my text, I think that there has emerged a tendency to hold too rosy a view of the economy and society of Tokugawa Japan, the 'revisionists' undoubtedly had a point. Tokugawa Japan's economy was more developed and dynamic than scholars focusing on the Meiji Restoration as a completely new beginning have long been willing to admit. I have therefore decided to systematically extend my analysis backwards – at least in those cases where that might make sense. Actually, most of my comments with regard to the pre-Meiji period will pertain to the second half of the Tokugawa reign.

Going back several centuries in time in my view is not very helpful, even though certain quite influential scholars do so and emphasize that Japan had already been 'like the West' and thus endowed with more dynamism long before the Meiji or even Tokugawa era. Yosaburo Takekoshi, the author of the influential and voluminous *The economic aspects of the history of Japan*, in another publication from 1939, claimed:

Japan has become a world power as a result, not of achievements of half a century or so, but of the developments made along the same path of progress, as has been followed by the peoples of the oldest history of Europe.[5]

Tadao Umesao, another quite influential author, in his *Ecological view of history*, wrote the following sentences that concisely express what he thinks about Japan's position in the world:

There are two regions of the Old World that remained unscathed by the violence emanating from the dry centre. These lie at the eastern and western extremes of the Eurasian continent: western Europe at the one end, and Japan at the other. In these areas civilization was nurtured in relative security. The very similar ecological circumstances of western Europe and Japan caused them to follow parallel paths of historical development. It was these two regions that fostered the development of modern civilization while regions such as China India, Russia and the Islamic world suffered the misfortune of repeated destruction.[6]

If Japan had not isolated itself in the seventeenth century, so he thinks, it would have industrialized at about the same time as Great Britain. Interesting as such perspectives of the *longue durée* may be, I think discussing periods further back in time than the Tokugawa period will not provide concrete extra information for answering the questions I would like to answer.

There is of course also the question of when to stop. On the basis of my reading, it seems there is a general consensus that with the end of World War One Japan was no longer a traditional pre-industrial society, or, for that matter, a weak state. All the usual indicators, e.g. growth rates of GDP or of production in manufacturing, the introduction of modern technology and sources of energy, point in that direction.[7] A decision to stop there would certainly have been tenable. But in the end, I decided to pursue my analysis till 1937, the year in which Japan's economy was turned into a war economy and Japan entered an escalating war which fundamentally changed its economy as well as the role of the state in it.[8] During my research, I became convinced that extending the period by twenty-five years after the end of Meiji rule would enable me to get a better view on structural transformations and continuities than only looking at the Meiji era and the period of World War One. I can only hope that the reader will, at the end of my book, agree.

So much about the demarcation in time, what about demarcation in space? Considering what is probably the most consequential change in historiography over the last decades, the rise of global history, it would be inexcusable not to set developments in Japan in a wider geographical context. Much of what happened in Japan in its period of economic acceleration cannot, or cannot optimally, be understood without reference to an 'international' context. Where possible and relevant I will try and trace international or even global 'connections'. Most global history is either connecting or comparing. Comparisons will play a crucial role in my analysis. The question of course then immediately poses itself: to what countries should industrializing Japan be compared? I decided to systematically compare information with regard to Japan in the period 1868–1937 with information with regard to several countries that successfully industrialized, the United Kingdom (Great Britain or Britain, depending on the available data), Germany and France, all of them countries that had gone through a process of industrialization and that were not too different from Japan in size and population. There will also be frequent comparisons to countries that did *not* industrialize. Here the comparisons will be more ad-hoc. Many countries at the time were not independent states but colonies or otherwise non-sovereign polities. That means that they did not have a state of their own that could influence their industrialization. Many countries, often the same ones, clearly were not in a position to industrialize as they were too poor and too underdeveloped. For many countries, again often the same ones, we do not have enough trustworthy data to make helpful comparisons. My choice of cases to compare in this context has been pragmatic and based on a wish to keep the analysis manageable and concrete. Via comparisons of economic *outcomes* and state *inputs* in different countries I hope to be able to chart to what extent Japan's state made a positive contribution to the country's economic development and learn more about the role of the state in 'catching up, forging ahead, and falling behind' in general.[9]

Most of my comparisons will be synchronic, in *chronological* time. They will juxtapose phenomena at the same moment in chronological time. That means that what went on in Japan at a certain point in time, say 1868–1937, is being compared to what went on in other countries at the same time. Several comparisons, however, will be synchronic in what I call *historical* time. That means that what went on in Japan at a certain moment in time, let us again say between 1868 and 1937, is compared to what went on in other countries when they were in a similar stage or at a similar level of their development. The reason for using these two kinds of comparisons is that they can complement each other. A country that catches up by definition started later, which should be taken into account, but on the other hand it is always contemporaneous with the countries it wants to catch up with, which determines to what extent it has indeed caught up.

My focus is on the importance of the state, not only of its explicit economic policies but also – and deliberately because I think these get far too little attention in the literature on comparative industrialization – of the economic implications of simply having or not having a certain kind of state with a certain structure, institutions and capabilities. In my analysis, I have tried as much as possible to underpin my claims with figures. I realize that many of these figures are and can only be approximations or estimates, in particular those referring to Tokugawa Japan, which moreover are often not easy to compare. I therefore as a rule use them as rough indicators of orders of magnitude and changes over time.

I have written this book even though I am not a Japanologist and do not read Japanese. That certainly is a risky endeavour but there are several reasons why I nevertheless decided to write it. Firstly, the book does not pretend much. Nowhere do I pretend to do original historical primary research or to come up with new original data about the history of Japan. I have confined myself to the – in my view extremely useful – task of charting, synthesizing and interpreting the information I could gather about Japan's state in languages that I do read, comparing those findings with those for other countries and trying to come to conclusions with regard to the economic history of Japan, but also more in general with regard to the question why Japan ended up 'at the good side' of the Great Divergence. I will certainly have missed some new insights and facts, and misinterpreted matters only accessible to the *cognoscenti*. But doesn't everyone who is dealing with such a big topic? The topic examined in this book is an important one, which to my knowledge has not been dealt with in the way I do so here. I hope, and firmly believe, as a form of compensation I can bring to bear my ample experience in studying the role of the state in other contexts in so much of my previous work. My book in 'Popperian' terms is a 'conjecture'. Everyone is free to try and refute it.[10] If one cannot, on the basis of an enormous amount of literature available in English, but also French, German and Dutch, write a decent textbook-like text on the role of the state in Japan's economic development, what then – of course my own errors aside – is the value of all that literature?

I will not start my book with the obligatory exhaustive overview of debates on the role of the state in economic development in general, nor for that matter in the economic history of Japan. Both topics have led to huge amounts of literature, in particular of course the first one in which just about any conceivable position has been defended. For debates on the role of the state in economic development in general, I will refer to literature when relevant and helpful. The number of publications on that topic, as to be expected, is limitless. I do not want to burden this text with wide theoretical excursions that in all probability would not only be fairly vacuous but also fairly repetitious as I have made my general position clear in many publications.[11] In this text I really want to be empirical and try to focus on representing basic data and let them speak for themselves. I am not so simplistic as to actually believe data can just speak for themselves. But considering the fact that when it comes to the role of the state in economic development there are so many preconceived ideas, I am willing to err on the side of naïve empiricism.[12]

This importance of Japan's state for economic development in the period 1868 to 1937 has been heavily debated, with scholars and observers of various kinds taking very – or, rather, incredibly – different positions and with major shifts occurring over time. In this chapter I will present a fairly random selection of quotes just to show *how* different positions have been, varying from the claim that the state would be the key to explaining Japan's economic development at the time to the claim that its importance in this respect was fairly minor, negligible or even negative. In that way, I hope to show that my analysis is not a matter of repeating what everyone already agrees upon. The importance of the state for Japan's economic development in that period is heavily contested. I also will not give a traditional, extensive historiographical survey. My approach here is formal and analytical, not historical. I just want to show the broadest possible spectrum of claims that has been put forward to then structure my argumentation in response to them.

There is a long tradition of suggesting the role of the state was fundamental and positive. Let me begin with some observations by foreign commentators. Already after Japan's victory against China and even more against Russia, foreign commentators connected Japan's military strength with its economic strength and both in turn with the way the country was ruled.[13] At a time when Western economies were hit by the Great Depression, foreign observers and scholars looked with a fascination at Japan where the economy apparently was more resistant to crisis and again pointed at the prominent positive role of the state in the country's impressively and certainly also frighteningly successful industrialization.[14] After World War Two the idea that Japan's industrialization was organized from above found its way into several very influential scholarly publications. I just refer to texts by E. Herbert Norman, George Allen and Thomas Smith.[15]

No person has put as big a stamp on the debates on the economic impact of Japan's state as Chalmers Johnson. He became famous thanks to his 1982 book on MITI and its industrial policy, in which he coined the phrase 'developmental state' and claimed Japan was one in the period discussed in that book because its rulers systematically gave priority to economic development. In his own words, 'the essence of the argument' of his book is the claim that 'credit for the post-war Japanese economic 'miracle' should go primarily to conscious and consistent government policies dating at least from the 1920s.[16] He focused on the post-1945 period but his ideas have been taken to apply also to earlier periods. Scholars such as Sidney Crawcour, Christopher Howe or Ian Inkster, to refer to just three acknowledged experts in the field of Japanese economic history, also frequently refer to the major – or even crucial – 'developmental' role of the state.[17]

All references so far were to non-Japanese. Many Japanese, however, agreed. In the work of Kaname Akamatsu (1896–1974), whose ideas about economic growth have become widely known, also outside Japan, the fundamental importance of state protection for the successful catching up of Japan cannot be overlooked.[18] Kyoko Sheridan in her book from 1993, *Governing the Japanese economy*, emphasized Japan's government's crucial role and claimed that 'unaided market forces' did not determine Japan's economic development.[19] In 1994 Kunio Yoshihara wrote:

The Japanese government's economic policy has been far from *laissez-faire*. Free market economists who believe that an economy performs best without government intervention give the impression that all countries, which have succeeded in economic development, had a laissez-faire government or a government, which was not actively involved in the economy. This, however, was not true of Japan.[20]

He then refers to government's model industries, the big share of government enterprise in the production of iron, steel machinery and armaments, its major responsibility for the construction of railways, communication facilities and infrastructure projects, and to a relatively large share of government in total investment. Chushichi Tsuzuki in his *The pursuit of power in modern Japan* from 2000 basically simply paraphrases George Allen's positive comments.[21]

But not everyone has been so positive. Several scholars have been more sceptical. David Flath, writer of a widely used textbook on the Japanese economy, sums up many examples of the Meiji government's encouragement of industry by referring to its pilot plants, the hiring of foreign experts, the heavy investment in railroads and telecommunications, the subsidies for ocean shipping and shipbuilding, the establishing of the first integrated steel factory in Japan but concludes 'it is hard to view any of these efforts as essential' and goes on to claim that 'the government promotion of steel and shipbuilding may have served a military purpose but was largely irrelevant to the main thrust of entrepreneurial activity in Japan'.[22] He clearly does not eschew firm statements as shown in this (somewhat caricatured) contrast: 'The spirit of the Meiji era was one of *laissez faire*, not government control.'[23] About the post-World War Two situation he writes: 'Industrial policy made virtually no measurable contribution to Japan's post-war economic growth.'[24] Considering these claims this programmatic statement will not come as a surprise: 'In spite of the country's fascinating strangeness, the principles of economics (i.e. mainstream neo-classical economics P.V.) apply in Japan as elsewhere.'[25] Frank B. Tipton, Jr. in his skeptical evaluation had already in 1981 pointed out: 'When the central government attempted to introduce new technologies, it generally failed. In fact, monetary and credit policies probably hindered development.'[26] Jim Powell in 2012 did not beat about the bush either. According to him it was entrepreneurs who created the great boom that made modern Japan during the Meiji era *not* Japan's rulers. Beyond protecting private property, providing an essential legal framework and eliminating many barriers to enterprise, the Japanese government was actually a minor player. There were dozens of government-owned businesses, but almost all of them lost money and were subsequently privatized. Prestigious heavy industries favoured by the government never added as much value as humble light industries such as textiles that thrived with few subsidies.[27] In his opinion Japan's economy really began to flourish after the 1880s, when it had acquired a pro-free market culture.[28]

In Japan too, one can find sceptical views. Let me again use quotes to give a flavour of the kind of arguments presented. Proponents of a rather negative view often explicitly refer to what they consider to be the negative impact of the Japanese government's military expenditures. Harry Oshima (not actually Japanese! bi-nationality) for example not only qualifies the role of, in his case Meiji Japan's government, but on top of that points out the negative effects of the fact that Meiji rulers extracted so much money from agriculture to then use it 'relatively unproductively for military purposes'.[29] Ryoshin Minami describes war and its preparation, which was so important in Meiji policies, as 'a waste of money'.[30] Yasukichi Yasuba endorses that view, stating that in any case during the period 1859–1899, when in his view Japan's economy was on the right track, it would have been 'close to … laissez-faire':

> The economy in this period (1859–1899 P.V.) was close to a laissez-faire one despite the contention of many historians to the contrary. The slogan of *fukoku kyohei* (the rich nation and the strong military) is at fault. It certainly suggests that the government must have played an important role, but actually the government was very small by any standard. The proportion of the expenditure of the central government in GNP was only 7.9 per cent in 1888–92, somewhat larger than in Great Britain (6.0 per cent) but much smaller than in Italy (13.2 per cent) or Sweden (12.5 per cent) for the same period. Even the size of the military expenditure (the strong military) was small at least until the Sino-Japanese War. The military expenditure as a proportion of GNP, 2.3 per cent in 1888–92, was smaller than the figure of 2.7 per cent in 1954–56 under the 'Peace Constitution'. Since many of the naval vessels were imported in this period, the strain on natural resources coming from the military expenditure must have been minimal.[31]

When government intervention increased again in the 1930s, in his view that was not a positive development.

Unsurprisingly, I am tempted to say, not all scholars endorse the claim that military spending would be bad for economic development. In a forthcoming publication Kyoji Fukao and Tokihiko Settsu, who think that overall 'public expenditures… played a crucial role in key areas such as the creation of the railroad network, the modernization of maritime transportation, and the introduction of postal and telegraph systems as well as a national banking system' not only connect economic booms to increases in government expenditure in infrastructures but also and explicitly point at the stimulating effects of government expenditures for wars, e.g. the ones with China (1894–1895), Russia (1904–1905) and later, beginning in 1937, again with China.[32] In the, in my view inconclusive, debate about the overall economic impact of military spending in Japan, in any case before the Asian Pacific War they are not the only ones who have come up with a rather positive assessment.[33]

Unsurprisingly many others seem to be of two minds: Lockwood, in his impressive study of the economic development of Japan between 1868 and World War Two, first published in 1954, was fairly prudent:

> The existence of a strong central government infused with imperial ambitions served in some respects to stimulate and facilitate the process (of modernization and industrialization P.V.); in other respects it operated as a decided drag; in still other respects it had little direct influence on what took place.[34]

In his opinion, 'the real drive and momentum of Japan's economic growth lay in large measure outside the realm of national political ambition and state activity'.[35] He is convinced that without 'the exercise of personal initiative and entrepreneurial responsibility ... the imperial ambitions of Japan's rulers would never have achieved any material foundation'.[36] Henry Rosovsky, writing in 1961, still thought the matter was 'undecided':

> although scholars generally share the view that government influence was widely felt throughout the economy. Most of the opinions are not backed by macro-economic facts – one can believe almost what one chooses, tending toward either extreme or the other.[37]

He then set out to provide that macro-economic data and focused on government investment. This led him to underline the heavy share of government in gross domestic fixed capital formation and to claim 'there can be no doubt about the unusual weight of public investment'.[38]

David Landes also seemed fairly ambivalent. He published an extensive comparison of the role of the state in economic development in Japan and Germany in 1965 and did not come to an unequivocal conclusion, which is somewhat surprising as he did emphasize the fact that government was responsible for an important share of gross domestic fixed capital formation; described government enterprises after the collapse of Tokugawa rule as 'serious and an indispensable prodrome to subsequent industrial advance' and pointed out that many government activities and investments occurred in the period of time in between those in which industrializing follower countries 'perceived the necessity and opportunity of an industrial revolution and the time when human and material resources and the institutional structure made such a revolution feasible'.[39] Carl Mosk, who dedicated so many studies to the economic development of modern Japan, is surprisingly reticent when it comes to making explicit claims about the role of the state in his *Japanese economic development* of 2008, whereas he was very outspokenly positive about it in his *Japanese industrial history* of 2001.[40]

Many scholars claim that one should not exaggerate the importance of government policies as against that of private enterprise. Admittedly, those policies may have been important in *enabling* development and growth but, so they claim, they would have been of no avail without specific responses and initiatives of private enterprise. Besides, so such critics often add, important parts of the economy developed and created growth with no or hardly any government support. Tessa Morris-Suzuki succinctly writes that the most important point to make about the state-centred approach, is that 'it is not the whole story'.[41] Janet Hunter seems to agree. For her, the scenario 'growth from above' is 'far from telling the whole story'.[42] She dedicates an extensive discussion to the role of the state and considers it very important but then in the end claims 'its significance lay largely in enabling the private sector to innovate and prosper'.[43] Kenneth Brown is more explicit and pursues this line of reasoning an important step further by flatly rejecting the claim that government intervention has been the main cause of Japan's progress: 'Growth was sustained primarily by small-scale, labour-intensive enterprises in the towns and countryside, rather than by government initiatives and big factories.' In the last analysis economic success depended, so he writes, 'on the response of private firms and individuals who proved receptive to modernization and organized themselves accordingly.'[44] Penelope Francks also holds a plea for more emphasis on 'the mass of small-scale and more labour-using household-based producers' and adds that 'the growth of by far the most important of Japan's nineteenth-century industries, silk and cotton textiles, was the result of a large amount of small-scale investment, much of it coming from rural and urban trading, landowning and early industrial interests.'[45] Agov, to give one last example, thinks that successful industrialization gave rise to overestimation of the role of the government. In his view, it is true that the involvement of the Meiji leaders was essential to the changes, but not as engineers of industrialization. Industrialization took place as a result of the interplay between macroeconomic and infrastructural (physical and legal) frameworks and the dynamics of private enterprise. The government was not creator of industrialization, rather facilitator. It was successful precisely because it learned what constructive steps it could take in order to assist in economic growth. In the end, so he claims, the real engine of industrialization was private business.[46] Qualifying the importance of government with these scholars at times tends to come close to denying it.

It is not only non-Japanese who (strongly) qualify the importance of the state for Japan's economic development. According to Mikiso Hane, 'The government did play a very significant role in the industrialization of Meiji Japan', but, so he explicitly adds, 'it was not the only force that was to contribute to a transformation of the economy'.[47] Ryoshin Minami claims that the 'basic attitude of the government after this period (i.e. the early Meiji period P.V.) was *laissez-faire*'. In his view, 'the importance of the actions of the government to Japanese industrialization has been overrated'.[48] Tomoka Hashino and Osamu Saito, in their overview of the literature on the history of Japan's industry, also tone down the importance of central government and emphasize the importance of small-scale enterprises and of local and regional governments.[49] Tetsuro Nakaoka emphasizes that the transplanting of technology by the Meiji government often failed and basically only worked when it harmonized with local domestic factors which, in their turn, changed under the influence of the transplanted foreign technology.[50] Kenichi Ohno points out that the role of the private sector was more important: 'While the official policies of introducing western institutions, building infrastructure, hiring foreign advisors, education and training, establishing state owned enterprises and research centres, organizing trade fairs, assisting *zaibatsu* and so on were important, it should be stressed that private sector dynamism was even more essential.' He then adds: 'Without … private sector capability, even good policies would have failed to produce results.'[51] My last example of a Japanese scholar who tends to tone down the importance of government is Akira Hayami:

> In Meiji Japan, as illustrated by the setting-up of government-run factories in the early years, the agent promoting industrialization was the government, but within a relatively short period of time, most of them were sold off to the private sector, and it is an indisputable fact that private-sector entrepreneurs became the principal actors. While the government-industry relations are often said to have been close

as compared to those in Western Europe, Japan's industrialization itself was brought about by competition in the market place.[52]

According to Hayami, the Meiji government Japan could 'leave it to competition among private-sector companies and agents in the market place' to develop the country because Japan already was an economic society, i.e. 'a society where the people of a country, down to the common people, can act in an economic manner'.[53] He does not deny though that state intervention would have played a substantial role in Japan's industrialization.[54]

The core of many of the qualifying claims of which we just presented some examples consists in the emphasis on the fact that the state did not 'do it' alone and could not have done so. There are several other critiques that I, for the sake of completeness, want to briefly mention here too. One lies in the comment that the policies of the Meiji state after the Restoration were not as new as scholars emphasizing the rupture of that Restoration like to suggest. Tessa Morris-Suzuki, for example, writes 'the government often relied less on radically new ideas than on reinterpretations of old concepts to suit new circumstances.'[55] But she is – as we will see repeatedly in this book – only one of a growing group of scholars who emphasize the existing continuity between Meiji and Tokugawa Japan.

Several scholars who want to qualify the importance of the state for Japan's economic development also point out that a lot of government support was not coming from *central* but from *local* and *regional* government. For them, it will not do to look at Japan's industrialization from an exclusively top-down perspective as that would ignore the importance of social networks for understanding Japan's economic developments and innovations.[56] Another point of critique on the traditionally rather heavy focus on the state – the last one to be discussed here – regards the fact that the policies of the successive governments in the period 1868–1937 would not have been the outcome of any predetermined, explicit and consistent plan but to a large extent were a matter of pragmatic and even ad hoc decisions. Government policies often changed fairly abruptly. In short, there would have never been a rational master plan. To again quote Tessa Morris-Suzuki: 'the Meiji government did not (as sometimes implied) possess preternatural foresight and vision in its pursuit of technological modernization.'[57] It learned by doing and it made many mistakes. In Kenneth Brown's words: 'It cannot be assumed … that those responsible for formulating Japan's economic policy in the Restoration period had a clearly thought out, consistent program which was successfully implemented.'[58] In his view, 'Meiji governments set out to modernize the country, although it is debatable as to whether the creation of an appropriate infrastructure can be regarded as the equivalent of conscious economic planning.'[59] Penelope Francks too has her doubts about 'the degree of planning and the efficacy of the state's actions' and thinks 'one should beware of overemphasizing … the extent to which the Meiji state pursued a concerted and successful industrial-policy strategy'.[60] Several Japanese scholars share this scepticism. One example would be Miwa Yoshiro, author of *Japan's economic planning and mobilization in wartime, 1930–1940s*, who on the back-flap of the book is described as a 'leading sceptic' of Chalmers Johnson. In the book, he discusses 'the competence of the (Japanese P.V.) state' to conclude it was only a 'myth'.[61] Miwa is not the only one having such doubts. Osamu Saito also has them:

> Since the political scientist Chalmers Johnson coined the term 'developmental state', an interventionist state whose *raison d'etre* is the attainment of economic development . . ., Japan's economic success has often been considered a product of the state's planning and guidance. The early Meiji government's industry promotion and the post Second Wold War Ministry of International Trade and Industry (MITI)s industrial policy are said to have been particularly effective and exemplary. However, the early Meiji policy models resulted in a total failure.[62]

Let me briefly address in any case all those qualifying comments that I have presented in the previous pages on a more *methodical* level before embarking, from chapter 2 onwards, on an *empirical* overview and assessment of the importance of the state in Japan's economic development.

When it comes to the emphasis on the importance of the private sector, I would want to point out that no one, not even the fiercest defender of the thesis that Japan would have been a 'developmental' state, claims it thus was a non-capitalist economy, in the sense of an economy where the market-mechanism and private enterprise would have been abolished, or in any case made so small as to become irrelevant at the level of the economy as a whole. Chalmers Johnson himself never said or implied that the state was *solely* (italics in the original P.V.) responsible for Japan's achievement or that it behaved like the state in command economies.[63] In principle, developmental policies by the state were meant to create enterprises that in the end could profitably survive in the market without state support and they actually were implemented in a way to reach that goal. For him, the developmental state clearly is 'capitalist'.[64] In Japan the state never abolished the market economy. Far from it, the bulk of economic activity was and continued to be private initiative co-ordinated by a market. Notwithstanding the many activities and interventions of government that impacted on Japan's economy and notwithstanding the fact that there were important state-run factories Japan's economy clearly was an economy dominated by private property, private enterprise, commodification in which supply and demand strongly impacted on prices. It was a country with, overall, decentralized economic decisions. An explanation of Japan's take-off therefore cannot be confined to referring to the central state; no scholar who uses the concept 'developmental state' in analysing the country's economic development would endorse such an approach and, as the reader can see for him- or herself, I will not either.[65]

Scholars formulating the critique that the state-centred approach is one-sided, usually, in order to lend further support to their argument, refer to the immense importance of small, traditional firms that till the end of the period under discussion here employed the bulk of the manufacturing labour force, produced a very substantial share of total GDP and for decades provided the bulk of Japan's (semi-) manufactured exports. The major importance of this kind of traditional, mostly labour-intensive industry is undeniable, as is the fact that they profited less from direct or indirect government support than big, more capital-intensive firms. But in my view the fact that the role of the state indeed is not as overarching as the 'industrialization-from-above-thesis', claims, should not lead to erring in the opposite direction. Firstly, those small- and medium-sized firms certainly *also* profited from the way in which the state functioned and from state policies, in particular those with regard to the material and institutional infrastructure of the country, the transfer of knowledge via education and otherwise, healthcare and all sorts of standardization and quality control. My analysis in the rest of this book will provide ample examples in support of this claim. My second argument is the fact that, relatively small, labour-intensive, or as I would prefer to call them, 'labour-absorbing' industries, inevitably run into decreasing returns and are bound to become dead-end streets. *Sustained* growth in the period under discussion in this book increasingly depended on major increases in productivity that required large capital-, energy- and technology-intensive production units. This general 'rule' also applied to the case of industrializing Japan, as I will try and prove in my forthcoming book on Japan's supposedly labour-intensive industrialization.[66] In the case of Japan, smaller firms could and indeed did less and less function as the main motors of development and growth, and there too, growth increasingly was a result of higher capital-, energy- and technology-intensity. For the emergence and functioning of capital-, energy- and technology-intensive production state 'support' in any case for Japan, but I would claim everywhere, was essential.

My point of departure, that I of course will try and substantiate in this and the following book just referred to, is that the emerging of modern economic growth requires a certain *kind* of firm that cannot easily develop spontaneously in underdeveloped countries. In that sense, as will be shown frequently in this text, I have certainly been influenced by the ideas of Alexander Gerschenkron, without, however, in any way claiming that Japan would be a perfect showcase for his ideas.[67] I fully endorse Joe Studwell's claim that: 'no big countries . . . have become rich off the back of small firms.'[68] To substantially increase the wealth of an economy the size of Japan's, substantial investments in manufacturing plants with a maximum efficient scale, in managerial and technological capabilities and in marketing are unavoidable, as Alice Amsden rightly emphasizes. In her view, an economy that tries to compete via low wages and hard work soon enters a dead-end street leading to pauperization. It simply cannot be a match for economies where innovation is the source of increasing productivity.[69] An economy that wants to catch up and have sustained and substantial economic growth simply cannot persist in producing low-added value, primary goods in highly competitive markets. It has to try and upgrade itself to producing high-added value goods for markets in which it can have some leverage, as Erik Reinert in my view convincingly argues.[70] Producing such goods and creating such markets requires high investment and innovation. Those in turn require a sophisticated material and institutional infrastructure and highly skilled labour, which in turn require a developmental state. It is not by accident that 'upgrading' production is at the core of Akamatsu's famous flying-geese model of Japanese economic growth.[71] I fail to see how such upgrading could have been realized in the case of Japan without substantial state intervention and steering – that may be unprofitable in the short run – and without substantial capital accumulation that in turn is hard to realize in a context of free and fair competition. Ian Inkster, in my view with good reason, points out that it would in all probability have been all but impossible for Japan's producers to upgrade their production if Japan's state had been weak:

> (the) actual workings of the Akamatsu model depended on the retention of economic sovereignty, particularly the move from government instigation of import substitution activity (1881–1896) towards protection of infant industries (1896–1914), an impossible shift in the absence of the gaining of tariff autonomy during 1897–1899, a result of official political, commercial and diplomatic activity whose character and effectiveness lies beyond the reach of formal economics.[72]

Upgrading implies import substitution which usually requires some protection, fairly large sums of capital and risky investment. It is not by accident that in Japan the state intervened in the market mechanism, by *allowing* and at times actively *promoting* market distortion through its support of specific sectors of the economy and of forms of monopoly and oligopoly. My comments, I would like to emphasize, are not meant to deny the contribution of labour-intensive and small-scale production to the growth of Japan's economy. I just want to point out that in the longer run labour-intensive growth in small firms peters out and that the state tends to play a very important role in efforts to avoid that. It in any case did so with unmistakable success in Japan.

The comment that the Meiji Restoration was not in all respects the major break with the past as which it is often presented and that, also when it comes to government policies, there were (certain) clear continuities with the preceding Tokugawa era in my view is simply correct. In this text, the reader will time and again find references to such continuities and similarities. In particular in the last decades of Tokugawa rule many initiatives were taken at the level of 'national' government and even more so at that of certain domains that can be considered precedents of government policies after the Restoration. In that respect too, Tokugawa Japan was not lacking in dynamism and development. But all that of course does not as such refute my thesis that after the Restoration the state had a fundamental part in Japan's transition to modern economic growth; nor does the mere fact that there was a lot of continuity exclude that with the Restoration certain things indeed changed revolutionary, even if it would only be in terms of scale and scope and official institutional arrangements. I hope to be able to show that all continuities notwithstanding, the state after Restoration in many respects changed fundamentally and instigated many unprecedented and portentous changes.

When it comes to the 'criticism' referring to the importance of local and regional governments, I think we can be brief: in post-Restoration Japan, these governments were well funded and well provided with personnel and they indeed took many fundamental initiatives, or were crucial to their implementation.[73] In the literature, initiatives and activities below central-state level get increasing attention and deservedly so. But both local and regional governments are part of what we call 'the government' of a country, so it would in my view be wrong to construct a sharp contrast between them and central government or look at their respective activities in terms of a zero-sum game.

The comments that government policies were much more improvised and much more *ad hoc* than in any case Chalmers Johnson's expression 'plan rational' would suggest, as such also are correct. The expression 'plan rational' to describe the strategy of the Japanese developmental state, is not a lucky one, the less so the earlier in the period one refers to.[74] Not only because it evokes the image of a centrally planned communist economy, which Japan evidently wasn't, as Johnson himself has emphasized; but also, because, as Osamu Saito correctly points out, the information as well as the macro-economic knowledge and concepts needed to rationally 'plan', were simply lacking.[75] Japan's rulers at the time we discuss here certainly did not have detailed 'econometrically specified', macro-economic plans: they had ideas, convictions, priorities and visions. Those in my view were quite influential and in their core quite stable – even though in their concrete implementation there have been even major switches – and they always centred around 'development'. Saito's suggestion, but that is just a comment on the side, that nowadays we know much more about the economy and thus would be able to better 'plan', strikes me as quite optimistic.

Obviously, over a period of some seventy years, there were conflicts and disagreements about how to reach 'development' and many changes of policy, voluntarily or forced upon Japan's rulers by shortage of money to make or sustain investments, by lack of profits, by all sorts of practical often unforeseen problems and of course because they simply had made wrong decisions. The Meiji Restoration and what came after it was not the systematic implementation of a pre-set masterplan by a specific group of ideologues, let alone a specific group of economic experts, although the role of experts became more prominent. Much of its outcomes were a matter of coincidences, accidents, trial and error, expected *and* unexpected outcomes, all with an (il-)logic of their own. In the 1860s there actually were at least three major camps debating Japan's future: the so-called imperial camp, the so-called shogunal camp and the so-called camp of public discussion. The people who took over power from the Shogunate – or the *Bakufu* (I will use these words interchangeably) – were anything but a coherent political entity.[76] There was much improvising and trial and error.[77] One of the most frequent criticisms of Meiji government policy making was the claim that 'a decree issued this morning is changed in the evening'.[78] One should not forget, for example, that in 1870, Japan still was a 'federal state system'. Even at the beginning of 1871, the Meiji leaders did not consider it urgent to abolish the domains, although the conviction existed that it would be a good idea. Controversy and policy changes continued to characterize economic policies over the entire period under discussion in this book. There were controversies about specifics and – in particular between the military and the world of business – about whether the primacy would have to be with the 'rich nation' or the 'strong army'; about the *extent* to which government should interfere, for example between developmentalist bureaucrat *par excellence* Okubo Toshimichi (1830–1878) and Matsukata Masayoshi (1835–1924), famous and notorious for his policies of austerity, or about the *sectors* of the economy that government should focus upon.[79] See, in that respect, for example the controversy between Maeda Masana (1850–1921) and (again) Matsukata who disagreed whether government should support small-scale agriculture and traditional industry and trust the market, local knowledge and initiatives (Maeda) *or* focus on large-scale infrastructure and heavy industry, employing a top-down approach (Matsukata).[80] In 1881 there was a shift towards more deflationist and 'austerity' politics. Meiji leaders in favour of free trade were ousted from positions and substituted by persons more inspired by the example of Germany and by mercantilist, i.e. nationalist economic ideas. A similar shift occurred at universities and in ministries. Many proponents of Westernization were side-tracked.[81]

There were controversies about *fiscal and monetary policies*, that at times tended to be 'Keynesian' and inflationary and at times tight and deflationary.[82] Just think of the difference between the policies of Takahashi Korekiyo (1854–1936) and his deflationist predecessor, finance minister Inoue Junnosuke (1869–1932), who made Japan return to the gold standard in 1929. There were differences of opinion about the choice of a *monetary standard* that was changed several times between the Restoration and the 1930s. Japan effectively had been on a gold standard since 1772. In 1858, when the country was opened economically, that became unsustainable as its gold to silver ratio (five to one) was so different from that in the West (fifteen to one) and gold massively left the country. This led to a situation in which the country *de facto* was on a silver standard. The Shogunate reacted by minting silver and copper coins. In 1863, more than half of the Shogunate's annual income came from minting. In 1870 the conviction still reigned that the silver standard would be better for Japan. In 1871, however, 'to follow the general trend', it was decided to adopt the gold standard. In 1878, the government permitted the silver yen, which was previously minted for international trade only, to be used in domestic transactions and payment of taxation. That meant Japan from then on *de facto* was again on a silver standard.[83] In 1897 there was a switch to a gold standard. In 1917 the yen started to float; a policy to return to a gold standard at the old parity of one dollar equals two yen was finally successful when in 1930 the embargo on exporting gold was lifted, but was then again left in 1931.[84] There were constant debates about 'social policies' and the extent to which one should protect certain sectors of the economy, e.g. rice agriculture and about the extent to which certain *zaibatsu* should be spared. Business and the military did not always agree, nor for that matter did the army and the navy. But here too, all those controversies and changes in policy did not alter the overall priority of government, i.e. the will to develop Japan and make it and its economy stronger.

Much more importantly: What interests me in the end is the *impact* of the existing state and its policies on Japan's economy. That is what over time and at a macro-level matters for development. What exactly state agents intended and why, and whether their ideas were coherent, consistent for that question is of secondary importance. The same goes for the question whether or not one wants to consider the policies that were implemented morally 'correct' or not and whether in the end Japan's rulers primarily wanted to develop the state rather than the economy. My focus is on the *outcome* of agency and on the effects of the structures it created.

Personally, I have a fairly outspoken position in the debate on the role of the state in economic development in general and that of Japan between 1868 and 1937 in particular. In my view that role was fundamental in the sense that without it Japan would not have known such a substantial economic growth over consecutive decades. The type of growth that Japan knew in the period from the late 1860s to the late 1930s depended on: 1) a sophisticated, extended and thus expensive material and institutional infrastructure, which required initiatives, funding, maintenance and coordination by government; 2) sustained innovation, which also required all sorts of infrastructures and thus investment in the development of knowledge and human capital that in any case in Japan at the time would be very hard, if not impossible, to realize without major government support and investment; 3) an institutional and political framework geared to maximizing growth and development and supportive of entrepreneurship and profit making. For all this the input of the state was indispensable, and in Japan's case major. In the rest of this book I will try to argue that position. My approach will be clearly in the tradition of scholars who think in terms of a developmental or entrepreneurial state and it will clearly build on ideas about the role of the state in economic development and in particular in the Great Divergence that I have developed in previous studies, in particular *Escaping poverty* and *State, economy, and the Great Divergence*. I will, however, not simply *assume* that tradition is right but try to *show* that with empirical data and plausible arguments. My position in debates about the role of the state in economic development does not imply that I would want to claim this role was *always* and *only* positive. In the case of the economic history of Japan there are undoubtedly instances of state intervention that deserve extra and extra critical attention, in particular the role of state enterprises, of state-initiated, -supported or condoned market distortion (monopolies, cartels, trusts et cetera) and of military, war and empire building. They will get that attention. Here it suffices to point out that the assumption that as a rule underlies those critical comments about state enterprises, market distortions, the military and empire – that is the assumption that they would *by definition* be bad for growth – as such is debatable.

1

Continuities and Changes

The importance of Tokugawa legacies

The focus in my text will be on the period between 1868 and the Meiji Restoration, that undoubtedly heralded a new era in the political history of Japan and 1937 that I have taken as the year in which Japan politically and economically became a society at war. I assume that not many people would want to question that these two years mark watersheds in the political history of the 'state' of Japan. One may of course question whether these years also mark clear watersheds in the economic history of Japan. If the answer to that question would be a firm "No", the plausibility that my analysis can show that things changed in Japan's economy because of changes in Japan's politics would clearly diminish. I will not enter into the debate whether 1937 indeed also was an economic caesura. As always in history one may refer to continuities – and scholarship indeed has increasingly done so between pre- and post-Second World War Japan – but I believe also taking on board developments in Japan after 1945 in a setting that in so many aspects was so different, would really stretch my analysis. I will therefore confine myself to discussing dis-continuities with the preceding Tokugawa period.

Among scholars specializing in the history of Tokugawa and Meiji Japan for quite some time the dominant view has been to regard Japan's take-off, i.e. its beginning industrialization and the breakthrough of modern economic growth as solely a Meiji affair. The economy of Tokugawa Japan was considered to have been too backward, poor, underdeveloped and static, to take off without the incisive revolutionary changes that Meiji Restoration and the ensuing opening of the country was purported to have brought. It is not much use to try and extensively document this long-existing consensus.[1] I will confine myself to providing a couple of telling quotes and refer the interested reader to the literature. Kazushi Ohkawa and Henri Rosovsky thought Tokugawa peasants were 'of a rather common Asian type . . . many of them . . . living on the border of subsistence'.[2] They, however, add on the same page that Japan on the eve of the Meiji Restoration was in a state of 'relative backwardness' but in a much more favourable position than under-developed countries at the time he wrote his book.[3] Elsewhere they claim about Japan on the eve of the Meiji Restoration: 'Islands of modernity existed and exist in most backward countries' adding 'A few spinning mills and iron foundries cannot be said to change the industrial structure of a country with a population of some thirty million inhabitants.'[4] This comment – correct as it is as such – does imply they tend to see the industrialization that took place after the Meiji Restoration as a break and that they do not expect much from going back in time in trying to understand Japan's industrialization. Jon Halliday, in his political history of Japanese capitalism, gave a 'perfect' textbook-like Marxist description of Tokugawa Japan as a strictly hierarchal and closed feudal society where the standard of living of the peasants, 'although varying considerably from one area of the country to another was on the average extremely low' and their status 'far worse than implied by their formal position in the *shi-no-ko-sho* four-class structure'.[5] That was in 1975. Three years earlier Mikiso Hane had written that whereas the peasantry was the segment of society that supported the national economy under Tokugawa rule it tended to endure hardships and miseries and that its plight got even worse over the eighteenth century.[6] Even though he has several positive things to say about the economy of Tokugawa Japan, Raymond Goldsmith nevertheless in his *Financial history* of 1983 discusses the period 1868–1885 under the title 'Out of the Middle Ages'.[7] As late as 1995, Wayne Nafziger wrote in his *Learning from the Japanese*: 'The overwhelming majority of Japan's twenty-eight to thirty million people (under Tokugawa rule just before the Restoration P.V.) were unfree, poverty-stricken peasants, living mostly in self-sufficient rural villages'.[8]

It was not just professional historians who could be quite negative about the economy of the Tokugawa era: John Orchard, an economist/geographer to whom we already referred earlier, in his book of 1930 argued that Japan's economy at the end of Tokugawa was as developed – or rather, undeveloped – as that of sixteenth-century England.[9] Freda Utley (1898–1978), an English scholar and political activist, clearly of Marxist inspiration, unsurprisingly for a Marxist who all tended to be quite negative about Tokugawa Japan, wrote in 1937 that Japan in the middle of the nineteenth century was 'in most respects more backward than Tudor England' and that 'her condition more nearly approximated to that of fourteenth-century England'.[10]

Stock in trade were references to the stagnating population.[11] This stagnation that set in sometime in the first half of the eighteenth century was interpreted as a sign that Japan at that time was already hitting its 'Malthusian' ceiling. The repeated occurrence of serious famines seemed to fit neatly in such a Malthusian interpretation of the history of (late) Tokugawa Japan.[12] There were various famines that claimed several hundreds of thousands of casualties. I only mention those that have become the most notorious: the *Kyoho* famine of 1732–1733, the *Tenmei* famine in the 1780s, and the *Tenpo* famine that occurred in the 1830s.[13] As a result of the *Kyoho* famine and other catastrophes of 1732–1733, the number of 'common people', i.e. by and large everyone except the samurai and the outcastes, dropped from 26.92 million in 1732 to 26.15 million in 1744, when the next census was taken. Just prior to the *Temmei* famine, there were 26.01 million commoners, but this number declined to 25.08 million in 1786, and then dropped even further to 24.89 million in 1792. Luke Roberts in his book about the Tosa domain shows the impact of several famines at a regional level. During the so-called *Genroku* famine period of 1697–1708, its population declined by some 25,000. During the *Kyoho* Famine of 1732–1734, by 22,000. Over the entire decade of the 1740s, in which from 1743 to 1749 the region was hit by the *Kanpo-kan'en* famine, Tosa's population fell by some 10,000. Crop losses in 1766–1767 caused a decline of population of more than 9,000. The notorious *Tenmei* famine of 1784–1790 led to a decrease of population of 24,000. To get a sense of what these figures mean: The entire population of Tosa during the eighteenth century hovered between 400,000 and 450,000 people.[14]

References to high levels of abortion and infanticide were rife. According to one source, in the Northern provinces the number of children killed annually in the early nineteenth century exceeded 60,000 or 70,000.[15] Even if one would like to interpret this as an effective way of (after)birth control, as several scholars are willing to do, it would be hard to regard it as an indication that all was well in the economy. There were references to serious ecological decline or even crisis, which of course can also easily be related to overpopulation. Conrad Totman, not himself a Marxist pessimist, in several of his publications has assiduously referred to an emerging shortage of agricultural land, of water for irrigation and of fuel, and his ideas have not been without resonance. In his view Tokugawa Japan from roughly the 1720s onwards entered a stage of ecological stasis – and an ensuing stagnating population – in which the Japanese undeniably learned how to deal with ecological constraints and population pressure and how to keep them in check but did not transcend them and did not set the country on a road to substantial growth.[16] Scholars wedded to the idea that not all was well in (late) Tokugawa Japan could also easily find confirmation of their pessimism in the frequent outbursts of peasant revolt and popular unrest.[17]

The image of Tokugawa Japan's economy – as well as of its society at large – has changed substantially or, to put it in David Howell's words, 'the tired image of Tokugawa Japan as a backward and stagnant society' has been finally put to rest.[18] The pessimist case has increasingly lost ground to an explicitly revisionist perspective. Let me illustrate that perspective by briefly synthesizing the view of its two most prominent promoters, Susan Hanley and Kozo Yamamura. For a more extensive discussion of the current revisionist position, which has become quite popular but has never convinced all scholars, I refer to the relevant literature.[19] Susan Hanley and Kozo Yamamura have made a plea for a complete reinterpretation of the economic and social history of the Tokugawa period, and they have done so quite successfully. According to their 'revisionist' interpretations the absence of substantial growth of the population to a large extent was not so much caused by Malthusian tensions, resulting in positive checks as famine or disease, as by preventive checks. In short, the most important reason for the low growth of population was that people did not want the population to grow much. There indeed were some serious famines that had a lot of victims. These, however, were not countrywide affairs, but regional in nature and effect. They appear to have been caused by specific environmental problems and problems of climate rather than by extreme population pressure. The same goes for various epidemics. Their appearance had a logic of its own and they cannot simply be related to population pressure or poverty.[20] Often natural disasters like floods or earthquakes acted as triggers to crises. The country was also plagued by fires.[21] Social unrest, especially the almost endemic rural revolts, must not simply be connected to a deteriorating of the economic situation. They must rather be linked to the financial problems of the rulers and to social tensions because of an emerging sharp differentiation between various social groups. At the end of the Tokugawa period such disturbances were increasingly directed against village leaders and merchants.

Moreover, so they point out, overall the growth of the population in Tokugawa Japan from the beginning of the eighteenth century onwards may indeed not have been impressive. But when one takes a closer look the picture becomes more variegated. Huge differences existed between regions. Some saw their population stagnate or even decrease, others had populations that increased substantially. Besides, from roughly the 1840s onwards, that is already before the Meiji Restoration, after some serious setbacks, total population *did* increase. The pessimist, 'Malthusian' interpretation of Tokugawa Japan's economic history hinged strongly on the claim that its agriculture could not cope with increasing population. Summarizing the findings of numerous case studies Susan Hanley and Kozo Yamamura, however, conclude that 'Tokugawa agricultural output and productivity as a whole grew more or less consistently throughout the entire period'.[22] In the work of Yamamura and in particular Hanley, Tokugawa Japan is turned into an advanced pre-industrial economy, where people were healthy and had a high life expectancy. Hanley sums it all up in her famous statement that 'the standard of living around 1850 was not only appreciably higher than that in the 1700s but also high in comparison to most of the industrializing West in 1850'.[23]

All this 'revising' by Hanley and Yamamura and others resulted in a much more positive image of Japan's economy and growth potential during the Tokugawa era. Hanley and Yamamura, with their extensive analysis, certainly were the most influential scholars propagating a new perspective but there are also other examples of an explicitly revisionist approach.[24] Judging by the work of e.g., in alphabetical order, Penelope Francks, Akira Hayami or Osamu Saito, what once was 'revisionism', seems to have become mainstream. In most of the recent literature Tokugawa Japan is portrayed as what E. A. Wrigley calls an 'advanced organic economy', a market economy with a sophisticated division of labour, high urbanization and 'Smithian growth'.[25] Kaoru Sugihara too could be considered a revisionist with his claim that Japan experienced an alternative labour-intensive route to its industrial society with clear roots in Tokugawa. I will discuss his ideas extensively in my forthcoming book.[26] The best brief description of the current view on the economy of Tokugawa Japan can be found in Penelope Francks' *Japan and the great Divergence*, to which I refer the reader.[27]

This means that the question to what extent the Meiji Restoration really implied a break in the *economic* history of Japan – to confine us to that aspect: one might also ask the continuity-and-change question for other aspects of Japan's society – now has become much more prominent and deserves a more empirical and in-depth analysis. Although there has been an overall shift in the direction of pointing out continuities, there, unsurprisingly I am tempted to add, still exist substantial differences not only when it comes to assessing the impact of the Meiji Restoration but also when it comes to interpreting that Restoration: more as a response to external pressure that basically consisted of borrowing or rather as an internal response to domestic developments? Again, I will not try to be exhaustive but just give a couple of quotes to show the wide range of positions taken here. Probably most striking is the position of the non-Japanese Eric Jones and David Landes as both of them are considered to be notoriously 'Eurocentric'. Let me start with the ideas of Eric Jones. Already in the first edition of his *European miracle* of 1981, he wrote: 'In deep-seated economic ratios and social structures Japan was a surprisingly "western" country' and added, in reference to an analysis by Norman Jacobs: 'Indeed, in certain respects Japan was as "European" as if it had been towed away and anchored off the Isle of Wight.'[28] In his *Growth recurring* he set out to show, and thinks he actually *has* shown, that:

> *intensive* growth did emerge gradually in early modern Japan and Europe, and did so independently, that is, that Japanese growth may have been helped but was not begun by the borrowing from the West after 1868.[29]

In a later publication, he comments that Commodore Perry's American fleet intruded before the experiment (of starting industrialization in Japan P.V.) could run its course.[30] Unsurprisingly considering the prominent place of capitalism among explanations of the rise of the West, he claimed that Japan under Tokugawa also has been capitalist.[31] John Powelson argues along similar lines: 'I will argue that Japan did *not* copy the West. Rather, the Japanese and the Europeans were independent progenitors of economic development.'[32] Stephen Sanderson defends the thesis that the 'European Miracle' also happened in Japan, and that considering the similarities between Japan and the West, the main question actually should be why Japan did *not* take off first.[33] David Landes held a similar view: 'they (the Japanese P.V.) had every prospect of industrializing, even without the Western challenge, on the eve of the Meiji Restoration.' Although he admitted he could not prove it he nevertheless wrote 'that even without a European industrial revolution, the Japanese would sooner or later have made their own.'[34] Reinhard Zöllner in his *Geschichte Japans* even claimed that not only did Japan not need the Western challenge and inspiration but that 'there can be no doubt that Japan would also have industrialized without the Meiji Restoration'.[35] If the claims presented in this paragraph were true the role of the state after 1868 that – in my view – so fundamentally transformed Japan and that was so keen on catching up with the West as the way to reach 'civilization and enlightenment' can only have been relatively small.

Other scholars in contrast emphasize the extent to which the Meiji Restoration implied a major break. Again, I will present a number of quotes, all by well-respected experts in the field, to show that describing and analysing what actually changed in Japan and its economy with the Meiji Restoration, is not a superfluous trivial exercise. I will do so in alphabetical order. Arthur Alexander is quite outspoken: 'it is important to emphasize that the late Tokugawa was not an industrializing economy, nor was it likely to become one without a radical transformation of political and economic structures.'[36] (That transformation in his view had to come from abroad. P.V.) So is Bernhard Bernier: 'In brief: Nothing allows us to claim that Japan would have become an industrial power on its own without western intervention.'[37] Akira Hayami, one of the most influential economic historians of Tokugawa Japan, is also convinced that Japan would not have been able to industrialize on its own.[38] Christopher Howe is just as outspoken and thinks that without the opening by foreigners no entry in the new world of industrial revolution and international trade would have been possible.[39] This is what Ian Inkster says about the potential to generate modern economic growth of the Tokugawa era: 'we would not go on to argue that such changes in themselves were sufficient to generate the industrial revolution of the Meiji era.'[40] For Alan Macfarlane the case is quite clear. Japan 'would never have developed science or industrialisation without the West – there was no sign of this'.[41] In the analyses of Kazushi Ohkawa and

Henry Rosovsky, and Ryoshin Minami, as already indicated, one would also search in vain for substantial 'sprouts of industrialization' in Tokugawa Japan.[42]

I have decided in this text to systematically compare pre-Restoration Tokugawa Japan with Post-Restoration Japan and to also systematically refer to the international context in which things in Japan occurred, as I believe (unsurprisingly!) Japan's economic development in the period under study in this book can only be understood by paying attention to continuity *and* change, internal *and* external factors. My position in this respect is quite similar to that of Janet Hunter:

> Notwithstanding the relatively 'positive' revisionist picture that we have of the Japanese economy in the latter part of the Tokugawa period, it is apparent that Japan was in 1850 on the Asian side of any Western-Asian divergence, and showed few signs of the divergence that was to occur later in the nineteenth century between its own fortunes and those of other Asian states.

But she then adds that:

> the undoubted foreign threat was hardly sufficient to in itself generate in Japan a response whose dynamism contrasts so strongly with that of many other Asian economies. We find ourselves back with trying to identify the 'native sources of Japanese industrialization.'[43]

Even if the technology for industry would have been amply available in Tokugawa Japan, which to a certain extent it was, the socio-economic and political structure required for massive industrialization and modern economic growth were *not*. I think it is fair to say that currently there exists a consensus that the fundamental economic changes that occurred in Japan after Restoration would not have been possible without the new socio-political order that came with that Meiji Restoration. One can already find that claim in the work of, for example, William Lockwood and Tessa Morris-Suzuki.[44] As an indication of the type of arguments put forward to underpin it – and that will all one way or another be dealt with later in this text – I here refer to Carl Mosk who wonders why it was Japan and only Japan that managed to simultaneously industrialize rapidly and build up its military prowess and who then highlights the following contributions of late Tokugawa Japan to development under Meiji rule: 1) national integration via good transport; 2) accumulation of physical capital; 3) a human capital-enhancing structure; 4) a financial infrastructure; 5) a relatively strong commitment to private property; 6) relatively high productivity in rice farming; 7) a widespread diffusion of proto-industrial production; 8) a bureaucracy.[45] Considering the strong and often justified emphasis on elements of continuity in the history of pre- and post-Restoration Japan I will in my analysis systematically and whenever that in my view makes sense refer to Tokugawa legacies or precursors *and* the lack thereof.

The aim of this book is to chart the structure, development and activities of Japan's polity and changes in the country's economic development and growth, in an effort to empirically grasp and connect them. What I want to explain is changes in the economy.

That means I have to begin my analysis by charting how wealthy and developed Tokugawa Japan was to then show how different the situation had become in the 1930s when my analysis stops.

How wealthy and developed was Tokugawa Japan?

To figure out what difference the post-Restoration state may have made for Japan's economy, we must first determine what the economy looked like at the eve of that restoration. As would be expected, there are clearly different accents and perspectives and different estimates of the main relevant variables, but the great majority of scholars at the moment seem convinced that Japan at the time of the Meiji Restoration was not underdeveloped, poor or static, when compared to China, India or parts of the Islamic World *and* large parts of Europe, although it was substantially poorer than North-western Europe, in particular Great Britain and the Netherlands.

Before we continue to try and give some basic information with regard to Japan's economy during the Tokugawa era, a fundamental caveat has to be made that applies to all the figures with regard to that economy – and often also other aspects of that society – in this book: We often lack hard data, certainly at an aggregate level, that would allow us to make solid claims about the economy at large. Often basic data simply are not or are no longer available, or not to such an extent that they can serve as a basis for the generalizations modern economists are so fond of. Tokugawa Japan was basically a pre-statistical and very fragmented society. That is not all. Often the data we do have are not suited to serve as buildings blocks for modern economic analysis. How to get solid figures about, e.g. real GDP per capita, when some three-quarters of the population are peasants; when many goods and services never enter a market and thus do not get a price; when often payments, including payment of taxes, are in kind; when monetary prices, including incomes and salaries, in as far as they exist, often do not reflect supply and demand but rather tradition or power relations; when wages and incomes often are extras and not even the main source of revenue; when we do not even know the exact number of people in the country? Asking for hard data here is asking for the impossible, suggesting one gives them an imposture. Most figures presented here about the Tokugawa era should be considered as no more than approximations and never taken at face value.[46] The situation in this respect only really improves from the 1880s onwards.

Let me present a couple of core data with regard to Japan's economy at the end of the Tokugawa era to indicate what the economy and society that the new Meiji rulers wanted to 'modernize' looked like. Japan's GDP per capita in the middle of the nineteenth century in all probability was at the level of Central and Eastern European countries. It in any case was much lower than in the wealthiest parts of Europe, in particular Great Britain and the Netherlands (see Tables 1 and 2). As indicated, all these figures can only be estimates. But they are the best and most recent ones available.

There seems to be a consensus for the case of Japan when it comes to orders of magnitude. A recent estimate by Osamu Saito and Masanori Takashima claims that GDP per capita in Japan would have been 556 US 1990 dollars in 1600 and 587 in 1721, after which it increased to 788 such dollars in 1846 and 860 in 1874.[47] All

Table 1 Estimates of real GDP per capita in several countries in 1850, expressed in 1990 US dollars

	Japan	GB	Netherlands	Italy	Spain	China	India
1850	933	2,997	2,397	1,350	1,144	594	566

Broadberry, 'Accounting for the Great Divergence', 23.

Table 2 Estimates of real GDP per capita in several countries around the beginning of Meiji rule, expressed in 1990 US dollars

	Japan	GB	Netherlands	Italy	Spain	Poland	China	India
1850	800	2,997	2,397				594	556
1870	737	3,190	2,755	1,542	1,207	946	530	533
1874	1,013							

For the figures for 1850 see Bassino a.o., 'Japan and the Great Divergence', Table 9. For the figures for 1870 see Van Zanden a.o., *How was life*, 67. For the figure for 1874, see Fukao and Settsu, 'Japan. Modern economic growth in Asia', Table 2. The figures, especially those for Japan, China and India are approximations, which may also explain the fairly big difference between the figure for Japan for 1870 and that for 1874.

Table 3 Average annual growth rates of GDP per capita, 1500–1870

	Japan	England	Holland	Northern Italy	Spain	India	China
1500–1700		0.15	0.19	0.02	−0.02	−0.08	0.00
1600–1700	0.00						
1700–1800	0.24	0.36	0.21	−0.08	0.12	−0.12	−0.07

The figures for Japan cover the periods 1600–1720 and 1720–1874, those for China the period 1700–1870.

Saito, 'Japan', 176.

revisionism notwithstanding, this still is not really impressive, at least as compared to countries in (Western) Europe and when one realizes that these are figures *produced* by or in any case *used* by 'revisionists' and not 'pessimists'. That is not changed by the fact that over the period 1720 to 1874 growth of Japan's GDP per capita looks 'respectable'.

Constructing GDP figures for an economy like that of Tokugawa Japan, for the reasons indicated earlier on, is a very tricky endeavour. We are therefore well-advised to try and also construct other indicators for the country's wealth. The first one that comes to mind would be real incomes in terms of real wages. This indicator too is not unproblematic as so many economically active people in Tokugawa Japan did not receive any money wages or were in any case not solely dependent on them. The fact that often payment was wholly or partially in kind further complicates measurement. Table 4 provides the best available estimates of real income of unskilled workers in terms of welfare ratios. Whatever the exact meaning of these figures, they do in any case not suggest Japan's workers were well paid. Figures calculated by Yuzuru Kumon, show a very similar gap between wages in England – where those of London are exceptionally high – and those in Japan.[48] As indicated, the problem here is to figure out what the height of wages actually tells us about total income as so few people were fully depending on them.

Tables 5 and 6 provide the core data for the Tokugawa economy. One can distinguish between developments in the long seventeenth century up until about 1720–1730 and developments in the second half of Tokugawa rule. Whereas in the first period land productivity increased somewhat but labour productivity decreased sharply, in the second period both land- and labour productivity increased. A second major difference is that in the second period population was rather stagnant, and at times even decreased, whereas it increased rather fast in the first period. Agricultural production grew because of the extension of cultivated land but also because there was a spread of best practices. Double cropping and crop rotation became more normal, techniques of

Table 4 Average welfare ratios of unskilled workers in Kyoto and selected European cities, 1700–1899. For Kyoto, there are two different calculations based on two different benchmark years, the first one based on data for 1742, the second one based on data for 1884. I refer to the article by Bassino and Ma for further details

	1700–1749	1750–1799	1800–1849	1850–1899
Kyoto	0.56	0.54	0.64	0.51
Kyoto	0.97	0.95	1.12	0.90
Florence Milan	0.70	0.51	0.39	0.50
London	1.58	1.42	1.41	2.15
Madrid	0.87	0.64	0.95	0.95
Strasbourg	0.57	0.61	0.85	0.79

Bassino and Ma, 'Japanese wages and living standards in 1720–1913', Table 4. The concept welfare ratio refers to the average annual earnings of a worker divided by the cost of a poverty-line consumption bundle for a family. For further explanation see Allen, 'Great Divergence', 424–432.

Table 5 Core data for Tokugawa Japan's agricultural development, 1600–1872

Date	Population (million)	Arable land*	Production**	Land/Labour (*tan*)	*Koku*/Labour (*koku*)	*Koku/Tan* (*koku*)
1600	12	2,065	19,731	1.721	1.644	0.955
1650	17.18	2,354	23,133	1.370	1.346	0.983
1700	27.69	2,841	30,630	1.026	1.106	1.078
1720	31.28	2,927	32,034	0.936	1.024	1.094
1730	32.08	2,971	32,736	0.926	1.020	1.102
1750	31.01	2,991	34,140	0.962	1.098	1.141
1800	30.65	3,032	37,650	0.989	1.228	1.242
1850	32.28	3,170	41,160	0.982	1.275	1.293
1872	33.11	3,234	46,812	0.977	1.414	1.447

Land* in 1000 *cho*. 1 *cho* = 0.99 ha

Production** in 1000 *koku*. 1 *koku* = 180 litres

A *tan* = one tenth of a *cho*.

Based on Miyamoto, 'Quantitative aspects of Tokugawa economy', 38.

Table 6 Growth rates of population, arable and arable output for the Tokugawa period

	Population	Arable land area	Arable output
1600–1650	0.72	0.26	0.32
1651–1700	0.96	0.38	0.56
1701–1720	0.61	0.15	0.22
1721–1730	0.25	0.15	0.22
1731–1750	0.16	0.03	0.22
1751–1800	0.03	0.03	0.22
1801–1850	0.10	0.09	0.18
1851–1871	0.11	0.09	0.59

Miyamoto, 'Quantitative aspects of Tokugawa economy', 38.

irrigation were improved and new rice plant breeds introduced. All these improvements tended to be quite labour intensive. Innovations that might save labour were not absent but more exceptional. What led to increases in labour productivity in particular in the second half of Tokugawa rule was the massive use of commercial fertilizer that tended to save labour. The exact causes of the levelling of population are a matter of debate in which some scholars prefer an explanation in which people voluntarily limited the number of their children to be able to improve their standard of living whereas others think more in terms of a defensive strategy to avoid having to feed too many mouths. Of course, sometimes even big regional differences are hidden behind these aggregate figures.

GDP and real income per capita only provide rough and sometimes even misleading indicators for the quality of life of the people involved. When we take on board other indicators such as consumption patterns, the quality of the goods consumed, the quality of housing or hygiene, especially when compared with Western countries at the same stage of industrialization, the outcome of the comparison turns out to be better for Japan.[49]

Life expectancy evidently is a very important indicator of well-being. Actually determining Japan's average life expectancy during the last century of Tokugawa rule is a quite complicated matter because of the existence of differences in the way in which it might be determined – by looking at life expectancy at birth, or at one year of age, or by looking at the average age at death – and because of the usual caveats regarding the data, their trustworthiness and representativeness, but the available estimates all suggests it must have been in the range of some thirty-five years at birth, which was not lower than overall in Western Europe.[50] Table 7 provides some data with regard to other parts of the world, which of course also have to be considered very generalized estimates.

As Hanley points out, a composite figure for life expectancy for males in western Europe in the nineteenth century, as calculated by the United Nations, was 39.6 in 1840, 41.4 in 1860 and 48.9 in 1900, and 42.5 and 52.1 for females in 1840 and 1900.[51] Table 8 gives some figures for the period 1860 to 1880, which suggest that *relatively speaking* the situation in Japan had deteriorated somewhat.

Table 7 Life expectancy at birth in a number of European and Asian countries

	Life expectancy at birth
Western Europe	
Germany before 1800	35
England 1550–1599	38
England 1650–1699	35
France before 1750	25
France 1750–1799	28–30
England 1750–1799	38
London 1750–1799	23
East Asia	
China (Anhui) 1300–1880	28
China (Beijing) 1644–1739	26
China (Liaoning) 1793–1867	26–35
Japan, countryside 1776–1815	33

In the period from roughly 1750 to 1800, of every 1,000 children born in France only 491 survived to become 15. For England that number was 736, for Sweden 612 and for Denmark 641.

Clark, *Farewell to alms*, 94; Livi-Bacci, *Population of Europe*, 113 and 135, and Wong, *China transformed*, 28.

Table 8 Life expectancy at birth, 1860–1880

	Japan	France	Germany	Great Britain
1860	36.4	41.6	38.4	41.1
1870	36.7	41.3	39.4	42.3
1880	37.2	43.5	42.2	44.6

Van Zanden, *How was life*, 109.

There are many caveats in interpreting all the figures presented so far but they in any case do not suggest that Japan, poorer at the time than the other three countries referred to, had a fundamentally different life expectancy.

Let us briefly discuss some other indicators of economic development, to wit levels of urbanization and marketization. Table 9 shows how many people in Tokugawa Japan were living in settlements of at least 10,000 inhabitants. This high level of urbanization implied that Tokugawa Japan must have had a substantial stock of capital goods in the form of material infrastructure (all sorts of buildings, roads and waterways) and a high level of division of labour and of institutional sophistication, which will have been helpful during industrialization. Towns as a rule are centres of innovation, skill formation, investment and major changes in consumption and they also played this role in Tokugawa Japan where they were home to daimyo, samurai and their followers. These, if possible, tended to spend lavishly, although their dynamism slacked somewhat during the second half of the Tokugawa era when many of the big towns lost population and much economic activity went rural. Differences with Qing China that was much less urbanized nevertheless are striking.[52] Such a highly urbanized economy almost inevitably is also highly monetized. As to be expected for a largely pre-statistical and

Table 9 Urbanization in Japan, 1650–1874, persons living in settlements of at least 10,000 inhabitants as a percentage of total population

1650	13.5
1700	12.0
1720	11.6
1730	12.1
1750	13.4
1800	13.3
1850	12.4
1874	10.5

Bassino and others, 'Japan and the Great Divergence', Table 4.

not fully integrated society, estimates of marketization and in this case monetization are tricky. For the 1860s, Sidney Crawcour came up with the following often quoted and credible estimate in which he *includes* tax rice because that in the end was also marketed: 'It seems safe to say that in Japanese agriculture as a whole over half and probably nearer two-thirds of output was marketed in one form or another.'[53] He adds, again for agriculture: 'The judgement that sales were nearer two-thirds of output is supported by what we know about rural cash expenditure.[54] Raymond Goldsmith, who in his estimate refers to figures by Sidney Crawcour, comes up with the following even higher estimate:

> It has been estimated that in the 1860s about sixty to seventy per cent of agricultural production, excluding tax rice, which may have constituted one-third of all farm output, was marketed. Because this proportion is likely to have been higher in the nonfarm sectors, the monetization ratio for the whole economy should have been on the order of three-fourths, excluding tax rice, but only about three-fifths including it.[55]

These estimates are quite high but considering the relatively high level of (marketed) agricultural taxes, the level of rural consumption of purchased goods and the high level of urbanization, they are not implausible.[56] Figures for the period just after the introduction of the new land tax, when there was no longer an obligatory transfer of rice as tax to the state, point to a similar level of marketization. In an estimate for 1877–1879, the national average for the marketed share of agricultural output was 48 per cent with variation from some 50 to 60 per cent in regions where commercial industrial crops such as cotton or silk cocoons were widely grown, to 30 per cent or less in places where production of grain and other subsistence food still predominated. By 1888–1892, agricultural sales represented 54 per cent of agricultural added value. By the late 1910s, this was 75 per cent.[57] One may assume that the share of marketed goods outside agriculture will have been higher. Whatever the exact figures, one conclusion seems unavoidable: the country that the Meiji reformers wanted to make rich and strong was already quite advanced when it comes to market integration, urbanization and monetization.

Another set of indicators would be provided by literacy and numeracy rates. Again, Tokugawa Japan does not 'score' badly. As for literacy, there is the often-quoted claim by Ronald Dore that at the end of Tokugawa rule some 40 to 50 per cent of the boys received some kind of schooling, against, it must be added, only some 10 to 15 per cent of the girls.[58] Herbert Passin thinks at the time 30 to 40 per cent of what he calls 'the lower peasant levels' were literate.[59] Literacy spread further after the Meiji Restoration as a result of which a Frenchman already in 1877 could write that 'primary education has reached a level which makes us blush'.[60] Indeed, literacy rates in Japan then were higher than in many countries in Europe and Asia.[61] Tests of conscripts in the early Meiji reveal sizeable differences in literacy with over half of those in the professional classes graduated from higher elementary schools, 40 per cent of artisans and farmers but only 10 to 20 per cent of fishers and labourers. Minimal definitions of literacy would have included 65 per cent in the 1850s and 76 per cent in the 1870s. However, a more stringent definition would drop the figures to 8 per cent.[62] For the sake of comparison, let me provide some figures for other countries. In France in 1860 some 65 per cent of children between five and fourteen years old attended a primary school (public and private); for Germany at the time the figure was 70 per cent (only public schools) and for England and Wales some 60 per cent (public and private schools). In Ireland at the time the percentage was only 30 (only public schools) and in Finland still less than 10.[63] Education and literacy have been subject to substantial research that of course cannot be discussed extensively here. I refer the interested reader to the relevant general literature.[64] When it comes to numeracy: according to recent research, the numeracy index in East Asia – which measures people's ability to report an exact rather than a rounded age – was at a level comparable to that for North West European countries. For Japan that index would have come close to the 100 per cent mark throughout the nineteenth century.[65]

The information presented above in my view indeed shows that Tokugawa Japan was an 'advanced organic economy', although, rather surprisingly in my view, even 'revisionists' seem to agree that at the end of Tokugawa rule Japan's GDP per capita in real terms was much lower than that in the wealthiest Western countries.[66] Being so advanced, though, did not make industrialization an inevitable or even predictable next 'stage' in its development. But it did mean that many conditions that tend to be regarded as enabling a country to more easily industrialize were present. Even if one wanted to defend the thesis, as I do, that the Meiji Restoration presented a major break in the history of Japan, when it comes to its economic development there was clearly much more continuity and 'preparation' than has long been taken for granted. I will therefore with good reason pay systematic attention to change *as well as* continuity and to differences *as well as* similarities between pre- and post-Restoration Japan.

What changed during the period 1868–1937?

To find out to how important the existence and activities of Japan's state were for Japan's economic development in the period from the Meiji era till 1937 we of course have to define it more precisely in empirical terms – although, unfortunately, the definitions given will still ultimately be open to differences in interpretation – what

exact continuities and of course in particular what exact changes we want to explain
and relate to the state.

Sixty years ago, the problem at hand would probably have been described as finding
an explanation for Japan's take-off. The concept 'take-off' as Walt Rostow (1916–2003)
initially introduced it, had a very specific and concrete meaning.[67] For Rostow it was
one of his stages of economic growth, namely the stage in which an economy enters
rapid, self-sustained growth. He focused on three related preconditions for an economy
to enter this stage:

1   A rise in the rate of productive investment from about 5 per cent or less to over
    10 per cent of national income or net national product.
2   The development of one or more substantial manufacturing sectors, that came to
    be called leading sectors, with a high rate of growth.
3   The existence or emergence of a political, social and institutional framework which
    facilitates the growth of the modern sector and gives growth an ongoing character.

In this very specific interpretation, the concept 'take-off' has been taken apart by
economists and economic historians and is no longer considered helpful. In the wider sense
in which Eric Hobsbawm uses it, referring to it as the process in which 'the shackles were
taken off the productive power of human societies, which henceforth became capable of
the constant, rapid and up to the present limitless multiplication of men, goods and services',
I think it is still useful.[68] It in any case describes the phenomenon that I want to describe and
explain in my analysis. In Hobsbawm's interpretation it refers more generally to the
transitionary period of time in which an economy develops what economists nowadays call
'modern economic growth', i.e. an increase of real income per capita that is substantial and
sustained. This means the best way to describe what I want to explain in this text would be
'the emergence of modern economic growth in Japan'. Usually Simon Kuznets (1901–1985)
is considered to be the creator of this concept. He identified six features of modern economic
growth as it emerged in the developed ('first') world.[69] He distinguishes between two
quantitative characteristics of modern economic growth that relate to aggregate rates (high
rates of increase in per capita product, accompanied by substantial rates of population
growth and high rates of increase in output per unit of all inputs); two that relate to
structural transformation (in particular a shift from agriculture to industry and services
and changes in the structure of society and its ideology, including urbanization and
secularization) and two that relate to international spread (the opening up of international
communications and the emergence of a growing gap between developed and underdeveloped nations). In particular, the two quantitative characteristics that Kuznets refers to
will play a big role in my analysis but I will also refer to the other characteristics when that
is helpful and enlightening. As we will see in the frequent comparisons of the developments
in Japan, Great Britain, Germany and France the way in which and the tempo in which
different economies become modern and grow could be quite different. It is only in the long
run, and at a high level of abstraction, that there are real uniformities.

As a rule, the phenomena that triggered this transition to modern economic growth
are collectively described as 'industrial revolution', or more broadly 'industrialization'.[70]
For that reason these concepts will also frequently appear in my text. I will use the

following 'definition' that David Landes coined for 'industrial revolution': 1) the substitutions of machines – rapid, regular, precise, tireless – for human skill and effort; 2) the substitution of inanimate for animate sources of power, in particular the invention of engines for converting heat into work, thereby opening an almost unlimited supply of energy; and 3) the use of new and far more abundant raw materials, in particular, the substitution of mineral, and eventually artificial, materials for vegetable and animal substances.[71] In the term 'industrialization', the emphasis on the supposedly 'revolutionary' nature of the developments under analysis is toned down.

In most of the recent literature, the transition to modern economic growth is set in the wider context of a major energetic and technological transformation, which brings us to a fourth concept or rather set of concepts. I here refer to the transition from what Wrigley calls 'an organic economy', or in specific cases 'an advanced organic economy', i.e. an economy that is almost entirely dependent on the productivity of its land, not just for its food but also for raw materials such as hemp, cotton, wool, hides or silk and, very importantly, for its energy in the form of muscle power of people and animals, wood or peat, to a 'mineral-based energy economy' in which this dependency on the land in any case for the time being is broken and production centres around the use of fossil fuels for energy and minerals as raw materials.[72]

The previous paragraphs provided some conceptual distinctions and clarifications that can be applied to the changes that occurred in Japan between the Meiji Restoration and World War II and that will provide my text with an analytical fame. But what did the transformation that we want to explain actually look like when we applied these concepts? In what respects had Japan's economy actually changed between the beginning of Meiji rule and 1937?

To know what the *explanandum* of this text is, i.e. to know what changes the Japanese state is supposed to have helped bring about, we have to determine to what extent Japan of the late 1930s can be considered an economy that had taken off, knew modern economic growth, had industrialized and had made the transition to a mineral-based fossil fuel energy economy.

The growth rates of Japan's economy were certainly impressive, as shown in Figure 1.

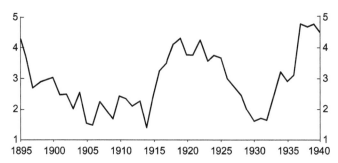

Figure 1 The growth rate of Japan's real gross national product, 1895–1940 in ten-year moving averages.

Alexander, 'Japan's economy in the twentieth century', Figure 1.

As I did for the Tokugawa period, I will now present some core data with regard to economic developments during the period from the Restoration to World War Two.

For the period till just before and just after Restoration Kyoji Fukao and Tokihiko Settsu estimated the following annual growth rates for population and GDP per capita in real terms. For the period 1846–1874, these are set at 0.28 per cent and 0.41 per cent and for the period 1874–1885, at 0.84 per cent and 0.64 per cent.[73]

Again, a comparison with France, Germany and Great Britain can provide the necessary perspective. As shown in Table 23, between 1880 and 1940 Japan's population roughly doubled. That is impressive. France's population barely increased at all in that same period of time, whereas total population growth in Germany and the United Kingdom was roughly 50 and roughly 40 per cent. Not only was Japan's population growth during the period in which its take-off took place quite impressive in comparison to that of France, Germany and the United Kingdom, so was its economic growth in per capita terms and even more in aggregate terms, as is shown in Tables 12 and 13. In the United Kingdom in the period 1820–1870, when with the end of the Napoleonic Wars and their aftermath, growth could really take off, per capita annual growth of real income was 1.26 per cent and aggregate annual growth of real income 2.05 per cent.[74]

Table 10 Average growth rates in percentages per annum of real GNP, population and GNP per capita, 1888–1938. Growth rates for GNP and GNP per capita are calculated on the basis of 1934–1936 prices

	GNP	Population	GNP per capita
1888–1890	3.53	0.85	2.68
1891–1895	3.12	0.92	2.19
1896–1900	2.25	1.10	1.15
1901–1905	1.84	1.18	0.66
1906–1910	2.29	1.14	1.16
1911–1915	3.35	1.36	1.99
1916–1920	4.77	1.11	3.66
1921–1925	1.93	1.26	0.67
1926–1930	2.53	1.50	1.03
1931–1935	4.98	1.36	3.62
1936–1938	5.07	0.95	4.12

Francks, *Japanese economic development*, 42 and 76.

Table 11 Annual GDP growth rates per capita in real terms in percentages: Japan as compared to France, Germany and the United Kingdom

	1870–1913	1913–1950
Japan	1.48	0.88
France	1.45	1.12
Germany	1.61	0.17
United Kingdom	1.01	0.93

Maddison, *Contours of the world economy*, 383.

Table 13 shows how high growth was in the sectors that we tend to associate with industrialization and economic modernization.

Investment, which played such a prominent role in many theories of economic growth, was quite high in Japan, as shown in Tables 14 and 15 that provide two estimates, also in comparison to developed Western industrial nations, as shown in Table 16. Some of the figures in Table 14 are substantially lower than those in Table 15. In my analysis, I will use the figures of Table 14, which are less favourable to my thesis about the fundamental importance of the state for Japan's economy.

Table 12 Annual aggregate GDP growth rates in real terms in percentages: Japan as compared to France, Germany and the United Kingdom

	1870-1913	1913-1950
Japan	2.44	2.21
France	1.63	1.15
Germany	2.81	0.30
United Kingdom	1.90	1.19

Maddison, *Contours of the world economy*, 380.

Table 13 Sectoral growth rates of Japan's economy. Annual average rates, in real terms, 1887-1938

	Manufacturing	Transport, Communication and Utilities
1887-1897	5.92	9.00
1897-1904	4.95	8.94
1905-1919	6.80	9.31
1919-1930	4.58	7.26
1930-1938	8.88	9.47

Francks, *Japanese economic development*, 42 and 76.

Table 14 Gross domestic fixed capital formation as a percentage of Gross Domestic Expenditure in Japan, 1886-1940

1886-1890	9.0
1890-1895	9.4
1896-1900	12.1
1901-1905	10.6
1906-1910	13.5
1911-1915	15.6
1916-1920	17.9
1921-1925	18.8
1926-1930	17.8
1931-1935	16.5
1936-1940	25.7

Mosk, *Japanese economic development*, 364. Based on Ohkawa, Shinohara and Meissner, *Patterns of Japanese economic development*, 256-260.

Table 15 Gross domestic fixed capital formation
as a percentage of GDP, 1885–1919

1885–1889	13.5
1890–1894	14.5
1895–1899	18.2
1900–1904	13.9
1905–1909	16.7
1910–1914	17.8
1915–1919	19.7

Alexander, *Arc of Japan's development*, 35.

Table 16 Gross domestic fixed capital formation as a percentage of GDP, 1870–1938, for eight countries

	Japan	France	Germany	UK	USA	India	Korea	Taiwan
1870–1889	13a	13		8	16	5		
1890–1913	14	14		9	16	6	5d	9e
1914–1938	16	16b	13c	8	14	7	7	16

a 1885–1889; b 1922–1938; c 1925–1938; d 1911–1913; e 1903–1913.

Amsden, *Rise of the 'Rest'*, 78. For further comparisons that also show that capital formation rates in industrializing Japan, comparatively speaking, were not exactly low, see Rosovsky, *Capital formation*, 89.

Table 17 Development of the components of Gross National Expenditure, 1919–1938

	Investment	Personal Consumption	Government Consumption	Exports	Imports
Shares in percentages of gross national expenditures					
1920	19.3 (13.1)*	77.7	8.6	11.1	−16.7
1930	17.0 (9.1)*	78.9	12.1	15.9	−23.9
1938	26.2 (14.5)*	63.6	13.0	20.1	−22.9
Average percentage growth in real terms					
1919–1930	1.23	2.60	5.73	4.97	5.64
1930–1938	10.95	2.23	5.98	8.05	5.34

( )*=Private investment

Francks, *Japanese economic development*, 76.

As always, a comparison helps to put things in perspective. As compared to Britain at the time of its take-off, gross fixed capital formation in Japan was clearly high. In Britain, it increased from 7 per cent of GDP in the 1760s when most scholars would claim its take-off began to just under 11 per cent in the 1840s, when most scholars would claim it was completed.[75] Table 17 shows the components of Gross National Expenditure, in the period 1919–1938.

Kuznets in his definition of modern economic growth claims that an economy that is experiencing modern economic growth becomes more open to imports and exports. That certainly is the case in Japan in the period discussed, as shown in Table 18. But one must realize that at the beginning of the Meiji period both imports and exports were almost negligible.

What is striking is that the final *outcome* of all this growth in terms of real GDP per capita and real wages as compared to major Western industrial nations was much less impressive than most people will have expected on the basis of the previous figures.

When we look at Japan's real wages for ordinary labour, we have to conclude that they increased much less than GDP per capita and thus continued to be quite low as compared to real wages in France, Germany and Great Britain. In this respect too, Japan, or rather the ordinary Japanese, continued to be fairly poor.

When we look at data with regard to structural change, often considered an inherent element of the process of taking off into modern economic growth, we see that the number of people working in agriculture in industrializing Japan continued to be

Table 18 Exports and imports as percentages of GDP

	Exports	Imports
1885	5	5
1895	10	11
1905	13	24
1915	20	16
1920	19	20
1930	17	17
1938	20	23

Hentschel, *Wirtschaftsgeschichte des modernen Japans*, Vol. I, 96. Based on Ohkawa, Shinohara and Meissner, *Patterns of Japanese economic development*, 251–255. For further information on Japan's foreign trade see also Tables 87 and 88.

Table 19 GDP per capita in 1990 US dollars in Japan, France, Germany and Great Britain, as decadal averages from 1870 to 1940

	Japan	France	Germany	Great Britain
1870s	737	1,876	1,839	3,190
1890s	1,012	2,376	2,428	4,009
1910s	1,304	2,965	3,348	4,611
1930s	1,850	4,532	3,973	5,411

Van Zanden a.o., *How was life*, 67. Saito, in his 'Japan' on page 173 comes up with estimates for Japan that look somewhat higher: 1874, 860; 1890, 1012; 1913, 1387 and 1935, 2120 US 1990 dollars.

Table 20 Real wages of building labourers, expressed in the number of subsistence baskets that a daily wage bought, decadal averages, 1870s–1930s

	Japan	France	Germany	Great Britain
1870	–	16	13	21
1890	7	28	20	28
1910	7	27	27	23
1930	9	19	27	37

Van Zanden a.o., *How was life*, 81.

Table 21 Structural change: Employees in agriculture, 1870–1950, in percentages of total labour force

	Japan	France	Germany	United Kingdom
1870	70	49	49	23
1913	60	41	35	12
1930	49	36	29	6
1950	48	28	22	5

Millward, *State and business*, 248.

surprisingly high. Here too the outcome is less impressive than growth figures may have suggested.

The share of industrial employment in total employment in Japan at the end of the 1930s was still less than 25 per cent. In France at the time it was a little over 40 per cent; in Germany some 50 per cent, and in the United Kingdom still over 40 per cent. Some fifteen million people were employed in Japan's primary sector in the 1870s; at the end of the 1930s, that number was still some fourteen million. The numbers for the secondary sector were less than three million at the beginning of the period under discussion in this book and some nine million at its end. The numbers for the tertiary sector were 3.5 million in the 1870s, and about ten million in the late 1930s.[76]

When we look at the kinds and amounts of products that were produced in Japan, it, all fast growth notwithstanding, still was something of an industrial 'dwarf' at the end of the 1930s. So as not to disturb the flow of my argument too much or drown the reader in figures, my examples are given in Appendix I. The figures shown above and in Appendix I indicate that we have to put Japan's industrialization in the right perspective. Even in 1937, after many decades of undoubtedly impressive growth and industrialization, Japan still was *relatively* poor, and in many respects only *semi-developed*.[77] As compared to the most developed Western economies, it still had, at least if it wanted to operate as a real *great* economic power, 'feet of clay', to use Freda Utley's expression. What Japan did in the roughly seventy years that are at the core of this book is impressive, in particular when compared to all the other countries outside the West, where industrialization progressed only slowly or not at all. But everyone trying to explain Japan's development over that period must be wary not to be misled by appearances. Even after so many decades of growth, Japan's economy had *not* caught up with the leading industrial nations in the West. Far from it. It would only do so after World War Two. This is a fundamental fact that is often overlooked. Robert Allen has rightly pointed out that, even if the average rate of growth of real per capita income for the period 1870–1940 had continued after World War Two, 'it would have taken Japan 327 years to catch up with the USA'.[78] As Table 22 shows, on the eve of the Asia Pacific War, Japan, at least in pure economic power, still was much smaller than the United Kingdom and a dwarf compared to the USA.

But to put things into perspective, we have to realize that even at the time of the Restoration, Japan was *not* a small country, in terms of population or in terms of size. Its population, then still counted excluding that of Hokkaido and the Ryukyu Islands,

Table 22 GDP of the Great Powers, 1938–1945, in international dollars and 1990 prices in billions

	1938	1941	1944	1945
Japan	169	196	189	144
France	186	130	93	101
Germany	351	412	437	310
United Kingdom	284	344	346	331
USA	800	1094	1499	1474
USSR	359	359	362	343

Harrison, 'Economics of World War II', 10.

was about thirty-four million people. At the end of the 1930s, it amounted to some seventy million people, then including Hokkaido and the Ryukyu Islands whose population together, however, was no more than a couple of million. Over time it substantially extended its total realm, by the incorporation of other territories and their inhabitants. The three core islands that formed Tokugawa Japan measured some 300,000 km²; Hokkaido some 80,000 km² and the Ryukyu Islands some 4,500 km². Together that is about as large as Germany (currently, in 2018, some 360,000 km²); smaller than, in rounded figures, metropolitan France (currently, in 2018, 550,000 km²) but substantially larger than the United Kingdom (currently in 2018, 240,000 km²). In the period discussed here the territorial extension of these three European countries with which we will regularly compare Japan in this text, France, Germany and the United Kingdom, underwent a couple of territorial changes that are substantial enough to be referred to here, even though they do not change the general gist of my comments. The German Empire at its foundations in 1871 measured some 540,000 km². Alsace-Lorraine, measuring some 14,000 km², belonged to it from 1871 to 1919, when it had to be returned to France. In that year, Germany besides losing Alsace-Lorraine, also lost several other regions. In total, its losses amounted to some 14 per cent of its land and some 12 per cent of its population. In the case of the United Kingdom there was one big change: in 1922 the Irish Free State became independent and left the United Kingdom, which thus became about 70,000 km² smaller.

Japan, France and the United Kingdom were the heartlands of overseas empires. In 1937 the surface of Japan's official empire, which then consisted of Japan plus Korea, Formosa, and Karafuto (Japanese Sakhalin), measured some 675,000 km². Its total population was about ninety-eight million inhabitants. The Kwantung leased territory and the mandated South Sea Islands, with an extension of some 6.000 km², although territories under Japanese control were not officially considered to be part of the Empire, but to most intents and purposes were treated as such. They had some 1.6 million inhabitants. Table 23 provides data for Japan, France, Germany and the United Kingdom to put these figures into perspective. Compared to much larger Asian polities such as the Qing and Ottoman Empires and 'India', but also European ones like the Russian or Austro-Hungarian Empires, Japan had the advantage that it was not *too* big. Ruling and developing a 'big' country *ceteris paribus* tends to be more expensive and

Table 23 The population of Japan, France, Germany and the United Kingdom and of their empires (*including* their motherlands) in 1880 and on the eve of World War Two, in millions, rounded figures

	Population 1880	Population 1940	Population Empire 1880	Population Empire 1937
Japan	36	70	36	100
France	38	40	45	110
Germany	45	68	45	68
United Kingdom	35	49	306	546

complicated than ruling and developing a smaller one – in particular when the smaller one is also quite homogeneous when it comes to its population. Not by accident, in literature on nationalism Japan has often been described as a historic state with a population that was ethnically almost or entirely homogeneous with a nationalism that could build on a tradition of proto-nationalism and therefore was 'strong'.[79]

The Meiji Restoration as the beginning of a new Japan

Japan's transformation into an industrializing nation with high economic growth and high rates of development in my view could not have taken place without the cluster of changes that we associate with the Meiji Restoration. But that does not mean that Tokugawa Japan and its rulers were immobile, nor does it mean that the people who defeated the (ex-) Shogun were a closed group of revolutionaries whose main goal from the very beginning would have been to modernize and industrialize Japan. In that respect, some more information about the actual occurrences of the Meiji Restoration is in order.

Many things done or proposed in the last decades of Tokugawa rule, in the lands of the Shogun himself as well as in several of the domains, clearly presaged or anticipated later reforms. Many important and influential people during the last decades of Tokugawa rule had already become convinced that Western institutions could be made consonant to Japan. Many Japanese one way or another had already set out to increase their knowledge of the West before Perry's 'black ships' arrived. The so-called *Bakumatsu* period from 1853–1867 was one of fierce discussion, experiments and real innovations. Perry's arrival and ships as such were not the shock as which they have often been presented, but they certainly were the beginning of a serious race between Westerners to open and enter Japan on good conditions to which Japan's elites simply had to respond. As such, they indeed can symbolize the beginning of a new era. Tokugawa Yoshinobu (1837–1913), who turned out to be the last Shogun, became the fifteenth shogun in 1866, and already tendered his resignation as shogun in November 1867. He was anything but a reactionary or even conservative. Actually, in the words of Mark Ravina, he was busy implementing a radical reform project, creating 'a unified national regime organized along the bureaucratic lines of Napoleonic France' so that 'by late

1867, the Shogunate was more "modern" than the imperial alliance'.[80] Robert Bruce van Valkenburgh, the US consul in Japan at the time, considered him 'the most progressive and liberal in his ideas of any Japanese official'.[81] The conflict between his supporters and those of the imperial court was not about deep ideological differences and fundamentally opposed views about the future of Japan. It was rather a question of factional strife and rancour, be it in a setting in which the changing position of the imperial court and the Emperor, the more self-conscious behaviour of certain domains and of course the question of how to deal with the Western powers whose presence simply could no longer be ignored, had become fundamental challenges to the Shogun and his power. The evolving conflict was not one in which the forces of progress combatted the forces of reaction. There actually were many similarities between those struggling to save the Shogunate and those trying to overthrow it and remarkably few staunch defenders of the old regime. When the Shogunate fell in 1868, many if not most, Westerners were concerned that the new Meiji government would be *more* instead of *less* xenophobic and insular than the old one.

Japan's new rulers, though, felt that they were not in a position to seriously antagonize the Western powers and that it would not be wise policy to let domestic antagonisms fester too long. But the lack of fundamental dissent may very well also have contributed to the fact that they behaved quite conciliatorily when it had become clear that they had indeed taken over power. Former Shogun Tokugawa Yoshinobu was permitted to go and retire to his Mito domain. His chief officers were also granted clemency and permitted to retire from public life. The new Meiji government gave Yoshinobu's five-year-old heir a large fief. He himself did not end up in prison but was allowed a quiet and comfortable retirement in a Tokyo villa. In 1902, he acquired the highest rank in Japan's peerage, that of prince, for his loyal service to Japan and a seat in the House of Peers from which he resigned in 1910. He died in 1913, wealthy and honoured.[82] In its very first years the new regime overall was averse to conflict. The *daimyo* were well treated. When in August 1871 the domain system was abolished, the new government took over the properties of the *daimyo* and their power, in the sense that they – or at least a number of them – became governors and thus mere officials. But it also took over responsibility for the debts of domain governments and for the stipends of their samurai. Domain debt at the time amounted to twenty-four million yen.[83] It, moreover, also spent twenty-five million yen, in paper notes, to buy up the domain paper notes that were still in use at the time. The new central government did all this *before* it had established institutions to generate revenue from the whole country.[84] As indicated, many *daimyo* became governors or were otherwise co-opted. Many of them were bought out. Many of them also seemed to be glad it was over. There was, in any case, surprisingly little resistance from their ranks. The new rulers had the luck that it seemed all but impossible to come up with viable alternatives to turning Japan into a strong and modern state and that almost everyone had begun to realize this. Powerful domain lords, e.g. those of Satsuma, Tosa and Echizen, had already in 1866 demanded the end of dual sovereignty in order to be able to stand up against the West.[85]

Time and again in this book too we will come across elements of continuity between Tokugawa and post-Tokugawa Japan. But that should not distract from the fact that the

Meiji Restoration in the end boiled down to a *radically* and *nationwide* abolishing of many *core features* of the existing regime – all of its references to tradition and 'restoring the old' notwithstanding – and actually implemented a broad range of fundamental changes. In their range, scale and scope and thoroughness, the institutional changes forced through during roughly the first ten years after the fall of the Shogunate dwarf everything that took place in Japan even during the last decades of Tokugawa rule. The Meiji Restoration in several respects stood for less revolutionary change than some who considered Tokugawa Japan immobile are willing to admit. In Japan itself, the new regime was described as *Meiji ishin* (renewed government oriented towards the light), which means that the new government, according to Pierre-François Souyri can best be considered as a 'Meiji Renovation'. The term revolution was considered inappropriate to describe what was happening. It would have reeked too much of a movement from below, which was clearly not the image one wanted to convey.[86] But as I hope to show in this book, this so-called Restoration in several respects undoubtedly had a very revolutionary and in any case fundamental impact.

That of course does not mean that without the Restoration as it actually took place, Japan's economy could not have taken off. It might have done so nevertheless but then, in my view, under the clear condition that the Shogunate or some other new ruler(s) would have unified Japan, turned it into a modern, national and centralized state, and would have implemented basically the same or quite similar policies to those of the Meiji and later regimes. I fail to see how Japan could ever have become the home of a modern industry – and of a strong state – while maintaining the fundamental institutional arrangements and divisions of Tokugawa rule. In my view sustained and substantial economic growth and even the persistence of Japan as an independent, sovereign polity were incompatible with the institutional order on which Tokugawa rule had always been based.

The way in which institutional changes were implemented had many Japanese characteristics and contained many references to real or invented Japanese traditions. But I think there can be little doubt that the bulk of the changes were *propelled* by the threatening presence of foreign powers. I endorse Mark Ravina, who in his recent work on the Meiji Restoration, claims: 'Modern Western imperialism destroyed the Tokugawa regime by destroying its international environment.'[87] In his view, responding to Western imperialism required national mobilization, whereas 'the great success of the Tokugawa dynasty had been avoiding war and thereby the need for such mobilization'.[88] 'Internationally', Tokugawa Japan seemed like a weak and a backward state that lacked clear sovereignty and clear borders and on top of that was very fragmented. It became a modern state with all that implies, operating as a 'normal' member of the international community of states under external, Western pressure. Neither the structure of its policy nor the way in which it dealt with neighbouring polities fitted Tokugawa Japan easily into the new 'international' order that Western powers were globally imposing over the nineteenth century. But it felt too vulnerable to not adapt to external pressure. In that sense, the transforming of Japan into a modern national state has to be seen as a response to global developments in which the country borrowed heavily and adapted institutions that at the time counted as 'Western'.[89] That in this response Japanese precedents or equivalents were often found or constructed does not alter this fact.

Without this external threat, it is hard to see why and how Japan's regime would have changed into the new polity that emerged with the 'Restoration'. In this text, we will try to pinpoint exactly what the changes and continuities in Japan's state and its policies were and how they can be linked to the changes and continuities in the country's economy.

2

A Sovereign and Modern State

A non-Western country that became a colonizer
rather than a (semi-)colony

What arguments can one provide for the thesis that the state was of fundamental importance in Japan's economic development in the period 1868–1937 and that, overall, its impact was quite positive when it comes to promoting growth? The first fact of immense importance that has to be pointed out is that Japan did not become a (semi-)colony but, to a very large extent, continued to be an independent 'sovereign' state. There are of course also reasons for that which have little to do with the policies of its government and one can only speculate what would have happened if one or more Western countries had seriously tried to conquer Meiji – or, for that matter and more likely, Tokugawa – Japan. The point I want to make here is that Japan's rulers, predominantly with a 'military' background, were, in contrast for example to those of China, permanently aware of the vulnerable position of their country and permanently engaged in trying to do something about it. Its new rulers after the Meiji Restoration understood full well that a polity like Tokugawa Japan had been was not likely to survive in the new global order.

Fortunately for Japan, the efforts of Western powers like Great Britain and to some extent Russia to actually and forcibly 'open' Tokugawa Japan had long been not very intense.[1] As compared to, for example India or China, it, overall, was considered less of a prize.[2] In 1819 the influential British intellectual journal *Quarterly Review* believed that 'the wants of the people are few and their superfluous produce neither great nor valuable' and that therefore any lost opportunities were merely diplomatic and marginal.[3] Many observers did not think the country had high economic potential. As late as the middle of the nineteenth century, the first British Minister to Japan described it as 'a cluster of islands on the furthest edge of the horizon, inhabited by a race grotesque and savage.'[4] Marx, with his usual self-assuredness, made the famous claim:

> Japan with its purely feudal organisation of landed property and its developed petite culture, gives us a much truer picture of the European Middle Ages than our own history books, dictated as they are, for the most part, by bourgeois prejudices.[5]

When the country was opened there still were many foreigners who did not think much of its economy and its people. The official guidebook to the French International Exhibition of 1878, in which Japan was a participant, contained this quote:

Unfortunately, for the Japanese to exploit their potential wealth themselves, they would need accumulated capital, which they lack, and also a sustained energy and enthusiasm for work, which they scarcely display at all.[6]

In 1881, in the *Japan Herald* it read:

The Japanese are a happy race, and being content with little, are not likely to achieve much.[7]

Whereas *The Currency of Japan* in 1882 published the following claim:

Wealthy we do not think it (Japan) will ever become: the advantages conferred by Nature, with the exception of the climate, and the love of indolence and pleasure of the people themselves forbid it.[8]

To think that Japan could rapidly catch up with the West was described as an illusion.[9] In the first half of the 1880s, the following claim was made in the Encyclopaedia Britannica:

By foreign observers ... this new departure (the opening of many new spinning factories P.V.) was regarded with contemptuous amusement. The Japanese were declared without organizing capacity, incapable of sustained energy, and generally unfit for factory work.[10]

Even in the early years of the twentieth century, some European observers were still sceptical of Japan's capacity for industrial expansion and most of them thought little of her chances of competing effectively with other countries in the world markets for manufactured goods.[11] But overall, the idea that Japan was quite primitive and poor, lacked economic potential or was just 'exotic' – *and* powerless – was quite drastically challenged with Japan's successful wars against China and Russia and in certain circles gave way to, at times, quite panicky fears of 'the yellow peril'.[12] This change was not confined to military matters. In the eyes of many foreign observers and writers – conservatives as well as liberals and socialists – Japan, in particular after it had beaten Russia, had now become a model of 'national efficiency'.[13]

Luck also played its part when it comes to explaining why Japan did not lose its sovereignty. It happened to enter the global stage at a time when Western countries often had more pressing engagements elsewhere, like the Crimean War (1853–1856), the American Civil War (1861–1865), the Austro-Prussian War of 1866, the Franco-Prussian War (1870–1871), and in Asia the First and Second Opium Wars (1839–1842 and 1856–1860) and the Indian Rebellion of 1857, just to mention the most obvious examples. Mutual jealousy among the imperialist powers that wanted to prevent one of them becoming too powerful and the 'open-door policy' of the USA also played their part.[14]

It is nevertheless of fundamental importance that Tokugawa and later Meiji, Taisho and Showa governments did everything in their power to avoid Japan becoming a semi-colony like China or even worse, a colony like British India or the Dutch East Indies, and already in the 1890s an all-out military confrontation with Japan would have been a risky endeavour for any great power in the world. Japan continued to be an independent state, politically and militarily as well as economically. The importance of this fact can hardly be exaggerated: colonies or semi-colonies – and almost *all* states outside 'the West' at the time were colonies or semi-colonies – simply could never have done what Japan did because they were not sovereign. They could not even have begun to think about it. The new rulers of Japan were all well aware of that.[15]

Everyone 'relativizing' what Japan's state did, ought to compare that with what the state in other undeveloped or developing countries did, or rather did not do and *not* to what some ideal state in ideal circumstances might have done. Frances Moulder has a point when she writes that the fact that Japan maintained its relative autonomy when it became incorporated in the evolving world economy made a major difference.[16] The Japanese themselves at the time, which I think is not irrelevant, were convinced of that. For them political sovereignty, military strength and economic development were intrinsically connected. This of course does not mean that Japan was a fully sovereign state. Few topics could excite Japan's public opinion during the Meiji period more than the so-called 'unequal treaties' that were enforced upon the country in the 1850s and 1860s. Because of them, several options of promoting the economy were not open to Japan's rulers for several decades.[17] They were 'unequal' as the Japanese did not get the rights in the countries of the other signatories that those signatories received with regard to Japan. They 'opened' Japan not only in the sense that any Westerner from a treaty country may trade – at least in the treaty ports – with the Japanese, but also in the sense that the Japanese may trade with foreigners at liberty and with no government interference, not only in treaty ports but also abroad. That meant that the Japanese were now allowed to leave the country.[18] This is not the place to discuss extensively what exactly these unequal treaties contained. For that I refer to the relevant literature.[19] These were the most relevant clauses of the unequal treaties as they in the end functioned when it comes to the questions that are central to my analysis:

- Certain Japanese ports were to be opened to foreign trade.
- Foreign citizens might permanently reside, have the right to lease ground and purchase the buildings thereon, and might erect dwellings and warehouses.
- A system of extraterritorially was created that provided for the subjugation of foreign residents to the laws of their own consular courts instead of the Japanese law system.
- Import-export duties were to be fixed at a low level, subject to international control. The rate would go as low as 5 per cent in the 1860s.
- Japan was subjected to a one-directional most favoured clause. It was to extend its treaties to all the countries it dealt with, but not the other way around.[20]

As it happens, those Japanese who actually signed them were not unduly annoyed by their content. They did not really mind that Japanese subjects had no extraterritoriality abroad because there were no Japanese abroad. Low import tariffs did not count as a major problem either: Japan hardly – at least up until then – imported goods. Overall, what happened outside Japan was not yet a major concern to Japan's rulers. Major irritation only emerged later. The treaties as they were signed, had no final date. In principle, they were eternal. The famous Iwakura Mission (1871–1873) had as its major goal to try and get them changed or preferably abolished. In the 1890s, they were re-negotiated with all the individual countries involved. This led to new treaties. In 1894, a new treaty was signed with Great Britain in which it was agreed that all extra-territoriality rights of that country in Japan would be eradicated by 1899. In that year Western powers all gave up their extraterritoriality privileges. In return, their subjects acquired the right to purchase property outside the old treaty settlements. The Western powers also started giving up their control of tariffs and allowed Japan to start increasing its import tariffs until in 1911 all tariffs imposed by the 'unequal treaties' were abolished. Now finally, after the transitional period of twelve years stipulated in the Treaty of 1899, autonomy was realized.[21]

These treaties certainly were a nuisance and Japan's rulers quite soon began to consider them extremely unfair and insulting. Their actual *economic* impact, though, was relatively confined.[22] Some scholars even turn them into something positive for Japan's economy as they enabled Japan's producers to cheaply import certain goods and, more importantly, forced them to be competitive.[23] The treaty ports themselves may have been a window on Japan for the foreigners, but they also were a window on the foreigners for the Japanese who managed to isolate them in those ports and keep them out of their hinterland. Carl Mosk, for example, points out that the 'presence of foreigners in the treaty ports was certainly a factor in the emergence of Osaka and Tokyo as innovating centres'.[24] It was not easy for the Japanese to get informed about the West, considering the distances and the language barriers. There certainly was a language barrier. In that respect too, the treaty ports could have positive effects.[25] The number of foreign firms that settled there was substantial. In the so-called Five Open Ports between 1874 and 1883 their number was 285 at its lowest in 1877 and 545 at its highest in 1883.[26] This is the way in which Inkster turns the disadvantage of the unequal treaties into an advantage:

> the decidedly unequal treaties ... and the consequent absence of control over tariffs reduced a potential source of revenue and removed the possibility of pursuing any direct export promotion under protection. The only focus left for the industrialising state was cost reduction and quality control over a wide front...
> (This) together with the Meiji internal policy decision not to import foreign capital, forced upon the entire industrialising system a concentration upon cultural engineering, technology transfer and human capital formation.[27]

Meiji Japan was not just independent: it quickly turned into an international power to be reckoned with. The idea, popular among its rulers that to become rich Japan also had to be strong, was generally endorsed and by no means odd considering the way in which the West had risen and become the world's ruler. Japan's strong army was not just meant for defence of 'Japan proper'. From the very beginning – actually even from *before* the Meiji Restoration – there were plans – or in any case ideas – to expand the realm. Already before the end of Tokugawa rule, there were people who argued Japan should confront Korea and begin to build an empire there.[28] Only eight years after that Restoration Japan signed a treaty with Korea that was exactly as 'unequal' as the treaties it had to sign itself with Western countries. Japan's new rulers not only wanted to avoid their country becoming a colony: many of them actually wanted to create a Greater Japan, a wider 'sphere of Japanese influence' or, less euphemistically, 'a Japanese empire'. In 1890, Prime Minister Yamagata Aritomo (1838–1922) explicitly pointed out that Japan must not only defend a 'line of sovereignty' but also protect a 'line of interest', which boils down to saying the country needed a safety belt or outer ring of surrounding territories.[29] No cleavages developed among policy makers along the lines of 'imperialist' versus 'anti-imperialist'. Everyone, from persons known to be fairly 'liberal', like Yukichi Fukuzawa (1835–1901), to the most extreme nationalists, was convinced that Japan sooner or later needed to expand in order to become a 'first-class country' rather than a (semi-)colony. The reasons could be various. Both pre-war and wartime Japanese imperialism were anything but a monolithic entity, but as an ultimate policy goal, expansion was never contested. There was an almost total consensus that Japan, being small, over-populated and surrounded by enemies, was a vulnerable country, militarily as well as economically and that one way or another the country should acquire autarky. Empire was considered a necessary attribute of every first-class nation and in acquiring it 'Might was right'. Considering the way in which Western imperialists behaved and had behaved, time and again using very flimsy excuses for their gunboat-diplomacy aggression, that too was not an odd idea.

The rise of Japan to great-power status was long facilitated or in any case condoned by the big Western powers. Reactions in the West to aggressive, or in any case firm, Japanese behaviour on the international scene, as long of course as it did not directly threaten one's own interests, could be quite understanding. When Japan in 1874 sent a punitive expedition to Taiwan to retaliate for the fact that a number of inhabitants of the Ryukyu Islands had been murdered there, the British did not seem to be 'amused', but in the *New York Times* Japan received praise for solving 'the irremediable nuisance of Formosa . . . combining oriental cunning and Western bluntness' (sic P.V.) and for 'a triumph of which the youngest member of the family of civilized nations (sic P.V.) may well be proud'.[30] When, shortly after that, Japan enforced an unequal treaty on Korea, a Western newspaper congratulated the country for opening Korea and wrote about 'a diplomatic achievement of which the Japanese may well be proud'.[31] The winning of the war against China had the effect of an earthquake in international relations. With it the country 'achieved the key international goal that had precipitated three decades of Meiji reforms: It had acquired the status of an international power. . . . Westerners were falling over themselves to applaud Japan's success'.[32] In 1902, Japan and Britain concluded the first treaty of an Anglo-Japanese Alliance. In its war against Russia, Japan openly and less openly, directly and indirectly, received support from Great Britain and the United States that did not want Russia and its then supporter Imperial Germany to become hegemonic. When Japan and Russia became engaged in war in 1905, they did not intervene or even protest. Actually no one really did. The London *Times* approved of Japan's 'preventive' attack.[33] After its victory, though, the idea that Japan might have become *too* powerful increasingly also gained ground outside Russia and Germany.[34] Meiji Japan at least was thus not only *not* colonized or seriously hampered in trying to develop its economy but often actually *helped* by several Western powers in trying to do so.

Strategic considerations that 'necessitated' conquering certain regions from the very beginning were popular with the military, whereas economic considerations that favoured informal imperialism were more prominent among certain business interests. Especially when, after World War One, Japan's industrialization entered a new phase in which the import of raw materials and sources of energy for its heavy industry became vital and when many in the military had become convinced that war had turned into *total* war, i.e. a confrontation of societies and all the resources they could mobilize, military and economic considerations could easily coalesce, as they in the end did in the 1930s. International status also played a role, i.e. the wish to be a 'first-class nation', which was considered to imply having an empire. As did the ambition to become 'the England of the East' and in any case strong enough to no longer have to put up with what one considered the repeated humiliation by arrogant foreigners.[35] Mistrust, fear and a sense of humiliation by the West always – and to a large extent, rightly so – were a fixed element in Japanese foreign policies. For whatever reason and with whatever justification, the idea that Japan ought to be strong and have a safety belt and an empire, probably weakest in the 1920s after which it came back with a vengeance in the 1930s, is a quintessential ingredient of Japanese policies in the period discussed in this book.

Japan happened to become a redoubtable military force and a successful imperialist which will have convinced many Japanese that their country was on the right track. It engaged in many conflicts in the period 1868–1937 and it did not lose any of them. The

Table 24 Japan's geographic expansion to the 1930s

	Incorporated	Till	How?
Ryukyu Islands	1872–1879	Present	Annexed
Kurile Islands	1875	1945	Exchanged with Russia for Sakhalin
Bonin Islands/Ogasawara	1876	Present	
Volcano Islands	1891	Present	Annexed
Taiwan	1895	1945	Via the treaty at the end of the war with China
Karafuto	1905–1910	1945	
Korea	1905–1910	1945	Turned into a colony in stages
Manchuria 1905-1932		1945	Turned into a colony in stages
Liaotung China (Kwantung, including Port Arthur)	1905–1910	1945	Ceded to Japan after the war with Russia
Shantung, China	1914	1922	Ceded to Japan when it entered World War One
Mariana, Palau, Caroline Marshall Island Group	1914	1945	Given as a protectorate, seized from Germany in World War One
Sakhalin	1917	1924	Seized during the Russian Revolution and aftermath

Alexander, *Arc of Japan's Development*, 42.

victories it obtained as such clearly had positive consequences for its economy. Those could be direct, material gains in the form of reparations, land, resources, additional labour or more indirect, such as an increase in power with all the economic advantages that could bring. But there of course also were enormous costs involved.

While opening Japan to the external world, the Meiji rulers did their utmost to stay their own bosses. They almost without exception – and for decades with impressive success – tried to keep their country's *dependence* on the outside world to a minimum. Freedom of movement of non-Japanese in Japan outside the areas designated for foreign settlement, was only recognized in the treaties between Japan and the United Kingdom of 1894. Foreign direct investment outside designated areas was only allowed in 1899. The Mining Law, which the new government promulgated in 1872, precluded foreigners from developing underground resources. They, moreover, were not entitled to own land. When it comes to patents, there was a strict control by the government over the amount of licensed manufacturing within the country. Until 1896 foreign patentees found it almost impossible to gain any protection within Japan or to enter manufacturing directly. Foreign residents, with exceptions, could not engage in any direct manufacture. Competitive tendering forced foreign firms that were active in Japan into competitive bidding and marketing. At the same time, the Japanese could reproduce foreign techniques with impunity and market the 'copies' they produced with them under trademarks identical to those of their foreign rivals. Moreover, which as such is rather striking, they could freely import machine tools.[36] In the rest of this book we will see that this effort to not become dependent was not confined to matters of sovereignty but also extended to the exchange of money, goods, services, technologies and ideas.

Elements of continuity with Tokugawa rule in these respects, as in many others, were quite strong. Tokugawa Japan too, and even more so, was an independent sovereign polity. Foreign powers had no noteworthy leverage on its economy and society. It was quite self-conscious in its dealings with other nations that it only wanted to deal with on its own terms. It did not formally recognize the Chinese Emperor as superior, nor did it engage in a formal, official tributary relation with his realm. As a matter of fact, it had no government-to-government relations at all with China. Admittedly, on the other hand it did not explicitly deny that country's central role, culturally and politically, in East Asia and was not intent on making the relationship with the Middle Kingdom problematic. Trade relations were never complexly severed.[37]

Regular contact with the West had begun in 1543, when the first Portuguese landed on the island of Tanegashima. Toyotomi Hideyoshi (1536/1537–1598) actually had a strong interest in foreign trade and foreign exchange and stimulated them. During his period of ascendancy, Japanese commercial vessels sailed as far afield as Malaya and Siam. Tokugawa Ieyasu (1543–1616), who initially was quite open to foreign contacts too, became increasingly suspicious of foreign powers and signed an act in 1614 ordering the expulsion of Christian 'missionaries'. The Tokugawa *Bakufu* became convinced that it had to have tight control over Japan's foreign policy, not only to guarantee social peace, but also to maintain its supremacy over the other powerful lords in the country, particularly the *tozama daimyo* or 'outer' *daimyo*, who were the ones most involved in foreign trade and exchange.[38] The Portuguese, who had been the first Westerners to enter Japan, were told in 1639 to leave and not come back. After receiving the news of the Portuguese expulsion, Philip IV of Spain (till 1640 also effectively King of Portugal) ordered that any further Spanish interaction with Japan was prohibited. That interaction had officially started with a treaty, signed in 1609. According to that treaty the Spaniards could establish a factory in eastern Japan, send mining specialists from New Spain, and visit Japan in case of necessity. It was also decided that a Japanese embassy would be sent to the Spanish court.[39] The first Englishman, William Adams, had set foot in Japan in 1600. In 1613 the English East India Company opened a factory at Hirado. But when it proved impossible to obtain Japanese raw silk for import to China and with their trading area reduced to Hirado and Nagasaki from 1616 onwards, the company closed its factory in 1623. People from the Dutch Republic came to Japan since 1600. In 1641, the Dutch East India Company's merchants were ordered by the *Bakufu* to relocate their factory from Hirado to Dejima. At that time contacts with the English, Portuguese and Spaniards had stopped and they were no longer allowed to enter the country. The Dutch, as the only Westerners, were permitted to have a tiny settlement in Dejima near Nagasaki from where they could, under tight restrictions, trade with the Japanese.

Over time Tokugawa Japan opted for a much more isolationist foreign policy that later became known as the *sakoku* policy. Relations and trade between Japan and other countries were now severely limited, nearly all foreigners were barred from entering the country and the common Japanese people were kept from leaving it for a period of over 200 years. The policy was enacted by Tokugawa Iemitsu (1604–1651) through a number of edicts and policies from 1633–39, and ended after 1853 when the American Black ships commanded by Matthew Perry forced the opening of Japan to American (and, by extension, Western) trade. The Shogunate engaged in this policy to be able to keep a close watch on what entered and what left the country, to keep their outer *daimyo* from engaging in lucrative trade and developing potentially dangerous contacts with foreigners on their own and to keep out foreigners, who were suspected of importing Christianity. In the end, the policy boiled down to a strategy of managing contact.[40] The country, as we will discuss later, was never fully 'closed'.

A functioning modern state

Under Meiji rule, which in my view also is highly important in an analysis of the contribution of Japan's state to the country's economic growth, Japan was quickly transformed into a polity that came to resemble an ideal-type *modern* state much more closely than its Tokugawa predecessor. The ideal-type modern state is a polity that:

- exerts full sovereignty over a defined territory and its citizens;
- is accepted as such in international law;
- knows a rule of law that applies equally to all its citizens;
- has a monopoly of legitimate violence in the hands of a professional army and police force;

- is administered by a professional bureaucracy;
- has a monopoly of taxation;
- has a system of legitimation; and
- is characterized by a shared sense of national identity.

In such a state there are no (semi-) autonomous power centres, corporations or status groups with specific privileges that are not subjected to central authority.[41] Modern state structures in particular when they, as Weber would put it, are legal-rational and thus transparent and predictable, are undoubtedly, in principle, more efficient and conducive to growth than traditional, 'non-rationalized' polities, in particular when they function quite smoothly. It will not be by accident that the emergence of modern economic growth and the formation of modern states as a rule were intertwined processes. Of course, Japan did not become a perfect, ideal-type state to all intents and purposes. But it came quite close to it, much closer – such as in the matter of centralization and marketization – than even many polities in Europe's economic periphery.[42] I already referred to the unequal treaties that were with good reason considered an infringement on the country's sovereignty. Contact with the West forced Japan's rulers to adopt the Western 'post-Westphalian' concept of statehood and thus to clearly and unequivocally define the sovereignty, subjects and borders of their polity in order to be accepted in the emerging 'international' order. The country's weakest spots were in its 'open' periphery, where, at least according to the Western definition at the time, sovereignty was not unequivocal and exclusive, which might provide Western imperialists with an excuse to extend their sphere of interest or even simply conquer 'Japanese' territory.[43] Unsurprisingly, therefore, Japan's new rulers quickly set out to fix those unclear, shifting borders and to claim exclusive sovereignty. They did so according to what in any case with hindsight looks like a certain logic: they started by exerting a kind of 'indirect rule', then turned the regions involved into quasi-colonies and in the end absorbed them in the mother country.[44]

The first major territory Japan's new rulers incorporated in their realm was Hokkaido.[45] That island officially became Japanese territory in 1869, although many Japanese were convinced that it had always been part of Japan. It was incorporated into the *Naichi*, the 'mainland', that till then had consisted of Honshu, Shikoku and Kyushu, only in 1903.[46] It also was only then that the right to vote was given, not to the entire population but only to the Japanese who had migrated to the island. Although in the formal sense Hokkaido may have never become a colony, its original inhabitants will certainly have felt it that way – and not just because the Japanese themselves long referred to the opening up and reclamation of the island as a process of 'colonization'.[47] The very name 'Hokkaido', meaning 'Northern Sea Road', was new and a Japanese invention. In 1899, the Japanese government passed an act labelling the Ainu as 'former aborigines' or 'former natives' and began to describe them as a 'dying race', assuming they would assimilate. The Ainu were 'granted' automatic Japanese citizenship, which meant they were effectively denied the status of an indigenous group. With the Ainu becoming 'Japanese', their homeland also became Japanese and a place that had never been held by a 'foreign' country. The Ainu were forced to learn Japanese, required to adopt Japanese names, and ordered to cease certain 'uncivilized' religious practices. The

Japanese government took the land where they lived, placed it under Japanese control and distributed it among Japanese migrants who initially were just tenants whom it had encouraged to settle on it.[48]

The Ainu did not just become a minority in legal terms, having fewer rights than real Japanese, but also numerically. According to estimates there were approximately 80,000 Ainu on Hokkaido in the early eighteenth century. In 1807, officials estimated the total Ainu population of Hokkaido at about 26,000. Forty-seven years later their number was reduced to almost 18,000. The main cause of the dramatic decline was epidemic diseases. In the beginning of the 1870s, their number had been further reduced to some 16,000. In that respect, the description 'dying race' could also be taken literally. The *total* number of inhabitants of Hokkaido, including the original population, is estimated at some 60,000 in 1869; over one million in 1900; over 2.5 million in 1925 and about 3.2 million in 1940. By then, the 16,000 Ainu still on the island constituted only one half of one per cent of Hokkaido's total population.[49]

In 1872, the Ryukyu Kingdom was reconfigured as a feudal domain. In 1879, Japan annexed the entire Ryukyu Archipelago, and abolished the Ryukyu *han* to replace it by the Okinawa prefecture. Hostility against mainland Japan increased immediately after annexation in part because of the systematic attempt on the part of mainland Japan to eliminate the Ryukyuan culture, including the language, religion, and cultural practices. Both land reform and conscription were introduced late here.[50] Japan introduced public education that permitted only the use of standard Japanese. In 1912, Okinawans first obtained the right to vote for representatives to the National Diet, which had been established in 1890.[51] By 1940 total population of the prefecture was some 600,000.[52] The so-called Bonin Islands had been claimed by Japan in 1862. In 1875 the Japanese government renamed them the Ogasawara Islands. They were put under the direct control of the Home Ministry in 1876.

When it comes to international recognition Japan's position was ambivalent. It undeniably was part of the international community in the sense that it was a country that concluded treaties and with which treaties were concluded. On the other hand, a number of fundamental international treaties of which it was a signatory, were 'unequal' treaties, which the Japanese interpreted as a sign that their country was not considered a full, 'civilized' member of the international community. Those unequal treaties were only fully and officially revoked in 1911.

How about the rule of law and equality before the law? In the Constitution that was proclaimed in 1889 and enacted in November 1890 after some two decades of discussion and at times serious conflict and that for almost fifty years formed the legal foundation of Japan's political system, the inhabitants of Japan did not become citizens but rather subjects, to whom, moreover, the law did not always apply equally. The Emperor clearly was not an ordinary citizen. In article 1 of the Constitution it read: 'The Empire of Japan shall be reigned over and governed by a line of Emperors unbroken for ages eternal.' In article 3, he was described as 'sacred and inviolable' and as such a godlike source of law and sovereignty.[53] He became *Tenno*, and as such had a position that combined – at least in the eyes of several observers – the powers of an Emperor like that of Germany and those of a religious leader like the Pope of Rome.[54] The fact that his position became described as that of a godlike source of sovereignty, implies that the country under his imperial rule cannot be considered a modern *nation*-state as nationalists ideally would define it. In such a state, sovereignty resides with the indivisible nation, not with some person and his lineage as embodiment of it. In so far as Japan under the Meiji Constitution nevertheless can be considered a nationalist society, its nationalism from the 1880s onwards increasingly became ethnic, which means that being a real Japanese became a matter of 'blood' and 'descent'. The more civic nationalist ideas propagated by the Freedom and Civil Rights Movement clearly lost support and in the end, were not integral to the Constitution.[55]

The law – which as such is a different matter – did not consider all subjects as equal. After the Meiji Restoration Japan still had its aristocrats. A new peerage was created that increased in number. After an initial phase in which there were four estates (as a distinction was made between higher and lower samurai) the population in the 1870s became classified in three estates. The highest was that of the peers. In 1869, under the new Meiji Government, this Japanese peerage was created by an Imperial decree merging the former *kuge* and the former *daimyo* – in 1868 together 427 families – into a single new aristocratic class, called the *kazoku*. A second imperial ordinance in 1884, grouped the *kazoku* into five ranks, equivalent to prince or duke, marquis, count, viscount and baron. In 1884, this class had 504 members; in 1911, that number had increased to 923. By 1928, through promotions and new creations, there were a total of 954 peers. The *kazoku* reached a peak of 1016 families in 1944.[56] The samurai became the lower aristocracy called *shizoku*, and the rest of the population, now entitled to have a family name, became the *heimin*, the common people. The legal implications of these differences were tiny as compared to the differences between estates under Tokugawa rule but it nevertheless should be pointed out that there was no full equality. The peers had the privilege of becoming members of the House of Peers. In 1889, the House of Peers Ordinance established the House of Peers and its composition. For the first session of the Imperial Diet (1889–1890), there were 145 hereditary members and 106 imperial appointees and high taxpayers. With the creation of new peers, additional seats for members of the former Korean nobility and four seats for representatives from the Japan Imperial Academy membership peaked at 409 seats by 1938.

When it comes to the former 'untouchables', always a quite substantial group of the population during the Tokugawa era, their official discrimination was abolished in 1871.[57] But in practice they continued to be second class, discriminated citizens. They were now called 'new common people', often ended up in specific hamlets and became known and discriminated against as *burakumin*, 'people of the hamlet'. Japanese family registration was fixed to ancestral home address until recently, which allowed people to deduce their *burakumin* origins.[58] In principle, Hokkaido, the Ryukyu Islands and the Osagawara Islands over time all became 'normal' parts of Japan and their inhabitants 'normal citizens'. In practice, however, in particular when it comes to the Ainu population of Hokkaido but also to some extent to the original inhabitants of Ryukyu, forms of discrimination were rife.[59]

After the Restoration, central government quickly began to acquire the famous monopolies that many political scientists, following Max Weber, consider constitutive for a modern state, i.e. the monopolies of legitimate violence, administration and taxation. Under Meiji rule Japan's government successfully set out to actually, exclusively and unambiguously govern over a precisely defined 'Japan' and over precisely defined 'subjects' and to do so by means of professionals. The monopolies referred to were in practice wielded by a *professional* military and police force and by a *professional* civilian bureaucracy that offered 'careers open to talent'. In 1876, the samurai lost their right to wear swords in public. Thereafter only active-duty military personnel and police officers were allowed to carry swords.

Like every modern state, Meiji Japan developed a system of legitimation. That too took some time and some improvising but the Constitution of 1890 may well be interpreted as its formal expression. When it comes to a shared sense of national identity, another important element in the definition of a modern state, there was a very intense effort to create it that to all intents and purposes has to be considered 'successful', even though one has to realize that the country was much less of a unified homogenous nation-state than has often been suggested, by Japanese and foreigners alike.[60] It was only in 1899 that the Nationality Act legally defined what it meant to be Japanese. At its core was a concept of the Japanese people, not as constitutionally defined 'subjects' but as a quasi-ethnic 'people'. Specifically, the Act stipulated that those born to a Japanese father would be the Japanese people, not the Japanese subjects as it read in the Constitution of 1890. This expressed a tacit understanding that everyone who lived on the Japanese archipelago prior to the establishment of the Nationality Act was Japanese, and completely sidestepped the question of Ainu or Ryukyuan identity.[61] In that context, it is interesting that inhabitants of Korea, Taiwan and South Sakhalin, in principle, just like the Chinese, were considered as peoples who *could* be assimilated.[62] That, however, did not mean that they, as clearly shows in the case of the Koreans who worked in Japan, would be treated as equals.

There of course were ethnic differences or 'nationality' issues in Post-Restoration Japan, increasing with further expansion, but the country itself did come much closer to the ideal of a modern nation state than it had done under Tokugawa rule. The Meiji Restoration can certainly be seen as 'the construction of a nation state'.[63] As indicated, a definition of who were the country's citizens or rather subjects, as a matter of fact occurred quite late, formally only with the Nationality Act of 1899, the same year in which a comprehensive civil code was proclaimed. That proclamation of that code, just like that of the Constitution, should not be interpreted as a sign of progress in terms of 'freedom and people's rights'. It certainly did not mean an improvement of the legal position of women whose position now in many respects as compared to that of adult male fathers or husbands was defined as one of second-class citizens.

Tokugawa legacies?

To what extent did the Meiji Restoration and its aftermath actually *modernize* the state-structure of Japan, i.e. to what extent had Tokugawa Japan *not* been a modern state? The question whether the Tokugawa 'state' exerted full sovereignty over a defined territory and specific citizens, in my view has to be answered negatively. From a modern perspective, it was also not unambiguous where sovereignty resided: With the Emperor, with the Shogun or even with the *daimyo*?

In practical politics, the Emperor to all intents and purposes was just a figurehead. But the fact remains that he was still seen as the ultimate source of both political and cultural legitimacy on behalf of whom the Shoguns ruled. Officially, the prerogative of appointing the Shogun resided with him whereas a Shogun only directly ruled part of Japan and the Emperor was emperor of all of Japan. As a rule, and with good reason, the Shogun is considered to have been the *de facto* ruler of Japan. One has to realize though, that the Tokugawa only exercised direct rule over their so-called house-lands. Those only covered part, roughly one-sixth, of Japan. The shogun's authority as a domainal lord was limited to the lands of the Tokugawa House. On top of that he ruled indirectly over a substantial tract of neighbouring land via his banner men vassals, whose rights to retain private armies and domains he always acknowledged. In total, he might claim to rule about one-fourth of the country. Apparently neither the first and very strong Tokugawa ruler Ieyasu, nor his many successors, felt the need to try and expand *Bakufu* authority vis-à-vis the outside *daimyo*. Had a Shogun claimed the imperial title for himself he would very probably have alienated friend and foe alike. Besides, there was no pressure to push the process of centralization to its logical conclusion as the outer *daimyo* almost till the very end of Tokugawa rule did not present much of a threat. What we see is rather the contrary: after the death of Tokugawa Ieayasu, the *Bakufu* more and more allowed the great lords to handle their own affairs, despite occasional criticism of this policy, permitting greater contact between men of the several domains and between *daimyo* and the court.[64] In a way the system, after some initial wrangling till roughly 1650, seemed in a balance with neither the Shogun nor the mighty *daimyo* apparently intent on extending their power.[65]

Nevertheless, the power base of the Shogun seems to have been somewhat eroded over time. This is how Totman describes the Tokugawa domain by the late Edo period:

> a chaotic maze of house land and liege vassal and *daimyo* lands loosely scattered about under varying types of control, with varying levels and methods of taxation and varying degrees of population pressure or insufficiency.[66]

If we are to believe Totman, over time Tokugawa house lands seemed to come off poorly in terms of productivity as well as strategic location, whereas in terms of food supplies, the *Bakufu* in the nineteenth century had a smaller advantage than it had had two hundred years earlier. In his view, there also was an overall decline of the military and strategic power of the Shogunate.[67]

Outside their personal domains, the Shoguns ruled very indirectly as overlords or suzerains of different types of (liege) vassals and *daimyo* to whom they could have different relationships. When it came to the sovereignty of their fief-holding vassals or *daimyo*, those, in normal circumstances and in day-to-day affairs, to all intents and purposes could act as sovereign rulers. Many *daimyo* in any case in practice could behave as if they were autonomous rulers and style themselves as 'a minor public authority' as long as they kept within the boundaries of the shogun's 'great public authority'.[68] Tokugawa Japan overall knew a lot of self-governing, self-organizing and self-disciplining organizations. There was a widespread practice of holding collectives responsible and of letting people carefully monitor one another via so-called five-men groups.[69] Public institutions engaged in social control tended to be relatively weak. Eleanor Westney points out that even though Tokugawa was a very 'controlled' society, it had hardly any people that one might call 'policemen'.[70]

When it comes to the borders of the Tokugawa realm, they were not sharply demarcated. The Ryukyu Islands were ruled over by a king who had become a tributary of the *daimyo* who ruled in the domain of Satsuma and who in turn held his domain as retainer of the shogun. That king also had a direct relation to the shogun and on top of that was a tributary to the Emperor of China. Ezo, or rather a part of it in the south, with certain exceptions, was ruled by the Matsumae clan that held a fief as retainer of the shogun. Relations with Korea were maintained via the clan that ruled the domain of Tsushima as retainer of the shogun. The position of Korea from a Western perspective was unclear as the country was ruled by a king who was also a tributary of China, a country with which Japan did not have any formal relations from the very beginning of Qing rule. The Chinese traders who came to Nagasaki, actually were closely watched by the Shogunate but officially it kept aloof and left all administration and negotiation to the so-called Nagasaki Chinese Translation Bureau.[71]

This unclear sovereignty and its porous, flexible borders would make Japan increasingly vulnerable to Western intrusion. In Japan 'Proper' itself, the lands under direct rule of the shogun and the lands administrated by the *daimyo* were not subject to the same rules, whereas the domains of the *daimyo* could also differ from one another in status, actual rights and obligations. Tokugawa Japan was not an integrated national state. There was no national – i.e. pan-Japanese – taxation, no national public treasury, no national bureaucracy, no national army, no national police force, no national school system. The Shogun's house lands were scattered throughout no fewer than forty-seven of Japan's sixty-eight provinces.[72] To ask whether Tokugawa Japan had been recognized as a state in international law is 'Eurocentric'. An Asian 'state system' functioning according to the Westphalian logic that had become predominant in Europe from the late eighteenth century onwards, simply didn't exist.[73] When in the nineteenth century the logic of the East Asian system was put to the test by Western imperialists, it soon became clear who would have to give in.[74]

The people over whom sovereignty was exercised in Tokugawa Japan were not all subject to the same law, nor were they equal to the law. One might say the Emperor in certain respects was outside the law, whereas the Shogun to all intents and purposes, was a dictator who made it. The *daimyo*, who on a day-to-day basis ruled most of Japan, were a variegated estate. The term '*daimyo*' refers to a direct retainer of the Shogun whose domain was valued at at least 10,000 *koku*, although there were cases where a retainer of a *daimyo* had a domain of over 10,000 *koku*, but was nevertheless not considered *daimyo*. Tokugawa Ieyasu divided the *daimyo* into two groups depending on their relationship to him at the time of the Battle of Sekigahara, in 1600, against the troops of Toyotomi Hideyori. These two groups were fixed as classes. This means that *daimyo* were not transferred from one class to another, although, especially under the first five shoguns, they were often moved around and many of them lost their position altogether. Those who were already, with a few exceptions, his vassals at the time of the battle were considered *fudai daimyo*, or 'vassal *daimyo*'. They were also called 'hereditary *daimyo*'. They included those who became *daimyo* during the Edo period, mostly bureaucrats whose stipends were raised. Relatives of Tokugawa Ieyasu were also included in this class. Their domains tended to be small as compared to those of so-called *tozama* or outside *daimyo*, i.e. all the others; allies, enemies, and neutrals at the time of Sekigahara and their descendants, who held a fief. Many of them, especially the greater ones, had close ties with the Shogunate, including marriage ties. The *tozama daimyo* tended to have bigger domains that were further away from the lands of the Shogun. They did not take part in the bureaucracy or concern themselves with national affairs, at least not publicly. They were normally the ones the Shogunate called upon to carry out any difficult or expensive undertaking. They were not taxed as such, though. Usually a third group of *daimyo* is distinguished, the collateral, related or *shimpan daimyo*, many of whom could and did partake in government functions. Normally they are classified in three categories: the 'three houses' (*sanke*), the 'three lords' (*sankyo*) and the other relatives (*kamon*), who might be involved in Edo government and politics. Of the thirty or more related houses established during the Edo period, twenty-four survived to 1868. In practice at the time, *daimyo* were classified and 'ranked' on the basis of a variety of different metrics. It would digress to try and do justice to the many differences in exact background, rank, status, function, source of income and power of these three categories and their subcategories. The most relevant point for me is the very existence of all these differences which made running the realm as a whole quite complicated.

As a matter of fact, the situation was even a little more complicated because of the existence of the so-called liege vassals who are usually identified as banner men (*hatamoto*) and housemen (*gokenin*), even though the exact meaning and relevance of these titles was not entirely clear.[75] Usually the *hatamoto* were valued at 100 to 10,000 *koku* and the *gokenin* at rarely more than 200 *koku*. The number of *hatamoto* was about 5,000 and that of *gokenin* about 17,000. Over time they increasingly became a salaried class living from stipends from *Bakufu* warehouses and not from any revenue from lands that they could consider their fief. Only about 2,500 of them were sustained by income from fiefs, which they administered privately with differing degrees of authority. They in principle *all* lived in Edo. They were expected to mount rear vassals in case of need. In their case that number decreased strikingly from 60,000 (many of them actually not mounted) in 1633, to only some 10,000 in 1862. In peacetime, they more and more became a police force and administrators and provided the bulk of *Bakufu* officials. Vassal *daimyo* employed by the *Bakufu* who still had fiefs were prevented from establishing strong roots in their castle region.

There were different degrees of trust from the shoguns when it comes to different *daimyo*. Till the very last they trusted their 'own' vassal forces most. Over time the number of domains ruled by *daimyo* – in particular, the number ruled by *fudai daimyo* with rather small domains, i.e. domains assessed at less than 50,000 *koku* – increased from over 200 at the beginning of Tokugawa rule to some 250 to 300 at the moment the domains were abolished.[76] As indicated, the number of collateral or related *daimyo* continued to be relatively small. The number of *tozama* in 1868 was about one hundred. The rest of the *daimyo* then were *fudai*.

Not only could the status of *daimyo* differ, but the size of their domains could be very different too. At the very end of their existence, these were the largest domains of Japan in terms of their annual output in *koku* of rice.

Table 25 The largest domains of Japan by output in 1869

Domain	Annual output in *koku*
Shogunate	4,000,000
Kaga	1,350,000
Choshu	990,000
Satsuma	870,000
Kumamoto	790,000
Owari	780,000
Saga	720,000
Fukuoka	570,000
Kii	540,000
Tosa	500,000

Koyama, Moriguchi and Sng, 'Geopolitics and Asia's Little Divergence', 9. The output of the Shogunate is based on an official estimate. The last Shogun after his fall claimed that his land had actually only amounted to two million *koku*. See Hillsborough, *Samurai revolution*, 11, note 4. Overall actual rice production of domains was higher than their official estimates. The other figures refer to actual outputs in 1869. The actual production of Japan as a whole has been estimated at almost forty-seven million *koku* for 1872. For a list of all the domains of 100,000 or more *koku*, at the beginning of the eighteenth century see Hall, '*Bakuhan* system', 151. Interesting information on the size of fiefs at differing moments in time can also be found in Samson, *History of Japan*, 210–228, and Totman, *Politics in the Tokugawa Bakufu*, passim.

The annual output of these nine domains and the Shogun's lands alone amounted to more than eleven million *koku* at a time when total output of Japan has been estimated at about forty-seven million *koku*. The other thirty-six million *koku* thus came from over 250 domains. That would on average be some 140,000 *koku* per domain. In the 1860s, according to Mark Koyama, Chiaki Moriguchi and Tuan-Hwee Sng, 166 out of 266 domains had annual outputs below 50,000 *koku*.[77] That means that the bulk of the domains were tiny. What should become clear even in my brief survey, is that Tokugawa Japan was a very fragmented country consisting of many different, in many respects all but autonomous parts of very differing sizes, administered by rulers of often different status. I fail to see how so many so tiny and so different polities could have survived as viable and independent entities, let alone as viable and independent *industrializing* entities in the new global 'order' that was created by Western powers in the second half of the nineteenth century.

Shogun and *daimyo* were 'members' of the warrior estate of the samurai, one of a number of different estates with different rights and, in any case officially, a quite restricted social and geographical mobility. According to the official classification, Tokugawa society was composed of samurai, peasants, artisans and merchants, that is if we ignore several minor groups outside this classification, the most important ones being the court nobility, the clergy and the outcasts. Samurai were placed at the top of society because they were the ruling class and set a high moral example for others to follow. Peasants came second because they produced the most important commodity, food. Artisans came third because they produced non-essential goods. Merchants held the lowest position, at least in the official system of values: they were assumed to not actually produce anything and to therefore contribute least to society. The rights and obligations of these different groups were very different. The core distinction was that between the warriors and the rest of the population.[78] The lines between artisans and merchants who both lived in cities were often blurred.

At the end of Tokugawa rule, at least some 5 to 6 per cent of the population consisted of samurai and their families.[79] Halfway through the seventeenth century the percentage for the entire country had been higher but was certainly still below 10 per cent. There were big differences in regions when it came to the number of samurai. In Edo, at least one-third of the population were samurai. In Satsuma, that was a special threat for the *Bakufu*, being the second biggest domain and located far from Edo, one in four adult men was a sword carrier at the end of Tokugawa rule. In Choshu the ratio of samurai to commoners at the time was one to ten. In Tosa, to give one last example, there were some 18,000 retainers on some 400,000 inhabitants during the eighteenth century. Very roughly two-thirds of the samurai were of higher, one-third of lower, rank. There were many finer distinctions. The bulk of the samurai lived by stipends although there also were so-called *goshi* or 'warrior farmers', i.e. samurai with land. In Satsuma, for example, their number was quite substantial. In principle, samurai were warriors but many of them became 'bureaucrats'. Often, they had to because of their dwindling incomes. Many of them became 'Jack of all trades'. A specific group of samurai that has to be mentioned here are the so-called *ronin*, samurai that for whatever reason – their lord having lost his domain, for example – had become master-less. They were quite a large group, numbering some 400,000. Under the third Tokugawa shogun Iemitsu (1604–1651), their number even approached half a million.[80]

At the end of Tokugawa rule all in all some 380,000 to 400,000 people were defined as 'base people' or 'outcasts', mostly known as *eta* and *hinin*.[81] This is not the place to analyse what exact categories there were, what differentiated them, what kind of work they did or did not do, nor what exactly turned them into outcasts. For that I refer to the literature. Here it suffices to say that there was a very substantial group of people who basically were *not* part of Tokugawa society.[82]

Can one claim that the rulers of Tokugawa Japan had a monopoly of legitimate violence that resided in the hands of a professional army and police force? I will discuss this question in more detail later and confine myself here to the comment that the military and those who, with some anachronism, might be described as doing 'police work' in Tokugawa Japan, were not working in a well-structured bureaucratic system based on merit and achievement. Apart from that, it would be hard anyhow to consider the samurai warriors after some two centuries of peace as professionals in the sense of well-trained and battle-hardened soldiers. Things were no different when it came to civilian officials, in so far as it is helpful to distinguish between military and civilian functions, that both were all but monopolized by samurai. Shogunate and *daimyo* tried all sorts of measures to give their administrations and military a more 'meritocratic' tinge, but the basic principles of the system of Tokugawa rule, that was based on ascription and status rather than achievement and competence, were only abolished after Tokugawa rule itself ended.

The question of whether the state in Tokugawa Japan had a monopoly of taxation can be answered unambiguously with 'No'. Every domain had its own system of taxation. The tax rates and methods of tax collecting were in principle set by the 'local' *daimyo*. The question whether it knew one 'national' system of legitimation is not easy to answer. I already pointed out that the positions and roles of the various rulers in this respect was not unequivocal, at least from our modern perspective. That brings us to the question whether Tokugawa Japan was characterized by a shared sense of national identity. One may discuss to what extent the idea 'Japan' was a lived identity under Tokugawa rule but I do not think anyone would want to defend the thesis that there was a national identity in Tokugawa Japan like that in post-French Revolution national states in the West or like it emerged in post-Restoration Japan.

A centralized and integrated state

In my view, it is fairly obvious that *from the perspective of its potential for economic growth* a modern state like the one that took shape after the Meiji Restoration was more efficient than a parcellized, hierarchic and fractured polity like Tokugawa Japan. Let me expand a little more on that with a focus on aspects of national centralization and integration. In my view, these contributed very substantially to the impressive economic growth of Japan in the period under discussion.[83] The cornerstone of that process was the abolishing in 1871 of the more than 250 domains and the division of the whole of Japan, the lands of the Shogun included, into a far smaller number of administrative units with overall an identical administrative structure and status and falling under a centralized organization.

After the defeat of forces loyal to the Tokugawa Shogunate, the new Meiji government confiscated all lands formerly under direct control of the Shogunate and all lands controlled by *daimyo* who had remained loyal to the Tokugawa cause. These lands accounted for approximately a quarter of the land area of Japan. They were reorganized into prefectures administered by governors appointed directly by the central government. In 1869, the lords of Choshu and Satsuma surrendered their domains to the Emperor. Fearing that their loyalty would be questioned, the *daimyo* of 260 other domains followed suit. Fourteen domains that failed to voluntarily 'return' their domains were ordered to do so by the Court, on threat of military action. In return for surrendering their hereditary authority, the *daimyo* were re-appointed as non-hereditary governors of their former domains (which were now called prefectures), and were allowed to keep 10 per cent of the tax revenues, based on actual rice production. The former *daimyo* had now become government employees, but still retained some military and fiscal independence. This was considered a threat to central authority. In August 1871, by Imperial Edict, the remaining domains were reorganized into three urban prefectures (*fu*) and 302 prefectures (*ken*). Their number was then reduced through consolidation the following year to three urban prefectures and seventy-two prefectures, and to three urban prefectures and forty-four prefectures by 1888. The number of villages was also reduced by some 7,000 between 1874 and 1886. Between 1888 and 1889, another 56,000 were 'extinguished'. When the new city code was enacted in 1911, there were 16,000 villages and towns.[84] Government was also streamlined by the creation over time of separate Ministries.

The construction of a centralized national state in Japan implied the creation of an institutional framework that, from the perspective of central government, made the country more 'legible' and thus easier and more efficient to rule. For the meaning of the concept 'legibility' I can do no better than quote James Scott who coined the expression:

> I began to see legibility as a central problem in statecraft. The pre-modern state was, in many crucial respects, partially blind. It knew precious little about its subjects, their wealth, their landholdings and yields, their location, their very identity. It lacked anything like a detailed 'map' of its terrain and people. It lacked, for the most part, a measure, a metric, that would allow it to 'translate' what it knew into a common standard necessary for a synoptic view. As a result, its interventions were often crude and self-defeating.[85]

Like governments of Europe at the time Japan's rulers began to intensively 'X-ray' their society to make it 'governable', as Foucault would say.[86]

Efficiently and effectively ruling the country meant knowing the size and composition of its population. In 1872 a nationwide population census, based on the Family Register was published. The first national census based on a full sampling of inhabitants was conducted in 1920, and repeated every five years thereafter. The introduction of universal and obligatory conscription in 1872 also increased the rulers' knowledge of and grip on their human resources. Efficiently and effectively ruling a country also means knowing its economic resources. In the newly created tax system, a land tax was to provide the bulk of all government revenue. It was decided that individual owners of land had to pay it in cash on the basis of an assessment of their land's value.[87] That required an up-to-date cadastre. Systematic survey work was started already in 1869 with the establishment of the Geography Division in the Ministry of Civil Services. The first modern cadastre survey was started in 1873 and would take several years. No fewer than 109 million properties were entered in it. Several cartographic projects were started.[88] A modern state that wants to be effective simply cannot function without 'statistics'. Unsurprisingly in 1869, the Ministry of Budget and Taxation was established, and in 1870, orders were given to produce a 'Table of Products by Prefecture'. In 1871, the then existing *Dajokan*, or Council of State, established the Statistics Division.[89] The introduction of a 'national' time, measured in years, months, weeks, days, hours, minutes and seconds, as well as national holidays, can also be seen in this light. The introduction of a new Gregorian calendar, which brought Japan's calendar into alignment with that of most of the Western powers, had the added advantage that it enabled government to not pay salaries over the two months that 'disappeared' in the process of calendar adaptation. Traditionally every first, sixth, eleventh, sixteenth, twenty-first and twenty-sixth day of the month had been a holiday, at least for people working in towns. In the Western, Christian calendar there was only one day off per week. In that respect too adapting to Western habits was 'advantageous' to government. The changes in this respect initially created more confusion than clarity. Well into the twentieth century, many villagers and merchants continued to work according to the old work schedule.[90] The actual development and fixation of a standardized language came into effect rather late, in the beginning of the twentieth century.[91]

When it comes to the institutional infrastructure of the new centralized and integrated state of Japan, the fundamental aspect is that administration now indeed became *uniform and national* with state institutions holding sovereignty. Whereas the domains were only abolished in 1871, the new rulers acted quite fast and firm when it came to taking over sovereign power from domain governments in monetary issues. In September 1869, the use of specie in domestic transactions was prohibited. Paper notes and coins minted by the previous domainal governments had to be exchanged for government notes. In that way, government excluded 'competing forms of money' and established a monopoly for its paper notes. These central government notes were non-convertible and actually imposed on Japanese society, although the promise was later made that government would use newly minted coins to redeem them.[92] Government in fact had no other option than to rely on issuing notes to cover its spending needs. During the period 1868 to 1871, it may have been ruling the entire country but as yet could only tax the shogunal lands. It would sooner or later have to find a way to redeem the notes circulating in the economy. That implied developing a centralized fiscal state.

The New Coinage Act of 1871 declared the yen as the standard unit of value and legal tender for transactions of any value.[93] In the same year, it was decided to create a Bank of Japan following the model of the centralized Bank of England. That, however, did not work out. In 1872, a decentralized national bank system was founded, this time following the model of the USA. In this system, government gave private banks, which somewhat confusingly were called 'national banks', the privilege to issue banknotes.[94] Between 1876 and 1879, no fewer than 149 of such banks were established. They were substantially larger than private banks or quasi-banks but most of them still were rather small. Half of them were set up by former members of the warrior class, which provides another clear example of continuity between the Tokugawa and the Meiji era. In 1880, such members invested 76 per cent of total capital inlay, merchants less than 15 per cent.[95] In 1882, one returned to the original plan and founded the Bank of Japan, a central bank modelled after Belgium's central bank. From 1886 onwards, that bank monopolized the issue of convertible banknotes which became legal tender.[96] Overall, the development of a banking system was fairly slow and certainly not without problems.[97] Before 1905, the traditional banking sector (money lending, rotating credit cooperatives, bankrolling of investments by friends and relatives) was as important in terms of flows of funds channelled through those institutions as was the new financial sector consisting of banks, the postal saving system and insurance companies. Government also established a series of specialized banks – saving banks, commercial banks, and banks concentrating on foreign trade and the handling of foreign currencies – that eventually took over many of the functions originally given to the national banks.[98] There seems to be consensus that Japan developed a satisfactory system of currency and money supply already in the 1880s, before industrialization got under way, and that a banking system was created in advance of industrial demand for its loans and other financial services. One may conclude that between 1868 and World War One, Japan developed an extensive, variegated, sophisticated modern financial system, well-structured to meet the needs of economic development. It has to be added, that Hugh Patrick from whom I take these claims somewhat relativizes the importance of the state in this context.[99]

It is important to note that the banking system through its loans to enterprises and individuals who then subscribed to new shares was the principal source of funds for industry. Banks did not just provide money, they also gave 'administrative guidance' and so exerted their influence. Japanese banks were almost all designed to direct most savings into industrial investment or into infrastructure on behalf of industry.[100] Small-scale enterprise and agriculture were residual claimants upon their funds for investment. Government too saw to it that some groups enjoyed a virtual monopoly on its largesse.[101] Under the policy of over-loan, the Bank of Japan, that had close ties with the Ministry of Finance that deposited its revenue with it, allowed certain banks to run negative reserves. This means it allowed them to become net borrowers. In that way, it ensured the credibility of the big investment banks.[102]

In this context, it is interesting to mention the fact that national banks were Japan's first corporations in 1871 and that the development of a business system, at least initially, also depended to a large extent, on government encouragement. Here developments were rather slow. Unlimited and limited corporate liability, for example, were only legally defined in 1883 whereas it was only in 1893 that government enacted a commercial code.[103]

But let us return to the building of a centralized (here implying uniform, monetized and supervised) tax system as it was started with the Meiji Restoration. Only by means of such a system, could the new government collect revenues to pay for the debts it had incurred in taking over power. The outcome was *one* polity with *one* uniform tax system instead of the fractured, differentiated tax system of Tokugawa Japan with its more than 250 fairly autonomous domains and its shogunal lands that all had their own systems of collecting and, to a large extent, spending tax income and other forms of revenues. There now emerged one central institution covering the entire country, which collected, managed and spent revenues according to general rates with standardized methods of assessment and payment. That payment would now in principle be in money. This new system made collecting, managing and spending revenue easier, more efficient and thus cheaper. Such a system could of course only function in an economy with a high level of commercialization and as such tells us something about the state of the economy. Management of government finance became highly centralized. Already by the late 1880s, Japan had a modern fiscal state. This is how Wenkai He defines such a state:

> the modern fiscal state has two closely connected institutional features. First, it centralizes tax collection, which allows the state to allocate spending out of a consolidated source of revenue. This greatly improves efficiency in managing government finance. Second, it can use centrally collected revenue as capital to leverage long-term financial resources from the markets. It thus achieves an economy of scale in mobilizing financial resources.[104]

By 1880, national banks and a number of major private banks handled up to 85 per cent of government tax revenue and expenditures.[105] The Bank of Japan was to centrally manage all government treasuries across the country and take care of central government's revenue and expenditure. Already in 1883, it began to remit government revenue and disburse government spending. The Meiji government now no longer was dependent on private banks to transfer official funds. This achievement put the entire government revenue and funds under the management of the Bank of Japan, which in turn strengthened the Ministry of Finance.[106] The possibility to now collect revenue in the entire country and, via credit, to increase state spending of course meant a serious strengthening, at least in principle, of the central state. More centralized institutions were also created for collecting indirect taxes, that became increasingly important. By 1880, Japan already had a centralized bureaucracy for assessing and collecting taxes on alcohol, which provided a substantial part of its revenue.[107]

In the follow-up to the Meiji Restoration, the institutional set-up was built that created the conditions in which Japan could effectively become one integrated economy with all the economies of scale that entails. The new centralized administrative regime led to a more formally integrated, borderless economy with – for reasons indicated above – lower transactions costs as against the previous situation, the more so as several domains had developed quite mercantilist strategies to protect and support their own economies. It also entailed more unification, standardization and interlinking of transport and communication systems. Private economic actors could now operate in a larger, more legible and uniform and, very importantly, more predictable setting. Better integration of the economy of what now indeed was the political and economic entity 'Japan' led to internal catching up and spreading of best practices. This in turn led to an increase of production and productivity.[108] During the Tokugawa period, agricultural productivity for example had varied between regions, partly because fief boundaries acted as barriers to the diffusion of best practices. Meiji policies set out to obliterate such regional differences in agricultural productivity through the systematic encouragement of the diffusion of such practices.[109]

It is far too easily forgotten that such an infrastructure is literally fundamental for economic growth and that many, if not most, states never manage to adequately build it. For an historical illustration of that thesis I can do no better than refer the interested reader to Larry Epstein's *Freedom and growth*, in which he shows how in Western Europe between 1300 and 1700 differences in centralization and integration led to differences in economic growth and economic potential. This is his conclusion, of course for his specific study, but in principle transferable to other cases.

> Centralisation … lowered domestic transport costs, made it easier to enforce contracts and to match demand and supply, intensified economic competition between towns and strengthened urban hierarchies, weakened urban monopolies over the countryside, and stimulated labour mobility and technological diffusion.[110]

To what extent was Tokugawa Japan an integrated and centralized polity?

The differences in this respect between Tokugawa Japan and Japan after the Restoration in my view can only have been striking. How striking of course depends on the question how centralized and integrated Tokugawa Japan actually was. That question has been hotly debated. Let us again for the sake of analysis distinguish between political and economic integration. For the extent of political integration, I here only refer to publications by Mark Ravina, Luke Roberts and Ronald Toby. In the end, I side with Toby when he claims that – all the 'sprouts' of state- and nation-building in the domains notwithstanding – under Tokugawa rule there existed a kind of Japanese state of which the Shogunate *de facto* was the sovereign ruler.[111] The Shogun unmistakably was the 'central' ruler and the *daimyo* unmistakably were his subjects. The Shogun's power over Japan as a whole via his grip on the *daimyo* was extensive and not disputed until the very end of the period of Tokugawa rule. The *daimyo* never developed into a countervailing power to the Shogun who had by far the largest economic and military resources. They were hindered in building a strong domainal power basis, in particular through the *sankin kotai*-system. They in any case initially were not allowed to have contact with one another and thus could not collude, which would have been difficult anyhow considering their differences in status. A protective ring of *fudai* and *shimpan daimyo*, moreover, kept the potentially more dangerous *tozama daimyo* at a distance of the shogunal lands. The obstacles to any vassal *daimyo* seizing the shogunal office itself were formidable. The position of the Shogun as such was legitimate and the Tokugawa house never lacked a candidate with some legitimate claim to the position.[112] In that respect one can argue that there indeed are good reasons to defend the thesis that Tokugawa already was a state, even if one can discuss whether it should preferably be called 'feudal' – as has long been the usage among Marxist historians – 'centralized feudalist', 'absolutist', 'composite' or 'compound'.[113]

But, it could be argued, even though Tokugawa Japan thus may have already been more of a state-like structure than scholars focusing on the indeed increasing 'autonomy' of different domains like Ravina and in particular Roberts would be willing to admit, it would be hard to deny that with the Meiji Restoration, Japan 'formally' as well as 'practically' became a *much more* fully centralized and integrated state. That Restoration inaugurated the transition from a realm consisting of some 250 distinct domains plus the *tenryo* lands that belonged directly to the Tokugawa Shogunate, to an integrated realm under one ruler and rule. Even though the country in the person of the Shogun may have had a central sovereign with substantial power over the entire realm, that realm was *not*, as I already indicated earlier, an integrated national *state*. How could it be as it had no national – i.e. pan-Japanese – taxation, no national public treasury, no national bureaucracy, no national army, no national police force, no national school system. After the *Kambu* and *Empo* eras, i.e. 1661–1681, no nationwide survey of land was ever again undertaken during Tokugawa rule.[114] One may even seriously doubt whether the realm became more integrated after the first shoguns had consolidated their position and their successors often developed an attitude of leaving well alone. It has to be pointed out though, that at the domain level, in contrast, there was increasing centralization. There the *daimyo* strengthened their position as against their retainers whom they when possible forced to live in castle towns. That made them loose their regional, rural base and made them fully dependent on stipends from their lord.

Its political fragmentation meant that from the perspective of political economy Tokugawa Japan in several respects clearly was *not* a unity. At the end of the Tokugawa era there circulated some 1,600, if not more, *han satu*, i.e. paper money currencies printed by *daimyo* that were used *in* their domains but hardly if at all *outside* them.[115]

Moreover, recent publications show that several domains in Tokugawa Japan developed all sorts of mercantilist economic policies, which could easily function as a break on wider and deeper economic integration of the entire realm.[116] Some domain rulers began to increasingly define their interests in terms of the prosperity of their own 'country' and to resent the subservience to the Shogun whom they increasingly regarded as no more than some far-away overlord. The costs of *Bakufu* duties were increasingly regarded as a weakening of the domain. Merchants started arguing along similar lines and began to justify their activities referring to their contribution to common wealth of their domain. Promoting exports of one's domain and hampering 'foreign' imports became a popular strategy. The heyday of the use of *kokueki* rhetoric, i.e. rhetoric that emphasized the 'national' interest of specific domains happened to be in the nineteenth century. The following quote from 1813–1814, made in a discussion about the silk industry, is 'mercantilist' *in optima forma*.

> It is a natural consequence that states that sell their produce to other countries and so bring in gold and silver should become rich and that the people of countries with little produce, which thus allow gold and silver to flow out to other lands, should become poor. Thus, by increasing production one enhances the flow of gold and precious metals into the country while suppressing their outflow. That is what is called 'economy'.[117]

Such rhetoric resonated in particular in large contiguous domains that were far away from the centre of Tokugawa Japan. Domain-sponsored commercial projects vastly increased and many domains created so-called 'country product offices'. All sorts of supportive and protective measures were taken. Domain rulers could support well-developed industries by freeing restrictions on merchants and producers or grant monopoly licences to merchants in minor and developing industries. In the process, they usually tried to collect more sales and export taxes to become less dependent on the land taxes or specific, *ad hoc* contributions. This strategy was quite successful although it as a rule did not solve the domain's financial problems. In Tosa, for example, the paper sales tax became the single most important source of domain cash income by the 1840s. At that time sugar, salt, eggs, and gunpowder had also become sources of tax revenue. The domain set up its *Kaiseikan*, a domain management office, which developed an aggressive industrial development programme after Perry's Black Ships had opened Japan. But it was not the only domain doing so. Similar initiatives were taken in, for example Satsuma, Choshu and Saga. Although clearly, as in European mercantilist policies, the goal was to create a strong and rich state, these policies were not exclusively endorsed by government bureaucrats and merchants. They could also find support from other groups in society.

A downside of this strategy was that domains at times explicitly tried to hamper development in other domains. The Awa domain did not allow its specialists to teach production techniques for producing indigo to foreigners. The domain of Satsuma complained about sugar production in the Tosa domain and filed a suit with Edo.[118] But such competition could also provide challenges and efforts at imitation. There was competition not only between domains, but also between domains and the Shogunate, which wanted to regulate trade and rice tax commutation by concentrating them in Osaka. Official central government regulations could make it hard to sell to the next-door domain and more or less force a domain to sell its exports via Osaka. Domain support for industries and exports to Osaka and prohibitions of imports in turn affected the market privileges of Osaka merchants. In that sense, there are indeed good reasons to endorse Landes' suggestion to 'consider Tokugawa as an approximate, rough miniature of medieval Europe' and his claim that 'Japan was in effect a competitive economic world of over two hundred fifty nations'.[119] With the Restoration, the policies of mercantilist domains were lifted to a higher level – that of Japan as a whole – often with a striking continuity of personnel – and in that sense too it meant *more* integration and *more* economies of scale.

But let us continue our analysis of the level of economic integration of Tokugawa Japan by discussing factors that may have had a *positive* impact on it. Akira Hayami, an influential scholar, is convinced there were strong unifying and centripetal tendencies in Tokugawa Japan's political economy that were fundamental in turning the country (nevertheless) into a unity that he calls 'a market society'. He in particular points at the integrating and market supporting effects of the *sankin kotai*-system (i.e. the alternate attendance system), of the peculiar system of collecting taxes in rice and then monetizing them at a central place, and of the castle-town system with its separation of *daimyo* and samurai from the peasants.[120]

The details of the 'alternate attendance-system' changed throughout the twenty-six decades of Tokugawa rule, but generally, the requirement was that the *daimyo* of every domain move periodically between Edo and his fief, spending alternate periods of time in each place. His wife and heirs were required to remain in Edo as hostages while he was away. The system was made compulsory for the *tozama daimyo* in 1635, and for the *fudai daimyo* in 1642. There were a number of specific rules, for example for certain *fudai daimyo* in the vicinity of Edo, and temporary dispensations might occasionally be granted due to illness or extreme extenuating circumstances. Aside from an eight-year period during the rule of Tokugawa Yoshimune (1716–1745), it remained in force until 1862. The expenditures necessary to maintain lavish residences in two places, and to pay for the procession to and from Edo, placed financial strains on the *daimyo*. But the frequent travel of the *daimyo* with his huge following encouraged road building and the construction of inns and facilities along the routes, and generated economic activity and economic integration.[121]

The transfer involved in terms of people, resources and money, was huge. Let me give one example, that of the domain of Tosa. In the spring of 1694, a time of Edo residence, the domain population statistics recorded 4,556 Tosa people in Edo. In 1697, there were 2,813 Tosa people in Edo who had made the journey with their lord. Total population of Tosa at the time was some 400,000. Additional porters, innkeepers, shippers and food suppliers had to be paid, as well as carpenters and artisans who built or maintained the mansions in which the *daimyo* and his 'followers' lived. The samurai who travelled needed extra stipends. Luke Roberts, from whom I take this information, claims that well over half of Tosa's expenses were related to costs of the alternate attendance system.[122] This is apparently true for nearly all domains for which we have data. Tsukahira, in his book on the system, claims that altogether costs that can be traced to the alternate attendance system regularly consumed 40 to 70 per cent of the budget of any domain administration.[123] Ravina comes up with an estimate that suggests these percentages are rather high, and claims that many domains spent 'only' between 30 and 50 per cent of their income on *sankin kotai* and related expense.[124] But that, of course, is still a staggering amount.

The integrating effect of the existing system of collecting, converting and spending of taxes and of regulating trade flows, in which in both cases Osaka played the role of linchpin, is fairly obvious. Osaka was the place where taxes that had been collected in the form of rice could be converted into cash.[125] The revenue collected in this way was then spent on goods and services that might come from all over the realm. The fact that some goods had to be brought to Osaka from where they then could be sold and distributed had an effect similar to that of the *sankin kotai*, by turning (parts of) the country into one market area. The *Bakufu* wanted a 'national' rice market in Osaka, or in any case one that attracted the rice from central and southwestern Japan.[126]

The castle-town system in which *daimyo* and samurai had to live in castle towns whereas peasants had to stay put in the countryside, also had its impact on the level of market integration. Such a social and geographical division of estates could only function when towns and countryside were connected by strong ties of exchange. In 1614, there were 186 castle towns. In 1868, according to different sources between 254 and 276. In total, during Tokugawa rule, 453 cities had been *Joka-machi* or castle towns, which actually does not necessarily mean they had a castle. A substantial number did not. To make things even more confusing, their size could be quite different. A substantial number of them actually were rather like a village.[127] But all this does not detract from the fact that Tokugawa Japan as we have seen in Table 9 was highly urbanized.[128] During the Tokugawa era, Kyoto, at its height, had some 400,000 inhabitants, Osaka probably as many as some 500,000 and Edo/Tokyo over a million. Kanazawa in Kaga and Nagoya, a castle town of one of the Tokugawa branch families, topped 100,000 inhabitants.[129] Urbanization, as also shown in Table 9, was not a linear process. Sometime during the eighteenth century, many middle-sized towns in particular actually began to lose population.[130] During the eighteenth and the first half of the nineteenth centuries, towns generally stagnated or lost population. But next to castle town decline there was country place growth. Thus, we see a combination of a decline of towns and pre-modern growth in the countryside, which meant increasing market orientation and market integration. The castle towns had to be fed with migrants to keep their population level. Whereas at the time in Western Europe population and foreign trade both grew, in Japan both did not.[131] Losses of inhabitants were not confined to such cities. Osaka, for example, was also hit. In 1860, the number of its inhabitants had decreased to 310,000. The population of Tokyo almost halved after the abolishing of the *sankin kotai*-system in the 1860s, with the number of inhabitants sinking to fewer than 600,000.

We have to realize though that the figures for Japan's urbanization comparatively speaking were and continued to be quite high. Whereas in 1800 more than 13 per cent of its population was living in towns with more than 10,000 inhabitants, this was only 3–4 per cent in China, 6 per cent in India and 8–9 per cent in Europe as a whole. Only in North-western Europe, in countries with far fewer inhabitants, were the figures substantially higher: for the Netherlands 28.6 per cent; for Belgium 16.6 per cent; for England and Wales 22.3 per cent and finally for Scotland 23.9 per cent.[132] As we have already provided information about the estimated level of monetization and marketization of the Tokugawa economy, we do not need to discuss them again, but it will be obvious that their level and that of the country's urbanization are not unrelated. We already pointed out that such a high level of urbanization implies a high rate of certain types of investment in material and institutional infrastructures. This again was a major positive legacy of Tokugawa Japan to Post-Restoration Japan and again provided a relevant difference with much less urbanized Qing China.

Over time the pattern of trade changed. Initially all the domains were or rather *had to be* oriented in their trade towards Osaka, Edo and Kyoto. Increasingly, however, there developed more inter-domainal trade. This is how Matao Myamoto describes the development: 'Thus, there was a change from the early Tokugawa radial, point-to-point distribution network between the domains and the central markets to the formation of a complex distribution network involving both inter-domainal routes and domainal-central routes.'[133] As already pointed out, the level and pattern of urbanization changed during the eighteenth century. After the 1730s, populations of larger towns overall alternated between stagnation and decline. Major towns such as Edo, Osaka and Kyoto no longer grew or witnessed a decline in population. Small towns knew stagnation or only slight growth. Whereas many towns lost manufacturing activities, there was an increasing involvement in non-agricultural activities and thus more marketization in the countryside. As small farm families became increasingly involved in market exchange, small market towns, in contrast to most other towns, tended to grow. The fact that many domains created monopolies hoping to be able to sell their produce all over Japan without interference of the Shogunate also meant that commodity production became increasingly geared to, in this case, more distant markets. All in all, there developed a more dense, fine-grained but also more extensive network of markets.[134] It has to be pointed out, however, that for money and labour the existing markets never became national during the Tokugawa era. According to Osamu Saito and Tokihiko Settsu, in the case of money 'late-Tokugawa local economies were never integrated into a national market.'[135] Tokugawa labour markets continued to be segmented along geographical, class and family and lineage lines, reflecting the political divisions, the cutting up of the land area into autonomous fiefs, and the social divisions between the four formally distinct status ranking groups.[136]

We again see an important Tokugawa legacy without which modernization under the Meiji Emperor and successors would undoubtedly have been much more difficult and again government policies play a role in the legacy. The following comments do not intend to deny but only to somewhat qualify that claim by pointing out that one may doubt whether the way in which Tokugawa rulers integrated Japan's economy would have been *optimally* efficient.

The alternate-attendance system, as many scholars of Tokugawa Japan, not just Akira Hayami, like to emphasize, indeed may have had a unifying effect on the economy and it indeed may have given a push to the economies of Edo and the regions through which the *daimyo* and their huge following had to travel. But it as such also had clear disadvantages – extracting resources from the regions from where the *daimyo* and their followers had to go to Edo. It was indeed meant not only to keep an eye on the *daimyo* and his family but also to drain their wealth.[137] It, moreover, enforced an allocation of people and resources that was not necessarily the most efficient. The fact that Osaka was selected to function and indeed often did function as the clearing centre for tax rice and many products meant for export from domains all over the country, from a national perspective yielded a similar mixture of advantages and disadvantages. The integrating effects Hayami refers to did exist, but one may seriously doubt whether the system of paying taxes in rice that then had to be sold in Osaka and in that way monetized and the obligation to bring certain commodities to Osaka actually were the most optimal ways to reach the effects that Hayami considers so positive for the development of a market economy. The fact that samurai and *daimyo* as a rule *had* to live in castle towns whereas peasants were not allowed to do so, also will have had negative, cost-enhancing effects.

What can we conclude after this fairly long detour through Tokugawa Japan? Scholars may debate the extent of political integration of Tokugawa Japan, but, in whatever way one would want to define it, there can be no doubt that after the Restoration Japan in a matter of years became a *far more* centralized, unified, and legible polity from the perspective of central government. This certainly as such had positive effects on the economy. When it comes to economic integration a similar conclusion can be drawn. Scholars have increasingly become aware that already under Tokugawa rule Japan to a certain extent had evolved in the direction of a unified polity with one fiscal, monetary and legal system, and of a unified market with substantial internal trading, shipping and communication. But the policies of the Shogunate didn't always lead to an optimal form of economic integration whereas those of many *daimyo* usually were meant to first and foremost develop their own fiefs, often even at the expense of other fiefs and 'Japan' as a whole. Turning Japan into one country the way its new rulers from 1868 onwards did, clearly facilitated better economic integration and thus higher productivity and overall growth. It is extremely unlikely or rather unimaginable that a fractured Japan as it existed under Tokugawa rule with overall 250 or more separate domains next to the lands of the Shogun could ever have achieved the level of growth and development that it achieved as the unified state created after Restoration. That is if it, being such a fragmented polity, would have been able to survive as an independent entity under increasing Western pressure.

3

A Powerful State: Politics, Ideology, the Military and the Bureaucracy

The concepts 'state power' and 'state capacity'

Japan's state was not only sovereign and even increasingly expansionist against the outside world, it was also quite powerful domestically. Overall, there can be no doubt that Japan's 'state' had a capability to get things done after 1868 that was quite high, again as compared to that of other developing and even many developed countries. Before trying to empirically validate this claim some comments are in order with respect to what it might mean to claim that a state is 'powerful'. Michael Mann introduced the concepts 'infrastructural' and 'despotic' power, which in my view can be quite helpful in this context. Despotic power concerns the range of actions that rulers can undertake without resorting to routine, institutionalized negotiation with civil society groups. It basically concerns the extent to which rulers can do as they please with their subjects. This should be distinguished from 'infrastructural' power, which can be defined as the capacity of rulers to actually penetrate civil society and to implement political decisions logistically throughout the realm.[1] Infrastructural power is about the ability 'to get things done. . .'[2] In Mann's view we are talking about two quite different kinds of power that often stand in an inverse relationship to each other: as a rule states with strong despotic powers have been infrastructurally weak and vice versa.[3] My claim would be that Japan's rulers over the period discussed in this book were powerful in *both* these meanings of the word. Japan's state in the period 1868–1937 was relatively speaking powerful despotically *as well as* infrastructurally. Mann, whose concepts have not found much resonance among economists, distinguishes four sources of social power: ideological economic, military, political power.[4] I will use this distinction in my analysis and sub-sequentially look at the political, ideological, military and economic power of the Japanese state. For pragmatic reasons, I will in my chapter on military power include a brief analysis of the bureaucratic power of the state in terms of personnel. It does not fit perfectly into the Mann's model but I preferred to discuss all of the states' 'manpower' in one chapter.

Economists, for whatever reason, tend not to use Mann's ideas and thus not to refer to 'state power' but to 'state capacity'. I will not use that concept in my own analyses but will, considering its popularity, briefly comment upon it. The concept has become popular thanks to the work of Timothy Besley and Torsten Persson. They give the following description:

For state capacity, we can distinguish two broad types of capabilities that allow the state to take action. One concerns the extractive role of the state. We call this capability *fiscal capacity*. Does a government have the necessary infrastructure – in terms of administration, monitoring and enforcement – to raise revenue from broad tax bases such as income and consumption, revenue that can be spent on income support or services to its citizens? The other type of capacity concerns the productive role of the state. Is it capable of raising private-sector productivity via physical services such as road transport or the provision of power? Or does it have the necessary infrastructure- in terms of courts, educated judges, and registers – to raise private incomes by providing regulation and legal services such as the protection of property rights or the enforcement of contracts? We focus on the later capability, which we refer to as *legal capacity*.[5]

The distinction between the extractive role of the state and the productive role in principle can be helpful but I fail to see that extraction would be identical to fiscal extraction. The way legal capacity is defined leaves out a wide range of productive activities of the state that in my view are important and should not be left out, and will not be omitted from my analysis. For the rest, the definitions are rather vague and open. In any case for legal capacity, it is not clear whether it has been exhaustively defined or whether only two examples have been given. Noel Johnson and Mark Koyama come up with the following description:

> State capacity describes the *ability* of a state to collect taxes, enforce law and order, and provide public goods. ... State capacity can be thought of as comprising two components. First, a high-capacity state must be able to enforce its rules across the entirety of the territory it claims to rule (legal capacity). Second, it has to be able to garner enough tax revenues from the economy to implement its policies (fiscal capacity).[6]

The reference to legal capacity and the way in which it is defined is basically identical to what Mann would call the state's political power; the exclusive focus on tax revenues again strikes me as needlessly confined. Why not also look at other sources of incomes or credit? They then add:

> State capacity should then be distinguished from either the size or the scope of the state. A state with a bloated and inefficient public sector may be comparatively ineffective at implementing policies and raising tax revenues. Furthermore, historians agree that the eighteenth-century British state had high state capacity even though it played a very limited role in the economy. Similarly, state capacity requires a degree of political and legal centralization, but it should not be identified with political centralization *per se*. The rulers of feudal society in which many legal and fiscal choices were devolved to local lords indeed had a low state capacity. But the concentration of political authority in the centre may cause inefficiencies and thereby undermine state capacity.[7]

The concept as indicated has become quite popular but when used in historical analyses it in practice has been almost exclusively used to refer to material resources and hardly to legal capacity. Attention to other state capacities or powers has been almost absent in that literature.[8] I have therefore chosen to structure my analysis in principle along the lines of Mann's sources of social power model.

My claim is not simply that the more power a state has in the senses described above the better it would necessarily be for the economy. At least two other things besides the scale and scope of a state's power must also be taken into consideration – *and will be in my text at least when that is feasible* – when talking about state power and its importance for growth: a) how efficiently does the state under analysis acquire and use its power; and b) what does it effectively do with that power that then in turn might be credited with a positive effect on growth? One cannot exclude that a state with high state power has acquired this capacity inefficiently and in a manner that is detrimental to growth and development. Nor can one exclude that it uses its powers in ways that do *not* have a positive impact on development and growth. There are so many examples of negative effects of what for the sake of convenience I will call 'big government', that claims about state power based on a state's scale and scope are often not very helpful without reference to its efficiency and to the nature of its activities. I will try and systematically deal with these in my analysis of the abilities of Japan's state. Just showing that a state has a lot of power is insufficient for ascribing a developmentally positive role to it. A reference to the *mechanisms* at work and the goals that are set is indispensable.

But that does not mean that a reference to the scale and scope of the power of certain states would by necessity be vacuous or 'sleight of hand'.[9] In the context of research into the emergence of modern economic growth the observation that a state had a very limited power *as such* can already be telling. There have existed and still exist many underdeveloped states whose state power is simply *too* low to do what even the most outspoken adherent of *laissez-faire* would admit that a state should do to function adequately, let alone facilitate modern economic growth. Even the most rigorous advocate of *laissez-faire* would admit that some things have to preferably or necessarily be done by the state, in particular providing defence, law and order, basic education and certain material and institutional infrastructure and that the costs of these state services in a modern economy are very high. I would want to emphasize that a surprisingly large number of states simply lacked and lack the resources to create an environment in which modern economic growth can emerge, let alone to actively promote it. In the period discussed in this book, many polities, especially outside the West, were so 'incapacitated', that they simply could not facilitate or contribute to growth – even if they had wanted to, which they often did not – and even if foreign powers had given them the necessary room to manoeuvre, which often was not the case. In such cases, reference to the sheer scale and scope of state power is sufficient in explaining why states with too little power knew no growth. Even a quick comparison of Japan and China in the crucial period 1850 to 1914, but also earlier, shows why China developed less than Japan. Its state was too weak to be effectively developmental and was more of a nuisance than of help.[10] Its government lacked the necessary means, motives and opportunities, to put it in criminalistics' turns, to trigger and support a take-off. Japan's government had them. High state power may not guarantee growth, but low state power guarantees it will not be impressive.

Another criticism that is ushered in with regard to the explanatory power of the variable 'state capacity' and that can also be made to apply to my power analysis, is that it would not *explain* growth but rather be an *expression* or *effect* of it.[11] That critique may indeed apply to many instances, but in my view, it is not valid for all cases, one of the exceptions being Japan. There is no universal, one-to-one relation between the level of income and development of a country and the powers or capacities of its state. Again, a comparison of the cases of Japan and China is telling, with the gap between Japan's and China's state capacity being bigger than one might expect on the basis of their levels of income and development. Another interesting comparison in this respect would be that between Germany and the United Kingdom in the period 1870–1914, when Germany became an industrial giant. Poorer Germany at that moment in time had a higher – and more efficient and effective – economic state power than the United Kingdom. The cases of post-World War-Two Korea and Taiwan could also count as examples of relatively poor countries with relatively economically powerful states. Why states of certain countries have more or less power than one might expect on the basis of their levels of income and wealth – I am thinking here in particular but not only of economic and military power – of course is an interesting question on which we will try to shed some light every now and then. Overall, I think one may claim that states in the process of trying to catch up tend to be more prone to big government than states that aren't. But dealing with that topic is not at the heart of our analysis. It would require a separate certainly quite interesting but again intensive and extensive analysis. I here confine myself to the observation that this is regularly the case. Finally, a comment that I think should be superfluous but that considering the critique by e.g. Caplan apparently is not: pointing out that state power or state capacity can be very important for growth does not, of course, imply that it would be 'the crucial factor that makes all the others possible' and as such in fact even its *only* explanation. I have never come across such a claim in all my reading and it would be strange anyhow: Who would want to claim of a historical phenomenon that it has *one* and *just one* cause?[12]

In the following chapters I will chart the powers of Japan's state and put forward the thesis that the state that emerged with the Meiji Restoration, after some initial serious problems, became quite powerful when it comes to *all* the four sources of social power that Mann distinguishes.

Political power

Let us first discuss its political power, i.e. its power in terms of its ability to enforce rulings. Admittedly, there were fierce clashes in the beginning of Meiji rule. Just think of the major armed conflict, the so-called Satsuma Rebellion or Southwestern War in 1877, fought with mainly samurai led by Saigo Takamori (1828–1877), who did not accept certain policies of the new government.[13] There was massive peasant or more broadly 'rural' popular unrest. In the period 1868–1878, there were no fewer than some two hundred uprisings in the countryside. The introduction of the new land tax and conscription in particular led to fierce resistance. No fewer than 300,000 people participated in a revolt in Fukuoka Prefecture in 1873.[14] It, as Ian Inkster has pointed out, required serious effort to control the country in order to be able to try and implement the programme of modernization. Government involved itself massively in social control measures during the late 1870s and the beginning of the 1880s. At times, for all investment in industry and education, such measures could absorb by far the greatest proportion of government expenditure. The following figures can illustrate their relevance: At a time when the total yield from the land tax was around forty million yen, the expenses for repressing the Satsuma Rebellion alone totalled forty-two million yen.[15] In the three years to 1878, government expended in total some 6.2 million yen on the Colonisation Department of Hokkaido; 2.5 million yen on direct loans to industry and 4.5 million yen through the Department of Education.[16]

Having 'solved' its initial 'problems' with rebellious samurai, did of course not mean that central government now had a fully free hand. Or that it was never divided in itself or uncertain about which course to pursue. It still had to face conflicts. One must be wary of the tendency to exaggerate the role of compliance and consensus in the history of Japan and to play down the role of contestation. Governments did often encounter fierce opposition.[17] The Freedom and People's Rights movement has already been referred to. There emerged oppositional political parties. There were efforts to create an effective labour movement. There also were more spontaneous, but at times massive, protests. In particular after 1905 the country's rulers clearly had to cope with the emergence of the masses, which meant a more active public opinion and more popular violence.[18] The so-called Rice Riots of 1918 lasted some three months and had some 700,000 participants. Thirty protesters were killed and about 25,000 people arrested. More than 8,000 of them were prosecuted for taking part and some 5,000 were found guilty. Two people received death sentences.[19] In the 1920s, Japan's political system became significantly more open, democratic and interested in international peaceful co-operation. Contention and contestation decreased substantially.[20] That development, as is well known, was reversed in the 1930s when political violence in the end became 'endemic'.[21] But overall, *as compared to other governments* of less developed *and* developed countries that may have wanted to push forward a process of modernization, from the late 1870s onwards till World War One, when the groundwork for Japan's take-off had been firmly laid, Japan's government had a lot of control and *relatively* little serious opposition that managed to really disturb the implementation of government plans. In his discussion of the country's speedy adoption of a new postal savings system Sheldon Garon points at the following explanation that in my view actually applies to most innovations that government initiated in Japan at the time: 'Meiji Japan was a technocrat's paradise. Leaders and elite bureaucrats governed with few challenges from the rest of society.'[22]

The first decade after the Restoration was a period of considerable open experimentation when it came to organizing Japan's political institutions. After the returning of the power to the Emperor, the question of course for those who had conquered power – and they were the *real* rulers, not the Emperor – was what to do with it. At first, they operated rather hesitantly and it was not evident what major changes might be implemented. But especially with the abolishing of the domains it became obvious that a new social order was in the making. Most scholars would agree that with the Constitution that was enacted in 1890, the new order was, finally, institutionalized in a specific, authoritarian way. That settlement, after some twenty years of often serious contestation, was not a predictable, obvious outcome of the Restoration although those who had a strong preference for a system of paternalist rule *for* rather than *with* or *by* the people, had always been quite a strong faction among the actual rulers of Japan during those two decades. Nor was the settlement stable. The Constitution not only contained an uneasy mixture of absolutism and representative government: on top of that the meaning of several of its articles was not unambiguously clear.

Opinions initially were quite diverse and several options seemed open. There were, for example, big differences between the caretaker government, that part of government that stayed at home when the Iwakura Mission went to explore the world, and the government members who joined this mission.[23] Those who stayed at home tended to be more radical, more populist, more positive about creating a broader-based, more representative government, but also more aggressive when it comes to Korea. Those who were visiting the West and often had already studied it before, became more aware of how backward Japan was. They were more prudent and gradualist and convinced that the people of Japan needed education and a strong guiding government in order to be able to catch up. Whatever one thinks of the conclusions that those who joined the mission drew, it definitely helped that so many of Japan's elite – in this and in other visits – got a first-hand acquaintance with the West. The difference with China, where far fewer people in high positions actually knew the West, will again certainly have made a difference.

In the period before the enacting of the Constitution quite radical representative ideas had been voiced. The Charter Oath promulgated at the enthronement of Emperor Meiji in April 1868, for example, explicitly referred to assemblies and open discussions.[24] Okubo Toshimici, who took part in the Iwakura mission, after the so-called political crisis of 1873, came in charge and dominated Japan's politics till 1878. His government was fairly reluctant to mobilize the people. He was more in favour of government guidance and tried a policy of co-opting and suppressing to keep opposition and demands for more freedom and people's rights in check. His strategy was only a partial success. The so-called Saga Rebellion of 1874 was still a relatively small affair. The Satsuma Rebellion of 1877 led to a serious war. As a rule it is known as a rising of samurai who were deeply dissatisfied with the abolishing of their specific privileged status and the lowering of their incomes. Actually, it was not just a conservative or even reactionary movement; among the rebels there also were people who were simply unhappy with the authoritarian style of governing of the country's rulers. After its victory, government took measures to curb the press even more, and began to lay more emphasis on loyalty and what, for the sake of brevity, I will call 'Confucian values'. Public debate, however, did not abate. The Freedom and People's Rights Movement undertook serious efforts to create citizenship and a more democratic, 'inclusive' politics.

After the death, or rather murder, of Okobu Toshimichi, there was again a crisis in 1881 that had all the traits of a modern political crisis as it evolved in an atmosphere of broad public debate. It brought Ito Hirobumi (1841–1909) to power and led to the promise in 1881 that there would be a Constitution and a national elected assembly by 1890. It also saw the emergence of Japan's first political parties, a liberal and a progressive one. Nevertheless, a shift was occurring towards a more authoritarian climate. Germany, rather than France, became the example the ruling elites wanted to follow in matters of politics and law. Those who wanted a sovereign people were pitted against those who wanted a sovereign monarch. Ito Hirobumi and other architects of the Meiji state had not started from a clear preconception of the new system of rule in which the monarch would be the supreme commander and the sole locus of sovereignty. Those who wanted such a type of sovereign monarch, the so-called Satsuma-Choshu clique, won. In that sense, the Constitution was a fairly contingent, 'authoritarian' settlement of disagreements among the ruling elites and between those elites and the Freedom and People Rights Movement. The state now was tantamount to a collection of imperially appointed ministers, supported by a bureaucracy.[25]

Apart perhaps from the period between the end of World War One and the beginning of the 1930s, Meiji, Taisho and Showa Japan in practice was ruled by a quite authoritarian oligarchy, that politically *as well as* economically was very exclusive and that in many respects did not even try to hide that.[26] That Japan had 'exclusive' political institutions will be shown in the following paragraphs. Its economic exclusiveness, which e.g. showed in a highly unequal distribution of wealth and income, a low and decreasing labour share, and a stark concentration of economic power, will be discussed later in this book.[27] Let me illustrate the exclusiveness of Japan's political institutions with just a couple of core data for the period 1889–1937, when the Meiji Constitution set the parameters of the political system. For an extensive description of the political structure of Japan during this era and of its internal power relations I refer to the bibliography.[28] Formal political representation for a 'larger' group of the population only came about with the Meiji Constitution of 1890 when some 450,000 men received the right to vote for the first Parliament. That right was initially, and for some decades, denied to everyone living on Hokkaido, Okinawa and Ogasawara[29] and to priests, teachers of religion, active servicemen and the insane. The franchise was limited to male subjects over twenty-five years of age who paid a national land or income tax of fifteen yen or more. Those who qualified numbered 1.14 per cent of the population. In 1898, the tax requirement for voting was lowered to ten yen; in 1919 to three yen. In 1919, before the lowering of the tax requirement, the percentage of voters on the entire population was some 2.6 per cent. With the lowering of the requirement to three yen it increased to some 5 per cent. The number of voters increased from 1.5 to 3.3 million. In March 1925, universal male suffrage was introduced: all males over the age of 25 who had lived in their electoral districts for at least one year and were not indigent, now had the right to vote. The number of voters increased to 12.5 million. That is some 20 per cent of the total population. There were no further changes till the end of the period discussed here.

It is important to realize that Japan continued to be ruled according to the famous Meiji Constitution of 1890 till the very end of the period discussed in this book, and actually even longer, till 1947. This constitution was presented as a gift of the Emperor to his people who were his subjects.[30] Actually when that happened *nobody*, apart from the very small group of people involved in writing it, knew its content.[31] It is significant that almost all signatories of the Imperial Rescript that accompanied the promulgation of the Constitution were high-ranking members of the new aristocracy and that they almost all came from Satsuma and Choshu. The Constitution was not a result of any consultation of the people and did not create citizens. The exact, concrete meaning of several statements in the text of the Constitution was unclear and open to differing interpretations. The decision of what the right interpretation was, often was made to depend on circumstances and on the power behind the different interpreters. Sovereignty resided in the person of the Emperor, by virtue of his divine ancestry, *not* in the people. As head of the Empire he united within himself all three branches of government, although legislation and the budget were subject to the consent of the Imperial Diet. In theory thus, the power of the Emperor was all but unlimited. In practice, he tended to be a mere figurehead with real power residing in the hands of a tiny oligarchy. The Emperor, who, as we saw, was described as 'sacred' and 'inviolable' and thus unassailable, became invested with a unique moral status that no Japanese could ignore and whose rule was claimed to come from an ancestral, 'sacred' lineage. His Japanese subjects were considered descendants of good and loyal subjects of this lineage. Being disloyal to the Emperor thus meant being disloyal to the ancestors and was thus immoral. This, as indicated, actually limited the right to religious freedom. In particular after the proclamation of the Rescript on Education in 1891, this created problems for Christians who, as Christians, could not worship the Emperor, which, among other things, led to anti-Christian sentiments.[32] Just after the Meiji Restoration there had still been openly and legalized xenophobic behaviour. By February 1870, more than 3,400 Christians were in prison.[33]

The Emperor held the right to appoint and dismiss all government officials and the sole rights to declare war, make peace, conclude treaties, dissolve the Lower House of the Diet and issue Imperial Ordinances in place of laws when the Diet was not in session. The Meiji Constitution provided for a cabinet consisting of Ministers of State and a so-called Privy Council. Both answered to the Emperor rather than the Diet. He was also considered the commander of army and navy. The heads of these services interpreted this to mean that army and navy only had to obey the Emperor, and not the cabinet and Diet. The army and navy ministers and the military high command had direct access to the Emperor via the Army General Staff founded in 1878 and the Navy General Staff that was approved by the Emperor in 1893. After 1900, both the army and navy ministers in the cabinet were required to be high-ranking serving officers. In 1913 regulations were changed. Now the selection of a reserve or retired general or admiral was also allowed. In 1936 the position of minister was again restricted to officers on active duty.[34] The military general staffs in many respects could act as if they were responsible to no one and claimed and acquired direct access to the throne.[35] The Prime Minister selected the (serving) military officers appointed to Cabinet as ministers, but only after the army and navy chiefs of staff had approved their appointment. The military could overthrow a cabinet by forcing the resignation of the army and/or navy ministers, and then refusing to approve replacements. The army always tended to fall back on its special relationship with the Throne for authority as well as legitimacy. Army leaders in the 1930s used appeals to the Throne to justify illegal acts at home and aggression overseas. The fact that war and the threat of war were so frequent in the decades we discuss here of course also contributed to its exceptional political leverage as did the fact that, except for a few years in the 1920s, 'the characteristic pattern of Japanese colonial administration was that generals held office as governors and had civilians as deputies'.[36] In particular in the 1930s, the military would often and with grave consequences ignore or interfere in politics.[37]

The legislature or Diet consisted of two Houses. The Upper House, or House of Peers, consisted of members of the Imperial Family, hereditary peerage and members appointed by the Emperor. The hereditary peerage here referred to was created in 1884 to form the basis of the Upper House and provide a check on the Lower House. Senior imperial government advisers, former *daimyo*, and high-ranking military officers were given titles that would make them eligible to sit in it. The Lower House, or House of Representatives, was elected by direct male suffrage, initially with qualifications based on the amount of tax paid, which kept the actual number of voters quite low. The Diet was given the authority to initiate legislation, approve all laws, and approve the budget. Both the Emperor and the Diet, however, had to agree in order for a measure to become law. The Diet could reject the budget but then government had the right to continue with a budget like that of the previous year. That means that the Constitution on the one hand declared there would be representative organs but that the most drastic action that those organs could undertake was to actually rather ineffectively reject proposed laws or budgets.

Up until the beginning of the twentieth century, real power in Meiji Japan's government was exercised by an elite group comprising the Imperial Family, the so-called *genro*, the Privy Council, the Cabinet of Ministers of State, the army and navy ministers, the military high command, and the House of Peers. The *genro* ('principal elders') is an unofficial designation given to certain retired elder Japanese statesmen who were considered the 'founding fathers' of modern Japan, and served as informal advisors to the Emperor. Their position had no official basis in the Constitution. They formed a group of nine, of which four came from Choshu and four from Satsuma. It was only in the twentieth century that their influence declined. The 'institution' was only abolished in 1940. The Privy Council was already created in 1888 to be the highest advisory body under the new Constitution to Emperor Meiji on domestic and foreign affairs. It was not responsible to Parliament for advice given to the Emperor, and the Emperor and his advisers selected its members. In 1885, again, already before the Constitution was enacted, a cabinet of ministers of state had been set up. A prime minister selected by Emperor Meiji and his advisers headed it. That prime minister chose the members of the cabinet. The cabinet was primarily responsible to the Emperor, and only secondarily to the proposed parliament.

A small clique of people thus for several decades basically ruled Japan. It came, in overwhelming majority from Satsuma, Choshu, and, to a lesser extent, Tosa and Hizen. Their rule that in fact already began with the overthrowing of the Shogunate in the 1860s, was called *hanbatsu*, the domain-clique rule. The government's position was that the people were not yet ready to share in the weighty affairs of state. The oligarchs considered their countrymen to a very large extent as unfit to do politics and attempted to control the formation of political associations and the free discussion of politics in publications and the press. They systematically excluded certain groups from political activity. Already in the 1870s, it was decided that not only no soldier, but also no upper-level bureaucrat or official in the local government was to associate with politics. The regulations on public meetings of 1880 barred 'public servants' – i.e. military men, active or reserve, police officers, teachers and students of public and private schools, and agricultural and technical apprentices were prohibited from joining any political association or attending political meetings. Women, minors and those deprived of civil rights were added to the list in 1890. Women and minors were even barred from simply attending public meetings. The rulings with regard to their attendance were in effect till 1922, those with regard to political organizations till 1945. These rulings were not a matter of 'institutionalizing' tradition, but a novel deterioration of the position of women, who were increasingly expected to confine themselves to becoming 'good wives and wise mothers'.[38] Politics was considered partial, a matter of interests and thus divisive. It therefore had to be a matter of officials, preferably with no interference of the people.[39] The power of the *hanbatsu* was only slowly eroded. It is only from 1898 that, at least officially, parties ruled.

With the Taisho reign a new era dawned in which the rise of mass society almost inevitably meant a further extension of public debate and increasing demand for real and more extended representation. The 1920s witnessed a clear move in the direction of a more 'democratic' and more open system: 'A triumph of a new Japan' as Dickinson calls it in a recent book.[40] The influence of the military in public life in this decade was much smaller; its status, that had been high after the war against Russia, was now much lower, its size and its budget were reduced.[41] The right to vote was substantially extended. The country became more firmly integrated in the international community of nations. But the Constitution with its hybrid character and its strong executive continued to be in place. Debates continued about where real power ought to reside. Simplifying those debates, two extreme positions can be distinguished: one in which real power ought to reside with representative institutions, which means the Emperor would become just an 'organ' of those institutions. Another one in which sovereignty resided entirely with the Emperor-ruler. The voices in favour of a very strong executive often belonged to ultranationalist, often Shinto radicals, whose ideas over time found substantial support among intellectuals, bureaucrats, and the military. From 1931 onwards, the political climate changed rather radically with a renewed rise of militarism, imperialist adventurism, ultra-nationalism, political violence and terror. Japan now slowly entered the era of the wartime 'dark valley':

> Between 1930 and 1936 there were twenty major domestic terrorist incidents, four political assassination, five planned assassinations, and four attempted coups, the March and October Incidents of 1931, the May Incident of 1932, and the Great Military Mutiny of 1936. Furthermore, the army's continual plotting in Manchuria destabilized those regions and helped to isolate Japan internationally. Military involvement to one degree or another in almost all these conspiracies undercut Japan's political process and enabled the army to gain dominant political influence.[42]

The text *Fundamentals of our national polity*, issued by the government in 1937, unmistakably epitomizes this change.[43]

Political rights were not just quite restricted for quite a long time in terms of voting. There is ample literature that describes how the freedom of political parties, labour organizations and the press was restricted and how difficult it was to create and sustain any form of organized dissent or opposition. In particular, the Public Security Preservation Laws are notorious in this respect.[44] The Social Democratic Party was banned on the day it was formed in 1901.[45] The communists, who founded a party in 1922, were permanently harassed by the police. Policies of government that explicitly focused on labour will be dealt with later.[46]

In as far as Japan's modernization could be and was steered from above it often was for lack of substantial countervailing powers. The following quote by Mikiso Hane may be exaggerated, but not by far:

> The Meiji leaders envisioned as the object of modernization, not so much the wellbeing of the people as *fukoku kyōhei*, the enrichment and strengthening of the nation. ... In the process ... the masses were treated merely as means to an end, as labourers and cannon fodder.[47]

Popular sentiment had to be tamed and the people guided rather than mobilized. Banno Junji calls this type of politics, which he considered typical for Okubo Toshimichi, 'developmental despotism'. I would claim that it typified many, if not actually most of, Japan's rulers in the period under discussion.[48]

But as I indicated earlier, my text is about the importance of the state, that is the *impact* on the economy of what the state was and did, not so much the actual *intentions*, let alone the morality of the rulers. So much attention here is devoted to the power of Japan's rulers to have things their way because without that power they would not have been able to push through so many 'modernizations', which I think – very importantly – would *not* have occurred spontaneously. To not interrupt the flow of the analysis even further I confine myself here to these general comments with regard to the political system. When it comes to certain specific policies, I will refer to them where my argument requires it.

Japan's state in the period under discussion here clearly was quite powerful and had a high capacity to enforce its policies. In Mann's categories, it clearly was strong overall in terms of despotic power, which in everyday language means that government had ample opportunities to do as it pleased.[49] Japan in that same period of time also had impressive growth rates. That is hard to square with ideas about the relationship between governance and economic growth that have become highly popular. I mean the ideas of Daron Acemoglu and James Robinson. Whatever definition and indicators one would want to use, for almost the entire period discussed here Japan certainly was *not* an inclusive state with inclusive institutions as these two authors suggest in their book on the origins of wealth and power and then adduce as explanation for the country's fast economic development.[50] This book has become such an enormously successful bestseller that their comments on Meiji Japan deserve separate attention. They claim, for example: 'This Japanese political revolution (i.e. the Meiji Restoration P.V.) enabled more inclusive political institutions and much more inclusive economic institutions to develop, and laid the foundations for subsequent rapid Japanese growth.'[51] Later in the book they write: 'By 1890 Japan was the first Asian country to adopt a written constitution, and it created a constitutional monarchy with an elected parliament, the Diet, and an independent judiciary. These changes were decisive factors in enabling Japan to be the primary beneficiary from the industrial revolution in Asia.'[52] For them the Meiji Restoration was 'a major turn toward inclusive institutions' and 'the empowerment of a broad coalition that could stand up against absolutism and would replace the absolutist institutions by more inclusive, pluralistic ones'.[53]

Much, of course, hinges on definitions. The authors distinguish between economic institutions and (supportive) political institutions. They provide the following descriptions.[54] Inclusive economic institutions are institutions that 'enforce property rights, create a level playing field, and encourage investments in new technologies and skills'. Inclusive political institutions are institutions that 'distribute political power widely in a pluralistic manner and are able to achieve some amount of political centralization so as to establish law and order, the foundation of secure property rights and an inclusive market economy'. Extractive economic institutions are 'structured to extract resources from the many by the few and ... fail to protect property rights or provide incentives for economic activity'. Extractive political institutions 'concentrate power in the hands of a few who will then have incentives to maintain and develop extractive economic institutions for their benefit'. Taking these descriptions seriously, the 1889–1890 Meiji Constitution would rather look like a turn towards a *less* inclusive society. But even if one would want to deny that: Everyone with even the slightest acquaintance with the history of Japan between 1868 and the beginning of the Asia Pacific War will be struck by the extremely naïve 'optimism' and historical incorrectness of Acemoglu's and Robinson's interpretation of the Meiji Restoration and its implications.[55] Here in this chapter I confine myself to political exclusion but economically too, Japan was a quite 'exclusive' society as, for example, is shown in its very unequal distribution of wealth and income.[56]

Japan, between 1868 and 1937, was a country with an institutionally strong and powerful government and in that sense, it was a strong state. Countervailing tendencies were not lacking and they were not always unsuccessful. But the fact remains that the authoritarian framework of Japanese politics, as expressed and set by the Constitution of 1890, basically remained intact, and, in the end, was succeeded by an even more authoritarian structure. The fact that Japan's rulers were so intent *on* and successful *in* developing ideological power over their subjects, on which more will be said later, certainly was a contributory factor in this respect. I emphasize the presence and the importance in industrializing Japan of a powerful state 'authoritarian' apparatus that could have things its way because in my view countries going through the first stages of industrialization *almost without exception* had such a powerful state, i.e. a state that has, to put Max Weber's definition in everyday language terms, 'the ability to exercise one's will over others'. In all the industrialized countries that I can think of, those first stages of industrialization have been characterized, in politics as well as in economic life, by the predominance of *extractive* and *exclusive* institutions. Japan is not at all exceptional here. A look at the development of the right to vote would already suffice to see that. *Even* if we would only look at male suffrage in France, Germany and the

United Kingdom, the countries that I systematically compare Japan with in this book, it is hard to deny that they too took off as societies in which large groups of the population were *not* included.[57]

This means that the thesis, infinitely repeated by Daron Acemoglu and James Robinson in their *Why nations fail*, that *inclusive* institutions would cause growth to emerge and perpetuate in any case for the phase of its *emergence* is completely at odds not just with the historical record of Japan but of *all* major industrializing countries.[58] The transition to a modern, more industrial economy has always been a complex, painful and disturbing process that most people would not want to endure voluntarily. I am pretty certain that most people would have voted against it if, during the initial stages of industrialization, governments would have asked them whether they were in favour of further industrialization. I am also quite certain that therefore governments did not hold such referenda. As much as we may regret it, almost without exception even in the West – I actually wonder what clear exception in the entire world I could come up with – countries *took off* in an extractive, exclusive setting. I am afraid we have to agree with Robert E. Ward when he writes about Japan's modernization that authoritarian forms of political organization 'can be extraordinarily effective in the early stages of the modernization process', and that such forms may have to precede 'the emergence of a political system which is both modern and durably democratic'.[59] Modernization in particular in its initial stages entails major shocks and strains. National governments often try to control the stress created, which tends to lead to their further extension and intervention. Inclusiveness normally only tends to have a chance of emerging *after* a certain level of wealth has been reached. In brief: modern economic growth did not begin with inclusive institutions. Whether it will end without them, i.e. whether growth can be sustained in an extractive, exclusive setting, is open to debate. China, the most populous country of the world and not exactly an inclusive society, has now had very high growth rates for forty years in a row, providing the biggest example of economic growth ever. That should be food for thought.

This is not the only respect in which the Japanese case throws specific light on general claims with regard to the relationship between institutions and growth. By the time the Meiji government opened the Japanese Diet with its very confined representation in 1890, the country strikingly enough had already acquired all the institutions that are usually associated with a modern fiscal state. Its fiscal system was not only centralized, the country's government already had huge amounts of long-term liabilities in the form of non-convertible paper notes *before* it had centralized tax collection. This indicates that the connection between the emergence of a strong fiscal state with its ability to float public debt on the one hand and political representation on the other, is less obvious than institutionalists like Douglass North, John Joseph Wallis, Barry R. Weingast and again Daron Acemoglu and James Robinson claim it was for England.[60] On the other hand, and that seems rather difficult to square with the claims made about the emergence of fiscal states that many scholars in the tradition of Charles Tilly and John Brewer have made, Meiji Japan already had its full-blown modern fiscal state *before* it had waged any major international wars.[61] In its case the sheer strength of the state and the firm conviction that one needed a strong military and a strong state in order to survive as a sovereign polity in an unfriendly environment apparently sufficed.[62]

Tokugawa legacies

When it comes to the government's 'despotic power', there is a clear continuity, in any case for the period 1880–1919 and 1931–1937, with Tokugawa Japan. Publications in which that polity is presented as an authoritarian 'police state' are legion. One of Japan's first social historians Fukuda Tokuzo, writing in 1900, referred to Tokugawa Japan as 'an absolute police state'.[63] Joseph Longford, in his *Evolution of new Japan* from 1913, described Tokugawa Japan as a country 'crushed under one of the most iron systems of feudalism that the world has ever seen'. According to him 'practically speaking' under Tokugawa rule, 'slavery, abject slavery, was the natural state of the great body of the people. They counted for nothing.' In his view, Japan's lower classes only sixty years ago were an 'abjectly spiritless race'.[64] Herbert Norman in his *Japan's emergence as a modern state*, in this aspect too, was quite explicit: 'This late feudalism represents one of the most conscious attempts in history to freeze society in a rigid hierarchical mould.'[65] Fairly recently in a textbook, in Dutch, Willy Vande Walle called Japan under Tokugawa rule 'totalitarian' and 'xenophobic'.[66] It would be easy to add many authors who even fairly recently, even though not always in such harsh terms, have expressed themselves in a similar vein.[67]

In practice, things may have been less rigid, but the *formal* rulings and regulations certainly point at a very strict and very regulated regime.[68] All *daimyo* had to be loyal to the shogun, who was their lord, and had to swear that they would rule just in their domains. The Laws for the Military Houses from 1615, in thirteen articles precisely indicated the obligations of the *daimyo* with respect to the shogun and announced severe punishment if they did not oblige.[69] From the fourth shogun onwards, they stayed almost unchanged. Their definitive codification was in 1635 when they consisted of, in total, twenty-one articles. The *daimyo* were not only expected to act in accordance with the Shogun's general rulings, they were also expected to show their lord signs of solidarity, in terms of money or corvee. They were not allowed to entertain contacts with other *daimyo*. In the *sankin kotai*-system they were basically held hostage by the shogun. The Separation Edict of 1591 had seen to it that they – and in time the great majority of their samurai – could not build a power base in the countryside. Especially in the beginning of Tokugawa rule many *daimyo* were expropriated and transferred.[70] When, over time, the threat of war became less acute, the Shoguns became less eager to increase their power and to decrease that of their retainers. But overall, and till the very end, the policies of the shoguns were meant to keep their *daimyo* in check and not let them become too powerful and autonomous. They, moreover, did not want to depend on them more than 'necessary'. This competitive and unequal relationship will not have contributed to strengthening Japan 'as a whole'. Shoguns continued to claim the right to enfeoff and grant the land they had entrusted to their *daimyo*, decide about their marriage and inheritance and impose extraordinary levies when they saw fit. Up until the very last decade of Tokugawa rule these rights were not normally challenged. In practice, certainly after the turn to the eighteenth century, *daimyo* could do as they saw fit in their fiefs, as long as they did not one way or another incur the wrath of their lord. It may not be surprising that the rights and obligations of the daimyo, who after all were retainers, were tightly described. The fact that this was also the case with the imperial court and court nobility in the so-called 'Regulations for the Imperial Palace and the Court Nobility' of 1615 indicates where power actually lay in Tokugawa Japan.[71]

That the bulk of Tokugawa Japan's population – the peasantry too were, at least in principle, subjected to a tight system of control – is less surprising. That does not mean that the Shogunate or the *daimyo* of the fief would, on a day-to-day basis, interfere in life in the more than 60,000 villages then existing in Japan. Those, to all intents and purposes, were quite autonomous and left alone on the condition of course that they paid their taxes and lived by the strict and elaborate rules that were imposed on them and enforced via mutual control and under a system of collective responsibilities. They were run by those who counted as owners of land.[72] The situation in towns of course was quite different, although there too strict rules prevailed.[73]

Open dissent and opposition were bound to be repressed and punishments were fierce.[74] Popular rebellions had only slight chances of success because the ordinary populace lacked arms. Already in 1588, Toyotomi Hideyoshi (1537–1598), with his so-called 'sword hunt', had divided Japan's population into two groups when it comes to the wearing of arms: the samurai, who were entitled to have two swords – but no longer any muskets, and the rest of the population who were completely disarmed. This did not change till the end of Tokugawa rule. Only government troops were still allowed to wear guns but as there were no wars against foreign, heavily armed troops, as was normal in Europe, we do not see much innovation in their weapons. To detect and investigate instances of maladministration, corruption or disaffection anywhere in Japan, Shogun and *daimyo* used censors and police officers.

Japan under the Tokugawa nevertheless was not always the 'realm at great peace' as which it has sometimes been known. Between 1590 and 1867, no less than 2,809 peasant disturbances were counted in the whole of Japan, 547 of them in *Bakufu* territory. In the latter half of Tokugawa rule, peasant disturbances increased substantially in number, in number of participants and with regard to the areas covered. Whereas 146 disturbances were counted in the territory of the *Bakufu* between 1590 and 1750, their number was 401 between 1751 and 1867. Such disturbances could be quite sizeable. In 1738, for example, 84,000 peasants in Iwaki province rioted. In 1754, no less than 168,000 peasants protested violently against unfair taxation in the Kuruke domain in Kyushu. In 1764, in the Kanto region 200,000 peasants rioted to protest the burden of corvee in the horse stations. In the year 1831, to give one final example, 100,000 peasants in Choshu demanded a reduction in taxes and protested against the domain's monopolistic policies in marketing industrial crops.[75]

When it comes to relations with other countries, there was indeed 'great peace'. The contrast with what occurred at the time in Europe, where in many countries war was an almost normal state of affairs, is striking. During the roughly 250 years of Tokugawa rule, Spain was at war for 160 years; Russia for 147; Austria for 130; Great Britain for 125, France for 115 and Prussia for 97.[76] *This* motor to strong state building, that was so prominent in Europe's history, was lacking in Tokugawa Japan. Its 'armed forces' – or rather its 'warrior estate' –nevertheless were quite substantial and its taxes quite high.

Here too, recent research has brought more nuance so that we now have a somewhat less oppressive image of Tokugawa rule. But there can be no doubt that neither those who were under the direct rule of the Shogun, nor those who were ruled by *daimyo*, had sufficient institutionalized countervailing power to protect themselves against their rulers. There in any case were no representative organs of any sort to curb the shogun's or the *daimyo*'s power, and there was no equivalent of 'natural law' or 'the law of god'. What law there was, basically amounted to a set of organic rules, general norms applied from case to case and from precedent to precedent. As indicated, these rules were quite repressive and often applied the principle of collective responsibility. The actual power of the Shogun in his house-lands and in Japan as a whole could vary significantly depending on the circumstances and the specific Shogun in charge. But up until the last decades of Tokugawa rule no serious threat to the Shogunal centre developed.[77] Non-samurai were subjected to samurai, samurai as vassals to their *daimyo* and *daimyo* to the shogun. There was no 'bourgeois' influence on government. In Tokugawa Japan, wealth may have increasingly been accumulated by merchants, but this economic power did not transform into political leverage as merchants were not permitted to hold government offices. Totman gave this characterization of the political system of the *Bakufu* (i.e. the Shogunate) that basically applies to Japan in its entirety:

> A government of the elite resulted, and it contained no avenue of approach for the increasingly affluent and socially influential members of the common populace.[78]

Ruling continued to be a monopoly of the warrior estate. The Meiji certainly inherited a 'successful' authoritarian tradition from their Tokugawa predecessors.

Ideological power

Politically, the state in the period 1868 to 1937 was quite strong in Japan. Let us now move to ideological power, meaning the power over – and thus by means of – concepts and categories of meaning, norms and aesthetic and ritual practices.[79] A state that manages to create, organize or even embody 'the nation's will' can certainly profit from it in terms of its strength, politically, militarily but also economically. Though it may not result in directly applicable skills and tends to be ignored by economists – though not by all of them – the contribution of this kind of winning and moulding 'hearts and minds' to building a strong army *and* a rich nation is often fundamental in economies in the midst of structural transformation. The following quote is by Walt Rostow, who usually is only quoted for his comments on investment rates and beginning industrialization:

> Although the period of transition – between the traditional society and the take-off – saw major changes in both the economy itself and in the balance of social values, a decisive factor was often political. Politically the building of an effective centralized national state – on the basis of coalitions touched with a new nationalism in opposition to the traditional landed regional interest, the colonial power or both was a decisive aspect of the preconditions period; and it was, almost universally, a necessary condition for take-off.[80]

He suggests that a mechanism of 'reactive nationalism' was the motivating drive behind the efforts at industrialization in Japan and Germany but also in Russia, and later the Soviet Union.[81] He thinks that this 'general mechanism' was even at play in the first industrial nation:

> An answer to these deeper questions places Britain back in the general case, to some significant degree. The general case is of a society modernizing itself in a nationalist reaction to intrusion or the threat of intrusion from more advanced powers abroad.[82]

Rostow is not the only influential economist pointing at the importance of (nationalist), pro-growth attitudes in order to make countries take off. Scholars such as Alexander Gerschenkron and William Arthur Lewis would agree. Gerschenkron emphasizes the importance of 'national mobilization', whereas Lewis claims that one of the tasks of government when it wants to promote economic growth is 'influencing attitudes'.[83] Among historians I could refer to are scholars such as David Landes and Liah Greenfeld.[84] The Japanese state certainly was very active and successful in this influencing of attitudes.[85] It in this context is striking that those contemporaries abroad who were impressed by 'the rise of Japan' often made a quite direct connection between the 'patriotism', 'national commitment' or 'self-sacrifice' – or whatever exact name they would want to give it – of the Japanese and their military *and* economic successes. Such references became stock in trade with the victory of the Japanese against the Chinese and even more so after they had won the war against Russia. It is only in the 1930s, that they were ousted by a more negative emphasis on 'exploitation of labour', 'unfair competition' and 'dumping'. Let me just give a couple of examples of that initial 'praise', in this case from British observers. Henry Dyer, a Scottish engineer, who had long lived in Japan and knew the country well, wrote the following about driving forces behind Japan's rise, in a book from 1904, with the telling title *Dai Nippon, The Britain of the East*:

> The sense of honour which cannot bear being looked down upon as an inferior power – that was the strongest of motives. Pecuniary or industrial considerations were only awakened later in the process of transformation.[86]

He thought that the secret of the developments which had taken place in Japan was to be found in the high sense of personal and national honour of the Japanese and in their ardent patriotism and intense loyalty.[87] Editor and writer Alfred Stead, in a book from 1906, with the no less striking title *Great Japan. A study in national efficiency*, claimed: 'Throughout the whole world, there is no such "national" nation . . . as Japan.' It is by their 'intense patriotism' and their 'affirmation of nationalism' that the Japanese scored their greatest success as a nation. A nation without national traditions 'could not have done what Japan has done'. Japan's triumph, so he writes in his permanent paean on the country, demonstrates one thing 'more than any other', that is: 'the absolute necessity for national efficiency, achieved by the unanimous effort of the entire people.' In his view, 'the patriotic impulse which has made Japan from a feudal into an industrial country, has enabled her to play the role of a first-class power instead of a third-class one.'[88] Twenty years later, to just give one more example, in this case from someone with first-hand knowledge of Japan's cotton industry, Arno Pearse wrote: 'one is forced to attribute a large portion of the unparalleled progress to this national patriotism.'[89]

When we look at ideological power, we can only conclude that Japan's rulers in the period under discussion 'had' a lot of it and moreover were quite outspoken about the importance they attached to it. This, however, as Carol Gluck, the major expert in the field, rightly reminds us should not lead us to commit two errors: to think they always agreed on everything and had a clear plan that they could implement without contestation and to think that Japan in this respect would have been unique. Although she admits that over time certain core concepts in the grammar of ideology transpired and that by the 1930s a clear monolithic orthodoxy prevailed, her book on Japan's modern myths shows that for decades there was diversity: there were different ideologues, different institutions and different audiences with different interests and ideas and many unplanned, unintended or unexpected effects.[90] Her admonition that we should not turn the Japanese case into something unique also is justified. The way in which ideologies emerge and spread and (can) turn into orthodoxies has a logic that is fairly common to modern complex societies. When it comes to the mechanisms of ideology-formation Japan was a good deal less than unique: 'the process of converting the Japanese into *kokumin* (countrymen P.V.) was as complicated and drawn out as turning peasants into Frenchmen, Germans into a Germanic *Volk*, or immigrants into 100 per cent Americans.'[91] Although one must, I think, admit that the efforts to turn the Japanese into one nation during the Meiji era and the 1930s were quite intense. In a way of course, Gluck's claim fits perfectly into my thesis: Japan evolved into a normal modern state like those in the West in contrast to all those (semi-) colonial states where the process of nation-building was *not* so successful and that – thus I would claim – did *not* experience fast development. As I rather heavily lean on Gluck in my description, one comment is in order here: According to her, basically all ideological elements of Japan's emperor-system were already present at the end of Meiji rule. They only became more dominant and more coherent in the 1930s. On the basis of my reading of Walter Skya, I think there are good reasons to believe that with the further spread of mass politics new elements and new forms of radicalization were introduced after the end of Meiji rule.[92]

The late 1880s showed a clear upsurge in ideological activity that had to deal with the two main issues that confront every modernizing and industrializing society. Firstly, what Gluck calls 'the sense of nation': the fact that imperial Japan with its new constitution and new place in the world needed to make up its collective mind and secondly, the question how to deal with the consequences of the country's fast modernization and all the concomitant social change.[93] All those concerned about the nation and the state considered it evident that the role of education and in particular of moral education in dealing with these questions was fundamental and that the purpose of the new general education was to serve the nation, by imparting practical knowledge, but also – and according to some even more importantly – by creating 'morality'. This is how the Governor of the prefecture Miyagi put it in 1890:

The purpose of moral education is to establish the foundations of the *kokutai* and teach the way of patriotism and ethics thus producing a people who are not ashamed to be Japanese.[94]

Yamagata Aritomo, for several decades one of the most important politicians and military leaders of Japan, thought along very similar lines, as shown in this quote:

The ways of loyalty among the people are the essence of the strength of a country. Unless the people love their country as their parents and are willing to safeguard it with their lives, though there are laws, both public and private, the country cannot exist even for a day. . . . society must also be maintained with morals and customs.[95]

Neglecting morality, so it was claimed, leads to deteriorating nationalism. Skills alone do not suffice: 'Elementary education should cultivate the moral character of the people.'[96]

The most famous product of this moral offensive in education undoubtedly is the so-called Imperial Rescript on Education that often and rightly has been described in terms of making 'good citizens' and of serving as the basis for loyalty and patriotism. Signed by Emperor Meiji on 30 October in 1890, it was distributed to every school in the Japanese empire, along with a portrait of the Emperor.[97] In primary schools, all pupils were educated 'in becoming loyal subjects.'[98] Government kept a close watch on education. From the time the first government texts appeared in 1903, through four subsequent redactions until the end of World War Two, the schools used uniform and official national texts, not only in the field of ethics but also in history, language and geography.[99] A lot of education amounted to indoctrination and drill with rather little clear effects on the economy, which by the way also applied to a lot of education in other countries.[100] The state increasingly managed to permeate daily life, to 'mould the Japanese mind' and to foster a strong sense of collective identity and destiny.[101]

The urge to inculcate patriotism was even more explicit, understandably, when it came to the military, the bulk of whom since the introduction of conscription consisted of young men of peasant background. The Imperial Rescript to Soldiers and Sailors of 1882 basically had to do for the military what the Imperial Rescript on Education was later supposed to do for pupils in schools.[102] It would be hard to find fault with Gluck's claim: 'The schools, along with the army, clearly constituted the most pervasive tutelary apparatus of the state.'[103] They could even merge their efforts. An army reform of 1925, for example, gave officers from inactivated units positions as military instructors in elementary and middle schools where they then could function as drill instructors.[104] In brief, one can safely conclude that the state in industrializing Japan with its grip on bureaucracy and the army, on education, and on the press and politics wanted to wield strong ideological power and to a large extent was successful.[105] The fact that the Emperor of Japan had a god-like status and that a variety of Shintoism became promoted as a kind of 'state-religion', will certainly at least in potential also have strengthened the ideological power of the ruling elite in the country.[106]

When it comes to ideological power, there again is continuity with Tokugawa Japan in the sense that in pre- as well as in post-1868 Japan, rulers were keen on moulding the hearts and minds of their subjects. Although after 1868 they did so with much more energy and a far broader reach considering the fact that in Meiji Japan modernization meant the 'nationalization' and thus 'mobilization' of the masses, whereas Tokugawa rulers were less interested in the hearts and minds of the bulk of the people as long as they obeyed and did what was expected of them.[107] That does not mean there would not have existed 'precursors' of Japanese nationalism in Tokugawa Japan. There was an embryonic proto-nationalism that later 'nationalists' did use. The emergence of nationalist ideas mainly was a result of the confrontation with the West, which basically already started in the late eighteenth century but became more explicit and politically relevant after 1853.[108]

The military

The military played a major role in public life in Japan during the entire period that this book deals with. Considering the number of wars in which it was actively involved between 1868 and 1937, that need not come as a surprise.

Considering the fact that it won the wars against China in 1894 and against Russia in 1904–1905, we may assume that its military was strong, so I do not have to expand on that. In the next chapter on the economic power of the state I will provide ample information on the military budget so that too need not be discussed here. My focus will be on its manpower, and that of the police, that as a rule and correctly so is considered a basic element in state power.

Let us begin with the army. In 1873 conscription was introduced and military service became universal and obligatory. At twenty years of age every Japanese subject, of whatever status, became liable for military service. Exemptions were given to criminals, those who could show hardship or were physically unfit but also to heads of households, heirs, students, government bureaucrats and teachers and those who could pay a – quite high – fee. Conscripts in the active army could be discharged before the expiration of their full service. In practice, this meant that the conscript army, at least initially, was

Table 26 Wars in which Japan's military was actively involved, 1868–1937

Boshin War	1868–1869
Southwestern War	1877
First War with China	1894–1895
Invasion of Taiwan	1895
Boxer Rebellion	1899–1901
War with Russia	1904–1905
World War One	1914–1918
Siberian Intervention	1918–1922
Invasion of Manchuria	1931–1932
Second War with China	1937–1941

mainly composed of second and third sons of poor farmers. The 1873 conscription ordinance provided for seven years of military service: three on active duty and the remainder in the reserves. In 1879, the terms of reserve duty were extended from four to seven years by creating a first (three year) and a second (four year) reserve. The fee to purchase a substitute was halved. In 1883, there again was new legislation that aimed at creating larger reserves: a first reserve with a four-year obligation to serve and a second one with five additional years of military commitment. The system of paid substitutes was abolished. Being exempted became much less easy. Of the large number of exemptions to conscription, in 1889 only illness and disability remained.[109]

On top of that, volunteer enlistments of one-year were introduced. A reform in 1925 reduced the terms of conscription from three to two years, but simultaneously built a larger pool of reserves for mobilization as conscripts would enter the reserves sooner.[110]

The seize of the now imperial army increased quickly. In 1871, it counted 15,000 people, in 1875 already more than double that number and in 1885 already 54,000.[111] It further increased till the beginning of the 1920s, as shown in Figure 2. Its growth then came to a temporary halt. In the second half of the 1930s, numbers again began to increase sharply. In mid-1937, the army numbered approximately 247,000 officers and men. But the number of regulars and reserves on active duty in total already amounted to 950,000. That number increased to 1,350,000 in 1940.[112]

The figures so far are figures for first-line active troops. They become much higher when all sorts of (other) reserves are included. Rough estimates of Japan's war strength made before World War One, gave 550,000 as the war strength of the first line army, plus 34,000 for garrisons overseas. But on top of that there were 150,000 special reserves; 370,000 second line reserves, and 110,000 trained troops in the territorial forces. All these branches could further draw upon half-trained elements to the number of about 800,000 to replace losses. In 1909, the Russian newspaper *Novoye Vremya* estimated Japan's available strength for home defence in the last resort at about three million. By 1930, when the system had produced its full effect, the first line would be 740,000 strong, the second line 780,000, and the third line about 3,850,000 (3,000,000

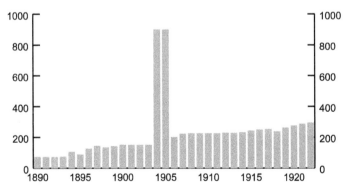

Figure 2 Personnel of the Imperial Army, 000s.

Schencking, *Making waves*, 104, 186 and 217.

untrained and 850,000 partly trained). That would suggest that the total available military strength at that time would have been over four million.

Conscription initially was highly selective. As indicated earlier, there were many exemptions. Over time though, their number was sharply reduced. Not all conscripts were 'equal'. In the regional garrisons, one would mostly find the second and third sons of impoverished farmers. Former samurai were in the Guard and Tokyo Garrison. The main selectivity resided in the fact that of those eligible to serve only a certain percentage were actually made to do so. Till the reforms in the 1880s, that percentage was only 3–6 per cent; in the period 1884–1890, 4 to 6 per cent, and in 1897, around 10 per cent. By 1904, the army inducted almost 20 per cent of the annual cohort and assigned double the number of those examined to the reserves. The percentage remained that high into the 1930s.[113] Apart from conscripts and reserves, there also was a substantial number of volunteers: between 1906 and 1916, for example, more than 35,000.[114]

Here too after the mid-1930s numbers increased again. The Navy basically was built on volunteers, who had to undergo very strict selection and received professional training. Overall the higher military echelons reached a high level of professionalism. The often sharply increasing numbers of Japan's military were not high, however, as compared to other countries as Table 27 shows.

Looking at the number of its regular military personnel, Japan, also *after* World War One, was not the heavily militarized society which it has often been portrayed as. Germany's army indeed officially remained small – till re-armament under Hitler in the 1930s. Under the Treaty of Versailles, it was only allowed to have 100,000 military men in arms, whereas its navy was reduced to a minimum. In the mid-1930s, before preparation for war had become massive, France, Germany and the United Kingdom all had regular *domestic* armies of between 300,000 and 350,000 men, with the German Army expanding very fast and already in 1936 probably passing the line of half a million.[115] Compared to those numbers, Japan's regular military as a percentage of total population at that time still was relatively modest. In 1936 that percentage was still below one.[116]

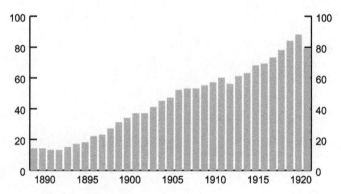

Figure 3 Personnel of the Imperial Navy, 000s.

Schencking, *Making waves* 104, 186, 217.

Table 27 Military personnel as a percentage of total population, for the years 1870–1910. The figures refer only to the indicated years

	Japan	France	Germany	Great Britain
1870		1.66	0.98	1.14
1880		1.44	1.07	0.96
1890	0.21	1.55	1.12	0.96
1900	0.41	1.59	1.05	1.51
1910	0.57	1.65	1.05	1.04

For Japan, the figures are calculated on the basis of figures in Figures 3 and 4 and of population figures as can be consulted under https://en.wikipedia.org/wiki/Demography_of_the_Empire_of_Japan. The rest of the figures are from Mann, *Sources of social power, Vol. II*, 806–810. For an overview of the absolute numbers of people in the armed forces of France, Germany and the United Kingdom for the entire period discussed in this book, see Flora, Kraus and Pfennig, *State, economy and society* volume I, 248–249. The figures presented there show how much more militarized than Japan these countries usually were, in particular France and Germany.

As yet we have mainly debated regular forces. In case of war huge numbers of men were mobilized.[117] During the Southwest War or Satsuma Rebellion, the national army expanded to at least 50,000 people. On top of that, some 90,000 civilians were involved in loading, hauling and distributing military supplies. Saigo Takamori, the leader of the insurgents, had some 30,000 troops, 6,000 of whom handled transport and supply duties. One in every three government troops was killed or wounded, and one in two of Saigo's insurgents. In the Sino–Japanese War of 1894–1895, the mobilized army grew to over 220,000. More than 150,000 civilian contractors, labourers, rickshaw men and coolies were employed to sustain this war machine. The number of Japanese soldiers killed in action was surprisingly low: 'only' 1,161. Almost 12,000 died of disease. One Japanese soldier was taken prisoner. When the Japanese had to confront 50,000 insurgents in Taiwan in 1895, 700 soldiers were killed in fighting, whereas diseases killed some 20,000. With the Russo–Japanese War of 1905, warfare again acquired new dimensions: the Japanese deployed some 950,000 troops, more than 25 per cent of them were involved in some kind of logistic duties. On top of that, some 700,000 Korean and Chinese porters and labourers figured as auxiliary quartermasters. In the biggest battle of this war, that of Mukden, over 300,000 Russians fought over 250,000 Japanese. This made it the biggest battle before World War One since the Battle of Nations in Leipzig in 1813. Now the number of Japanese military men killed in action was some 60,000; the number of people who died because of disease amounted to 22,000, whereas more than 136,000 men got wounded. In World War One, Japan was only marginally involved: it lost some 400 soldiers killed in action during the Qingdao campaign. In the intervention in Siberia after that war some 70,000 troops were involved. By the end of 1937, Japan to all intents and purposes was waging a full-blown war in China, in which already at that moment no less than 600,000 men were involved. I already mentioned that the total number of regulars and reserves on active duty at the time amounted to 950,000 and that in 1940, that number had risen to 1,350,000. With Pearl Harbor, warfare again reached new dimensions. When Japan surrendered in August 1945 the total number of people in the military amounted to almost seven million. The number of military fatalities, i.e. of military personnel and civilians working for the army, killed in combat, by war-related injuries and war-related fatal disease in the Asia Pacific War from July 1937 to August 1945 was also of an entirely different scale. It amounted to about 2.3 million, excluding tens of thousands of military men missing and never accounted for.[118]

Japan's Navy, which in principle became such a formidable weapon, deserves further attention. In 1869, it was formally established that Japan should have an Imperial Navy. In 1870, an Imperial decree determined that Britain's Royal Navy should be the model for development. In 1872, the Ministry of War was replaced by two separate Army and Navy Ministries. With often extensive help in terms of experts, material and examples from France, Germany and the United Kingdom, a modern navy was built. Naval cadets were sent overseas, and foreign experts invited to teach at newly established naval training schools. This contributed to building a well-educated officer corps. Foreign technology was welcomed but at the same time domestic development was promoted.[119]

In 1896, a major program was funded for a 260,000-ton navy to be completed over a ten-year period at a total cost of 280 million yen. The acquisition of warships alone accounted for over 200 million yen. Roughly 70 per cent of the program was financed from the Chinese indemnity paid after the Sino–Japanese War of 1894–1895. Public loans and existing government revenue provided the rest. In 1920, The Japanese Navy was the third largest in the world, behind the navies of the United Kingdom and the United States. Such a navy of course cost serious money. By 1921, Japan's naval expenditure amounted to nearly a third of the national budget. The Washington Naval Treaty of 1922 set a cap on expansion. A system of ratios was set up between the five signatory powers, the United States, the United Kingdom, Japan, France and Italy.[120] In the 1930s, new ambitious plans were proposed and started to further expand the Navy. Developing a modern army and, relatively speaking, even more so developing a modern navy, was quite expensive. Figure 4 shows how expensive.

Again, in the second half of the 1930s military efforts in financial terms also reached new dimensions. Only a strong, effective and technologically advanced state could

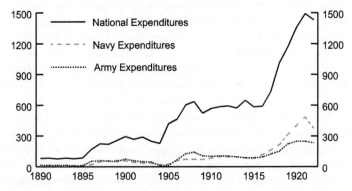

Figure 4 Army expenditures, navy expenditures and national expenditures, 1890–1922 in 000s of yen.

Schencking, *Making waves*, 104, 186 and 217.

have such a large and modern military, make it wage wars against formidable enemies *and* win them. Warfare had become industrialized, its outcome depending more than ever on the mobilization of huge amounts of people, of specific industrial resources such as iron, steel or gunpowder, and of the most advanced technology.[121] A modern army ideally became an army of a fairly small group of professional officers combined with a mass of trained and motivated troops. In that respect too, it was important to have a military that was well-embedded in civil society. In 1910, a group of army officers founded the Imperial Military Reserve Association. Their goal was to ensure that the role of the military and its ideals were not neglected by society. It set out to spread its ideals, such as obedience, frugality, diligence cooperation, bravery, hierarchy and a belief in the divine Emperor. It established branches in 14,000 communities. At its height, it had some three million volunteers, half of whom had no military experience. By the 1930s, the organization and its members had become the backbone of rural Japan.[122]

Tokugawa legacies

The military, as we have seen, was quite prominent in post-Restoration Japan. The country built a quite substantial army and navy. Here too, next to important changes, there are striking continuities. Discussing the military in Tokugawa Japan means discussing the samurai. Their total number doing service in the various domains of Tokugawa Japan and in the lands of the Shogun may have been as high as 350,000. In theory, the Tokugawa regime could, when all its 'retainers' answered its call, field 400,000 men, but this capacity was never tested.[123] Two comments are necessary here. When discussing Tokugawa Japan's military, we have to realize that the country's navy was tiny and that its warriors increasingly *de facto* became civilians.

The figure of 400,000 armed men of course only gets significance when it is put in perspective via comparison. It is in any case high. Azar Gat in his book on war in human history calls it an iron rule throughout history 'that no more than one per cent of a state's population (and normally less) could be sustained economically on a regular basis, as fully professional troops'.[124] The figure for Tokugawa Japan, with some 400,000 military men on a population of, at its lowest, some twelve million inhabitants and at its highest some thirty-two million, is certainly higher. Depending on the estimates of population and army size that one wants to accept, at the very beginning of Tokugawa rule under Tokugawa Ieyasu no less than 3.3 per cent of total population would have been 'in the military' and at the end, in 1868, some 1.25 per cent. But again, these were troops on paper. Even if they had been real, they did not fight and in the second half of Tokugawa rule the number of retainers that was expected to answer a call declined very substantially. The effective army thus became only a fraction of its former size.[125]

Table 28 can provide some idea of Tokugawa Japan's 'militarization' from a comparative perspective. With all the caveats that also apply to this comparison, I think it is safe to say that Japan under Tokugawa rule was not exceptionally militarized compared to European 'states', that at times could indeed be real war machines.

Table 28 Military personnel as percentage of total population, 1760–1910

Year	Great Britain	France	Prussia-Germany
1760	2.36	1.78	4.14
1770	0.58	0.82	
1780	2.76	0.89	3.76
1790	0.97	0.85	3.42
1800	4.91	2.93	3.73
1810	5.30	3.66	3.88
1820	1.02		1.33
1830	1.01	1.23	1.15
1840	1.10	1.02	1.05
1850	1.20	1.09	1.04

Mann, *Sources of social power, II*, 393.

During campaigns or on 'special occasions' impressive amounts of troops could be mobilized. In 1586, Toyotomi Hideyoshi led 250,000 men against the great southern domain of Satsuma.[126] When he invaded Korea in 1592, his expeditionary force numbered 158,800 men. When he invaded that country for a second time in 1597, he did so with 141,000 people. Throughout the entire conflict with Korea, the Japanese mobilized a total of 320,000 troops. In the Battle of Sekigahara in 1600, between the troops of Tokugawa Ieyasu and Toyotomi Hideyori (1593–1615?), in total some 170,000 men were involved. In 1634, Shogun Iemitsu visited the imperial court with some 300,000 troops, in what Ravina describes as 'a show of force thinly disguised as a gesture of respect'.[127] These are all quite impressive numbers, but from 1615 onwards, Tokugawa Japan's warrior elite did not wage any wars for some 250 years. For all those years, the proud, sword-wearing samurai were never engaged in any real military action. They often took up all sorts of jobs or in any case 'occupations', preferably in 'bureaucracy', just to do something and, which is very important, to add something to their usually shrinking stipends. But whatever exactly they did or did not do at whatever reward: till the very end of Tokugawa rule, and in several respects even some years longer, they continued to be a hugely privileged, and subsidized estate, with all the disadvantages that go with that for the civilian (and the military) side of Tokugawa government. The part of expenditures of the Shogunate that went to paying its personnel was quite high.[128] In this respect, things would certainly change after the Restoration.

Having large armed forces and spending substantial amounts of money on them was not a post-Restoration invention. Building a large navy certainly was. But again, the last decades of Tokugawa rule were a period of transition that witnessed several new initiatives. As soon as Japan opened up to foreign influences, the Shogunate recognized the vulnerability of the country from the sea and initiated an active policy of assimilation and adoption of Western naval technologies. In 1855, it acquired its first steam warship, which it used for training and establishing a naval training centre at Nagasaki that relocated to Tokyo in 1859. Samurai were sent to study in the Netherlands for several years. The Shogunate acquired its first screw-driven steam warship in 1857. In 1865, it hired a French naval engineer to build the country's first modern naval arsenals. The Shogunate also allowed and then ordered various domains to purchase warships and develop naval fleets. The Satsuma domain had already set up a naval centre by itself. In this case too, students were sent abroad for training and a number of ships were acquired abroad. The domains of Choshu, Hizen, Tosa and Kaga joined Satsuma in acquiring ships. By the mid-1860s, a small Japanese fleet had been created: the Shogunate had eight warships and thirty-six auxiliaries. Satsuma (with the largest domain fleet) had nine steamships; Choshu had five ships plus numerous auxiliary craft; Kaga ten and Chikuzen eight. Many smaller domains had also acquired a couple of ships. It would be exaggerated to already speak of a genuine fleet: all these ships functioned as transport ships as well as combat vessels, and they were manned by personnel who lacked experience except for coastal sailing and had virtually no combat training. After the Restoration, however, in particular from the 1890s onwards, the history of Japan's maritime power entered a new era.

In an analysis like this some references to the police must be included. For Japanese officials, the police system was an essential part of a modern state apparatus, a sign of civilization, and a necessary element in their effort to convince the Western powers to abolish the unequal treaties.[129] Already in 1871, Tokyo's Western-style police was established. The police system chosen as model for the country was that of France. That means that it was highly centralized and standardized and penetrated the entire country. Its organizational structure was made quite similar to that of the army. Its professionalization proceeded rapidly. In some respects, the Japanese police system actually anticipated later developments in Western police. What is surprising is the high turnover rate and the low level of financial resources. The total number of police officers became substantial. In 1876, there were some twenty-three thousand civilian police officers; in 1912 over forty thousand, spread over seventeen thousand police posts. Next to the civilian police there was the *kempetai*, the military police, founded 1881. It was part of the army and fell under the Ministry of War. It was used for service in colonies. In 1912, this police force numbered over ten thousand in total.

With regard to the police in Tokugawa Japan we can be brief. The country had no real national police. What came closest to it were the *ometsuke*, high-ranking samurai and their subordinates whose mandate was the surveillance and control of the *daimyo* and senior Shogunate officials.

The bureaucracy

Historically speaking the overwhelming majority of persons working for the state has always been in the military. How about civilian personnel? Table 29 shows the number of civilians working for Japan's government in the period 1880 to 1940.

Table 30 provides a comparison with the situation in France, Germany/Prussia and the United Kingdom, now counting state employment of civilian personnel at the central level as a percentage of total population.

The information in Tables 29 and 30 only refers to officials working for central government. But, as can be deduced from the figures about local taxes and local expenditure, there must also have been a substantial number of officials working for local government. According to Harry Harootunian, their number already amounted to 14,000 in 1882.[130] Again, a comparison with China can be instructive here. For this country, we know that in the 1880s there were *in total* some 27,000 officials, counting Han *and* non-Han Chinese, civilian *and* military officials. That number hardly changed till the end of Qing rule in 1911. That would mean at that time there was one 'real'

Table 29 Employees working for central government, *excluding* members of the armed forces and people working for local government

	Number of employees in 000s	Ratio of employees to total gainfully occupied population
1880	37	.19
1890	75	.33
1900	89	.35
1910	185	.71
1920	308	1.13
1930	705	2.38
1940	1,043	3.21

Emi, *Government fiscal activity*, 5.

Table 30 State employment of civilian personnel at the central level as a percentage of total population

	Japan	France	Germany/Prussia	United Kingdom
1850		0.41		0.24
1860				
1870		0.60	1.15	
1880	0.10	0.87	1.56 1.51	
1890	0.19	0.91	1.70 1.80	0.32
1900	0.20	1.10		0.40
1910	0.36	1.40	2.35 3.92	0.64
1920	0.55	1921 1.85	1923 2.25	1921 0.96
1930	1.10	1931 1.80	1930 1.83	1928 0.72
1940	1.42	1938 3.00	1933 1.69	1940 1.09

The figures for Japan are calculated on the basis of the information in Table 29. The figures for France, Germany/Prussia and the United Kingdom are from Mann, *Sources of social power, Volume II*, 806–810 and Flora, Kraus and Pfennig, *State, economy and society*, Volume I, chapter 5. According to Kyoko Sheridan, central and local government employees, excluding the military, amounted to 0.6 per cent of total workforce in 1880. That percentage increased to 2.6 in 1910 and 4.8 in 1930. Sheridan, *Governing the Japanese economy*, 64, note 22. She does not indicate how she has arrived at these percentages, which seem fairly high. Much of course depends on how she defines 'workforce'.

Table 31 General government employment as a percentage of total employment, in this case *including* the military

	Japan	France	Germany	United Kingdom
1913	3.1	3.0	2.4	4.1
1937	5.0	4.4	4.3	6.5

Tanzi and Schuknecht, *Public spending*, 26.

central government official per 14,000 inhabitants. Such officials amounted to 0.007 per cent of total population.

In debates on the role of the state in Japan's economic development, scholars have pointed out that the number of people working for government, in which case they in particular meant people working for government in government enterprises, would not be so high.[131] One can always discuss what 'high' or 'low' would mean in this context but I think it would be an error to reduce the importance of the state in this context to just its quantitative dimension. What set Japan's officials, to begin with them, apart from many contemporary officials in developing countries, was that they were working in a rationally organized bureaucracy. In discussing bureaucracy, it is always helpful to refer back to Max Weber. According to him, in brief, a bureaucratic system has the following characteristics:

- Officials are free, subject to authority only in their official tasks.
- Officials are organized in a clearly defined hierarchy of offices.
- Each office has a clearly defined sphere of competence.
- Offices are filled by free contract.
- Candidates for office are selected according to their qualifications, normally examinations and technical training.
- Officials are salaried and granted pensions.
- The office is the sole or primary occupation of the incumbent.
- The office constitutes a career involving promotion by seniority or for achievement.
- The official is separated from ownership of the means of administration.
- The official is subject to systematic discipline and control in official conduct.[132]

Of course, here too there often may have existed a gap between theory and practice, but nevertheless in theory as well as in practice post-Restoration Japan developed an administration that was much closer to Max Weber's ideal-type bureaucracy than that of Tokugawa Japan and that – which is highly important – when it comes to efficiency and effectiveness could stand comparison with Western bureaucracies at the time. Many of Japan's officials were highly educated professionals. Higher ranking officials tended to be university-trained specialists.[133]

To illustrate the importance of a well-staffed well-functioning bureaucracy for Japan's developmental state it might be helpful to quote the scholar who introduced that concept, Chalmers Johnson. In his book on MITI and the Japanese miracle, Johnson pointed out that 'all states intervene in their economies for various reasons'. Hence what matters most are the purpose and mode of state intervention. He then differentiated between a 'developmental state' and a 'regulatory state'. In the former, of which Japan is a prime example, the state has a predominantly 'developmental orientation', taking an active part in setting 'such substantive social and economic goals' as 'what industries ought to exist and what industries are no longer needed'. By contrast, the latter, exemplified by the United States, eschews explicitly developmental goals, concerning itself instead with the forms and procedures of economic competition. A developmental state, in Johnson's words, is 'plan rational', whereas a regulatory state is 'market rational'. The plan-rational, developmental state employs 'market-conforming methods of state intervention in the economy'. Nonetheless, the degree of state intervention is necessarily greater in such a developmental state than it is in a regulatory state. And that brings us to the importance of government bureaucracy for growth: the greater the degree of state intervention in the economy, the more salient the government bureaucracy, a quintessential embodiment of state power. A 'natural corollary of plan rationality', in Johnson's words, therefore is the 'existence of a powerful, talented and prestigious economic bureaucracy'.[134] We should add that it is not just the economic bureaucracy but the entire state bureaucracy whose role is magnified in a developmental state. Examples of inefficiency and corruption abound but in principle Japan's bureaucracy was well functioning, that is *as compared to* other underdeveloped or developing countries and *as compared to* how Japan as a whole was ruled *before* Meiji.[135] It was, however, not well paid. Before World War Two, the wage level of government employees, when represented in real terms, gradually decreased.[136]

When discussing people working for government in government enterprises, I would like to point out two things. The first is that their number was not low. George Allen, who wants to emphasize how relatively small the government sector had become, points out in support of that view that in 1912, *after* the much-discussed sale of many factories in the 1880s, only some 12 per cent of all 'factory' operatives in manufacturing industry were working in establishments that were owned outright by government.[137] Apart from the fact that it is not clear what makes him come up with this figure, that in light of other figures I referred to seems quite low. Even this figure is not really low.[138] The second one is that they almost without exception worked in big, modern and skill-intensive factories.[139]

Tokugawa legacies

When it comes to the importance of state officials, continuities between the period before and that after the Restoration are more important than one might expect, assuming that the Meiji Restoration implied a regime change after a violent conflict. A first striking continuity lies in the fact that Japan, *pre*- as well as *post*-Restoration, was a country with a quite substantial bureaucracy and army. When it comes to Tokugawa 'bureaucracy', I found no statistics covering the entire country. Even if I had had found them, it would still be hard – if not all but impossible – to determine who should count as a 'real' government official and on what grounds.[140] According to Conrad Totman, the early Shogunate had about 17,000 supra-village officials for its own realm. Assuming that *daimyo* administrations were similarly dense, that would suggest there were 50,000 to 60,000 officials in Tokugawa Japan in its entirety, a country with, in his estimate, at that moment, fifteen to seventeen million inhabitants.[141] Dowdy claims that in middle of the nineteenth century, the total number of officials working in the Tokugawa bureaucracy still was 17,000, of which some 5,300 persons were working in intendancy and finance offices.[142] It would be naïve to draw firm conclusions from these figures considering all the problems of reliability and interpretation involved. But in my view, it is telling that in Qing China the total number of *central* government officials never surpassed 30,000 before 1850, whereas the number of its inhabitants then had already surpassed the 400 million. Again, Japan seems to have been more like Western Europe. Great Britain at the end of the eighteenth century had some ten million inhabitants and some 20,000 central government officials. For Prussia, the figures at that time were some five million and some 14,000 and for France almost thirty million and some 60,000.[143]

The 'bureaucracy' of Tokugawa Japan in principle was monopolized by the samurai estate. Only men of samurai status (meaning those who had entered vasallic relationship with a lord) could hold government offices.[144] As a matter of fact the reservoir from which the *Bakufu* took officials was even more restricted: the bulk of them were liege vassals. According to Totman, of the total of 22,500 liege vassals about 12,200 were in positions with some military or police duty.[145] *Fudai daimyo* and *shimpan daimyo* could also have jobs as *Bakufu* officials, though less frequently, in particular in the case of *shimpan daimyo*. *Tozama daimyo* were completely excluded from *Bakufu* functions, as were aristocrats, monks or clerics and merchants. In the country as a whole there occasionally was some participation of merchants in town government. At the village level, non-samurai could act as headmen and samurai 'officials' were all but absent.

But even with these 'restrictions' the supply of samurai was too high. About one-fourth of the liege vassals actually had no real job but just performed *sankin kotai* duties and other ceremonial affairs, and were simply maintained within the net of the *Bakufu* organization.[146] The *daimyo* could not easily afford to reduce the number of their vassals as Tokugawa vasallage was 'a long-term, transgenerational bond between the *ie* of the *daimyo* and that of the vassal'.[147] Which means that often administrative posts were rather scarce of content because there was not enough real work to employ so many samurai. Higher offices were usually reserved for samurai with higher honour rankings, the lower ones crowded with men from lower ranking houses. There thus were ample restrictions when it came to choosing officials. It will not come as a surprise, that, as Ikegami indicates: 'The problem of efficacy remained to plague the system ... because the samurai were confined in a secure cocoon of life-long employment.'[148]

Samurai were aristocrats, bureaucrats and military men at the same time. The difference between military and civil officials therefore was rather ambiguous. Their social position tended to rest on a mixture of three indices: their honour ranking, that was primarily determined at birth, their office or position, and their income. The inflexible nature of the honour-ranking system made it hard to systematically recruit people on the basis of merit. The high born did not necessarily get a high, powerful office and certain very talented or appreciated samurai could be 'unconventionally' promoted. But such promotions remained exceptional and problematic. Preservation of the status quo was the basic principle of organization.[149] The fundamental traits of the system stayed in place till the very end of Tokugawa rule which means that, following Ikegami, one can justifiably claim that Tokugawa Japan was not ruled by a meritocratic professional bureaucracy that provided a career open to talent but rather by a 'caste'. Totman in a book from the 1960s agrees:

> by present-day standards the *Bakufu* was a most imperfect bureaucracy, particularly in personnel practices.[150]

bureaucratization did not lead to the predominance of objective criteria of appointment and promotion, and it neither broadened the basis of political recruitment nor significantly facilitated mobility amongst most office holders, despite a growing debate on the need for merit-promotion nexus and general approval of the slogan 'promoting the able'. Rather, the value structure which emerged during the seventeenth century preserved both elitist government and a close correlation between office and hereditary rank.[151]

The *Bakufu* had almost no objective bureaucratic means for selecting office holders although the question of competence was not ignored. For higher functions the crucial factor in personnel selection was political preference.[152] As it was the beginning of a systematic effort to 'professionalize' officialdom, the Meiji Restoration in that respect indeed was a break.

Two further facts with regard to Tokugawa bureaucracy deserve specific attention. Firstly, the fact that in Tokugawa Japan at the higher levels the distinction between politicians (elected state officials who assist in deciding and formulating policies) and officials (appointed departmental official who carry out routine administrative tasks) was not strict. Often the political as well as the bureaucratic functions were discharged by the same official.[153] Secondly, the fact that in the *Bakufu* the growth of bureaucracy was accompanied by the development of an informal administrative power structure, the vertical clique, which enabled a single group of men to control both political and administrative functions.[154]

When it comes to choosing personnel, the system may not have been bureaucratic. When it comes to actual work practices, however, there were clear signs of bureaucratization. The work of officials became more formalized and based on an increasing number of written rules and codes that standardized e.g. procedures, office hours or office supplies. We see a growth of written law and an increased use of exams. Among those in office, literacy was high. The administrative systems of *Bakufu* and domains became more impersonal as *daimyo* often were not in their domain but in Edo whereas samurai were not in the countryside with 'their' peasants but in castle towns. In the middle and lower echelons, capability often could not be ignored. The number of offices and duties with differing salaries multiplied.[155] There were repeated efforts at reform and the introducing of meritocratic elements. For details, I refer to the literature. But as with the tax system and so many other elements of the Tokugawa 'system', the fundamental structures were not changed, which means that Tokugawa Japan continued to be administered in a way that, at least economically speaking, had fairly clear shortcomings.

The Meiji Restoration did signal a clear step in the direction of the building of a modern professional bureaucracy. But, again, it was not a clear-cut break. There also was continuity. Not just in the formal sense that Japan before as well as after the Restoration had a very substantial number of people engaged in administrating it. Also in the sense that many members of the samurai estate continued to be involved in administration *after* Restoration. Let me give just a couple of examples: In 1877, ex-samurai occupied more than 77 per cent of the functions in the state apparatus and

Table 32 Composition of government officials, 1872–1882

Year	Central all	Central samurai	Local all	Local samurai
1876	23,135	17,935		
1882	96,418	59,041	14,171	8,148

Harootunian, 'Progress of Japan', 260–261.

more than 70 per cent in local administration.[156] According to an estimate for the 1880s, over 90 per cent of senior government officials were of samurai origin.[157] Sonoda, in a text about the decline of the Japanese warrior class, comes up with the following figures:

> In 1881, the ex-samurai and their families made up 5.3 per cent of the total population. This small group occupied 68,556 of a total of 168,594 official posts, or 40.7 per cent. Moreover, the higher the official post, the higher the rate of occupation by former samurai.... In 1885, among ninety-three high-ranking officials above the bureau heads of the central government, we find four members of the peerage, eighty-eight ex-samurai, and one commoner.[158]

As late as 1890, when 5 per cent of total population had *shizoku* rank, one third of all the members of parliament was *shizoku*, as were almost all ministers and high officials, and two-thirds of professors at institutes of higher education and of those who finished their studies there.[159] In Ikegami's words: 'The Meiji Restoration thus tapped into and aroused the dormant meritocratic and achievement-oriented aspirations of the Japanese people.'[160] The fact that under Tokugawa rule having multiple offices and frequent job rotation was so normal in any case had the mostly unintended positive effect of building a reserve of skilled officials that could switch jobs easily.[161]

4

A Powerful State: The Economy

State property

An institutional framework as such may be quite helpful in implementing policies, but when the state lacks sufficient resources ultimately it will not make a lot of difference. In that respect, it is important to emphasize that Japan's state in the period discussed here also was strong in the sense that its rulers had the necessary means – in terms of resources and personnel – to seriously try and implement their plans. They could not only, in principle, try and do what they *wanted*, which means they were fairly autonomous, they also had a fair amount of chance of being *effective*.

Any comparison of Japan's state capacity with that of other non-Western countries in material and human resources speaks volumes. Recent studies focusing on a comparison with the situation in China and India show how much weaker these states were.[1] It needs no further comment that this capacity to get things done is tightly connected to the quantity and quality of the means at the state's disposal. Let us begin with the most important capital good of (semi-) agricultural societies, to wit land. Japan's post-Restoration state owned a lot of it. To illustrate how much, let me first provide some general information about Japan's geography. Japan in its current extension counts some thirty-eight million ha. In the period discussed here, the percentage of this land that was used as arable never corresponded to more than some 16 per cent: roughly five million ha of paddy and upland fields and about one million ha of plain and pastures.[2] According to Willy Vande Walle at the beginning of Meiji rule only some 2 per cent of Japanese soil was state property. In 1881, this was 31 per cent and in 1890 63 per cent. He, however, gives no sources for this claim.[3] Haruki Yamawaki gives the following figures for the beginning of the twentieth century: Of the total amount of land of thirty-eight million ha, only some fourteen million ha, less than 40 per cent, was in private hands. About thirteen million hectares of it were taxable. Over twenty-one million ha, which is some 55 per cent of Japan's entire landmass, belonged to the Emperor and the state. Of this area, some three and a half million ha, almost 10 per cent of the entire country, belonged to the Imperial Court, mausoleums and shrines. Land, forests, plains, and premises that were government property, amounted to seventeen and a half million ha, i.e. some 45 per cent of all land. The rest, some three million ha, consisted of highways, places under water and various other minor categories.[4]

The government was the biggest forest owner in the country. National government, local government and the Imperial Household, here for the sake of convenience included in government, came to own over two-thirds of it.[5] In the beginning of the twentieth century, the total forest area of Japan measured about twenty-three million ha. At that time, national and local government owned thirteen million ha of it, the Imperial Household two million ha, and 'the people' almost eight million ha. In 1899 Imperial forest had still been some three and a half million ha. The 'people's' forest consisted of 160,000 ha owned by Shinto and Buddhist Temples; 1.7 million ha of communal forest and some six million ha of private forest. On top of that there were also *Genya* lands (plains and moors, which would mostly become forest). Almost 1.5 million ha of them belonged to the state, 150,000 ha. to the Emperor and about one million ha was either private or communal property.[6] For changes over the next decades, see Table 33.

In an economy like that of Japan, where land continued to amount to such a high percentage of total capital, holding such a high percentage of it as the Japanese state did, was quite significant.[7] Again, a comparison might be enlightening. In China, under Qing rule that lasted till 1911, the state had never owned more than 3 per cent of total arable land.[8] When it comes to arsenals, shipyards and big factories, it also, relatively speaking of course, was less well-endowed.

The changing position of the Emperor deserves some further separate attention. He and his family certainly profited from his Restoration. Not only did the Imperial Family, as already indicated, acquire a huge amount of land, which at its height amounted to some 10 per cent of the surface of entire Japan,[9] it also held other substantial forms of wealth. Its holdings in stocks and bonds increased substantially and in 1887 they were worth almost eight million yen.[10] The General Headquarters of the Japan Occupation Army reported that just after World War Two, the household of the Emperor accounted for 1,590,615,000 yen at current prices. That would mean the Emperor was the biggest landowner and capitalist of pre-war-Japan.[11]

How did the state acquire so much land? With Meiji rule a modern property regime was introduced. The new civil code guaranteed the protection of individual private property but also, in principle, protected the *collective* private property of the so-called *iriai* rights, the pre-1867 village common property rights, consisting of entry use and extraction of products. There were now three varieties of land property: privately held, commons and state land. Multiple ownership and joint ownership of arable were to cease in 1873, which did not mean that they actually ceased to exist everywhere.[12] The first step in land registration was to distinguish between land of the government and

Table 33 Forest ownership in Japan, in millions of hectares

	Imperial Household	State	Public authorities	Shrines and temples	Private
1913	9.2	38.4	16.7	0.6	35.1
1936	5.8	31.9	18.4	0.6	43.4

Penrose, 'Japan, 1920–1936', 198. The total forest area in 1913, including so-called wild lands, amounted to twenty-one million ha. In 1936 it was twenty-four million ha.

land of the people. In the initial set of guidelines and instructions it read that village *iriai* land should, when in doubt, be registered as land of the people. As the original criteria would result in very little state land, government changed the guidelines so that only villages whose *iriai* rights had been disputed in the Tokugawa court and for which there were extant records would be able to save their *iriai* land from nationalization. Another strategy to eliminate *iriai* rights was to amalgamate the more than 60,000 villages of Tokugawa Japan into a much smaller number and, in this process, to get rid of *iriai* rights. In the permanent struggles that ensued after land reform, the bulk of those rights disappeared. The real attack on *iriai* rights came not from people selling them and therewith eliminating the structure but from government that over time nationalized large tracts of common lands. One can only endorse David Howell's claim: 'The flip side of the systematic recognition of property rights by the state was the dispossession of those whose rights were *not* recognized.'[13]

In a society like Japan, that still was agricultural, the value of land continued to be a large portion of total wealth. In the period from 1905 till 1935, for which I found data, it amounted to on average about one third of total national wealth (the highest percentage was in 1913, with 43 per cent, the lowest in 1924, with 22 per cent). In England, it had been as high as 55 to 60 per cent in 1688. It then declined to 43 per cent in 1800, and had dwindled to only 10 per cent in 1932–1934. For France, I only found information for 1890 (34 per cent) and for Germany for 1911 (23 per cent).[14]

What about other forms of government property?[15] Government with the Meiji Restoration took over all assets of the Shogunate and all assets *and* liabilities of the *daimyo* and samurai, to whom it in principle guaranteed an income. That means it acquired all the modern shipyards, military arsenals and armament factories that had recently been founded by their *daimyo*. Those arsenals, shipyards and armaments factories were the places where Japan's first modern, government-operated manufacturing machine plants were set up. With Restoration, the new government also took over all gold, silver and copper mines. Not for very long though. Its copper monopoly was already repealed in 1869 and several major copper mines were consequently sold to private entrepreneurs. In the 1880s, government began to divest itself fully of mine ownership when most of the important mines it still owned were sold cheaply to emerging *zaibatsu*. Already in 1870, government had taken over all coal deposits, although actually most private small mines remained. Two decades later the right to mine was separated from government ownership, which enabled highly-capitalized private firms to enter the field.

In the 1880s, when government was short of money, it indeed did sell many of its enterprises. That, together with the deflationary policies of the 1880s, is often presented as a fundamental break, a moment of 'state-withdrawal', especially when it comes to ownership or direct intervention in the economy. But government did not give up all its enterprises. It kept several factories, shipyards and mines, and related operations that were considered of fundamental strategic value for the military power of the country. The telegraph system and later the telephone system came under central government direction from the very outset and continued to be state property. In 1895, government founded the Kure Naval Armoury. It was unwilling to see the Yawata Iron Foundry, which was founded in 1897, in private hands. In 1904, it founded the Tobacco-manufacture enterprise and in 1905 the Salt-manufacture Monopoly Enterprise. After the Russo–Japanese War the major railway trunk lines were, finally and permanently, nationalized. In 1906 the Imperial Railway Bureau was founded to run them.[16] The firms that government ran, as a rule were large, as shown in Table 34, modern and concentrated in capital-intensive, 'heavy' industrial sectors, in particular shipbuilding, the production of railroad cars and production for the military. As we will see later, government did *not* withdraw from the economy in terms of taxation, expenditure or capital formation after the 1880s either. It also acquired a number of monopolies such as the sale of salt, tobacco and camphor, which provided a substantial income.

Table 34a lists the ten largest factories by employment in 1902 and clearly shows how important government in this respect was. Table 34b lists the ten largest enterprises by employment in 1907.

According to Yoshio Ando, in 1890, government-operated factories still accounted for 75 per cent of the total horse power employed and 88 per cent of employees in what he calls Japan's heavy, i.e. capital goods and armaments, industry.[17] In 1934, to give an example much more towards the end of our period, the total number of people working

Table 34a Ten largest factories by employment in 1902

Ranking	Factory	Number of workers	Ownership
1	Kure Naval Factory	12,378	State
2	Yokosuka Naval Factory	6,761	State
3	Tokyo Military Factory	6,152	State
4	Mitsubishi Shipbuilding	5,058	Private
5	Sasebo Naval Factory	3,612	State
6	Osaka Military Factory	3,120	State
7	Kawasaki Shipbuilding	3,060	Private
8	Shimbashi Factory (railroad cars)	1,721	State
9	Japan Railroad Omiya Factory	1,700	Private
10	Osaka Steel	1,623	Private

Ohno, *Economic development of Japan*, 79.

Table 34b Ten largest enterprises by employment in 1907

Ranking	Enterprise	Employees	Ownership
1	Ministry of Communication	152,869	State-run
2	Railroad Agency	88,266	State-run
3	Furukawa Mining	30,125	Private
4	Mitsubishi Mining	24,245	Private
5	Kure Naval Factory	21,056	State-run
6	Monopoly Bureau, Ministry of Finance	20,563	State-run
7	Tokyo Army Weapons Factory	19,688	State-run
8	Mitsui Mining	17,472	Private
9	Mie Spinning	13,393	Private
10	Kanegafuchi Spinning	12,204	Private

Ohno, *History of Japanese economic development*, 67. The numbers are exclusive of office personnel

Table 35 Government's capital goods as a percentage of national capital goods

	I	II
1913	15.2	13.3
1919	14.5	24.0
1924	15.6	30.4
1930	16.4	25.4
1935	17.6	26.4

Column I for *all* capital goods and column II only for *reproducible* capital, which I personally think is more informative for my analysis. The figures are of course estimates.

Emi, *Government fiscal activity*, 10. Lockwood, *Economic development*, 238–239 and 508, looking at all capital goods, comes up with a very similar figure for 1930: 16.9 per cent. Of these 16.9 per cent, some 40 per cent was land and forest, the rest consisted chiefly of public buildings, ships and the Imperial Railways. I found no comparable estimates for France, Germany and Great Britain. I am sure they must exist and will discuss them in my next book, where capital formation and capital stock play a central role. Lockwood, *Economic development*, 238 claims that in the USA in 1935 government-owned property amounted to about 15 per cent of national wealth.

in the engineering industries was 465,000, including office staff, foremen and others. Some 100,000 of them were working in government factories.[18]

We would of course like to somehow add up all the capital goods government owned to know its share of total national capital stock. Table 35 gives some figures.

Tokugawa legacies

Here too, the question can be asked to what extent there was continuity with Tokugawa times. Let us begin with land. When I refer to land owned by the state here, I mean land actually held by the Shogun for creating income. In principle, all the land in Japan was property of the Shogun but in practice he entrusted it to his retainers giving them the right to collect taxes on it from peasants who were allowed to hold it in possession and use it.

As shown in Table 36, the Shogun's granary lands, which were located in forty-seven of the sixty-eight provinces, around 1700, accounted for roughly a sixth of the country's agricultural land. If we add the banner men's holdings, the percentage rises to close to a quarter. The land was, comparatively speaking, well-located and fertile. Much of it had been confiscated. Tokugawa Ieyasu (1543–1616, effectively ruling from 1601 till 1616) alone had taken over the land of eighty-seven *daimyo*. During the rule of the first five Tokugawa shoguns in the period 1601–1705, land assessed at over thirteen million *koku* of rice, i.e. about half of the total assessed production, was confiscated and reallocated: in the process 200 *daimyo* lost their 'position', 172 new ones were created; 200 received increases in their holdings and 280 had their domains transferred.

Table 36 Distribution of taxable landholding land at the end
of the first century after the founding of the Edo Shogunate
in assessed *koku* of rice

Shogun's house land	4,213,000 *koku*
Banner men	2,606,000 *koku*
Fudai and collateral *daimyo*	9,325,000 *koku*
Tozama daimyo	9,834,000 *koku*
Total	25,978,000 *koku*

Based on Hall, 'Bakukan system', 152. The extension of registered land of course
was not stable. It tended to increase over time. The imperial household at the
time owned land at a value of 141,151 *koku*.

After 1705 expropriation and transfers of fief land were much more uncommon.[19] If,
from now on, the tax assessment and/or the production of the lands of Shogun or
daimyo changed, that was because of the cultivating of new fields and/or increases in
productivity.

As indicated, the relative position of the Shogun had decreased over time – much
more than shown in Tables 36 and 37 – as there was less room in his domain to increase
the actual productivity of the land that had been high to begin with, add new land to
his arable or maintain a tax level as high as many *daimyo* could.

The Shogun's revenue did not just consist of land tax. He could also impose
extraordinary levies on *daimyo* and gift taxes on merchants. On top of that, he had the
right to mint coins for the whole of Japan, which brought a substantial revenue, in
particular considering the fact that those coins were so often debased. At the end of
Tokugawa rule more than 20 per cent of *Bakufu* revenues were the consequence of
such debasements. The *Bakufu* itself did not print any paper money before the 1860s.
Daimyo, after 1730, were again allowed to have their own paper money (*han satsu*) for
use in their own domain. These paper notes, however, were of little value and use
outside their fief.[20] Their amount was nevertheless quite substantial: of the total amount
of currency circulating in Japan in 1867, about 15–21 per cent consisted of paper notes
issued by domain governments.[21] The minting of coins by the domains, which the
Shogunate as a rule opposed, remained exceptional. The major gold and silver mines
were in the Shogun's hand, who moreover directly administered Edo, Kyoto and Osaka,

Table 37 Distribution of taxed land among warrior
groups at the beginning of the nineteenth century in
officially assessed *koku* of rice

Shogun's House lands		4,120,000
Banner men	(2,250)	2,600,000
Fudai daimyo	(151)	6,360,000
Collateral *daimyo*	(21)	3,370,000
Tozama daimyo	(108)	9,490,000
Total		25,940,000

Totman, *Politics in the Tokugawa Bakufu*, 33.

and had jurisdiction over the highways, even if they passed through a domain.[22] He, finally, all but monopolized foreign relations and controlled foreign trade taking place in Nagasaki and the Ryukyu Islands. One may conclude that under Tokugawa rule too, the central 'state' could control a substantial part of the country's wealth. Not unimportant in that respect is the fact that one third of the people in Tokugawa Japan would eventually live in territories of the Shogun. But here too it has to be added that the wealth of the shoguns tended to decrease, even in absolute terms, as the gold and silver mines already after 1660 started to produce less and foreign trade became only a trickle.

State revenue

Let us now pass from government *wealth* to government *revenue*. How high was government revenue in the period 1868–1937? Kazushi Ohkawa, Miyohei Shinohara and Larry Meissner provide ample information, so ample that I have decided to put it in an appendix, to wit Appendix II, to which I will refer the reader when that comes in useful. In modern states government revenue as a rule is associated first and foremost with tax revenue. Let us therefore start with taxation. As such, of course, the figures on taxes in Appendix II do not tell us much about the importance of taxation for the economy as a whole. To appreciate that, Table 38 presents an estimate of tax revenue as a percentage of net domestic product.

National taxes belonged to the central government and included land taxes, customs and indirect taxes on major consumption goods. Local taxes were at the disposal of municipal and prefectural government. They constituted a prefixed ration of land taxes and some indirect taxes that were difficult for the centre to collect.[23] Three comments are in order here. The first is that we have to realize, and this applies to all the figures in the coming pages which refer to a rate of gross or net national or domestic income/ product or expenditures, that the values of those aggregates themselves increased enormously between 1880 and 1938. The second is that collecting, managing and spending tax revenue became more effective and efficient and, in that sense, cheaper in post-Restoration Japan than they had been in Tokugawa Japan because of centralization, standardization and monetization. The entire process also became better supervised. Double entry bookkeeping was introduced into government finance and it was ordered that all government offices and prefectural governments must regularly submit the

Table 38 Taxes (national and local) as a percentage of net domestic product

1888	11.0
1900	9.7
1920	9.6
1938	10.7

Minami, *Economic development*, 256.

account books and budgets for inspection to the Ministry of Finance. Surveys and field investigations were undertaken to compile statistical data to thus get better estimates of potential revenue via indirect taxes. Officials were sent out for supervision.[24] Meiji Japan acquired a national financial system with a national budget and draft proposals in which public finances were centrally coordinated and checked. Local governments were, in practice, reduced to little more than administrative officers of the central government. A *Standing Committee of Budget* was established in 1890 to ensure the national budget was adequately scrutinised.[25] The third comment is that the part of taxes in total government revenue in Japan in the period discussed here, steeply *decreased* over time.[26]

How high was the tax revenue of Japan's government as compared to other countries? Let us again make a comparison with the situation in France, Germany and the United Kingdom. First for the period from 1870 till World War One, that in many respects was a caesura, and then for the Interbellum period. For the period from 1870 till World War One, we have data for *total tax revenue* as well as for *total government revenue* as a percentage of GDP in Great Britain and France.[27] As so often, the figures are not unequivocal but the conclusion seems justified that for both countries the average for this period for both types of revenue has not been above some 10 per cent of GDP. For Germany as a whole, we do not have the required data for that entire period. We do, however, have information for Prussia, where more than 60 per cent of all the inhabitants of the Reich founded in 1871 lived. Total tax revenue, *plus* the revenue surpluses of the operating of government monopolies, was about 6 per cent of national income in 1855, to increase to about 12 per cent in 1913. For the much less populous German state Württemberg, the figures for roughly that period were almost identical.[28] Considering its relative poverty, Japan's government tax revenue in the first decades of its economic transformation must thus be considered fairly high as compared to that of much wealthier developed countries.[29] During the period between the two world wars, tax revenues as a percentage of GDP in France, Germany and the United Kingdom rose substantially: to above 20 per cent for France, to 18 per cent in 1932 and 23 in 1938 for Germany and as high as about 30 per cent for the United Kingdom, during the whole period of 1930s.[30]

What can we conclude when we compare Japan's tax revenue to that of other countries than the European countries referred to so far? Let us first look at a couple of big empires. For the case of Qing China there are many uncertainties and one basically can only make educated guesses. Those all lead to a figure for the share of government revenue in total output that is much lower than that of Meiji Japan. For the half century between the Second Opium War (1856–1860) and the fall of the Qing in 1911, my educated guess would be that it was below 5 per cent of GDP.[31] Total government revenue from all sources in 1908, when it was not low for Qing standards, is estimated to have been some 2 to 3 per cent of net national product.[32] For the Ottoman Empire, Şevket Pamuk estimates that the revenues of the central administration rose from about 3 per cent of GDP in the second half of the eighteenth century to 5–6 per cent of GDP by the middle of the nineteenth century and more than 10 per cent of GDP in the decades before World War One.[33] In Russia government tax revenue per capita as a percentage of national income per capita during the period 1885–1913 went up from

Table 39 National government tax revenue as share of GDP in percentages for several countries in Latin America

	1900	1910	1920	1930	1940
Argentina	10	7	5	7	8
Brazil	10	11	9	8	10
Mexico	5	4	n.a.	6	7
Venezuela	n.a.	n.a.	8	9	12

Engerman and Sokoloff, *Economic development in the Americas*, 203.

about 12 to almost 17 per cent, which is a surprisingly high rate. In 1860, it had already been more than 12 per cent.[34] Table 39 gives an estimate of the share of GDP that that national governments acquired via taxation in several Latin American countries. Again, it should be emphasized that these figures are rough estimates.

The result of these comparisons in not unequivocal, but it would seem that Japan's government had a fairly high, but as compared to several other non-developed or developing countries, not exceptionally high tax revenue income.

The countries just referred to were (semi-)independent. How about colonies? When we look at India, we find very low tax revenues. According to Tirthankar Roy, the British Raj, i.e. the British government of India, was a small government, also in relation to its own national income. He estimates government revenue as a proportion of national income at 2 per cent in 1871 and marginally higher at 3–5 per cent in the period 1920 to 1930.[35] The available information about colonial Africa does not point at high tax incomes either. Let us distinguish between British and French colonial Arica. Considering the fact that there are no trustworthy figures for the GDPs of the British African colonies I will, following Ewout Frankema, refer to their tax pressure in terms of working days required of a native urban unskilled worker to equal annual average per capita tax revenue. Frankema present figures for all these colonies for the periods 1910–1913, 1919–1921, 1925–1929 and 1938. The unweighted average hovered between 7.1 days, the lowest figure for 1910–1913, and 14.6 days, the highest figure, for 1938.[36] This is including customs duties; excluding them the number of days would only be a fraction.[37] Table 40 provides information for the entire British Empire for the year 1911.

For the French Empire, to give another example, we have information on net public revenue as a percentage of GDP over roughly the period 1890–1940. In Algeria, that percentage barely passed 10 per cent at its height in the 1930s. For Tunisia, it hovered between 10 and 15 per cent in that same period of time. In the Federations of French West Africa and French Equatorial Africa, Togo and Cameroon, even in the 1930s at its highest level, it still was substantially below 10 per cent. In Indochina, it hovered between 6 and 14 per cent during those five decades. For Madagascar in the first four decades after 1890 it on average was about as high.[38] Collecting these tax revenues involved large costs, in particular a high wage bill, so that despite at times impressive increases in fiscal capacity the colonies remained under-administered.[39] It in this context probably is just as, if not even more, important to point out that the revenue

Table 40 Working days by adult male urban workers required to fulfil the per capita tax revenue in the British Empire in 1911

United Kingdom	19.2 excl. local taxes		
United Kingdom	28.5 incl. local taxes		

Dominions		British Asia and Pacific	
Australia	10.5	India	10.6
New Zealand	14.9	Ceylon	14.8
Canada	9.2	Federated Malay States	44.5
Union of South Africa	5.5	Hong Kong	28
		Fiji	24.6

British Africa		British West Indies	
Nyasaland Protectorate	7.2	Bahamas	9.2
Kenya	6.9	Barbados	17.5
Uganda Protectorate	5.9	British Guyana	24.3
Somaliland Protectorate	3.1	British Honduras	15.1
Mauritius	22.9	Jamaica	13.8
Gambia	7.8	Trinidad and Tobago	18.9
Sierra Leone	5.7		
Gold Coast	10.3	**Mediterranean**	
Nigeria	3.1		
		Cyprus	13.8
		Malta	12.6

Frankema, 'Raising revenue', 458.

collected in colonies tended to be spent in a very 'biased' way in the period discussed. Spending almost in principle was in the interest of the motherland and its colonial settlers. In all of France's colonies, between one third and half of public expenditures went to infrastructure, in particular transportation, first and foremost railways, and to communication such as post and telegraph or transfers to concessionary companies. Revenue had to serve the interests of French colonists and capitalists, also by providing settlers with urban public services at metropolitan standards. In 1925, public civilian expenditure per capita in the metropolis of the French Empire was more than eight times as high as in the rest of the Empire and public employment more than five times. On the other hand, public workers in the Empire received quite high wages compared to what was average in the countries where they worked.[40]

Let us now look at the situation in Japan in more detail. After the Restoration, Japan's system of tax collecting was fundamentally reformed. With the abolishing of the domains, a new national, uniform tax system emerged in which assessing and collecting of taxes occurred according to nationally enforced norms and procedures and payment in principle was in money. This does *not* mean – far from it – that local taxes would have become irrelevant. Table 41 provides information on the ratio of local tax revenue to total tax revenue over the period 1880–1940.

Table 41 Local tax revenue as a percentage of total tax revenue, 1880–1940

1880	33	1915	31
1885	34	1920	39
1890	31	1925	37
1895	32	1930	36
1900	37	1935	35
1905	23	1940	16
1910	24		

Based on Ohkawa, Shinohara and Meissner, *Patterns of Japanese economic development*, 376–377.

Interesting, and a clear indication of progressing industrialization, is the fact, that in 1890, of total government tax revenue, 86.8 per cent was collected in the countryside and 13.2 per cent in cities, whereas in 1940 these figures were 30.4 per cent versus 69.6 per cent.[41] The following tables indicate how total tax revenue was spread over different types of taxes. Table 42 provides information for *direct* taxes and Table 43 for *indirect* taxes.

What is striking in these tables, apart from the exceptionally high initial contribution of land taxes, is the rise of indirect taxes and, particularly, the importance of taxes on liquor.[42] As mentioned earlier, after 1880 the collecting of these taxes had become highly centralized and was executed by professional bureaucrats of the Ministry of Finance.

Table 42 Composition of central government tax revenue in Japan, 1872–1940, *direct taxes*, percentages in seven-year moving percentages

	Land	**Income**	**Corporation**	**Business**	**Inheritance**	**% of total**
1870	90.1					90.1
1900	34.6	4.3	1.2	3.9		44.0
1920	10.2	23.5	11.8	6.6	1.1	53.2
1940	0.9	34.0	11.7	2.6	1.6	50.8

Minami, *Economic development*, 258.

Table 43 Composition of central government tax revenue in Japan, 1872–1940, *indirect taxes*, in percentages in seven-year moving averages

	Liquor	**Sugar**	**Customs**	**Gasoline**	**Others**	**% of total**
1870	1.5		3.3		5.1	9.9
1900	38.0	1.3	10.9		5.8	56.0
1920	22.6	6.8	11.1		6.3	46.8
1940	8.9	3.2	2.9	0.3	33.9	49.2

Minami, *Economic development*, 259.

Land tax and agricultural development

During the crucial decades of the Meiji era, in which Japan initiated its industrialization, by far the most important tax was the land tax. Therefore, a more extensive discussion of this tax is in order here. In the Land Reform of 1872, it was stipulated that the land tax would have to be paid individually by the owner of the land. That meant it had to be unequivocally determined who owned the land, which implied that a new national cadastre had to be made. Land titles were issued to whomever could prove ownership. In 30 per cent ownership did not go to the cultivator, who then became tenant.[43] A quite complex system was developed to assess the amount of tax – in principle to be paid in money – that was due. The new tax assessment would be determined under reference to the 'legal' value of the land to be taxed, which was derived by applying the following formula:

> First, the money value of the average yield (over a five-year period) from one *tanbu* (0.245 acres) of land was calculated on the basis of the price of rice prevailing in that area. From this was deducted the cost of fertilizer and seed rice (legally fixed at fifteen per cent), the land tax, and the local tax which was usually one third of the land tax. What was left was called the 'net profit' despite the fact that no deduction had been made for the cost of labour. Then the 'net profit' was capitalized at as rate ranging from six to seven per cent, giving the 'legal value' of the land.[44]

The land tax was to be 3 per cent of this value. It was thus in principle based on the capitalized value of 'normal' net farm income rather than market value. Basically, it was not fundamentally different from the Tokugawa idea of paying according to the capacity of land. The interest rates and prices used in the application of this formula were reportedly chosen so that revenues from the land tax system would be not less than, but also not more than, they were prior to 1874.

Most estimates suggest that the new Meiji land tax, enacted in 1873 but already adjusted, i.e. lowered somewhat from 3 per cent of assessed land values to 2.5 per cent in 1877 – indeed was not higher than the old one and scholars agree that it declined over time. For those agriculturists considered to be owner of their land, the new land taxes initially were roughly as high as they had been for ordinary 'peasant-proprietors' under Tokugawa rule. That does not mean that the introduction of a new system of tax assessing and collecting was irrelevant from the perspective of the taxpayers. Peasants often were cash poor. Now that land taxes had to be fully paid in money, millions of them had to sell a substantial amount of their products at about the same time, which of course tended to lead to low prices. The obligation to fully pay in cash therefore often was loosened and in practice peasants often were allowed to pay one half of their taxes in kind. A large part of peasant production, moreover, was for subsistence. Peasants therefore did not have much room for manoeuvre in responding to price developments. Besides, the new national system was less flexible than previous, more local or regional arrangements. According to the plan, the land value on which the tax payment was based, would be fixed every sixth year. But this plan was never carried out, so the assessed land values remained unchanged. That meant that the actual impact of taxation now depended much more on the monetary yield of the harvests, and could fluctuate substantially. It indeed did, initially for worse and only later on for better, as Table 44 shows. Whereas the tax level in money terms was constant, the actual tax rate was quite different during the 1880s-period of deflation from what it was later when prices began to rise. For government, the new scheme in any case had the advantage that revenue became more predictable.

Land taxes were paid by landowners. Their number relatively speaking declined as the number of peasants who had to rent part or all of their land increased fairly steadily and substantially, as shown in Table 55. Although more land tended to be accumulated in the hands of landlords, this did not lead to a substantial rise of wage labour or the emergence of large estates. Most landlords simply rented out their land in small parcels to small peasants. Japanese agriculture thus continued to be based on peasant farming by peasants who generated a substantial amount of their income by combining agriculture with other, proto-industrial activities.[45] It is important to realize that the landlord-owner only paid the land tax and that all other farming expenses had to be paid by the tenant. Rents, paid in kind, could easily be as high as 50 per cent of the harvest.

Taxes on land also were a very substantial part of local government revenue. As *a percentage* of total tax revenue, land tax revenue clearly became less important: in *absolute terms*, however, it was first fairly stable before then, in the beginning of the twentieth century, increasing quite substantially.[46] The tax burden on agriculture, however, was always *at least* twice as heavy as on other sectors of the economy till World War One.[47]

The Meiji state taxed agriculture heavily in comparison to other states. Paul Mayet, Professor in Tubingen in Germany and consultant to the Meiji government, undertook a series of surveys in its employ. In a book that he published in 1893, he claimed that

Table 44 The impact of the land tax

	Land tax as percentage of central government tax	Direct taxes on agriculture as percentage of net agricultural income*
1868–1872	87	
1873–1878	88	
1879–1883	64	17 (8)
1884–1888	62	22 (12)
1889–1893	56	16 (9)
1894–1898	40	12 (8)
1899–1903	32	12 (8)
1909–1911	27	13 (9)

Bird, 'Land taxation and economic development', 163.

*Figures without parentheses are from Ranis, 'Financing of Japanese economic development'. The figures in parentheses represent Nakamura's correction for the undervaluation of agricultural production in the official statistics. (See Nakamura, *Agricultural production*, 161) Other scholars think this correction is too large, though most would probably now agree that some downward revision of the conventionally accepted figures is desirable. In his analysis of Meiji fiscal policy Harry Oshima claims that over the entire period 1879–1911, direct land taxes amounted to one tenth of income originating in agriculture, which is a rather low estimate. See Oshima, 'Meiji fiscal policy', 358.

Table 45 The land tax as a percentage of the net proceeds on land in Meiji Japan and several other countries

Japan, 1878	30% of the net assessed proceeds	
France, since 1789	20% of the net assessed proceeds	6% of actual proceeds
England, 1693–1798	16.25% of the net assessed proceeds	
Austria, 1857	16% of the net assessed proceeds	
Belgium, 1859	11% of the net assessed proceeds	9% of actual proceeds
Prussia, 1865	9.5% of the net assessed proceeds	4.2% of actual proceeds

Mayet, *Agricultural insurance*, 230.

government continued to take – like its predecessor – about 30 per cent of the harvest. He considered this taxation level 'out of all proportion higher than it is in any other civilized state'.[48] To substantiate that claim he came up with the estimates presented in Table 45.

He concluded that land tax as a percentage of *net* agricultural proceeds in Japan in the late 1880s was 'from double to seven times what it is in the states of civilized Europe' and added that if one were to look at gross produce the comparison would be still more unfavourable for the Japanese tax payer. If one were to compare total land tax (that is national and local land taxes combined) in Japan as a percentage of gross produce with total land tax in Prussia, he claims it would be thirty times as high in Japan (more than 25 per cent) than in Prussia (less than 1 per cent).[49] This apparently was not a wild exaggeration. The German agricultural expert Dr Georg Liebscher, who visited Japan extensively, claimed that, ignoring exceptional circumstances, the total amount of taxes a Japanese farmer had to pay would have been no less than some forty times as high as the land tax for a Prussian farmer in the 1870s.[50] There can be no doubt that the Japanese peasant was comparatively highly taxed. In Qing China, taxes on agricultural produce were traditionally expected to never be more than 10 per cent of the harvest. Normally they amounted to even less. At the time that Paul Mayet did his research in Japan, land taxes in China amounted to an estimated 2–4 per cent of the harvest.[51] One can only agree with Mark Metzler when he concludes:

> Thus, once the Meiji government had fiscally cut loose the hereditary military retainers and their households, it had considerable fiscal leeway compared to most mid nineteenth-century states.[52]

Land taxes undeniably were of major importance for government in the first decades of Japan's industrialization. In particular, in classic Marxist stories about Japan's state-led industrialization, they are considered as one of the two distinct 'ways' in which Japan's peasants made a fundamental contribution to their country's industrial take-off. They were supposed to have done so firstly, by providing their 'surplus' labour cheaply to industry and in that way keeping industrial wages down and secondly, which would be a clear example of the kind of 'primitive accumulation' that Marx liked to talk about, by paying the bulk of the taxes, at least in the first decades of Japan's industrialization, and thus providing the state with the money it needed to invest in the development of industry. For those who think that government investment was fundamental in the early stage of Japan's industrialization – and I am one of them – the connection between tax payments by all those who owned agricultural land on the one hand and industrial development on the other is an undeniable fact, even if one must admit that the agricultural tax rates declined quickly and that the number of people earning their living in agriculture in Japan simply was so high that land taxes almost by necessity had to be a highly relevant source of government revenue. Without the land tax revenue, government would have been less able to develop all sorts of initiatives. I fail to see who – other than agriculturalists, who in Meiji Japan always formed more than half of the entire labour force – could have borne the brunt of paying for industry in the first decades of industrialization. The fact that this extraction probably was necessary – as were the low wages (ex-)peasants received in industry – of course does not mean it would be pleasant. From the perspective of tax collection, a country like Japan with many small peasant-owners will, all practical problems of tax collection notwithstanding, be preferable over a country with a small number of big landlords and a huge number of (semi) landless labourers, the first ones being too powerful and the second ones too poor to pay much in taxes.

Assessing the effectiveness of this policy of heavily taxing agriculture implies determining how bad high taxation was for agriculture and how helpful government spending actually was for creating and supporting industry. Harry Oshima was quite outspoken in this respect:

> In particular, the extraction of large sums of money from the farm population was generally detrimental to the healthy development of agriculture, especially as so much was used relatively unproductively for military purposes.[53]

I will here only comment, briefly, on the effects of the land tax on agriculture. The state took more from agriculture than agriculture received in return. According to Oshima, under Meiji rule only some 4 per cent of state expenditure was in support of agriculture, whereas tax payments overall took some 10 per cent of net total agricultural income. In his view, that would have presented quite a substantial burden for poor peasants.[54] How burdensome taxes were – which were only paid by landowners but which one may assume were then when possible passed on to tenants – in the end depended on how poor peasants were. Oshima had a quite bleak picture of the standard of living of ordinary peasants in Japan's countryside. He was not the only one. For Marxist historians, rural poverty and exploitation, that in their view already became more extended under Meiji rule but led to a real general crisis of the countryside in the 1930s, were and are crucial for understanding Japan's industrialization as well as the rise of Japan's fascism. As indicated, for them industrialization has been borne by cheap rural surplus labour whereas Japan's 'fascism' could only become so strong because poor peasants and parts of the military in the end jointly endorsed extremely nationalist and aggressive polies in order to save 'the countryside' as 'the essence' of Japanese civilization.[55]

This is not the place to present an extensive analysis of the standard of living in Japan's countryside over the 70 years that are discussed in this book. For extensive coverage, I refer to the relevant literature.[56] I will confine myself to a couple of general comments. Firstly, one should not forget how poor Japan as a whole and not just its peasants continued to be, all growth notwithstanding. The figures in Tables 1 and 2 illustrate that quite clearly. Secondly, it is important to realize that over the entire period under discussion, agriculture and the secondary sector in Japan were not two neatly separated sectors with one-directional exchange in which the one (agriculture or rather the agriculturists) provides resources to the other (manufacturing or rather manufacturers). Agriculture and manufacturing often, certainly till the 1930s, were intertwined in the household economy. Non-agricultural activities only rarely became so dominant that peasants entirely gave up basic agriculture activities meant to provide subsistence and that working members of the household actually became proletarians. But they were certainly important. In practice, the linkages between the agricultural and non-agricultural activities of rural households often led to a substantial synergy. A rise of income and dynamism in one sector could at least often compensate for possible problems in the other one. Before World War One in any case, the net private capital outflow from agriculture into industry and services was negligible. The major surplus transfer, which via the land tax, as we have seen, declined as a proportion of rural incomes. Besides, there also was a flow in the opposite direction. By the early 1920s, even solid agricultural households with one to two hectares of land, derived some 30 per cent of their income from outside agriculture.[57] For the period 1918–1922, it has been calculated that for agricultural households, non-agricultural labour income amounted to about one quarter of total income.[58] Thirdly, it would appear that agriculture as a sector and the people working in it overall did not fare badly. That in any case is suggested by the information in Table 46.

Rice yields, in *koku* per *tan*, increased substantially over the longer run. Whereas they had only been 0.7 *koku* per *tan* in the seventeenth century, they rose to 1.3 *koku* per *tan* in the next one. From then on, they changed only slightly until after the middle of the nineteenth century. In the 1890s they reached 1.39 *koku* per *tan*. In the late 1910s, the national average was again higher, 1.9 *koku* per *tan*.[59] The average rice yield in 1933–1937, to use another measure, was about one third higher than in the years 1898–1902.[60] Double cropping on paddy land was 27 per cent in 1884 and 47 per cent

Table 46 Rates of growth in agricultural output, inputs and productivity 1880–1935 (annual average rates in %; 1934–1936 prices)

	1880–1900	1900–1920	1920–1925
Total agricultural output	1.6	2.0	0.9
Rice output	0.9	1.7	0.4
Other crop output	2.0	1.4	0.7
Livestock output	6.8	3.8	5.6
Sericulture output	3.9	4.7	1.7
Commercial fertilizer output	1.6	7.7	3.4
Output per worker	1.8	2.1	1.1
Output per work-hour	0.6	1.5	1.6
Output per hectare of cultivated land	0.7	1.5	1.1

Francks, *Rural economic development in Japan*, 139.

in 1907, when it was already 70 per cent in the most advanced regions. From then on there apparently, at least until 1933, was not much change anymore.[61] Overall, *what* was grown did not change much, apart from the fact that till the 1930s, sericulture continuously increased its popularity whereas indigo ceased to be cultivated when synthetic alternatives became available.

It would appear then that in any case part of the explanation of how government could extract so much money from agriculture via taxation without causing an overall clear impoverishment of that sector, resides in the fact that taxation tended to increase less than production and productivity. The fact that the class of wealthier landlords no longer consisted of *daimyo* and samurai, who tended to consume much and invest little but now included more landowners who ploughed back money into agriculture, may also have played its part here.

All in all, a fairly dynamic and 'positive' picture has emerged of the rural economy, certainly for the period till the end of World War One. Penelope Francks is a clear exponent of this optimist perception and approvingly refers to studies that claim that between the late 1880s and the late 1920s, daily and annual wage rates in agriculture approximately doubled in real terms.[62] That is quite a revision as compared to the pessimist interpretation that long was dominant, in particular among Marxist scholars who claimed that rural overpopulation and economic stagnation kept real wages fairly stable and low and who focused on the rise of tenancy that they interpreted negatively. It, however, is important to realize that even such an optimist interpretation as such does not exclude the possibility that agricultural wages rose *less* than industrial wages – which they indeed did.[63]

To show what the revisionist, much more positive interpretation of Japanese rural development – that as far as I can see has become predominant – actually looks like, I can do no better than extensively quote Penelope Francks. This is her conclusion when it comes to the nineteenth century till 1890:

> As such, the rural economic system by and large functioned to generate rising incomes for much of the rural population. It undoubtedly imposed costs on some; it created new forms of differentiation and conflict and Totman (= Conrad Totman, P.V.) in particular has cast doubts on its environmental sustainability, given the much more intensive exploitation of natural resources that it involved. But, in the terms that would be used to describe development processes in today's Third World, it created employment, raised rural living standards and probably narrowed urban/rural differentials; it did not generate the levels of concentration and inequality in the ownership of land and other forms of wealth which have been observed elsewhere and it enabled the small-scale cultivator and manufacturer to survive and develop; it involved the application of improved labour-intensive techniques to the production of 'appropriate' food and other consumer products destined for relatively low-income and predominantly rural markets, and it provided the basis on which localities were able to resist, or at least be selective about, centralizing and 'globalizing' (where the world, for much of the period was represented by Japan as a whole) economic, political and cultural forces.[64]

She describes the period from 1890 to 1920 as one of transition but one in which the positive still seems to predominate:

The years up to 1920 represented in many ways the golden age of the Japanese rural economy: agricultural prices were rising, non-agricultural employment opportunities were abundant and the threat which the burgeoning cities, with their new kinds of industry, might pose to the traditional ways of rural areas was as yet a relatively distant one.[65]

There were signs of change but diversification in the countryside had not disappeared, although industry that had been a side-line now for some slowly became the most important source of income. The inter-war years as a whole for Francks were a period of structural transformation and modernization. In the 1920s, agriculture slowly entered a phase of more structural trouble as total demand for food tended to increase less than total agricultural production, which, as the number of agriculturists did not decrease, could only mean lower agricultural income. When we look at the entire period 1921–1940, average real rural household income, from agricultural *and* non-agricultural activities combined, while fluctuating, continued on a generally rising trend until the later 1920s. It, however, dropped sharply during the depression years, to then recover to pre-depression levels in the second half of the 1930s. The fact that increases in labour productivity in industry, and therefore often wages, were substantially higher than in agriculture made agricultural work less attractive. In 1920 output per person in agriculture was 46 per cent of that of the entire economy and 34 per cent of that in manufacturing. In 1938 the figures were 36 and 20 per cent. There was a steady decline in the level of wages in agriculture in nominal as well as real terms as compared to manufacturing and the economy as a whole.[66] The countryside now relatively and at times in absolute terms impoverished, the government felt forced to massively support it.[67]

The previous discussion of the land tax and rural economic development was quite extensive but considering its fundamental importance for state finance in the first decades after the Meiji Restoration and considering the fundamental importance of agriculture for Japan's economy as a whole at the time, it does not seem disproportionate. The conclusion apparently has to be that taxation did not impede economic growth in the countryside till the 1920s and that when in the 1930s the countryside indeed found itself in a state of depression, that had fairly little to do with taxation.

With regard to other taxes, we can be briefer and confine ourselves to a couple of comments. The Japanese government introduced a comprehensive income tax system already in 1887, which is remarkably early.[68] A form of income tax had been introduced in Britain during the Napoleonic Wars, but was abolished in 1816, immediately after those wars had ended, to be re-introduced in 1842. In the mid-nineteenth century, there were fewer than half-a-million people paying this tax; at the start of the twentieth century, still fewer than a million.[69] In France, a general income tax was only introduced in 1914, whereas the German Reich even then still did not have an income tax covering all its member states. In the Netherlands, to give one last example of an advanced economy, a national income tax was only introduced in 1893.[70] As the figures in

Tables 42 and 43 show, overall, the existing tax system was supportive of capital accumulation in the secondary and tertiary sector. Capital and wealth there were only taxed lightly. What is striking in the figures for Japan, to wit how little wealth, incomes and business were taxed, again, however, is not exceptional in industrializing countries. Business tended to be spared when it came to paying and spoiled when it came to receiving. The claim that Guenther Stein, at the time a foreign correspondent for several British and American papers who had visited Japan, made for the 1930s, applies to the entire period discussed in this book: 'The system of taxation is obviously directed quite consciously towards the development of Japan's industry and commerce.'[71]

Other public revenue

Even though taxes of course are a very important source of government revenue – for several decades undoubtedly the most important one – it would be quite misleading to confine our analysis of government revenue in post-Restoration Japan to just them. Initially taxes were indeed the biggest source of revenue. But over time their relative importance declined steeply. In the 1930s, government bonds even became the primary source of government 'revenue'. I put the term 'revenue' between parentheses, but this is how they indeed were classified. By relying on them, government could avoid tax increases and absorb private capital. As shown in Appendix II between the 1870s and the 1930s, the share of taxes in total government revenue decreased from some three-quarters in the 1870s and even more in the 1880s to some 60 per cent in the 1920s and less than half in the 1930 till 1937, whereas in particular the share of securities as new debt issue increased steeply in the 1930s.[72]

Here, a brief excursion is in order on how and by whom those securities or bonds were bought. That means that we have to briefly discuss the history of Japanese saving.[73] Already under Tokugawa rule frugality had been promoted as a major virtue. Being frugal meant restricting or regulating one's consumption. Shoguns and *daimyo* liked to call on their subjects to reduce spending and refrain from aping the ways of their superiors.[74] In that way, the Japanese became accustomed to governments and communities vigorously trying to shape their economic behaviour. Merchants too were often advised to be parsimonious. Frugality tended to be considered beneficial to the community and then, for example, could take the form of granaries run by confraternities that saved rice for hard times. In the nineteenth century, agrarian reformer and 'peasant saint' Ninomiya Sontoku (1787–1856) not only became famous for his philosophy of 'Work hard, spend little. Gather much firewood, but burn little', but he also stood at the beginning of the so-called *Hotoku* – repaying virtue – movement. That movement spread over entire Japan and was at the basis of numerous saving organizations whose members were expected to deposit – without interest – a certain amount of money or percentage of their income.[75]

Under Meiji rule, thrift, already accepted as an individual and communal virtue, would be mobilized for the nation's good as well. An important role in that respect would be played by savings banks, in particular postal savings banks. The first savings banks – whether postal or private – did not appear until the 1870s, but from then onwards their development was fast. Already in 1875, Japan adopted the British model of postal savings, and started a postal service that took care of mail delivery, money orders and postal savings. There was not much competition from rival banks, as banking as yet was only weakly developed and officials tended to privilege 'their' postal savings banks while inhibiting the development of private banks. Instead of attracting foreign capital, the state did its utmost to mobilize the savings of its own people or rather of Japan's heads of households. Anyone not legally heading a household needed the family head's approval to make deposits and withdrawals. Already in 1884, bureaucrats seized control of postal deposits. Finance Minister Matsukata Masayoshi arranged for all postal savings to be transferred to the Ministry of Finance, where they ended in a Deposit Bureau. Henceforth, officials of the Ministry of Finance could invest the country's postal savings, in Garon's words, 'with nearly total discretion'.[76] With the passing of time, the funds of the Deposit Bureau of the Ministry of Finance almost exclusively came from the postal savings system.[77] Baron Kenjiro Den, who lived from 1855 to 1930 and held many important positions in politics and in business that gave him first-hand knowledge of the subject, in 1909 had put it in almost identical terms:

> The mode of investing the postal savings is left wholly to the discretion of the Finance Department, which generally applies them to buying up or consolidating the national debts.'[78]

A practice, so he adds, that will be changed and improved 'when the proper moment arrives'.[79] Self-help, industriousness and thrift were systematically promoted, idleness and debauchery systematically denounced. The Home Ministry even employed Protestant social workers and clergy men to spread its – and their – message. Farmers were now told to deposit money in individual saving accounts, not just because saving benefitted them but also because it was 'one's duty to the State'.[80]

As a matter of fact, the postal savings system had a somewhat slow start when we look at actual deposits. It was not very important to public finance until the early twentieth century. It was only halfway through the 1890s that the number of postal depositors passed the one million mark. In 1912, though, it amounted to over twelve million.[81] A system of regulated saving emerged in which officials and local elites exerted compulsion and used group pressure to *make* people save. A lot of saving therefore can hardly be called 'voluntary'. During and after the Russo–Japanese War, there was a barrage of exhortations to save, culminating in a piece of moral education called 'the Boshin Imperial Rescript' of 1908, sometimes referred to as the 'diligence and frugality rescript'. Already then it was claimed, in this case by the Minister of Agriculture and Commerce that luxury is 'enemy of the nation', which would become a famous motto during the Asia–Pacific War.[82] The efforts to make the masses save and so put their money at the disposal of government were quite successful. Between 1903 and 1910, the number of postal savings accounts arose from 3,562,000 to 11,266,000. Aggregate savings increased more than five-fold. By 1910, postal savings depositors held 17.5 million accounts. Only Germany, with 21.5 million, had more of them. The number of savings accounts per capita in Japan was one of the highest in the world.[83]

Table 47 Tax revenue of government and total government revenue – i.e. revenue including securities, and revenue from government enterprises and other non-tax revenue – as a percentage of net domestic product

	Tax Revenue of Government	Total Government Revenue
1888	11.0	15
1900	9.7	13
1920	9.6	16
1938	10.7	32

Approximation based on information in Minami, *Economic development*, 256–258 and indirectly on information in Appendix II. The figures give seven-year moving averages apart from the figures for 1938 that are five-year averages.

In the 1930s, the pressure on people to 'rationalize' their behaviour and save further increased. Savings organizations and saving-promotion schemes multiplied. Authorities could found such organizations and did their best to see to it that everyone participated. Again, group pressure and compulsion of all sorts abounded. During the Asia–Pacific War pressure increased further. Government set savings quotes for prefectures, financial institutions, and later also for cities, towns, villages and individual savings organizations. At the end of the war, the national savings target had become eight times that of the beginning. The Japanese apparently preferred to transfer their money to the state via bonds, that at least still were their 'property', over paying extra taxes. In fact, however, their 'voluntary' savings, transferred into government bonds, increasingly resembled simple taxation.[84]

The fact that the importance of (official) taxes in total government revenue decreased so strongly of course means that government revenue as a whole formed a much bigger part of the national produce than the percentages in Table 38 suggest. Table 47 provides information with regard to the rate of *total government 'revenue'* to net domestic product. The percentages in this table, again with all the necessary caveats, show that public revenue was a quite substantial part of net – and gross – domestic product.

Tokugawa legacies: A tradition of high taxation

To what extent are there continuities and/or similarities between pre- and post-Restoration Japan when we look at government revenue? Tokugawa Japan was infamous for the high taxes it levied on agricultural income. Reading the literature about those taxes always yields some quotes like the following ones: Tokugawa Ieyasu advised his rural intendants to govern the peasants by 'making certain they can neither live nor die'. Honda Masanobu (1538–1616), a *daimyo* closely allied with Ieyasu, apparently heeded this advice and is claimed to have said: 'The proper way to govern is to ensure that peasants don't accumulate wealth yet don't starve either.' Kan'o Haruhide in 1749 compared peasants to sesame seeds: 'The harder you squeeze them, the more you can extract from them.'[85] Whatever the ruling warriors may have thought of agriculture, they did not hold peasants in high esteem. There was a common saying among them: 'A good peasant is one who does not know the price of grain.'[86]

It is only too easy to assume that the frequent peasant revolts and popular unrest in the last century of Tokugawa rule to which we referred earlier on, can be blamed on high tax levels. We will not discuss here to what extent that indeed was the case and focus on the actual height of tax levies.[87] Most scholars are now convinced that actual taxes rates already from the very beginning were lower than all the quotes just presented suggest and that they tended to decrease. To be able to determine the actual tax rates we will first need to briefly discuss the way they were (supposed to be) collected. The height of the land tax was determined on the basis of a calculation of the potential rice output of a particular parcel of land, whether or not rice was actually cultivated on it.[88] This system for determining land value for taxation was called *kokudaka*, as that value was then expressed in terms of *koku* of rice. Such a *koku* equalled some 180 litres or about 150 kilos of rice, which was traditionally assumed to be the amount of rice a man needed to feed himself during one year. In principle, the tax was not only *assessed* in rice but also *paid* in it. In practice, only wealthier peasants could directly pay in rice. In dry fields, where no rice was grown, payment normally was in cash. Such payment in cash became increasingly normal but could be problematic for poorer peasants who did not have much cash. People in cities as a rule paid substantially less of their income in taxes and trade was not subject to regular taxes although merchants were often 'asked' to give large contributions.[89] The height of taxes was decided per domain and the bulk of the tax revenue stayed in the domain. Differences in rates could be substantial.

Considering the major importance of this land tax some more information is in order, the more so because, as Totman comments: 'The real nature of Tokugawa land tax affairs is difficult to assess because theory and fact were so often at variance, because practice differed so from place to place, and because so many records have been lost or never were kept.'[90] Determining the height of taxes and collecting them became more difficult. There developed a tendency to collect more of them in money, but the percentage of total taxes for which this was the case often varied between domains and periods. Things were further complicated by the fact that the purchasing power of money could fluctuate. How to pay taxes, moreover, in practice often was a bone of contention: When rice was expensive, peasants liked to pay in money, when it was cheap they preferred payment in rice. For the tax collector, it of course worked the other way around. Over time, the part paid in money increased, for the lands of the Shogun, to 45 per cent or even more.[91] It is critical to distinguish between actual and assessed *kokudaka*. The latter refers to an officially recognized figure upon which the annual tax was based, whereas the former, as the name implies, refers to an actual assessment of production for private records or intra-village tax distribution. The assessed *kokudaka* was readjusted only a few times, if at all, after the initial survey conducted under Toyotomi Hideyoshi. The process of registering land and realistically assessing its production was onerous, difficult and expensive.[92] Besides, as Charlotte von Verschuer has shown in her book on food supply in what she calls 'premodern' Japan, a substantial part of the food produced did not consist of the taxed 'five grains' and did not come from taxed land, i.e. irrigated fields, dry fields, or gardens near built surfaces, but from swidden fields used for shifting agriculture, from foraging, hunting or fishing.[93]

There of course always were differences between theory and practice and all sorts of adaptations but the basic underlying principles of tax assessment and tax collecting persisted throughout the entire Tokugawa era. Its main adaptation was part of the *Kyoho* Reform of 1716–1736 and consisted in the decision to no longer base the tax rate on an annual or in any case fairly regular inspection of the harvest and to collect taxes in kind and not in money. Before this reform, peasants were allowed to negotiate a margin of exemption in cases of poor harvests.[94] Now taxes were fixed for a longer period of time, on the basis of the assessments of yields over a couple of good harvests and such exemptions were no longer allowed. After a couple of decades, however, payment in money and exemptions re-emerged.

The *kokudaka*-system proved not very suited to assess new sources of rural wealth, which meant that its actual impact tended to decrease. It was complicated to change the tax levies for practical reasons but also because that could easily lead to social unrest. It has been documented that fierce and massive resistance contributed to keep the real height of land taxes in check.[95] This turned them into customary, more or less fixed levies, whereas productivity went up. Much new land that was used for agriculture, moreover, escaped taxation or was, for whatever reason, exempted from it.[96] The fact that *daimyo* and (most) samurai were no longer part of the agricultural communities that had to pay the land taxes and were thus unable to directly oversee village land-use patterns and effectively extract the growing rural surplus also impeded effective tax assessment. Corruption had a similar effect, as those who were in charge of tax assessment were bribed to come up with a low assessment.[97] All this led to a situation in which taxes amounted to a decreasing part of total production. In the process, the position of the samurai, most of whom no longer lived in the countryside, and were paid a stipend on the basis of the assessed *kokudaka* of their fief, became increasingly problematic, as their superiors, who frequently were short of resources, often simply and one-sidedly lowered the stipends. Unsurprisingly *Bakufu* as well as *daimyo* soon started looking for income from other sources than the rice taxes.[98]

But how high were tax rates actually? It would lead too far to go into much detail here. Let me confine myself to giving a couple of different estimates that all come up with quite similar outcomes. Before I do, one very important preliminary comment is in order that refers to the difference between tax and rent. In Japan, the land tax paid to 'the state' included what in Europe would have been the rent one had to pay to one's lord, feudal or otherwise. The landlord in Japan was a representative (in case of the *daimyo*) or the embodiment (in case of the Shogun) of the state that in the last instance owned all the land. This means that the difference between tax and rent in practice did not exist and that peasants in Japan thus had extra 'room' to pay more tax than their counterparts in Europe. Determining how high land taxes actually were as a percentage of actual agrarian income and crop yields is quite a complex endeavour, with substantial room for interpretation and estimation. When it comes to orders of magnitude, though, there appears to have emerged a consensus. I can do no better than present a couple of estimates by experts. Conrad Totman, in his book on early modern Japan, claims that land tax as a percentage of crop yield for *Bakufu* house lands over the period

1720–1840 hovered between roughly 25 and 35 per cent.[99] James White, in his book on social conflict and political protest in early modern Japan, presents a graph in which he claims that what he calls 'the real land tax rate of *Bakufu* administered lands' declined from over 50 per cent in 1630 to about 30 per cent in 1850.[100] According to Penelope Francks, the total tax rate on village land in Tokugawa Japan declined from some 50–60 per cent at the beginning of Tokugawa rule to around a third of total output by the end of it.[101] Matao Miyamoto presents a calculation of tax rates in shogunal territory during the period 1700 to 1840: at its highest, the rate was about 38 per cent, at its lowest about 30 per cent.[102] That is quite in accordance with the estimates by Yugiro Oguchi for the period 1716 to 1788 that lie between a highest rate of 38.9 per cent and a lowest of 29.2 per cent and with those of Mark Metzler who claims that *assessed* tax rates in the shogunal domain averaged about 34 per cent across the eighteenth and early nineteenth centuries.[103]

A major problem one encounters in all such calculations/estimates is to figure out the relationship between tax assessment and actual agricultural output, and between agricultural output and other forms of peasant income. Masaki Nakabayashi provides an estimate in which he assumes that the increase of land productivity in the Tokugawa lands would be equal to that in the country as a whole – as estimated by Matao Miyamoto. Comparing the 'real' output with the tax assessments enables him to estimate the *effective tax rate*, again, for the Tokugawa lands and measured as a percentage of agricultural yields. In this estimate made for the period 1716–1841, effective tax rates dropped below 30 per cent in the early nineteenth century. The highest estimated effective tax rate in his period of study amounted to 37 per cent, the lowest to 21. The trend was clearly downwards.[104] One can only make rational guesses about how much income peasants earned *apart* from their strictly agrarian activities, but it is clear that for many peasants this extra income was substantial. That would imply that their tax payments amounted to an even lower rate of their total income.

In principle, every domain could set its own tax rates. This meant that there could be substantial differences. Taxes are understood to have been lower in shogunal territory than in the domains. Tax rates in Kumamoto domain in Western Kyushu between 1650 and 1850 on average were about over 40 per cent of agricultural income. The lord of Aizu domain in Northern Honshu taxed his peasants at 55 per cent between 1637 and 1764. In Choshu domain, agricultural outputs were taxed at an average rate of 40 per cent in 1840.[105] A straightforward comparison can be misleading here. The Shogun had several important sources of extra revenue that *daimyo* did not have, but on the other hand he had the additional burden of being – at least in several respects – the actual ruler of *entire* Japan. That means he was responsible for the upkeep of the national road and transport system, paying stipends to Tokugawa retainers and maintaining costs of rudimentary central administration to manage its fiefs. There was a clear tension here: the bulk of the Shogun's revenue came from his 'private' lands, whereas several of his obligations were 'national'.

The previous paragraphs discussed land tax rates, but what about their absolute value? Mark Metzler, basing himself on work by Toshio Furishima, presents the following stylized trends and figures with regard to land tax revenue of the *Bakufu* expressed in *koku*:

Table 48 Land tax revenue of the *Bakufu*, 1716–1843

1716–1736	Low	1.4–1.4 million *koku*
1737–1764	Rising with a height in the period 1740–1760	1.6–1.7 million *koku*
1765–1786	Declining to a point in 1780 below	1.4 million *koku*
1787–1819	Rising again in the 1780s and maintaining a level of	1.5 million *koku*
1820–1843	Declining with a low in the 1830s of	1.3 million *koku*

Metzler, 'Policy space', 225–226. See also Sng and Moriguchi, 'Asia's Little Divergence', Figure 8.

Table 49 Trends in non-land tax revenue, in million golden *ryo**

1716–1736	Low	Less than one million *koku*
1736–1787	Increasing to as much as	Two million *koku*
1788–1818	Decreasing till about 1800, increasing after that, and in 1810 at parity with land tax	1.4 million *koku*
After 1818	Increasing and high, in the mid-1820s temporarily	More than three million *koku*

*The weight and gold content of the *ryo* were quite often changed, mostly lowered, during the Tokugawa period. In principle, one *ryo* was meant to be the price of one *koku* of rice but in practice prices fluctuated.[106]

Metzler, 'Policy space', 227–228.

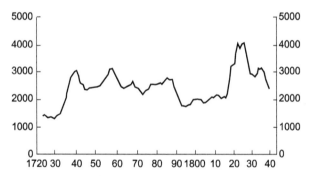

Figure 5 Annual revenues of the Shogunate, 1720–1840 in 1000s of *ryo*.
Miyamoto, 'Prices and macroeconomic dynamics', 125.

In the 1650s, the land taxes amounted to somewhat over one million *koku* of rice.[107] The *Bakufu*, however, and this applies even more to many domains, did not only acquire revenue from land taxes, as shown in the stylized figures in Table 49. Figure 5 provides information on the annual revenues of the Shogunate over the period 1720–1840, whereas Table 50 provides information on the composition of the revenue of the Tokugawa Shogunate expressed in *ryo*. According to the information in Table 50, land tax amounted to 79 per cent of the total general account revenue in 1730; in 1843, the percentage had decreased to 71 per cent; in 1844 to 44 per cent. Of total revenue (general account plus special accounts), as indicated in the table, the percentages were sixty-four, thirty-nine and twenty-five.[108] Considering these percentages, the heavy

Table 50 Revenue structure of the Tokugawa Shogunate, 1730–1844, in thousands of *ryo*

		1730	1843	1844
General account	Land tax, officially in rice	509.0	603.7	646.8
	Direct tax for state public works in cash	24.9	20.2	7.2
	Direct tax for small public works in cash	26.9	22.4	23.3
	Direct tax for special civil service in cash	55.0	45.9	71.3
	Indirect tax, paid in cash	29.0	158.0	706.4
Subtotal		644.8	850.2	1,455.0
Special accounts	Surplus from selling tax rice	112.9	45.7	32.1
	Repayment of loans, in cash	20.8	208.8	165.7
	Surplus from re-coinage	10.4	394.4	856.4
	Other revenues	9.8	43.4	66.3
Subtotal		153.9	692.7	1,120.5
Total		798.7	1,542.9	2,575.5
Land tax of total %		64%	39%	25%

Nakabayashi, 'Rise of a Japanese fiscal state', 385.

emphasis on the land tax in discussions about taxation and government revenue during the Tokugawa era seems rather misleading. The tax system clearly was developing in a more 'modern' direction in any case when it comes to a decreasing dependence on land taxes.[109]

The impression often given in general literature is that taxes – which as a rule then refers to *land taxes* – were always or mainly paid in kind also is incorrect. Tables 51–54 show how, for the years 1730 and 1844, the revenues of the Shogunate were divided between payments in rice and payments in cash.

Shogunate as well as individual *daimyo* tried to increase their tax revenue by, for example, extending territories via land reclamation, which could provide them with more land taxes or by developing strategies that might enable them to better determine production and thus better assess their land taxes. The possibilities to increase the land taxes, however, were rather limited because with the diverging of incomes and wealth in many villages trying to collect more taxes inevitably meant that the wealthier agriculturists who ran the village community would have to contribute more. That was

Table 51 Rice accounts of revenues in the shogunal finances for 1730

Item	Kokudaka	Percentage
Tax rice	500,019	58.5
*Agemai**	72,661	8.5
Other rice submissions	234	0.0
Purchased rice	281,326	32.9
Total	854,240	100.0

The *agemai* is a levy to be paid by all *daimyo* of 100 *koku* per 100,000 *koku* of the assessed agricultural yield of their land.

Oguchi, 'Finances of the Tokugawa Shogunate', 194.

Table 52 Monetary accounts of revenues in the shogunal finances for 1730

Item	1000 *ryo*	Percentage
Annual tax (gold)	509.0	63.7
Kuniyaku	24.9	3.1
Kofushin	26.9	3.4
Yakusho osame	55.0	6.9
Rice sales	112.9	14.1
Agemai	29.0	3.6
Loan repayments	20.8	2.6
Others	9.8	1.2
Reminting profits	10.4	1.3
Total	798.8	100.0

Kuniyaku refers to duties to be paid by tozama daimyo
Kofushin refers to payments for repair and maintenance
Yakusho osame literally means 'officials payments'

Oguchi, 'Finances of the Tokugawa Shogunate', 195.

Table 53 Rice accounts of the revenues in the shogunal finances for 1844

Item	*Kokudaka* (rice assessment)	Percentage
Income		
Tax rice	595,045	97.1
Other rice submissions	11,072	1.8
Purchased rice	7,416	1.2
Total	613,535	100.0

Oguchi, 'Finances of the Tokugawa Shogunate', 209.

Table 54 Monetary accounts of the revenues in the shogunal finances, 1843–1844

Item	1000 *ryo* (percentage)			
	1843		**1844**	
Income				
Annual Tax	603.7	(39.1)	646.8	(25.1)
Kuniyaku	20.2	(1.3)	7.2	(0.3)
Kofushin	22.4	(1.5)	23.3	(0.9)
Yakusho osame	45.9	(3.0)	71.3	(2.8)
Rice sales	45.7	(3.0)	32.1	(1.2)
Forced loans	158.0	(10.2)	706.4	(27.4)
Loan repayments	208.8	(13.5)	165.7	(6.4)
Others	43.8	(2.8)	66.39	(2.6)
Reminting profits	394.4	(25.6)	856.4	(33.3)
Total	1,543.0	(100)	2,575.5	(100)

Oguchi, 'Finances of the Tokugawa Shogunate', 210.

not a very enticing strategy because Tokugawa rule depended on the co-operation of exactly this group of people. The Shogunate employed very few officials in rural areas and delegated the process of assessment to the village notables. A certain understanding had emerged that as long as those villages paid the prescribed taxes they kept their autonomy and frequent tax rebellions reminded Shogunate as well as *daimyo* that there were limits to what the peasantry were willing to endure. This meant that when harvests failed, the requests by villages for tax cuts often met with success. Incremental increases in production, however, often escaped the tax collector. To increase taxes on handicraft income, that became an at times very important part of total income in villages, proved not easy. The Shogunate in any case did not manage to turn such taxes into a major source of income. What it could do in contrast to ordinary *daimyo* and what it increasingly did, was using its specific rights and monopolies. It collected very substantial amounts of revenue by reminting coins, as shown in Table 54; by demanding service fees or special contributions from its *daimyo*, e.g. for river 'repair' or for repairing its castles; or by forcing merchants to provide it with loans. Charter fees were levied on privileged merchants mainly residing in big cities such as Osaka, Edo and Kyoto. The Shogunate increasingly tried to find ways to transfer the burden of its 'national' tasks, such as taking care of river works, calamity relief, or infrastructure maintenance, to the domains.[110] In comparison to several daimyo in their fiefs, the Shogunate during the last century of its existence was less active when it came to promoting manufacturing and reforming its economy.

In an overview of government revenue of Tokugawa Japan, reference to corvee labour cannot be missed. It chiefly took three forms. One was labour for public works projects, usually provided at the direction of a domain in order to contribute to construction or repair of castles or river-related projects in lands held by the Shogun. A second form was labour provided by towns and villages to aid in the travel and transport of official journeys, in the context of *sankin kotai* or of Ryukyuan and Korean embassies to Edo. Here villagers and townsmen had to serve as porters and provide horses, baskets, inns, and so forth. A third form of corvee was provided by fishermen and other peasant/commoner boatmen, who were obliged to use their boats to help escort or unload samurai vessels, among other similar tasks. The burden of river work and highway service tended to increase, as did the resentment against them.[111] The following example from a book by Arne Kalland shows how burdensome corvee labour duties could become. This is what he writes about the amount of labour that coastal villages in the province of Chikuzen, currently Fukuoka district, had to invest in receiving Korean envoys.

> The preparations as well as the lavish entertainment became steadily more elaborate. Whereas around 20,000 working days are likely to have been spent on the Koreans by the inhabitants of the coastal villages in 1682, at least 120,000 days were required for the visit in 1748. During the latter visit, 433 boats with 1,625 crew members plus another 1,174 *kako* were mobilized from the coastal villages to transport officials and provisions to Ainoshima, to mark shallows in order to make the journey safe for the envoy, to tow the Korean and Tsushima ships, and to secure fresh sea food for an elaborate reception for 1,000 people or more.[112]

The Shogunate did not incur any serious debts in the sense that it, as a rule, with a lot of improvisation and extraordinary revenue, could make ends meet in the period from the 1740s till its downfall. The situation in the fiefs was different. Many, if not most, *daimyo* were heavily indebted.[113] As they lacked the possibilities to increase revenue that the Shogun had by virtue of his position, they often, more than the Shogunate, took all sorts of initiatives that in a western European context would be described as 'mercantilist'. They tried to lessen their dependency on the regular land taxes by stimulating and often – directly or indirectly – controlling production of and (export) trade in certain 'market-oriented' goods like indigo, sugar, rape-seed, cotton, silk, wax or paper. Many domains established offices to co-ordinate their 'commodity-promotion policies', which often entailed a monopoly over the production or in any case the sale of certain commodities. Their rulers often introduced their own domainal notes to facilitate trade in them.[114] Their policies are not only strongly reminiscent of the policies of Western European governments in the age of mercantilism but also, for that matter, those of Japan's post-Restoration governments. They were characterized by import substitution, export promotion, quality control, standardization, the acquiring and spreading of knowledge and techniques: all, to promote the interest of the country, i.e. the domain.[115] They were often explicitly meant to circumvent the guilds or cartels of wholesale traders from Osaka or Edo that were authorized by the *Bakufu* to control 'national trade', i.e. trade between fiefs and the lands of the shogun or among fiefs themselves and to divert that trade via their warehouses.

These domainal policies without any doubt were a precursor of the developmental polies for which post-Restoration Japan would become famous. Again, we come across an important element of continuity with respect to an important element in Japan's economic growth after 1868. In the work of the early Meiji rulers too we see a similar focus on import substitution, export promotion and efforts to float paper notes. The Ministry of Finance, erected after the Restoration, became the most powerful of all ministries. It was a bastion of Westernizing officials. Among the thirteen members of the Office of Reform, its think-tank, nine were former Shogunate bureaucrats.[116]

It has not been my goal to write a detailed history of government revenue of Tokugawa Japan. I just wanted to find data that are sufficiently reliable and sufficiently 'detailed' to make claims that are relevant for my research questions. With all possible caveats and all justified scepticism when it comes to exact figures, I think that it is beyond any reasonable doubt that in Tokugawa Japan, central government (i.e. the *Bakufu*) and regional government (i.e. the *daimyo*), as compared to other polities in the world at the time (and later on), collected an impressively high percentage of 'GDP' as its revenue.[117] It would of course be misleading to come up with very precise figures, but I allow myself the following approximation: if we assumed that in the lands of the Shogun land tax at the end of the Tokugawa period amounted to 20 per cent of actual agricultural produce – which is a low estimate – and that agriculture would amount to 50 per cent of total produce – which also is not a high estimate – then land tax alone would have amounted to some 10 per cent of 'GDP'. As we have seen, the land tax as such was only a, decreasing, part of total Tokugawa government revenue. It only amounted to 39 per cent of that total revenue in 1843 and to 25 per cent in 1844. I must assume that last percentage is exceptionally low because of the big re-coinage income in 1844 and that one third to 40 per cent would be more 'normal'. On the basis of those assumptions I would hazard the guess that the Shogunate had at least some 20 per cent of the 'GDP' of his lands at his disposal. I would guess the percentage was not lower for the *daimyo*.[118] These are very high percentages, that, I have to immediately admit, will *to a certain extent*, have been 'compensated' for by the fact that, as pointed out before, the land tax levies in Japan can be considered as tax and rent in one and by the fact that there was quite a high number of people whose maintenance in principle had to be provided by government grants. The total number of samurai, including the *daimyo*, amounted to some 5–6 but, according to other estimates, even some 8 per cent of the entire population of Japan, i.e. if we include their families. In principle, they depended on the stipends their lord gave or allowed them, which was not an enviable position to the extent that Shogun and *daimyo* frequently cut those stipends, often with no less than 30–40 per cent, frequently under the euphemism of 'borrowing'.[119] Moreover, as we will see, in any case central government paid all its expenses out of its income. In Europe, where almost all governments at the time were heavily indebted, that was quite exceptional. But nevertheless, when it comes to revenue, I can only fully endorse the following conclusion by Mark Metzler:

> in the world of the eighteenth and nineteenth centuries, the Tokugawa state system, 'compound' as it was, presents a picture of 'big government' (notwithstanding the claims of some prominent historians . . . that the Tokugawa and early to mid-Meiji eras were times of 'small government').[120]

To show how high 'government' revenues were in Tokugawa Japan a comparison with the situation in other countries may be helpful. We will focus on the situation in the eighteenth and nineteenth centuries. For Britain, we have many estimates.[121] Tax revenues as a percentage of national income are claimed to have fluctuated between 9 and 13 per cent throughout most of the eighteenth century. During the Napoleonic Wars this ratio rose to over 20 per cent. After the Napoleonic Wars, tax revenues as a percentage of Britain's (increasing) GDP declined. In the 1830s, they amounted to just some 10 and in the 1840s to some 11–12 per cent. We have to realize that in (Great) Britain like in most other countries in Western Europe government expenditures as a rule were substantially *higher* than government revenues.[122] For France, a country for which our information is less unequivocal and reliable than we would want to, one can nevertheless be certain that in the 1780s, tax revenue as a percentage of national income was less than 10 per cent. After the Napoleonic Wars the ratio overall was somewhat lower still. In 1840, after more than ten years of increasing taxes, it still was less than 10 per cent. For Prussia, central government revenue will have amounted to, at its peak, some 12–15 per cent of national income in the 1780s. After the Napoleonic Wars, total government income is estimated to have been less than 10 per cent of GDP.[123]

Making claims in this respect for China, a country with which Japan is often compared in texts about state-capacity, is even trickier than it is for various countries in Western Europe. Actually, the figures we have about its GDP for the entire period before 1880 are no more than (sometimes even wild) guesses. Our figures for total government income are fraught with uncertainties too and differences between various estimates are huge. Figures that express the ratio of government income to national income therefore can only be broad approximations. For the eighteenth century, estimates vary between 4 and 8 per cent. For the first half of the nineteenth century this percentage will certainly not have been higher. The estimates that we have, show a much lower per capita tax income for Qing China than in any case for the Shogunal lands. Average land tax income per capita *alone* in the lands of the Shogun expressed in koku of rice amounted to almost 0.35 koku per capita in the 1650s to very slowly decrease to about 0.3 koku per capita in the 1840s. For China as a whole *all* tax income per capita in the same period of time, measured in the same way, decreased from 0.2 koku per capita to less than 0.05 koku.[124]

Continuities, reforms and real changes

Considering their intention to squeeze the peasant population as much as possible and considering the high level of their tax rates, it may come as a surprise that from the end of the seventeenth century onwards, rulers at the level of the domains almost constantly faced financial crises.[125] As a rule, the short-term response then was to combat those crises by cuts in spending which often meant the lowering of payments to samurai. In the longer run, as we have already indicated, one tried to (also) with variable success increase revenue. When it comes to the composition of government revenue a lot of it did *not* – or no longer – consist in traditional land tax and was *not* in kind but in money. In that respect, the tax system of Tokugawa Japan, as we already pointed out, had already evolved in a much more modern direction than has often been suggested. But it has to be emphasized that the system as such was never structurally overhauled. There was no official structural change. New sources and forms of income resulted from improvisation and *ad-hoc* measures, such as impositions on *daimyo* or merchants, or currency re-coinage. In that respect, the Meiji Restoration indeed was a break with the past. The existing tax system had become inadequate and was in need of structural innovation. But it apparently under Tokugawa rule was considered too dangerous to create a fundamentally new system.[126] In that respect I think one must somewhat qualify the conclusion by Chiaki Moriguchi and Tuan-Hwee Sng in their text about the state capacity of early modern Japan and China that 'Tokugawa Japan's legacy of a strong state might have prepared Japan better for the age of industrialization' and that 'the proactive Meiji government' must be seen as 'a product of Japan's history, not a radical break from the past'.[127] The Tokugawa state, whether one looks at the shogun's lands or at the fiefs, indeed overall was powerful and proactive and as such a prefiguration of the post-Restoration state but with Restoration its power and policies unmistakably became more systematically and more radically geared towards national development.

Not that efforts at reform had been lacking under Tokugawa rule. Usually reference is made to three major reforms. The first ones were the so-called *Kyoho* Reforms, instituted by the eighth shogun, Tokugawa Yoshimune (1684–1751) who ruled from 1716–1746. His reforms received their name after the Kyoho era (1716–1736). We already referred to his tax reform. He increased government income by substituting cash for corvee, appointed new officials to posts in finance and rural administration in order to increase government efficiency, reduced the number of *hatamoto* and *gokenin* and kept the number of new retainers entitled to a stipend in check. He was keen on cost reduction and austerity and proclaimed sumptuary laws. As an emergency policy, he ordered all *daimyo* to make rice contributions (*agemai*) of 100 *koku* per 10,000 *koku* of their incomes, which he then allotted to the *hatamoto* to supplement their stipends. As compensation, the *daimyo*'s stay in Edo was reduced to half, which meant a substantial reduction of their costs. He also wanted the *daimyo* to increase their contribution to the defence of the realm. He undertook efforts to increase land tax yields by opening new lands to cultivation and attempted to popularize new crops, such as sweet potatoes and sugarcane, that could be grown in soil not used for rice cultivation. In an effort to find other sources of income, he licensed commercial monopolies and attempted to regulate rice prices. He successfully revalued and standardized the currency. By 1744, the year before his retirement, the receipts of the *Bakufu*, both in total land taxes and in tax receipts, reached their highest level for the entire Edo period. His reforms were a mixture of many conservative elements with their emphasis on frugality and austerity, but he also tried to find new ways of acquiring revenue and new ways of organizing things. His efforts, however, in the end did not herald a fundamental break and transition to a new economic order, but rather a temporary respite.[128]

A second cluster of reforms were the so-called *Kansei* reforms, undertaken by Matsudaira Sadanobu, the Shogun's chief councillor, between 1787 and 1793, that is largely during the Kansei era (1789–1801). They boiled down to a general policy of frugality with strict limitations on the expenditures of all classes. Curbs were placed on the migration of farmers to the cities, and debts to merchants incurred by retainers of the Shogun were either reduced or cancelled. Matsudaira dismissed officials and instituted qualifying examinations for new appointees. He sought to foster the traditional agricultural economy by curtailing foreign trade and severely restricting the growth of the merchant class, while limiting fiscal expenditure through a vigorous program of economy. Again, and even more than with the *Kyoho* reforms, all these measures brought some relief to the government in its financial difficulties. His efforts to alleviate famine temporarily averted serious peasant unrest. But his policies of austerity did not bring any fundamental and lasting innovation.[129]

In the *Tempo* reforms, (1841–43), named after the *Tempo* era (1830–44) in which they occurred, again the emphasis was on restoring the old agricultural society and its old order. Again, there was an emphasis on frugality in governmental and personal affairs. Many officials lost their position in the administration. Debts incurred by the shogun's followers to merchants were cancelled, further migration to the cities was restricted, merchant guilds were discouraged, and price controls were encouraged. Attempts to consolidate the shogun's land around Edo and Osaka aroused the opposition of the landowning classes and had to be dropped. The reforms in the end proved ineffective.[130]

Assessing the literature, I think that with regard to the Tokugawa revenue system one has to conclude that even though it collected quite substantial amounts of money and resources, it was fairly inefficient and un-transparent, quite vulnerable to forms of corruption and evasion and, at least in principle, too much focused on agricultural revenues. It would certainly not suit an industrializing economy. What is striking and relevant considering the many debates on the importance of secure property rights and contract for economic development, is how easily and one-sidedly Shogun and *daimyo* could cancel debts and lower stipends.

The Meiji rulers inherited a state that, even though regular tax revenue relatively speaking tended to decline and even though many *daimyo* often were in serious debt, had always been able to collect, comparatively speaking, very substantial amounts of revenue. Considering the fact that catching up requires massive infrastructural investment, a lot of which can best or only be provided by the state, Meiji Japan in this respect certainly was in a good starting position. Its population was already used to paying a lot to the state. In that sense too, post-Restoration Japan could fall back upon a positive legacy from Tokugawa times.

5

A Capitalist State, Friendly to Employers but Much Less so to Workers

Creating a capitalist society: What does capitalism mean?

With the Meiji Restoration fundamental changes occurred in Japan's political economy. They were enforced, enabled or allowed by state. To claim that they turned Japan into a 'fully' capitalist society would be exaggerated and one-sided, suggesting that economies are either capitalist or not and that government only took measures that strengthened capitalism. But the thesis that Japan overall became far *more* capitalist because of the policies of its new rulers seems irrefutable. Ultimately, of course, it all depends on the definition of capitalism one uses. In my minimalist definition, a capitalist society is one characterized by private property, private enterprise and the commodification of goods and services including capital goods, in which supply and demand determine prices via the so-called market mechanism. In such a society entrepreneurs invest in order to make profit, which they then in turn invest in order to make a new profit.[1]

In my view, it wouldn't make sense to describe a society as capitalist in which private property, private enterprise, commodification and a market mechanism are *not* quite prominently present. Scholars have from its very introduction discussed the concept and have come up with often different opinions about how a capitalist market economy actually works and whether it really is the motor of wealth that its proponents think it is. The fact that in those debates references to an ideal-type and references to 'reality' often were mixed up, tended to cause more heat than light, as did the fact that from the very beginning the concept was a political as much as an analytical concept. Many debates have been waged about the importance and the effects of the role of the state as non-private owner and actor; about the importance and the effects of commodification for different commodities, in particular the effects of the commodification of labour, and about the extent to which competition on 'capitalist' markets actually has been and should be free and fair.

In my view, one can distinguish between four varieties of capitalism. I will first briefly introduce those varieties and indicate why I think Tokugawa Japan in none of these varieties can be called capitalist to then present a more in-depth analysis of both the economic systems of Tokugawa and post-Restoration Japan. The first variety one can distinguish is one, that, after Adam Smith, may be called 'Smithian' capitalism. In this interpretation, the focus is on the dominant mechanism of *exchange*. Capitalism is here defined primarily over the existence of the free exchange of commodities on an abstract market with an extended division of labour. To call Tokugawa Japan a capitalist society according to this definition, in my view, would be exaggerated because *for society as a whole* the role of the capitalist logic of commodification and accumulation was certainly not dominant. In particular, because commodification of capital (in the form of capital goods as well financial means) and labour was so exceptional. In practice, Smithian capitalism often tends to be simply equated with the existence of a commercial society and extensive commercialization. In this quite loose, rather unspecific sense, Tokugawa society might be called 'capitalist'.[2] There were extensive markets in which even small peasants were integrated not just as selling and buying agriculturists but often also as producers of manufactured goods. What has become, rather unfortunately, known as 'proto-industrialization' was a widespread phenomenon in Tokugawa Japan.[3] Personally, though, I do not think using the term 'capitalism' in such a loose sense is very helpful.

In Karl Marx's definition of capitalism, the second variety I would want to distinguish, the focus is not so much as it was with Smith on the mode of *exchange* but on the mode of *production*. According to Marx, the essence of capitalism has to be sought in its specific organization of production. The critical difference between commercialization and what Marx and his followers would consider 'real' capitalism, lies in the impact that capitalism *à la Marx* has on social relations. Whereas in commercialized economies agricultural products and many other goods are commodified, under full-blown capitalism this also and to a grand scale is the case for labour and for capital goods. When this is predominantly the case one can characterize a society as a whole as capitalist.[4] Marx's emphasis on the commodification of labour and capital goods entails a mode of production in which wage labourers work for capital-accumulating, profit-oriented employers who systematically invest their profits in capital goods. None of this was very common in Tokugawa Japan – which does not mean that it would be entirely absent, as we will point out in our brief discussion of David Howell's ideas in this respect.[5]

Max Weber's definition – the third one – actually is quite similar to that of Marx but he has become famous for the explicit and extensive attention he dedicated to the 'mentality' of capitalism. I already referred to the fact that such a mentality can be found in Tokugawa Japan too, but that it would certainly be exaggerated to consider it dominant or hegemonic. Tokugawa Japan therefore in my view was not capitalist in this third sense of the word either. As is well-known, Fernand Braudel came up with a fairly idiosyncratic definition of capitalism – in my perception a fourth one! – in which long-distance trade, high finance, supernormal profits, monopoly, manipulation, and collusion of 'people of power' and 'people of profit', are key words.[6] Braudel actually was fascinated by similarities between the economies of Tokugawa Japan and Western Europe and discussed the question to what extent Japan might already have been capitalist before the Restoration.[7] He comes to the conclusion that 'the creation of capitalism succeeded in Europe, made a beginning in Japan, and failed (with some exceptions that prove the rule) almost everywhere else – or perhaps one should say failed to reach completion.'[8] Considering the central importance of long-distance trade in his interpretation of capitalism it will not come as a surprise that he thinks capitalism in Tokugawa Japan could not 'reach completion' because its rulers 'closed' the country.[9] But his claim that it came closer to completion than anywhere else, except Europe, implies – and rightly so – that there were markets on which wealthy merchants and financiers did all sorts of complex transactions and accumulated substantial amounts of resources. It also means there were examples of collusion between state power and 'capital'. In a very broad interpretation of the word, in which the presence of any kind of capital accumulation by merchants or entrepreneurs via collusion (also with the state), manipulation and market transactions is a sufficient condition to talk about 'capitalism', one may defend the thesis that Tokugawa Japan had 'Braudelian' capitalists. In my view that, however, does not imply it would have been a capitalist society. Too many elements that Braudel considers typical were lacking.[10]

My thesis here is that in Tokugawa, Japan government often acted as a brake on the development of capitalism in all of the varieties presented above, which it in several respects also, but then rather *unintentionally*, promoted, whereas after the Restoration Japan's rulers systematically promoted or even enforced capitalist forms of exchange and production.[11] Why is discussing capitalism in this context important? The exact connection between capitalism on the one hand and modern economic growth and industrialization on the other, that had so long been assumed to be fairly unproblematic as the first was supposed to lead to the second, has over the last decade become a hot issue in economic history. Debates have become very complex and this is not the place here to elaborate on them. Let it suffice to say that most economic historians would now agree that there is *not* an automatic, stage-like transition in which capitalism in any of the varieties portrayed above, would be smoothly succeeded by modern economic growth and industrialization although a capitalist 'pre-history' is certainly considered helpful.[12] In my view in the Japanese context, the post-Restoration state more or less simultaneously officially institutionalized capitalism and set out to try and industrialize the country. The two processes were closely intertwined. To put it in Marxist terms, that state destroyed the shackles that hemmed in capitalist development and created the institutional structures it requires, in the meantime actively promoting industrialization.

Tokugawa Japan as an anti-capitalist societal order

To show that Japan indeed became *more* capitalist thanks to the Meiji reforms, which in this case means that its growth potential was enhanced, it is probably better to reverse the 'normal' order of my analysis and start by showing more in detail in what respects Tokugawa society was *not* or even *anti*-capitalist. I will here focus on the general criteria I indicated above on page 139. I will not separately discuss private enterprise as a characteristic for capitalism here. *In practice*, private property and private enterprise were inseparably connected. This means that Weber's comments on 'the spirit of capitalism' and Braudel's considerations on capitalism as the top-layer of economic life will not be separately discussed. I assume that is not problematic as it has already been briefly indicated to what extent they do and in particular do not apply to Tokugawa Japan.

In Tokugawa Japan, there were no individual, modern i.e. in-alienable and absolute property rights when it comes to land. It was legally speaking difficult to determine who actually 'owned' it. Under Tokugawa rule, in principle the Shogun owned all the land in Japan which he then in turn entrusted to his retainers in the form of fiefs. Those retainers did not in any way own the land in their fiefs. What they 'possessed' was the right – that the Shogun could and as we saw often *did* withdraw – to collect taxes in their fiefs which had to be paid by peasants who worked the land but also did not own it. The amount of taxes depended on the assessed agricultural production of that land. The retainers who were entrusted with a certain fief, as *daimyo*, held an exclusive right to administer it. They did so with the help of their samurai retainers, the bulk of whom lived in castle towns, and who in turn received stipends. It had become the policy, symbolized in the Separation Edit of 1591 by Toyotomi Hideyoshi, to try and separate warriors and cultivators and to force samurai to live in castle-towns. That resulted in a situation in which many of them became absent 'landlords' who could not control what went on in villages and had no actual property there.[13] They in principle were expected to live from the stipends they received from their *daimyo*. By the beginning of the eighteenth century, rural property possession by samurai had become the exception. Incoming *daimyo* often used a new cadastral survey of their region to weed out landed retainers of their predecessor.

Shogunate and *daimyo* in practice had hardly any grip on what was going on in the more than 60,000 villages of (late) Tokugawa Japan. That not only shows in the fact that their tax assessments became somewhat 'fictitious' in the sense that they did not reflect the extent to which productivity increased and new sources of income became important, but also in the sense that many of their rulings with regard to land 'ownership' were actually ignored. Peasant-cultivators in the villages whose holdings were registered, soon behaved *as if* their villages were autonomous and *as if* they owned the land they cultivated. The registers that contained lists with all the plots of cultivated land as well as the names of their holders with their titles, were kept by village officials and village citizenship was awarded to the peasants who in that sense owned land and, according to their arable lands, paid taxes. It is important, though, to realize that such *de facto* recognition of 'holdership' is not identical to what we now consider full *de jure* private property. The peasant-holders officially did not have the right to sell the land in their possession 'forever' or 'in perpetuity'. Sellers and buyers of land had to take recourse to specific 'constructions', if they did not want to trespass existing rules. A registered farmer held exclusive right *to cultivate* his farm and to its *output* net of tax. When he sold (or collateralized) his farm, that transaction was legally governed by the village official only if the other party was also resident of the village in which he was registered. This was done in order to ensure tax payment for which the village as a whole was responsible. Otherwise buying and selling land was not legally governed and had to be completely self-enforced. People from outside who had bought land in a village as a rule had great problems in enforcing their property rights, if they managed at all.

There were also constraints on land owners as a consequence of the fact that in villages mainly living from agriculture and collectively assessed for paying taxes, there existed practical and 'moral' limits to the extent to which one individually could decide how to manage one's business, in particular as an agriculturist. Those restrictions were quite explicit in the case of the so-called 'commons' and jointly owned arable land. 'Commons' here refers to land under common property with regard to entry use and the extraction of products. They were held by villages or groups of villages. Their extension was enormous. Cultivated acreage in Japan is estimated to have trebled between 1600 and 1868, reaching a total of 4.4 million ha in 1868. Even in the late 1930s, total cultivated area in Japan in its entirety was only some six million ha. The extension of the forests – the bulk of all common lands – and uncultivated mountain meadows communally held and managed by thousands of villages during the Tokugawa era, has been estimated at no less than twelve million ha. Common lands of whatever nature were of fundamental importance to village agriculture as supplier of e.g. fertilizer, fuel, construction material or wild foods. Officially, a distinction was made between the lord's forests, forests held by the village in common and forests held by individuals. In practice, the situation was more complex and rights were often overlapping. Villages paid a much lower tax on their commons and were free to determine their own rules when it came to individual tax shares. Not all commons consisted in land: irrigation networks, hot springs and coastal fisheries could also be common property.[14] Apart from that, there was arable land that was held in joint ownership. Again, we are talking about a very substantial amount of land. Philip Brown, who wrote a monograph on commonly owned arable land in Japan, provides this brief explanation of the logics according to which it was cultivated.

> In some thirty per cent of Japan, no direct link existed between a farmer and the land associated with his cultivation rights. Especially in many parts of Hokuriku, Shikoku and Kyushu regions, the land one farmed at any given time was determined by village or baronial domain (*han*) policy employing one of three mechanisms: allocation of cultivation rights linked to family composition, a fixed order of rotation, or lottery. Although there are three major variants of these systems (per capita allocation, allocation per family and per share allocation), and many lesser ones, I subsume them all under the most widespread Japanese moniker *warichi*, literally 'dividing the land' and under the term 'joint ownership' in English. These forms of tenure applied to arable lands, not to the commons (*iriai-chi*) which sometimes employed similar mechanisms to allocate access to a resource. Depending on which variant one discusses, these tenurial regimes not only determined who farmed which plots, but also imposed severe restrictions on alienability of rights in land.[15]

Whatever their exact implementation, all these forms of communal or joint ownership shared the characteristic that individuals could not claim personal and full ownership of the land they used. In the sentence directly before this quote, Brown, to contradict the position of classical and neoclassical economists, emphasizes that these forms of ownership did not impede 'economic diversification and growth', which in my view is hard to believe for the long run.[16]

Efforts undertaken by Shogunate and *daimyo* to keep peasant possession intact and so guarantee social stability and tax revenue, like the 1643 edit against the sale of land, in the end failed. That was virtually admitted when in 1723 the Shogunate recognized forfeiture of peasant land. Regulations by the authorities to protect and/or control small peasant holdings notwithstanding, selling and renting of land actually became quite normal, be it often under some disguise.[17] The ban on permanent sale, for example, was interpreted to mean that peasants were allowed to sell a parcel of land for a limited period of time. The pawning of land in many instances actually meant its selling or renting. Often, however, buying and selling simply took place in complete disregard of shogunal laws.

Tokugawa Japan thus developed a land-market with especially in some regions a (further) polarization between those holding tiny plots of land and larger landlords. Increasing fragmentation as well as concentration of land possession were facts of life.[18] Small land-holders who managed to keep some economic independence, increasingly did so via by-employments. Parcels of cultivated land usually changed 'owner' in the village, but at times also outsiders could acquire land. This 'rise of the market' was accompanied by an overall increase of land as well as labour productivity, at least until a couple of decades into the eighteenth century. Unsurprisingly, at least to me, this was a process with winners and losers. One of its most striking social effects was the rise in tenancy, which would rise even more after Restoration (see Table 55). The emerging land market tended to take the form of tenancy contracts. At the beginning of the Tokugawa period as a rule peasant-cultivators *de facto* owned their fields. Over time, as much as almost 30 per cent of the total land area came under some form of 'tenancy'. The national tenancy rate in 1873 was already 27.4 per cent. In 1916, it had increased to 45.3 per cent.[19]

It is no longer disputed that a quite lively land market developed in several regions of Japan. What is disputed though, is how to interpret this development when it comes to causes and consequences. Simplifying the debate one can distinguish between two contrasting positions: that of Susan Hanley and Kozo Yamamura, who present a quite positive, 'neo-classical' interpretation of the 'rise of the market' as a rational response of all actors involved to incentives leading to a general improvement of the economic situation and that of Grace Kwon, who, in her clearly Marxist interpretation, points at relevant differences between developments in and outside the Kinai region and who, unsurprisingly for a Marxist scholar, focuses on differences – and similarities – in

Table 55 Regional tenancy rates in Japan in 1873 and 1916

	1873	1916
Tohuku	14.6	41.6
Kanto	23.6	46.0
Kyushu	26.3	42.7
Toyama	31.0	47.4
Kinki	33.0	50.2
Tokai	33.7	47.7
Shikoku	41.0	40.7
Yamakage	42.7	53.8

Kwon, *State formation*, 72 and 115.

evolving class relations and on the deterioration in the position of the semi-landless and tenants, in particular in that Kinai region.

A real 'class' of landless agricultural workers, however, did not emerge.[20] Wage labourers were never more than just a tiny percentage of the agricultural labour force. They never comprised more than 10–15 per cent of total agricultural population. According to Yuzuru Kumon, by 1700, only 13 per cent of the people in Japan's countryside were landless.[21] According to Jan de Vries, as late as 1879, no more than 5 per cent of Japan's *entire* labour force worked for wages.[22] Osamu Saito has come up with two explanations for this near absence of agricultural landless proletarians. One is the very possibility for those having no or only very little land to become tenant. As he himself points out, overall in the Tokugawa period rents were well over 50 per cent, at least in the case of rice fields. That would suggest that tenants could easily end up with financial problems, find it impossible to pay their rents and thus turn into 'proletarians'. But, still according to Saito, until the beginning of the twentieth century, tenant–landlord relationships and village customs were such that it was very unusual to actually make or allow people to become completely landless. The second explanation is the widespread existence of by-employment in the late-Tokugawa countryside, which enabled people, especially when they were part of a household, to earn a living even when they only cultivated a tiny plot of land.

Like in all non-capitalist societies, the situation in Tokugawa Japan when it comes to defining property and property rights was extremely complex and characterized by often overlapping, multiple and changing claims. What is clear, however, is that in any case when it comes to land – by far the most important capital good – property rights were not absolutely and individually fixed by law, if they were formally described at all. The Meiji Restoration in this respect brought major changes as it clearly favoured and where possible enforced modern, i.e. absolute, individual and inalienable property rights in land and the freedom to buy and sell it. It now became policy to classify properties as either private or public and, in case of doubt, nationalize them. I have already referred to nationalization – that many would consider as *non-* or even *anti-*capitalist, because capitalism would in essence be a system of private property – earlier on.[23] Here it suffices to say that joint arable land was officially abolished even though it in practice might persist, whereas commons were not officially abolished but in practice often privatized and, in far more cases, *nationalized*.[24] What I am concerned with here is the effects of the introduction of modern property rights on GDP as economists measure it. Like by far the majority of economists, I would claim that in any case the *introduction* of modern property rights is conducive to a growing of GDP. That means that in this respect too, the role of Japan's state after 1868 was a quite positive one. This is not meant to deny that modern property rights can and often do have negative effects for specific groups. In the case of Japan discussed here there also were such negative effects.

Land was thus increasingly turned into a pure factor of production, i.e. a commodity already during the Tokugawa era, but only all but fully with the Meiji Restoration. What about labour? It is assumed that about 80 per cent of the labour force in Tokugawa Japan worked in the countryside and there at least to a substantial extent in agriculture. We already indicated that virtually no households in the agricultural sector were wholly dependent on wage labour although many members of those households had by-employments in manufacturing, commerce or other service occupations. Live-in service in other households as compared to Western Europe, was relatively less common.[25] By implication wage labour, certainly *full* wage labour, i.e. wage labour on which the worker is fully dependent, must have been quite exceptional in the economy of Japan as a whole. Far more exceptional than for example in England, where in 1851, 73 per cent of those working in the countryside were wage labourers and where, according to Gregory King, already in 1688, two-thirds of the rural population was landless.[26]

In towns, guild-like structures eroded in the late Tokugawa period whereas the importance of casual work for wages increased. In the 1860s, according to Saito, the proportion of live-in servants who had a longer-term contract to the town population hardly reached 10 per cent in provincial towns and in all Edo boroughs. He suggests this figure had been higher and as such was fairly low, but the contrast in this respect with England is not very striking. Apparently between 1574 and 1821 about 13 per cent of the population of English communities were servants or apprentices.[27] Saito refers to some Edo evidence that would suggest that the enforcement of apprenticeship became ineffective and regulation of wages difficult. Interestingly enough, the reason he adduces would be that the numbers of both journeymen and migrant, part-time craftsmen from the countryside increased over time. That would mean that all the rulings to restrict mobility, about which some more will be said later, were not very effective or not taken very seriously. In circles of tradesmen, in contrast, the employment of servants who learned their skills in the trade expanded in the eighteenth and early nineteenth centuries, which meant that in this sector the importance of 'the market' declined. Overall, however, Saito is of the opinion that during the latter half of the Tokugawa period the tendency towards 'casualization' outweighed that towards in-firm training and forms of apprenticeship. The state, so he claims, in practice tended to leave reasonably wide room for the spontaneous growth of labour markets from below.

Commodification of labour implies that workers are free to move around and settle. Going by the official rulings freedom of movement and residence in Tokugawa Japan were very restricted. For peasants, it was officially forbidden to leave their village. They could not, officially, settle in towns. Samurai in turn as a rule had to stay in castle towns. Overall, however, the rulers must have become rather permissive when it comes to mobility. As indicated, Japan had a high urbanization rate. Towns as a rule could only grow or even just keep their population size – which in the second half of the Tokugawa era *not* all towns did – when they received an inflow of immigrants that could compensate for their high mortality rates. Migration and the taking up of new jobs must have been substantial in the latter half of the Tokugawa period. That means that the prohibition to change job must also to a large extent have been ignored. Besides, considering the fact that, especially in the countryside, many people combined all sorts of activities, the idea of having a job cannot have entailed much for most people.

Restricting geographical mobility and choice of job was part and parcel of the many efforts by Tokugawa Japan's rulers to freeze the social status quo. That also transpired in the fixed distinction between the four estates of samurai, merchants, artisans and farmers. In practice, the distinction between them was not always clear-cut and 'estate-barriers' were not always impermeable. For the warrior estate Tokugawa's 'realm of great peace' – and the frequent cuts of their stipends – meant that they had to take up all sorts of jobs to not be completely idle and to make ends meet.[28] I already indicated that not all warriors had moved to towns. There were several hundred thousand of master-less samurai roaming around. There was intermarriage between members of the merchant and the samurai estates. Mikiso Hane and Luis G. Perez point out that in the beginning of the nineteenth century, wealthy farmers, the so-called *gonosho*, started taking up surnames and wearing swords and that some even had yearly allowances.[29] The fact that sumptuary regulations were repeated time and again indicates they often were honoured primarily in the breach.[30]

The four-estates discourse thus became increasingly detached from reality. Samurai were no longer actual warriors, and those living in cities had become deeply involved in the urban commercial economy as they had to sell their stipend, which existed of a share of agricultural income, to a broker and then buy what they needed with cash income. They were often indebted to merchants, who gave credit and market services. Peasants had often become farmers selling cash crops who in that respect acted like merchants.[31] Merchants who were supposed to be members of the lowest estate could be very wealthy and hold indebted samurai in their grip. But all this blurring of distinctions notwithstanding, the samurai remained 'the sole political officeholders and the commoners continued to be shut out from the political process', whereas the sons of townsmen and peasants 'lacked any significant possibility for true upward mobility in the form of gaining entrance to the community of honour'.[32] Merchant capital that was so important in the state formation of several European state did not play a significant role in the formation of the Tokugawa state. Tokugawa Japan, I would conclude, certainly was not a capitalist class society as Marx defines it. David Howell's thesis that Tokugawa Japan already knew capitalism – in a Marxian meaning of the term – to my view, considering all the comments I made before, therefore is not very convincing, even if he would have good reasons to claim that in Hokkaido fisheries: 'the fundamental transformation to capitalism was complete before the establishment of a regime dedicated to Western-style economic development.'[33] As he admits himself, the situation in the fisheries sector was not 'normal'. I would not, like him, claim that the difference in dependence of labour on the market, was 'only in degree', not 'substance' as compared to the *Bakufu* and other domains.[34] Hokkaido was a fishery region where rice cultivation was impossible, and as such different from the beginning and somehow 'un-Japanese'. The migrant fishers that came to Hokkaido, filled a space that was economically and socially empty as Howell himself points out.[35] In the rest of Japan under Tokugawa rule and even during the Meiji era, dependency on wage labour, the essence of Marxian capitalism, continued to be quite rare.

When discussing capitalism, some comments on money are unavoidable. In Tokugawa Japan, minting coins in principle was a monopoly of the Shogunate, which owned all the large mines. Export of bullion from the end of the seventeenth century onwards was almost completely forbidden as there often was scarcity of bullion.[36] Many fiefs printed paper money that could only be used inside the fief. When we look at the height of interest rates, as a rule a good indicator of the efficiency of the financial markets, we must conclude that they were fairly high.[37] There is no need to again discuss the commodification of consumer goods. It had already been quite widespread during the Tokugawa period, in particular during the second half of it. I confine myself to referring to my previous comments on commercialization, monetization and marketization.[38]

Let us synthesize our findings with regard to the Tokugawa period. It would be incorrect to suggest that Tokugawa Japan, all the transferring and renting of land notwithstanding, had a smoothly, let alone optimally efficient functioning land market. When it comes to the market for labour: that was small. The bulk of the labour force in the countryside, where at least some 80 per cent of the working population lived, continued to work in the setting of farming households, even though the importance of by-employment in non-agricultural activities increased steadily. All this working for wages hardly ever led to the emergence of a wage-labouring class. In towns, overall the importance of the labour market increased, as very probably did the number of wage labourers. The increasing ease of buying and selling land, the development of a widespread proto-industry in the countryside as well as the casualization of labour in towns, the weakening of the restrictions on geographical and social mobility, they all will have contributed to Smithian growth in Tokugawa Japan, but they should not distract from the fact the legal-institutional framework of Tokugawa Japan in principle was anti-market. The market was not a Meiji innovation. But it would be hard to claim that the Tokugawa rulers intentionally promoted it. They never formally abolished most of their original rules, institutions and organizations, that we would now characterize – anachronistically – as *anti-capitalist* in the sense of *anti-laissez-faire*. In as far as the market for land, labour and capital grew, that mostly occurred because existing rules were bended, evaded, or just ignored. Several of them, for example the rulings hampering trade between fiefs among each other and in particular those prohibiting trade with foreign countries were applied quite strictly almost till the very end of the Tokugawa era.

The reality of Tokugawa Japan thus could be quite different from the rules and norms that were supposed to shape it. But here too, it is, in my view, evident that those rules and norms were not without effect and clearly impeded an optimal functioning of the market mechanism. There can be no doubt that abolishing those norms and rules will have had a positive effect on Japan's economic development. One may debate the extent of 'proto-capitalism' in Tokugawa Japan, but in my view the Meiji Restoration heralded the coming of a really new age. Even David Howell, with his emphasis on continuity, in the end admits that 'the origins of capitalism lay in the Tokugawa period, but the transformation was not complete until well into the Meiji era'.[39] It was only with Meiji rule that 'scattered instances of capitalist productive relations gave way to a capitalist mode of production' as it brought 'a decisive end to the institutional barriers to capitalist development'.[40] After that, 'economic change proceeded at a rapid pace, so that Japan was a genuinely capitalist economy by the beginning of the twentieth century'.[41] What is important for my thesis about the importance of the state for economic and in this case capitalist economic development, is that Howell with good reason claims that the institutional structure in which economic life takes place – and thus in the last instance the state as 'key variable' – is determining whether a society as a whole can become capitalist.[42]

Institutionalising capitalism

With the Meiji Restoration, Japan officially, i.e. legally, became a modern capitalist market economy, which overall made its economy more efficient from a macro-economic perspective. Modern property rights were officially introduced which, in particular for the ownership of land, was a major change. Owners in future were free to buy and sell land and to use it as they pleased. This does not mean property rights became 'inviolable'. In 1871, the *daimyo* returned their fiefs. The overwhelming majority did so 'voluntarily', but one may question their willingness. A couple of years into Meiji rule, the bulk of the samurai had to accept that their incomes were systematically reduced. Although fiefs and stipends had never been 'properties' in the modern sense of the word, the *daimyo* and samurai concerned will certainly have felt expropriated. That also applies to those villagers who lost common lands to the government. The property rights of the Ainu were simply ignored. The land of Hokkaido effectively became property of the Japanese government that gave it or rented it out to Japanese settlers. We are talking about a substantial amount of territory here. As indicated, the island measures some eighty-three thousand square kilometres, and thus is about as big as the whole of Austria.

In the secondary sector guilds and monopolies were abolished. Labour now became officially free to choose any job and residence, and to travel. In that sense there was now free enterprise. There were no longer any macro-economically relevant, legally fixed distinctions between different 'estates'. Post-Restoration Japan certainly did not become a society where all careers were open to all talent and where meritocracy ruled, as was suggested in article three from Charter Oath of 1868: 'The common people, no less than the civil and military officials, shall all be allowed to pursue their own calling so that there may be no discontent.' But, and that is of major importance, it was certainly much more open and meritocratic – and thus efficient – than Tokugawa Japan. That of course does not mean there would have been no clear distinctions in practice. In the famous 'duality', for example, that became so characteristic for its developing industry, even though it became only became firmly institutionalized and widespread in the 1920s or rather the 1930s, there certainly were different 'statuses' of labour.[43] There emerged a difference between those core workers in large firms who enjoyed long-term or even life-time employment and seniority-based wages and who might be represented in their company or enterprise unions and on the other hand the many 'second tier', temporary workers in those firms and all the others working in small to very small workshop-like enterprises, who earned much less and whose existence was far more 'volatile'.[44]

The coming of Meiji rule also meant that something was done about the monetary chaos that existed at the end of Tokugawa rule. At the beginning of the 1870s the following currencies were circulating in Japan: non-convertible Meiji paper notes, coins minted by the late Shogunate, counterfeited versions of these currencies issued by some domains, new government's paper notes, notes issued by domains and foreign currency, i.e. Mexican dollars that were circulating in treaty ports.[45] In 1871, the yen was introduced to replace the *ryo*. Now the whole of Japan had one standard, universal currency, not – as had been the case – a broad variety of currencies with often changing values. Again, it would be wrong to suggest that the changes were quick, always consistent and effective, but after the usual adaptations and trial and error Japan as a whole acquired a functioning monetary system. This, again, must have led to higher efficiency and lower 'transactions' cost. The new state now set out to acquire 'monetary sovereignty', i.e. the exclusive and unlimited power to create its own sovereign currency.[46] On top of that, the economy became more monetized as the land taxes, that for several decades were by far the most important ones, were now collected in money although, as we have indicated, in practice many people long continued to pay them in kind. Collecting taxes in money is more efficient than doing so in kind, which means that the new tax system would be more efficient. At last in my view: Japanese economic historian Kozo Yamamura claims there were good reasons why Japan's system of in-kind tax payments lasted so long.[47] In his view agriculture, especially rice production, was both the dominant activity of Japan and a reliable tax base. Rice output could be measured fairly accurately, whereas the tax rice could be levied and collected with minimum transaction costs. It, moreover, was a storable and standardized product. Measuring, assessing and collecting taxes based on income from commerce, services or the production of other kinds of goods, still in his view, suffered from serious drawbacks. In my opinion Yamamura, as well as Arthur Alexander, who endorses his position, both seriously underestimate the *disadvantages* of assessing and collecting tax in rice in a developing economy.[48] Collecting, transporting, storing and then selling a bulky and fairly basic good such as rice is not exactly cheap and easy. The yield of rice-taxes in terms of money was not easily predictable and often varied sharply over the years. A country like Britain already in the eighteenth century was able to collect the bulk of its taxes in the form of excises and customs, and in money. Why would this have been impossible or inefficient in Japan? The existing tax system in Tokugawa could certainly also in itself be a hurdle for development. In rice-growing regions local authorities often were unwilling or unable to appreciate the value of industry and wanted the people to grow rice because under the *kokudaka*-system that was the form in which peasants were expected to pay their taxes.[49] What one certainly can discuss, is whether it was wise – from the perspective of collecting taxes fairly and efficiently, with minimal damage to the economy – to create a new tax system in which land taxes figured so prominently in total tax revenue.[50]

Overall, the importance of the market mechanism in which supply and demand determined prices increased. There were no longer government rulings indicating where to bring and to whom to offer one's merchandise. Japan domestically now became a more integrated market that moreover was far more open to foreign trade. As I indicated earlier, over time Tokugawa Japan, when it comes to trade, indeed had become all but closed. Its opening made a substantial difference as the figures for foreign trade on page 191 show. One may assume that the resulting new allocation of the factors of production after the country's opening, increased efficiency.

The comments so far regarded the extent to which post-Restoration Japan became more capitalist according to the definitions of capitalism we referred to as Smithian and Marxian. Post-Restoration Japan, however, also became much more capitalist in the Weberian sense of the word because of the increased, often government-instigated promotion of, on the one hand, thrift and 'industriousness', basically already old virtues, but on the other hand also of 'efficiency', 'self-help' and being an entrepreneur. The position of the 'merchant' now officially was no longer at the bottom of the scale. 'Capitalists' were looking for and given a more respectable place in society.[51] As Japan's new rulers now explicitly began to favour collusion of power (of the state) and profit (i.e. the capital of large capitalists) and explicitly condoned or even supported all sorts of rigging of the market that Braudel found so characteristic for 'his' form of capitalism, we may conclude that with the Meiji Restoration and its aftermath Japan's economy also became more capitalist in the 'Braudelian' sense.

That already suggests that competition would not become completely, as economists define it, free and fair. Competition certainly did not become entirely free: there was state intervention of all sorts, with often market-distorting effects. In agriculture, private ownership now became much more normal whereas the importance of commons and of joint arable diminished. But, on the other hand, there was a substantial increase of the amount of land in ownership of the state (central government or local government) and the Imperial Household. Competition certainly also did not become entirely 'fair': all sorts of arrangements existed by which it was restricted. A dual economy with, on the one hand, very big players who could distort the market (first and foremost of course the so-called *zaibatsu*) and on the other hand many thousands of tiny firms that, while they were in murderous competition with each other, at the same time often were heavily dependent on such big players. The monopolistic trade organizations and guilds that were so important in Tokugawa times did not survive the transition to the new economic order after Restoration. But fairly soon many forms of association and co-operation became reinstated in somewhat different guises. Some further comments are in order when it comes to the attitude of Japan's rulers towards competition and labour.

A regulated and regulating capitalism

Even though of course neither politicians nor bureaucrats, nor for that matter business men, in Japan have ever formed monolithic groups, each with their own very specific interests, one may, nevertheless, claim that Japan's rulers and bureaucracy overall tended to be pro-business in their policies during the period 1868–1937. Politicians and bureaucrats often were personally acquainted with or even actively involved in business. As compared to, for example, China or the Ottoman Empire, in Japan the worlds of business, government and bureaucracy seemed less separated from each other. In a country that wants to modernize its economy that can certainly be helpful although – as indeed was not uncommon in Japan – connections between the different spheres can also be *too* close.[52] Examples of collusion and corruption were legion.[53]

The spectrum of policies in support of business was very broad and diverse, ranging from very general policies from which in principle every Japanese might profit to measures with a very specific goal and directed at a very specific group of people or interests. The provision of an infrastructure in the widest sense of the word in which business can function efficiently would be an example of the first category. As has already been discussed, Japan's state did create such an infrastructure institutionally – in terms of e.g. legal, financial or monetary arrangements – as well as in material terms. The provision of such 'public goods' is of fundamental importance for the smooth functioning and growth of an economy. How important is normally only fully realized when they are lacking.

But there were also measures that were more specifically targeting business. The data provided in our analysis of Japan's system of taxation showed that government allowed, facilitated and even stimulated capital accumulation. Business was taxed only very lightly whereas in any case certain sectors of it received subsidies. Our brief discussion of trade policies on pages 190–202 will show that government protected business via a policy of 'buy Japanese', and as soon as it was possible, via tariff policies. In the 1930s, to just give one example of more specific policies, industrial and trade associations were relieved of all taxes.[54] Government, although it continued to run several strategic enterprises itself, also after the sell-out in the 1880s, in principle considered Japan a country of private enterprise and competition. But it always kept certain general, 'developmental' goals of its own that it wanted to push. It did not hesitate to regulate competition when it believed that the existing practices had negative consequences for the competitive strength of the nation 'as a whole'. Japan's rulers in the period we discuss here without notable exception were convinced that government should have an industrial policy, which Chalmers Johnson defines as 'a concern with the structure of domestic industry and with promoting the structure that enhances the nation's international competitiveness.[55] Actually such industrial policies were only a part, be it the central one, of government's concern with the strength of the economy as a whole. They targeted particular sectors, in particular of industry, for development and as such involved extensive government guidance. This meant that in practice competition quite often was neither free nor perfect according to the textbook definitions of economists.

Never before World War Two did government enact any 'anti-monopoly' or 'anti-trust' laws. Nor did it show any *principled* objection against the existence of all sorts of 'combinations', whose effect or even goal was to 'regulate' or even abolish competition. Rather the contrary, it in many instances supported their existence or even instigated their creation. A clear example here would be its tolerance *of* and even support *for* the so-called *zaibatsu* and, in particular later on in the period, for cartel building.[56] In the direct aftermath of the 1868 Restoration, to refer to a probably less well-known example, there were many *seishos*, merchants by the grace of political connections', e.g. Yataro Iwasaki who ran the Mitsubishi company.

It would lead too far to here discuss in detail the *zaibatsu's* complex structure and history. I refer the interested reader to the relevant literature and confine myself to a couple of brief comments.[57] By definition, the *zaibatsu* were large family-controlled, vertical monopolies, that consisted of a holding company on top, with a wholly-owned banking subsidiary that provided finance, and several industrial subsidiaries that were active in specific sectors of a market, either solely, or through a number of subsidiary companies. No *zaibatsu* as such held a monopoly over any specific sector of the economy and it would therefore be a serious error to think they *eliminated* competition. Government would in many cases not have approved of that. But their size and structure did strengthen their competitive advantages. As interlocking conglomerates, they could do all sorts of things that independent firms could not and endure all sort of things that independent firms would not have been able to endure.

The Big Four *zaibatsu*, in chronological order of founding, Sumitomo, Mitsui, Mitsubishi and Yasuda, were the most significant *zaibatsu* groups. Two of them, Sumitomo and Mitsui, had roots in the Edo period, while Mitsubishi and Yasuda originated after the Meiji Restoration. Beyond the Big Four, there is no consensus as to which companies can be called *zaibatsu*, and which cannot. In particular, after the Russo–Japanese War, a number of 'second-tier' *zaibatsu* emerged, mostly as a result of business conglomerations and/or the award of lucrative military contracts. Japanese industrial expansion on the Asian mainland in the 1930s saw the rise of a number of *new zaibatsu*, which differed from the traditional ones. They weren't controlled by specific families and didn't have banks of their own, whereas in the old *zaibatsu*, as 'financial cliques', finance and financial control had always been paramount. Their core business was in heavy metal and chemical industry and their founders were engineers with work experience in those sectors. Whereas the old *zaibatsu* were viewed with increasing suspicion by both the right and the left of the political spectrum in the 1920s and 1930s, the new ones developed good contacts with the bureaucracy and with the military in Manchuria.

This is not the place to extensively describe the powerful position of the *zaibatsu* in Japan Proper and later on its Empire. Suffice to say that the *zaibatsu* were at the heart of economic and industrial activity within the Empire of Japan, and held great influence over the economy and over Japan's domestic and foreign policies.[58] The following two quotes give an indication of their 'power':

> Even if the seventeen leading combines (i.e. *zaibatsu* P.V.) are defined so as to include only companies in which they held twenty-five or more per cent of the stock, their aggregate paid-in capital was nearly one-fifth (eighteen per cent) of the paid-in capital of all Japanese joint-stock companies in 1935. Even greater was the concentration of control in the banking, insurance and trust business.... On the eve of World War Two, the seven big private banks of the county ... held nearly sixty per cent of the total assets and the depositories of 'ordinary' (private commercial) banks. Together with the six leading government banks, they accounted for over half of the capital and deposits of *all* banks. Four of the seven were the Mitsui, Mitsubishi, Sumitomo and Yasuda banks.[59]
>
> By 1929, the firms owned or controlled by the Mitsui, Mitsubishi and Yasuda *zaibatsu*, along with the giant nationally-owned Yawata produced 93,6 per cent of the total output of pig iron, 83.1 per cent of the steel and 83.5 per cent of processed steel products. In the ammonium sulphate industry, the Mitsui and Mitsubishi firms by 1930 virtually divided the total output between them. In the cement industry, 83.1 per cent of the output was accounted for by eight firms under the control of Mitsui, Mitsubishi and Asano-Yasuba *zaibatsu*. Oji Paper and Fuji Paper, both directly controlled by Mitsui, produced 65.4 per cent of the total output in paper in 1929. In sugar, flour milling, mining and other major industries the pattern was similar. The textile industry, in which the financial penetration of the *zaibatsu* group was weak, was one major sector of industry which was not as highly

concentrated as the other industries described above. However, in that industry too, the so-called Big Six, accounting for over forty per cent of the total paid capital of the industry emerged by the end of the 1920s to lead effectively organized cartels.[60]

The financial sector with its powerful old *zaibatsu* became heavily concentrated. The five largest banks, Mitsui, Mitsubishi, Yasuda, Sumitomo and Daiichi, increased their total capital from 12.7 to 19.0 per cent of the total of commercial banks between 1914 and 1927. The Big Five's share of total deposits of all commercial banks in that period increased from 22.5 to 31.2 per cent. The number of commercial banks decreased from 1615 to 876 between 1911 and 1929.[61]

Throughout the entire period we discuss here, the government employed the financial powers and expertise of *zaibatsu* for various endeavours, including tax collection, military procurement and foreign trade, whereas it on the other hand, in particular in the first decades after Restoration, tended to support them in all imaginable ways, in the form of subsidies, specific rights or monopolies, favourable deals, exemptions and so on and so forth. Actually, the *zaibatsu* as they operated in the period we discuss in this book, would have been unimaginable without government support, active or passive, in particular in the first decades of Meiji rule.[62] In the last decade of the nineteenth century, they increasingly attracted capital via equity-based lending. In the next stage of their financial history, they avoided stocks and foreign capital – which they had *always* avoided – and increasingly financed their endeavours via their well-endowed in house banks. Capital accumulation was the essence behind *zaibatsu*-led expansion.[63] It allowed the *zaibatsu* to keep their autonomy with regard to foreigners, family members and the government. The old *zaibatsu* initially always combined family capital, family management and government support. Over time salaried professional managers became increasingly important and direct government support less so.

Prior to the 1920s, the large companies that spearheaded Japanese development often dominated their respective markets. This means there was little need for collusion. Apparently, there were no more than three formal cartels predating 1920. During the 1920s and 1930s, with economic depression and militarization of the economy, they became much more numerous. In 1925, cartels were legalized by legislation that mandated compulsory adherence by members.[64] In 1931, a law was enacted authorizing the government to compel all firms in an industry to join a cartel when a certain number of them requested that. Government now increasingly was in favour of cartels and started to act as a driving force behind their foundation. In 1932 their number had reached eighty-three.[65] At the beginning of the Meiji era, government had abolished all guild-like organizations in order to promote free enterprise. But over time it increasingly allowed and stimulated the return of organizations that were meant to coordinate and supervise production and trade. In particular so-called '(general) trade organizations' come to play a very important role in Japan's economy.[66]

In the 1920s, in particular their second half, and the 1930s, government in the context of its policies of 'rationalization', encouraged the founding of associations for production or export, that regulated or even completely eliminated competition. Such organizations received state support and protection.[67] In the 1930s, direct government intervention in the economy (again) became commonplace.[68] In the beginning of the decade two laws were passed: one that affected all important branches of industry, both those working for the domestic market and those working for export, and another one that was primarily enacted to promote export associations. Nearly 500 industrial associations were formed, some of them reorganized and officially recognized. According to the *Oriental Economist*, the functions of these associations were as follows:

> Survey of productive facilities of members; designation of raw and partly manufactured materials; production control and price fixing; establishment of cooperative institutions and lending of machinery for lowering production costs; finishing and distribution of products of member-firms on a co-operative basis; co-operative purchases of raw and partly manufactured materials; accommodating operation funds; technical advice regarding business management.[69]

At the end of 1934, sixty-seven organizations were functioning under the Export Guild Law. Guenther Stein, in his *Made in Japan*, gives the following description of their aims:

> The usual aims of such associations are all or some of the following: fixing export quantities or prices according to markets; inspection of export shipment and enforcement of a fair standard of quality; maintenance of agents abroad; investigation of new markets; advising inexperienced exporters; elimination of middle men causing a reduction of sales prices; negotiating sales for members, or outright buying from members and direct selling to foreign customers.[70]

The state supported such industrial and trade associations with certain subsidies and guarantees, cheap credits or tax exemptions. The application of these laws in practice was not as strict and as general is it was declared on paper. According to Stein, government, at least when he wrote his text, was not strong enough to really enforce such laws. Interestingly enough, he clearly was in favour of all this planning and co-ordinating. With a strong government, the associations would flourish. If Westerners would also organize their trade like the Japanese, so he concludes, 'world trade might be planned and developed on a more efficient basis.'[71] He already in 1935 mused about the development of absolute government control 'in proportion as Japan's domestic and foreign difficulties increase.'[72]

Again, this is not the place to expand on the minutiae of all sorts of specific institutional arrangements. I will confine myself to two general conclusions that one, in my view, can draw from a survey of the history of competition in Japan and the role of the state in it for the period 1868–1937: Whatever their exact origin and history and whatever the exact role of the state in them, state policies stimulated 'regulated competition' and, to a substantial extent *by means of* that regulated competition, contributed to the emergence of many large firms and factories in Japan, which gave the country its famous dual economy. Both regulated competition and large-scale enterprise, in my view, *in the specific setting of Japan at the time* overall had positive effects on its economic growth and development as they facilitated capital accumulation, innovation and protection against risk.[73] The existence of *Zaibatsu* did not eliminate competition or stifle innovation. It was the government's strategy to encourage the growth of competing oligopolies that were large enough to exploit economies of scale but were nevertheless forced to be 'competitive'.[74]

Let us also give some further examples of regulation and concentration, now primarily for sectors where the *zaibatsu* were less involved. In the silk industry, i.e. the production of silk yarn and later on also silk textiles, for many decades the biggest 'industry' of post-Restoration Japan, the level of concentration was very low. In the 1920s the largest company, Katakura, still only produced 8 per cent of the total amount of silk reeled in entire Japan.[75] The cotton textiles industry, in contrast, from the 1880s with the founding of the Cotton Spinner's Federation onwards, was a sector with large factories and firms, a high level of co-operation and collusion, and a very high level of concentration. Basically, cotton spinning was organized as a cartel from the moment it became a modern industry. According to George Allen in his chapter on Japanese industry in the 1930s, the country's iron and steel industry had also been in the hands of a tiny number of concerns from the very beginning, whereas the engineering industry had become concentrated in a few firms of the *zaibatsu* groups that ran large plants and produced a wide range of products.[76] Several other important sectors of industry are also portrayed as heavily concentrated in the 1930s. All the leading shipbuilding yards were owned by a few great industrial and financial groups. In the new sector of rayon production, six companies accounted for three quarters of output. One firm turned out four-fifths of foreign-style paper. Eighty-eight per cent of crude and refined sugar production was in the hands of five firms. The cement industry in Japan and Korea was in the hands of some twenty-five firms. Beer brewing was monopolized by four companies. The whole output of sheet glass in the empire came from a few large factories, owned by three companies. This high rate of concentration was not just the outcome of a process of competition in which economies of scale and scope advantaged larger units, it quite often was also the outcome of political decisions.[77]

There is not much doubt that the *zaibatsu* were efficient as firms. The way they were set up gave them distinct advantages in competition. They were able to only refer to the most important of those advantages, to profit from economies of scale and scope and from synergy; from diversification and risk minimization and from internal capital markets. For the rest, I refer to Schenkein's analysis.[78] The *zaibatsu* banks had huge capital resources in comparison to average banks. In capital-scarce Japan that certainly was a major asset.[79] The final litmus test are their profits. They as a rule were high but, as indicated earlier, not the result of the absence of competitors.

Overall, the existence of *zaibatsu* for the period discussed here, at least *when it comes to their macro-economic effects,* has been assessed positively, although one has to realize that not all *zaibatsu* were the same and that changes occurred over time. Public opinion in the 1920s and 1930s often turned against the powerful cliques as did parts of the army, from which the *new zaibatsu* profited. All *zaibatsu* contributed greatly to the rapid accumulation of capital and modernization of technology. Full-scale industrialization is impossible without large-scale enterprises and sustained technological progress. Capital-intensive projects like shipyards, mines or heavy industries needed large amounts of money that only monopolizing *zaibatsu* firms with their banks could provide whereas *zaibatsu* firms played a major role in introducing new, expensive technologies.[80]

When it comes to employment though, it is easy to exaggerate the importance of the *zaibatsu*. By far the majority of the labour force in manufacturing (but also in agriculture and the service sector) worked in small entities, as shown in Table 56.

Productivity increases and innovation were not lacking in more labour-intensive endeavours but those did tend to run into decreasing returns more easily and faster. As I hope to show in my next book, in Japan's industrialization the future belonged to capital-, technology- and energy-intensive production. As Japan's new rulers did not want to, or felt unable to, run the economy themselves and thus to entirely eliminate the market and private enterprise, they from the very beginning opted for a policy of supporting forms of regulated competition, including *zaibatsu*, and later on cartels. The only other alternative would have been to just wait till certain firms spontaneously became large enough to be able to catch up with firms in more advanced and wealthy economies and to withstand their competition. That did not – and does not – seem to be a very efficient strategy for a semi-developed country that wanted to develop quickly and become wealthy and strong. In the context in which Japan wanted to take off, that of the second and later third industrial revolutions, size and capital mattered a lot. That of course does not mean that the contribution of small- and medium-sized firms to employment but also to production and growth, and even to innovation, would have been irrelevant – far from it.[81] It just means that small- and medium-sized firms as a rule were not big and financially strong enough to produce commodities with a high added value with the possible exception of the production of luxury goods.[82]

Over the seventy years covered in this text government of course also provided direct and indirect support for specific businesses in the form of subsidies, cheaply selling them enterprises, factories, or machinery: by giving them monopolies or preference when it comes to buying material or by helping them with the transfer of knowledge or people. In the context of a book like this, it is impossible to try and express the impact of these activities in a nice balance sheet. There are, as with every type of policy, success stories and clear failures.

Table 56 The labour force of private manufacturing industry in Japan Proper, by size of establishment, 1930

Size of establishment	Number of establishments	Persons engaged, principal occupation	
		Number	Per cent
Total	1,240,038	4,759,921	100
Independents	665,533	655,533	14.0
1–4 operatives	512,271	2,106,650	44.3
5–99 operatives	59,643	988,465	20.8
100–499 operatives	2,178	504,512	10.6
500 or more operatives	413	494,761	10.4

Lockwood, *Economic development*, 204.

There also is no need to point at the many continuities that existed with the Tokugawa era when it comes to government interventions, regulations, monopolies and the like. They were omnipresent then and again with differing effects. What is important though to point out is that in particular the Shogunal interventionist and regulatory policies focused on control much more than on change and growth.

Government policies in the period 1868–1937, overall, did not only support capital; they as a rule also were quite repressive towards labour. That will also have had 'positive' effects on capital accumulation, investment and competitiveness and as such also on the potential of the economy to grow. Labour legally had hardly any protection, certainly not before the 1910s. The position of (young) women, who were of such fundamental importance for Japan's economic development but were considered legal minors, was even weaker on the labour market than that of men. Child labour, at least officially, was relatively scarce. But one may wonder how anyone can really know, considering the importance of family-enterprises in all sectors of the economy. From 1911, in any case, children under the age of twelve were no longer allowed to work in factories.[83] Laws were very employer friendly. The famous labour laws of 1911, that only came into effect in 1916, at first applied only to 'factories' with more than fifteen employees and later, from 1923 onwards, to 'factories' with more than ten employees. Considering the fact that even in 1930 more than half of all people 'principally' engaged in private manufacturing were estimated to have done so in establishments with a total labour force of fewer than five people, many hundreds of thousands of people in principle were not protected by them at all.[84] In 1911, night work was officially abolished. The implementation of that decision, however, was postponed till 1926, and in the end only became effective in 1929. It is overall hard to determine how many workers were actually 'covered' by government rulings, as the labour laws also applied to firms with fewer than ten workers when they were using power-driven machines, which many did, whereas some laws on the other hand only applied to firms with over fifty workers. Overall, exceptions were rife and inspection was not exactly strict or effective. For the year 1929, Guenther Stein claims that 21 per cent of workers included in statistical records were not covered by labour laws i.e. on top of those workers who officially were not covered by the law as they worked in workshops that were too small.[85]

The activities of trade unions were legally very circumscribed and in practice it often was all but impossible for them to operate effectively. Left-wing organizations were kept under close watch, if not simply forbidden. So-called Peace-Preservation Acts were passed in 1900 and 1925 to inhibit labour organization, and in 1928 it became a capital crime to agitate against private property or the Japanese 'national polity'. Beyond the suffrage act of 1925, politically and institutionally no advances were made, while the Peace-Preservation Laws of 1928 established a special police corps to ferret out 'dangerous thoughts.' Laws restricting, 'dangerous meetings', or 'seditious publications', also served to hinder the labour movement. All these labour-repressive policies certainly did help Japan's entrepreneurs in their efforts to make their businesses profitable. None of this of course is peculiar to Japan. In none of the countries that had already industrialized when Japan started to take off had there been a labour-friendly political climate and 'good' labour conditions during early industrialization.

Trade unions or, maybe less anachronistically, 'workers organizations' had been weak to begin with in late Tokugawa Japan. There are historical reasons for that, which we do not have to discuss here. What is striking, is that notwithstanding Japan's fast industrialization they *stayed* weak and that membership *continued* to be low. Union membership was less than 8 per cent of the industrial workforce at its peak in 1931. Among women it was less than 1 per cent.[86] Most trade unions, moreover, were organized vertically per firm and not horizontally according to sectors or branches. Their membership existed almost entirely of a male 'labour aristocracy' of workers with a fixed job and an interest in the firm for which they worked. The condition under which they came to be employed in the so-called Japanese labour system can be described as paternalistic. Considering the large amount of repression that in particular the rest of the workers were confronted with, the following claim by Henry Rosovsky's: 'The great proof of paternalism's strength was the weakness of the Japanese labour movement during the pre-war period', looks rather naïve.[87] What is striking, in comparison to industrializing Great Britain but also to what happened in China and India, is the fact that although radical ideas certainly were not lacking in Japan, machine-breaking was all but unknown.

Women, who were of fundamental importance for the textiles industry – and of course also children when they were still allowed to work – had a very weak legal position. That seems to have been the case *a fortiori* for women working as prostitutes. After the Meiji Restoration, the practice of public prostitution spread everywhere. In 1896, Ito Hirobumi said he thought public prostitution was a splendid arrangement which, among other things, enabled filial daughters to help their poverty-stricken parents.[88] Poverty was a permissible reason for being granted a license to work as a prostitute, or rather the *only one*. As so often in the case of young Japanese female workers, there was a system of advances that were very hard to ever pay off. As courts did not allow women with debts to leave the brothels, they often were trapped. The number of women involved is substantial. In 1897, national records listed over 49,000 prostitutes. In 1899, they numbered over 52,00. In 1901, the number had declined to some 40,000. At the beginning of World War One, again some 50,000 registered women worked in public brothels. Such figures do not, of course, include the unlicensed prostitutes, entertainers, or women in eating and drinking establishments who worked the sex trades.[89]

Another group of workers who had to work in extremely bad conditions were prisoners who performed forced labour.[90] Total prison population according to Botsman was less than 25,000 in 1876, to then in the 1880s quickly rising to on average 80,000 in the first half of the 1890s. The number of people who passed annually through jail was much higher. At its height in 1886, the Miike coal mine on Kyushu accounted for about 20 per cent of Japan's total coal production. In total, several thousands prisoners worked there, coming from a prison newly created for that goal. On Hokkaido, prisoners were massively used for clearing land, working in mines and creating infrastructure. Its so-called 'five prisons' in the period 1886 to 1903, on average kept some four to five thousand prisoners at a time.[91] According to Daniel Botsman there can be no doubt that 'prison labour played a crucial role in the colonization of Hokkaido and more generally, in the early development of Japanese capitalism.'[92] He immediately adds: 'all this came at a terrible human cost. Between 1844 and 1894 close to 44,000 people died in Japanese prisons.'[93] Only a relatively small percentage of the prison deaths resulted from (epidemic) disease. Not everyone apparently thought there was a problem here. This is a comment by Kaneko Kantaro, Ito Hirobumi's Harvard-educated adviser, made in 1885 after he visited Hokkaido:

> When there are large numbers of serious criminal as there are today, government expenditure on prisons increases uselessly, and so if we put prisoners to work on necessary projects and they weaken and die because they cannot cope, then, ... when we are told of the difficulties of paying prison costs, the reduction in numbers should be thought of as a helpful measure.[94]

Interestingly enough the way Meiji Japan treated its prisoners was inspired by Western European, in particular French and English, thinking about function and nature of punishment. The distinction between prisoners and free labourers could be quite fleeting: workers who replaced prisoners or worked jointly with them often were housed in the same dormitories under constant supervision by guards who saw to it that they worked and did not leave before their contract expired. Corporal punishments were long routine.

Labour conditions in mines in general were described as horrible. The situation of many miners strongly reminded of that of serfs.[95] The numbers involved were quite high. Among these miners there were a substantial number of women. Almost all of them worked in coal mines. In 1920, after the recession of 1919, there were almost 100,000 of them. From then onwards their number declined. In 1924, it was some 65,000.[96] The actual protection of former outcastes, of Koreans working in Japan, and of the Japanese and non-Japanese working in Japan's colonies was bad.[97]

Not only were there hardly any protective laws: there also were hardly any social security arrangements. As will be indicated on pages 171–2, the amount of money government budgets devoted to social transfers was small. All of this led to low incomes and relatively high profits. Japan, between the Meiji Restoration and World War Two, had a quite unequal distribution of income and wealth and a labour share of GDP that tended to decline. This concentration of income and wealth kept the purchasing power of large groups of the population at a low level, which also had negative consequences for the economy. The state was responsible for all this in the sense that it legally allowed a lot of coercion, repression and the payment of low wages and did not do much against

Table 57 Number of miners in Japan

1886	36,000
1900	131,000
1917	434,000
1940	>500,000

Totman, *Environmental history of Japan*, 223.
Totman here refers to all miners, not just those working in coal mining.

it in practice. A substantial amount of what several scholars like to call Japan's 'industrious' or 'labour-intensive' path to industrialization, though not *all* of it, was a matter of coercion and pressure, made possible or even endorsed by Japan's rulers, or simply necessary because of lack of alternatives.[98]

Again, it must be emphasized how 'normal' Japan was in this respect as a country that was successfully trying to 'catch up'. Such countries, without exception, knew major government interference and market 'distortion'. As a matter of fact, that has been the case in *all* countries where government has ever been interested in growth. Capitalist countries as they appear in mainstream economist textbooks actually *only* appear in such textbooks.

6

A Developmental State

The intention to develop

The state in Japan was not only sovereign, modern, centralized and integrated, strong and resourceful when it comes to its political, ideological, economic and military power and in principle in favour of capitalism; it also, as has already transpired, *wanted* to develop Japan. Japan's state in the period discussed undoubtedly was a developmental state in the sense that its rulers shared the goal of making the country rich, and its army strong.[1] I use the term 'developmental state' here in a broad general sense, not in Johnson's fairly confined definition.[2] I of course do not claim that governments in Japan over the entire period discussed here would have followed one – and only one – strictly defined course of policies.[3] Their policies, however, continued to be fairly consistent when it comes to their overall *goal* and *priority*, i.e. to modernize Japan's economy and make the country rich and strong. It of course is entirely legitimate to point out that what in the end counts is *results* and not *intentions*. But I would want to counter this claim by emphasizing that, strikingly enough, many if not most governments in underdeveloped states did not even have the *intention* to develop their country. I am therefore convinced that one should not belittle the relevance of the sheer fact that Japan's rulers were 'developmentalists'. David Henley in a recent book seems to agree when he claims that there is, 'a simple, radical explanation for the great divergence in development performance between Asia and Africa' and then refers to 'the absence in most parts of Africa, and the presence in Asia, of serious developmental intent on the part of national political leaders'.[4] Most governments of less developed countries, whether colonies, semi-colonies or 'free', were interested first and foremost – and often exclusively – in extracting resources on behalf of themselves, their followers and/or their motherlands. It would be highly naïve or rather simply false to suggest that Japan's rulers worked solely and selflessly to promote modernization. There are far too many examples of self-enrichment for that. But it would be simply wrong to deny that the will to modernize provided a strong drive behind their actions. 'Modernization', in whatever terms it was referred to (e.g. 'enlightenment' or 'civilization'), implied higher efficiency and efficacy, and thus a systematic analysis of production processes, organizations and institutions in order to 'improve' them. This drive to improvement and rationalization was present from the very beginning in 'the new Japan'. It became very explicit in the promotion of 'rationalization', 'industry policies' and 'scientific management', which started in the 1920s and behind which the government was the main driving force.[5] The importance of the state in providing supportive legislation for standardization in the broad sense of standardizing measures, weights, time and money has already been referred to. But government also played a leading role when it comes to industrial standardization in terms of the specification of quality levels, production methods or engineering standards.[6]

Again, a comparison with China is illuminating. There, the will to modernize and the group of modernizers were never strong enough during Qing rule to systematically overrule more conservative or simply 'extractive' opponents.[7] The so-called 'Self-Strengthening Movement' undoubtedly could boast several successes when it comes to modernizing military production and infrastructure, though most of these were provincially rather than nationally based. In the end, however, one has to conclude that the reformers failed to realize the goal they had set themselves, i.e. to be strong enough to ward off the country's foreign enemies and that this at least to a substantial part was due to the fact that they often lacked sufficient support and were themselves unwilling and/or unable to *radically* change Chinese society. In as far as they wanted modernization, that as a rule was confined to military and specific economic affairs but did not include broad social or political reforms.[8]

In the Ottoman Empire, the so-called Tanzimat Reforms (1839–1876) were wide ranging and the reformers not hesitant to try and implement radical changes. But the resistance they encountered was such that in the end their efforts had only partial success.[9] A comparison with the situation in Latin America but even with that in the Russian and Habsburg Empires, which both had their 'modernizing' movements, shows that, at least after 1877, the support for radical economic and military modernization in Japan was exceptionally high and far-ranging. Even when the initial drive at radical *Westernization*, that rightly or wrongly is often associated with 'the young' Yukichi Fukuzawa, had subsided, to make place for an emphasis on the uniqueness and in any case 'otherness' of Japan, the drive to create a wealthy country and a strong army and the willingness to subordinate other goals to this one persisted.

Whatever else it may have been, Japan's state in the period 1868–1937 certainly was a developmental state in the sense of a state that systematically wanted to 'develop' the country's wealth and power and that was willing to do what it takes to reach its goal. This is clearly reflected in the dominant styles of thinking about economic development. After some initial flirtations with *laissez-faire* ideas, most people in Japan who wrote about economics, in particular when they were in government or bureaucrats, preferred ideas like those of Friedrich List (1789–1846) or Henry Charles Carey (1793–1879) over those of Adam Smith (1723–1790) and other proponents of the free market. The initial deregulation at the very beginning of the Meiji Restoration was generally applauded as it destroyed the fetters of the *Ancien Regime*, but no important thinker about the economy and no important politician or bureaucrat ever believed that to develop Japan's economy it would suffice to simply leave things to the market.[10] Adam Smith's economic ideas were considered 'cosmopolitan', i.e. they would ignore differences between countries. They might be suited for advanced economies like that of Great Britain, but for a developing economy like Japan's, List's national system of political economy, with its emphasis on the active promotion of a country's productive powers – and all the protectionism and subsidizing that implied for the time being –

were considered far more appealing and adequate. David Landes, with good reason, describes the Japanese as 'the mercantilists of the nineteenth century', whereas Okubo Toshimici was generally known as 'Japan's Bismarck'.[11]

I could give numerous examples but I will confine myself to a couple of quotes by Yukichi Fukuzawa, who, which makes them even more telling, certainly wasn't the most 'nationalist' or 'mercantilist' among Japanese politicians and scholars during the Meiji period.

> If one looks at the trade between Japan and foreign countries, one sees that Western countries are the manufacturers and Japan is the grower. . . . In economy, the wealth of a nation depends far less on the surplus of natural produce than on the skill of human arts. For example, there is India, on the one hand, where land is fertile and yet people are poor, and there is Holland, on the other, where there is scarcely any natural produce and yet the people are rich. Therefore, in trade between a manufacturing country and a growing country, the former makes use of unlimited human power and the latter of the limited produce of land . . . This is exactly the case with the trade between Japan and foreign countries. We can only be at the losing side.
>
> When exports are small and imports are large in value, the balance between the two must be our debts. Our imports are mostly manufactured commodities and our exports are natural produce. For that reason, our nation will lose not only the advantages that accompany manufacturing industry but also the skill with which to produce manufactured commodities. This is undoubtedly a great barrier to the very source of wealth.
>
> Regarding foreign trade there is a theory that foreign commodities should be freely admitted into the country so that anything that is inexpensive might be bought and consumed. There is another theory that claims that, by importing manufactured commodities from abroad and exporting natural home produce, the nation cannot fail to lose the profit that would otherwise be gained by manufacturing the produce and will eventually lose the manufacturing art itself. . . . Therefore, it is asserted that these imports should be either restricted or heavily taxed. I, for one, agree with this latter opinion.[12]

Time and again Fukuzawa emphasized that free trade suits the developed countries and protection the less-developed ones. Perfectly in tune with classical mercantilism, he tended to look at economic competition between countries in terms of a zero-sum game. He even compared it to warfare: 'there are many foreigners who want to enrich themselves by keeping us poor and ignorant.' He did not hide that he considered war with those 'foreigners' quite likely: 'Postponing a military battle with foreigners to some future day, at the moment we merely want to fight a trade battle'.[13] In light of the previous quotes, it will come as much less of a surprise that Fukuzawa devoted his whole life to 'implanting the concept of *nation* in the minds of the people of the entire country'.[14]

The approach to economic affairs in general was eclectic and pragmatic. What mattered was what worked in practice and solved practical, concrete problems. In this context, it is not irrelevant that in the 1880s, industrializing Germany increasingly began to replace other foreign countries as a source of institutions, ideas and techniques. In references to the economic history of the West, its mercantilist past was mentioned far more often than 'the rise of the market'. When discussing the strength of the British economy, for example, the favourite reference was to the Navigation Acts. Most 'experts' in Japan were convinced that different times and different places require different economics and that Japan needed economic ideas that were good for Japan. Economic nationalism without any doubt was a central and invariant defining principle of Japan's political economy. As so often with nationalism, that of Japan too liked to revel in the past. But this nostalgia, however radical, was never a serious hindrance to economic innovation.[15] Japan's rulers after 1868 wanted to protect and promote the national economy as a matter of principle. There certainly were differences of opinion and changes in the policies chosen to reach that ultimate goal. Those policies at times were more and at times less successful. But development and modernization were never given up as ideals and continued to guide government's actions. That certainly had an impact.

Here again there existed continuity with the previous era. In Tokugawa Japan, the classic Confucianist and moralistic thinking about what we nowadays call 'economics' continued to be strong, but it did not have a monopoly. We see an increasing reflection on the role and activities of merchants and a more positive appreciation of that role, often, unsurprisingly, by merchants themselves.[16] There also emerged a more positive attitude towards work, saving and frugality. This more positive appreciation is not irrelevant. But one should not overlook the fact that in Japan the idea that commerce and private-wealth accumulation were respectable activities overall only found wider support in the eighteenth century, and even then, it was only fairly timidly. That is centuries after this occurred – more extensively and more explicitly – in parts of Europe. To suggest that Meiji Japan inherited a 'bourgeois' or 'mercantile' mentality from the Tokugawa era therefore seems exaggerated. There were discussions *of* and pleas *for* industriousness, which seduced Robert Bellah and David Landes to look for and in the last case simply write about 'a Japanese version of Weber's Protestant ethic'.[17] And there were many forms of mercantilist thinking and mercantilist policies, in particular from the late Tokugawa era onwards, that the architects of the new Japan could and did build upon. Of course, the motto of the Tokugawa 'developmentalists' was not 'civilization and enlightenment', nor the goal 'catching up with the West', but as already indicated earlier, in particular in certain domains there emerged a set of policies strongly reminiscent of mercantilist developmental policies of early modern and nineteenth-century Europe.[18]

A spending state

The state of post-Restoration Japan was not poor when it comes to resources and revenue and it was eager to develop the country. That, of course, does not necessarily imply its presence and activities would be positive for economic growth. Much depends on how it spent its money. To what extent can Japanese government spending have had a positive impact on Japan's economy?

When we look at government expenditures in Japan at the time, we have to distinguish between two broad categories: expenditures of the general account and expenditures of the special accounts. These two accounts in turn were divided into ordinary and extraordinary sections. These divisions were established in 1890. In the general accounts one finds financing of normal government activities. Special accounts deal with special government activities, formally classified in six categories, and the individual accounts of each ministry.[19] It is very important to realize that, as Table 58 shows, the special in a way became the normal, i.e. special account expenditures over time became larger than general account expenditures.

The general account essentially depended on tax revenue, while the special accounts had various other sources of funding.[20] Information about expenditures of the general account therefore tends to give a better idea of the development of tax income of the state. The following two tables give estimates of total government expenditure as a percentage of gross domestic product and gross national expenditure at current prices. Because the differences are not always minor, I decided to reproduce them both.

From 1937 onwards, government expenditure increased steeply. The figures in Tables 59 and 60 refer to current prices. In real terms the figures are also impressive. The average pre-World War Two growth rate of real government expenditure was 7 per cent, higher than the growth rate of real GNP (3.6 per cent) and of real national income (3.7 per cent). If we look at these growth rates on a per capita basis, the figures would

Table 58 General account expenditures and special account expenditures as percentages of total expenditure

	General	Special
1890	75.9	24.1
1900	65.4	34.6
1910	40.8	59.2
1920	42.0	58.0
1930	37.3	62.7
1940	37.3	62.7

Emi, *Government fiscal activity*, 85.

Table 59 Government expenditure as a percentage of GDP

1885–1899	12.6
1900–1906	20.3
1907–1919	13.4
1920–1931	17.2
1932–1938	23.1

Hentschel, *Wirtschaftsgeschichte des modernen Japans*. Volume I, 113. On the basis of information in Ohkawa, Shinohara and Meissner, *Patterns of Japanese economic development*, 251ff, 348ff and 370–372.

Table 60 Government expenditure as a percentage of gross domestic expenditure in average annual value

1875–1913	11.9
1914–1918	10.9
1919–1930	15.1
1931–1940	22.2

Based on Fukao and Settsu, 'Japan. Modern economic growth in Asia', **. Government expenditure is here taken to be the sum of government consumption, excluding military expenditure, military expenditure and public investment. The website *Our World in Data* gives figures for total government spending for Japan, including interest on government expenditures, as a percentage of GDP. According to the graph presented there, https://ourworldindata.org/public-spending, the figure for Japan would have been lower than 5 per cent during the entire period from 1880 to 1940. That must be a mistake.

be roughly 5.6 per cent; 2.4 per cent and 2.45 per cent.[21] The fact that from the year 1880 till 1910, government expenditure in real terms was steadily growing, again contradicts the popular thesis that the deflationary policies of the 1880s and the selling of government factories in that decade started a period of government 'withdrawal' from the economy.

How do these figures of Japanese government expenditures compare with those of Western economies? For Great Britain/the United Kingdom, government expenditure over the entire period from the 1830s to the first decade of the twentieth century on average was less than 10 per cent of GDP. That is quite similar to the percentage for France, at least till the 1870s, when the French percentage started to rise to on average some 15 per cent of GDP during the decades till the coming of World War One.[22] Again, it is hard to come up with figures for Germany. That became one *Reich* in 1871 but actually even then continued to consist of different polities that in many respects were autonomous. Aggregated expenditures for the entire German Reich for the period 1881 to 1913 have been estimated to have increased from 10.5 to 18 per cent of national income.[23]

During World War One, government expenditure in France, Germany and the United Kingdom of course went through the roof, to also stay quite high in its direct aftermath. The Great Depression, and then in particular after 1933, in Germany rearmament also had a strong impact on government expenditures. It therefore is hard to describe a clear trend. In France, in the beginning of the 1920s, total government expenditure was still over 30 per cent of GDP, to then decline steeply decline to little below 20 per cent and with the Great Depression again rise to 30 per cent. At the end of the 1930s it hovered around 25 per cent.[24] For Germany we only have 'meaningful' and reliable post-war data for total public expenditure from 1925. Till 1933 they amounted to at least a quarter and in a higher estimate even almost a third of GDP. From then onwards expenditure, unsurprisingly, increased steeply.[25] For the United Kingdom total public expenditure has been calculated at 20.5 of GDP for 1920, 23.6 per cent for 1924 and 26 per cent for 1937.[26]

It is fundamental though, to realize that for Japan *government* expenditure is not identical to *public expenditure*. Very important was the role of all sorts of public corporations that were owned by government but were independent when it comes to their management and financing and as such 'off budget'. They were responsible for a substantial part of total public spending but their spending did not count as government spending. One should think here of post offices, with their large saving accounts, public pension funds and insurance funds, government banks and various public finance corporations.[27] Public expenditure therefore was certainly higher than government expenditure, at times substantially higher. Kyoko Sheridan, from whom I took the information in Table 61, comes up with very high figures.

It of course is not inconsequential on what government spent its money. Table 62 gives a first broad categorization. Whereas initially, Japan's new rulers after Restoration had been quite lenient in their treatment of representatives of the old regime and in particular many of the last *daimyo* had been co-opted with generous severance packages, tight finances made government increasingly frugal. The conversion of stipends into bonds that was finalized in the 1870s and that for once and for all fixed government's obligations towards its 'personnel', was very disadvantageous for the 'former' samurai, in particular for the wealthier ones. Again, we do not need to go into detail. Suffice to say that when the government decided to completely eliminate their hereditary stipends, the overall reduction amounted to roughly 45 per cent.

Table 61 Total public expenditure as a percentage of GNP

1880	10.9
1890	21.1
1900	21.5
1910	46.9
1920	30.1
1930	40.3
1935	47.1

Sheridan, *Governing the Japanese economy*, 184.

Table 62 Composition of current expenditure in Japan, 1870–1940, by local and central government and by government enterprises, in percentages. Seven-year moving averages, apart from 1870. The figure for that year gives a five-year moving average

	Purchases Goods/Services	Military expenditure only	Transfers*	Capital formation
1870	53.1	26.6	29.5	17.4
1900	65.9	33.7	11.5	22.6
1920	65.4	39.2	7.7	26.9
1940	82.9	80.2	5.7	11.4

* including transfers to former samurai.

Minami, *Economic development*, 261.

Samurai with an annual stipend of fifteen *koku* or less lost some 2 per cent of their income. Samurai earning 250 *koku* annually lost some 40 per cent of their income. But those samurai in the highest bracket, of 7,000 *koku* and above, lost 75 per cent of their income or even more.[28] Tables 63 and 64 provide more details about expenditure.

Policies affecting industry were made at all levels, national and local. The figures in Table 64 show that the role of local government was substantial.[29] When we subtract military expenditure from the national account, the share of local government in national spending of course increases. If we also subtract payments connected to national debt, local government expenditure appears to be approximately equal to or in excess of that of central government.[30] Again, a comparison can put things in perspective. In Britain, in 1840, local expenditure amounted to 21.9 per cent of total government expenditure; in 1890 to 38.4 per cent and in 1910 to 47.9 per cent.[31] At the end of the 1930s, it again, after the shift during World War One, was almost half as high as expenditure of central government. To weigh the importance of local, i.e. in this case municipal budgets, as compared to central budgets for Germany, or rather Prussia and Württemberg, I had to

Table 63 The composition of Japan's gross domestic expenditure. Average annual values for each period in percentages

	Private consumption	Military expenditure	Government consumption	Private investment	Public investment
1875–1913	78.2	1.6	4.9	11.3	2.5
1914–1918	68.6	3.7	4.1	14.0	3.1
1919–1930	75.4	3.4	6.3	11.1	5.4
1931–1940	66.7	9.3	8.4	11.9	4.5

Fukao and Settsu, 'Japan. Modern economic growth in Asia', **. The total percentages are not equal to 100 as they have been corrected for net exports.

Table 64 Local government expenditure as a percentage of all central government expenditures (i.e. including central government's military expenditures and its expenditures related to government debt)

1880	30.7
1885	32.9
1890	35.2
1895	19.7
1900	27.8
1905	12.8
1910	19.0
1915	26.1
1920	23.8
1925	30.3
1930	30.4
1935	29.0
1940	16.5

Emi, *Government fiscal activity*, 97.

fall back on figures about tax revenue. Here the rate of local taxes to total tax revenue in the first decade of the twentieth century had reached a level of over 30 per cent; in Prussia, it was even over 40 per cent.[32] In the period 1913–1933, roughly half of the expenditures were by central government.[33] France, over the entire period 1815–1914, as one would expect, but also later on, seems to have been more 'centralized', in this respect. Local tax revenue here never amounted to more than a quarter of total tax revenue.[34]

Total public expenditure as a percentage of GDP in Japan was certainly high for a fairly poor country but overall not high as compared to that of wealthy countries. As Inkster wrote: 'The Meiji government was probably the most industrially active in the world at the time, but it was never a big spender.'[35] That means we have to dig somewhat deeper and indicate on what exactly government in Japan spent its money. When doing so, it is quite striking to what extent all sorts of government tasks apparently were delegated to local government and in particular how much of total expenditure for education was paid for by local government.[36] What is also notable is the importance of government purchase of goods and services, also comparatively speaking e.g. as compared to the situation in the United Kingdom.[37] Table 65 shows their value as a percentage of Japan's GNP.

Government, when placing orders, always gave preference to home-made goods, regardless of price. The purchase of goods and services by government as a percentage

Table 65 The purchase of goods and services by government as a percentage of GNP

1890	10
1900	15
1910	18
1920	17
1928	20
1933	20
1938	28

Emi, *Government fiscal activity*, 43. Emi in his text refers to purchase of government in its entirety. There is a somewhat different estimate by Stein who claims that in the mid-1930s government purchases amounted to 14–16 per cent of GDP. Stein, *Made in Japan*, 126–127.

Table 66 Transfers and subsidies, 1880–1940, in million yen

	Transfers	Subsidies
1880	18.8	0.8
1890	16.1	3.2
1900	27.5	10.6
1910	45.2	19.7
1920	160.9	6.0
1930	204.0	2.0
1940	516.0	77.0

Emi, *Government fiscal activity*, 73.

of total government expenditure always was much higher than that of transfers and subsidies. Over the period 1880 to 1940, goods and services on average accounted for more than three quarters of total government expenditure.[38]

Subsidies were quite small as compared to transfers. Transfer payments for Japan are defined as social insurance expenses, pensions, annuities, welfare expenses and interest on deficit covering bonds.[39] *Social* transfers, here defined as transfers for welfare, unemployment, pensions, health and housing subsidies, as a percentage of GDP, were almost negligible in Japan as compared to Western countries. In Table 67 I only give the figures for a couple of countries and refer the interested reader to the book by Peter Lindert from which I took these figures.

Kyoko Sheridan goes as far as to claim that what she refers to as the low ratio of government budgetary expenditure to GDP was mainly due to 'the low level of government payments to households for social security purposes'.[40] That may be exaggerated, but it is clear that the priority of Japan's government lay with investing in the economy and not with supporting the workers. Table 68 shows which sectors of the economy received subsidies.

Shipping and shipbuilding received around 75 per cent of all government subsidy payments in the period from 1897 to 1913.[41] That was not without effect. With the coming of World War One, Japan suddenly rose to third place after the USA and the United Kingdom when it comes to tonnage produced in shipbuilding. In 1938, only the USA produced more in tonnage than Japan.[42]

Table 67 Social transfers* as a percentage of GDP in Japan, France, Germany and the United Kingdom, 1880–1930

	1880	1890	1900	1910	1920	1930
Japan	0.05	0.11	0.17	0.18	0.18	0.21
France	0.46	0.54	0.57	0.81	0.64	1.05
Germany	0.50	0.53	0.59			4.82
United Kingdom	0.86	0.83	1.00	1.38	1.39	2.24

* Social transfers are defined as transfers for welfare, unemployment, pensions, health and housing subsidies.
Lindert, *Growing public*, 12–13.

Table 68 Subsidies to different industry groups in Japan, 1880–1940, in percentages

	Primary	Construction	Mining/ Manufacturing	Electricity/ Gas/Water	Transportation/ Communication
1880	0.2	71.3			12.8
1900	4.4	4.3		2.0	83.0
1920	21.2	26.5	14.1	2.8	31.3
1940	52.1	3.9	25.1	3.0	5.7

The table includes only subsidies in the general account budget. The figures are seven-year moving averages, apart from the figure for 1940, which refers to a five-year moving average.

Minami, *Economic development*, 263.

A specific category of government expenditure, a bone of contention in many analyses of Japan's growth, is military expenditure. Let us first discuss its size. There is little discussion that it was high. Koichi Emi describes it as 'the most important factor influencing the amount and direction of total government expenditures'.[43] I would agree with Henry Rosovsky and his comment that it is impossible to understand the process of Japanese industrialization if military demand for construction and equipment were arbitrarily eliminated. About one third of all public durable expenditures went into some form of armament. The procuring of military equipment became a branch of capital-intensive, heavy industry and had a major impact on the development of that quintessential industrial sector.[44]

In debates on the role of the state in Japan's economic development, those who are less positive about it almost without exception claim that the country's military expenditures – which they tend to consider as economically all but unproductive – would have been too high. The question, of course, is too high *as compared to what?* As a percentage of total GDP, the figure for military spending in Japan always was relatively minor: 4.5 per cent for the period 1875–1913; 3.7 per cent for the period 1914–1918; 3.4 per cent for the period 1919–1930 and 9.3 per cent for the period 1931–1940. That last, high percentage was mainly due to the explosion of spending since 1936. In 1931, military spending still 'only' accounted for 3 per cent of GDP, in 1936 for 4.7 per cent.[45]

One may always discuss what *too* high might in general mean. I will not do that here, as I think such a debate in absolute terms does not resolve much. What one can

Table 69 Ratio of total military expenditure by government to total government expenditure, in selected fiscal years, 1880–1940

1880	14.9
1890	17.6
1900	29.5
1910	14.2
1920	25.0
1930	9.9
1940	39.5

Emi, *Government fiscal activity*, 31.

Table 70 Defence expenditures as a percentage of total public spending, 1891–1935

	France	Germany	United Kingdom	Japan
1891	24.9	26.3	26.7	17.6 (1890)
1900	27.2	25.2	48.0	29.5
1913	28.8	26.6	29.9	14.2 (1910)
1925	21.4	4.4	12.5	17(average 1920/1930)
1935	20.5	24.8	12.6	25 (average 1930/1940)

Ferguson, *Cash nexus*, 47, for France, Germany and the United Kingdom, and Emi, *Government fiscal activity*, 31, for Japan.

meaningfully do, is try and determine whether Japan's military expenditures were high as compared to other countries.

If we would take a simple average of figures in Table 70, Japan's military expenditure as a percentage of government expenditure would be about 17 per cent. The average for France would be about 24 per cent; for Germany 19 per cent and for the United Kingdom 26 per cent. Of course, this is a primitive calculation. But I think it is good enough to show that, at least until 1935, Japan's government's military expenditures were not 'extra-ordinary'. When we look at military spending as a percentage of GDP, as presented in Table 71, Japan does seem to have been fairly militarized, the more so when we realize that it was much poorer than the countries we compare it with here. There are, however, some caveats.

Differences between years and, in particular, between years of war and years of peace were enormous, which makes it hard to come up with overall and informative averages. During World War One, average military spending as a percentage of government spending in France, Germany and the United Kingdom was no less than 77, 91 and 49 per cent. As a percentage of GDP in those same years it amounted to 43 per cent in France and 22 per cent in the United Kingdom.[46] In Japan World War One had barely any impact on military expenditures: military spending as a percentage of the country's GDP, at the time, as indicated, was only 3.7 per cent. But even looking at the figures in Table 71, it is far from obvious that industrializing Japan *from a comparative perspective* spent extraordinarily on military affairs that this expenditure – on average some 5 per cent of GDP – was so high that it can have been a serious brake on economic development.[47] In the decade the country had the highest military spending, the 1930s, it also happened to have the highest economic growth.

If we take the period of 1780 to 1850 as the period in which Great Britain took off, Japan's average expenditures on the military as a percentage of GDP in the period

Table 71 Military spending of the major powers 1870–1938, annual average for the indicated periods in percentage of GDP and of central (or federal government) gross expenditures

	1870–1913		1920–1938	
	% GDP	%CGE	% GDP	%CGE
Japan	5	32.2	5.7	20.1
France	3.7	25.9	4.3	22.4
Germany	2.6	54.1	3.3	23.8
UK	2.6	37.5	3.0	16.3

Eloranta and Harrison, 'War and disintegration', 138. For Japan see also the figures I gave on page 173. Eloranta and Harrison refer to the periods 1870–1913 and 1920–1938 as 'peacetime', which for the case of Japan of course is quite misleading, especially for the period 1870–1913 in which Japan was engaged in major wars with China and Russia. The figure for the period 1870–1913 also seems to be rather high as compared to the figure of 4.5 per cent for the period 1875–1913 that we mentioned on page 00. Not taking on board the period of World War I in which Japan did not participate and in which military spending exploded in France, Germany and the United Kingdom of course also distorts the results substantially. For figures with regard to that period see later in the text. For further information see Eloranta, 'Military spending patterns'. The figures about central or federal gross expenditure are somewhat 'misleading' to the extent that the relation of central to decentral expenditure could be quite different in the countries discussed. For other data, which again are very hard to trace to any source and to interpret, see Tanzi and Schuknecht, *Public spending*, 28.

discussed in this book, also were not exactly high. Over the entire period from the late seventeenth century till the 1820s, Great Britain was an 'exemplary' fiscal-military state. Defence spending reached 20 per cent of GDP during the War of Spanish Succession (1701–1714), the Seven Years War (1756–1763) and the Revolutionary Wars with France (1792–1802). During the Napoleonic Wars (1803–1815) it even rose to over 20 per cent. These were only the biggest of the many conflicts the British were engaged in during that period.[48]

I will not enter into the very abstract debate here on whether military spending is good or bad for growth in general or the somewhat more concrete but still undecidable debate whether it was good or bad for growth in Japan, a topic that could be and has been extensively discussed. I notice here that Japan was not a very exceptional case and therefore does not need very exceptional attention in this respect.

Or rather, an investing state

For a text dealing with the role of government in economic growth it is of fundamental importance to be able to determine how much of total capital formation was the result of governmental (military and non-military) expenditure. My claim would be that Japan's state played a fundamental role in the economic development of Japan between 1868 and 1937, as it was responsible for a very substantial amount of total investment in the economy. Total capital formation in Japan during that period was substantial, not just for the fairly poor country that Japan still was, but even as compared to the most developed countries. This is a fact of fundamental importance. On pages 33–4, I presented tables with estimates of the level of gross capital formation in Japan at the time and compared that level to the levels of other countries at the same period in time and with the level of Britain at the time of its take-off. The conclusion was that the level of fixed gross capital formation of industrializing Japan was high.

It now appears that of this high investment quite a substantial part was investment by government. Unequivocally determining levels of capital formation is anything but easy. It therefore is fortunate that most experts in the field do not seem to have any major disagreements here. Again, scholars are not in full agreement, which need not come as a surprise as problems of availability of data, measurement and definition are substantial. Nevertheless, here too I think there has emerged a rough consensus on orders of magnitude. Henry Rosovsky, who very intensively studied the subject, claims that government's share in gross domestic capital formation during the period 1887–1940, 'never averaged less than 40 per cent, and it was only very rarely that low'.[49] In a book written together with Kazushi Ohkawa, he and his co-author claim that government investment was larger than the private sector's until around 1915. They suggest it was not until 1917 that private investment in producer durables overtook the government's share.[50] David Flat thinks that government spending accounted for about 35 per cent of capital investment in Japan over the period 1885-1915.[51] Figures provided by Masaki Nakabayashi suggest that government investment over the period 1868 to 1914, amounted to at least some 40 per cent of all investment.[52] Takafusa Nakamura and Konosuke Odaka, who write about the inter-war period, claim that in that period 40 per cent of capital formation was accounted for by public investment.[53] Carl Mosk, who covers the period 1904–1930, comes up with very similar figures.[54] The following tables come from publications by Ryoshin Minami (Table 71) and Koichi Emi (Table 72). The periods discussed are different, as are the ways in which the data are presented and the exact way in which gross capital formation is defined and measured. That estimates clearly also are different but those differences do not 'fundamentally' impinge on the gist of my thesis.[55] Finally, Table 74 gives a quite detailed and specified analysis of private and public fixed capital in the period 1913–1939.

Actually, the impact of government on capital formation may have been even bigger than aggregate figures suggest. Kyoko Sheridan reminds us that the government, not just in her calculations, was responsible for between 28 and 40 per cent of total capital *formation*, but that this amounted to more than half of total capital *accumulation*, as government had a tendency to invest in longer-lasting infrastructure and that it, on top of that, did a lot to influence private investment.[56]

Table 72 Contribution of total government investment to total gross fixed capital formation, in seven-year moving averages at current prices in percentages

1890	17.5
1900	33.2
1910	35.1
1920	31.2
1930	45.3
1938	46.0

Minami, *Economic development*, 133. The number for 1938 is a five-year average.

Table 73 Government's share of gross domestic capital formation

1887–1896	31.7
1892–1901	46.7
1897–1906	51.6
1902–1911	50.2
1907–1916	49.5
1912–1921	42.3
1917–1926	43.7
1922–1931	47.1
1927–1936	48.4
1931–1940	48.3

Emi, *Government fiscal activity*, 55. Emi bases his calculations on Rosovsky, *Capital formation*, 2 and 9.

Table 74 Private and public gross capital formation in percentages of total real investment from 1913–1915 to 1937–1939, in 1934–1936 prices

	Private			Local Government	Central Government	
	Electricity	Railroads	Other		Non-military	Military
1913–15	5.8	6.9	38.5	19.3	15.8	13.7
1916–18	10.3	0.6	62.0	9.7	9.0	8.4
1919–21	13.5	2.0	42.8	9.1	11.1	21.5
1922–24	12.7	5.6	30.7	16.2	16.8	18.0
1925–27	25.6	3.8	21.8	19.0	16.9	12.9
1928–30	14.7	11.7	17.3	25.3	19.2	11.8
1931–33	10.8	3.0	30.2	23.0	15.8	17.3
1934–36	9.4	0.4	47.6	16.8	15.3	9.3
1937–39	10.2	0.2	48.4	6.6	4.9	29.1

Nakamura and Odaka, 'Inter-war period', 33. Investment increased in yearly averages from 607 million yen in 1913–1915 to 7,791 million yen in 1937–1939, in current prices. In yen of 1934–1936, the increase over the period was from 893 million yen to 6,746 million yen.

The share of government investment in gross domestic investment apparently was very substantial *and* did not decrease after the 1880s, as is often suggested under reference to the sale of government enterprises and the austerity policies of the Matsukata period in the 1880s. The figures given here refer to *total* government investment. If we confined ourselves to *industrial* investment, the share of government would be even higher. Not just the amount of investment is important, but also its timing. In that respect, it is interesting that Takafusa Nakamura and Konosuke Odaka see a clear inverse relation between the variation in private and public investments: at the end of the nineteenth century, but also in the 1930s.[57] Public expenditures were implemented during sloughs in private investment, which most likely pre-empted possible crowding out effects that might have occurred had the investment pattern been reversed. According to the authors this, however, was not a matter of conscious policy. They describe it as 'by coincidence'.[58]

Although one might discuss whether growth is *driven* by investment and innovation or whether increasing investment and innovation are *a sign* of growth, there is as far as I can see consensus that modern economic growth and increasing investment and, in a higher stage of development, modern economic growth and sustained innovation presuppose each other. In that respect, it is crucial that the share of government in total investment was not only substantial but also concentrated in sectors with major innovative spin-off and impact like transport, communication and heavy industry. Undeniably a lot of growth and development took place in the private sector and in small-scale and labour-intensive enterprises in the light industries sector. The almost exclusive emphasis in much of economic historical analysis on the modern and quickly modernizing sectors of Japan's economy and on the state as driving force behind industrial modernization has, with good reason, been abandoned whereas the role of more labour-intensive and private, often small-scale, traditional industries now with good reason has begun to figure much more prominently in the literature. But one should beware of erring in the opposite direction. To reach a level of income as became normal in the West since the end of the nineteenth century, industriousness and labour intensity simply do not suffice, especially not in small-scale settings. Such a level of income requires massive investment, a high level of material and institutional infrastructure and concentrated efforts to increase the level of knowledge-intensity and innovativeness of the economy. In an underdeveloped country like Japan in the period discussed in this book, those are impossible to realize without state support and coordination. That of course is quite a claim but I hope that the comments in this book about the functioning and activities of the state will sufficiently corroborate it.

Government in the West not only had a tendency to become bigger but also to incur large debts. Figure 6 gives the relevant information for Japan. Great Britain had been a seriously indebted country ever since the Glorious Revolution of 1688–1689. Between 1750 and 1850, its national debt as a percentage of GNP had never been lower than 100 per cent. Just after the Napoleonic Wars, it had even been over 250 per cent.[59] In France *public* debts as a percentage of GDP between the 1830s and the eve of World War One, had hovered between roughly 40 and 100 per cent, depending on the circumstances.[60]

Table 75 General government expenditure on public investment, 1870–1937, as percentage of GDP, for specific years

	Around 1870	1913	1920	1937
Japan	1.3	3.7	4.3	3.3
France	0.5	0.8	2.7	6.3
Germany	–	–	–	–
United Kingdom	0.7	2.1	1.7	4.1

Tanzi and Schuknecht, *Public spending*, 48. As so often in their book, it is not entirely clear what their categories refer to. It seems that general government here refers to all government.

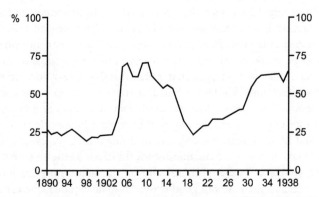

Figure 6 Japan's government debt as a percentage of nominal GDP 1890–1938.
Oguro, 'Seventy years after the defeat in World War II', Figure 1.

Table 76 Gross Public Debt 1870–1937, percentage of GDP

	Around 1870	1913	1920	1937
Japan	0.6	53.6	25.6	57.0
France	51.4	66.5	136.8	137.2
Germany	26.9	47.1		>40
United Kingdom	40.2	30.4	132.0	188.1

Tanzi and Schuknecht, *Public spending*, 65 and for Germany, for which the figures by Tanzi and Schuknecht strike me as improbable and that I could not trace to any concrete source, Spoerer, 'Öffentliche Finanzen', 106 who refers to total public debt.

For Germany, for obvious reasons it is only possible to come up with overall figures from the 1870s onwards. For Prussia, the debt ratio (= debts as a percentage of national product) was 14.2 per cent in 1872. It tended to increase from then on, but in 1913 it still was only 31.2 per cent. For the German Reich as a whole, it increased during this period from 0.4 per cent to 16.6 per cent, which does not mean that much as the government of the *Reich* had only circumscribed competences and a ditto budget.[61] Table 75 extends our comparison to the period after World War One.

After the 'devaluation' in 1931, a new line of policies was implemented that led to a sharp increase in government indebtedness. In the period 1932–1936, debt of central and local government together increased with 5.4 billion yen. Over the period 1937–1941, when Japan's economy became even more geared towards war, that increase was 30.9 billion yen.[62]

A comparison of expenditure with *non-borrowed* revenues, over the period 1892–1930, shows that there were twenty-six years when government on its *general* account had a budget deficit and thirteen in which it had a surplus.[63] Overspending will often have had 'Keynesian' effects.[64] The most famous example undoubtedly was the policy of Finance Minister Takahashi Korekiyo in the period 1931–1936. The core of his policy existed in keeping exchange and interest rates low and expenditures high.[65] His measures were so much in line with the ideas that Keynes was about to propagate that they in time earned him the name 'the Japanese Keynes'.[66] I will not enter into the debate to what exact extent this can be considered a result of his policies, but the fact is that Japan's economy during his mandate, when global capitalism went through a very severe crisis, had a period of high growth of total GDP and to a lesser extent of GDP per capita, even if many ordinary Japanese will not have noticed any improvement in their material situation. It seems highly unlikely that his policies would have been completely innocent to that. But already earlier on there had been examples of government spending that stimulated effective demand.

The 'original sin' of government debt in post-Restoration Japan was the fact that government with the Restoration took over all assets *and* liabilities of *daimyo* and samurai and in principle guaranteed them an income. That meant very high, in practice unsustainable costs. The debts that the new Meiji Government accumulated because of its historic obligations, amounted to in total 272 million yen, primarily for pension redemption. During the period 1868–1875, the costs of 'liquidating the old system' amounted to 50 per cent of total government expenditure. Its obligations to the ex-samurai, however, could fairly quickly be reduced or even fully redeemed, by carrots, sticks and luck, so that government could begin to work with a cleaner slate and lower fixed costs. But even so, as late as 1890 still some 20 per cent of total government expenditure took the form of income transfers.[67]

Tokugawa legacies?

To what extent was there continuity and change with regard to the Tokugawa era when it comes to expenditures and debts?[68] Tokugawa rulers, as we have seen, had large revenues and thus could in principle afford to have large expenditures. Tables 77–81 provide an overview of what we know about expenditures of the Shogunate for three different years in the Tokugawa era.

For an early modern government, the Shogunate, not only had a substantial revenue: The same goes for its expenditure. Striking in the spending of the Shogunate, but also of separate domains, are the large sums devoted to 'personnel'. A large number of retainers employed as warriors or officials, and their families, had to be provided for.

Table 77 Rice accounts of expenses in the shogunal finances for 1730 in *koku* of rice

Item	Kokudaka	Percentage
Stipends	151,264	25.5
Wages	161,077	27.1
Household expenses	11,277	1.9
Bureaus	12,933	2.2
Local officials	8,356	1.4
Sell off	203,323	34.2
Others	44,768	7.6
Total	592,998	100.0

Oguchi, 'Finances of the Tokugawa Shogunate', 194.

Table 78 Monetary accounts of expenses in the shogunal finances for 1730

Item	1000 *ryo*	Percentage
Stipends	297.3	40.7
Household expenses	60.4	8.3
Administrative costs	149.5	20.4
Reconstruction repair	68.5	9.4
Purchased rice	103.5	14.2
Aid	12.1	1.7
Loans	34.9	4.8
Others	5.2	0.7
Total	731.2	100

Oguchi, 'Finances of the Tokugawa Shogunate', 195.

Table 79 Rice accounts of expenses in the shogunal finances for 1844 in *koku* of rice

Item	Kokudaka	Percentage
Stipends	304,192	46.4
Wages	229,836	35.1
Household expenses	6,964	1.1
Bureaus	27,108	4.1
Local officials	41,233	6.3
Sell off	19,881	3.0
Others	26,125	4.0
Total	655,371	100.0

Oguchi, 'Finances of the Tokugawa Shogunate', 209.

Table 80 Monetary accounts of expenses in the shogunal finances, 1843–1844

	1000 *ryo* (percentage)			
Item	1843		1844	
Stipends /Salaries	405.0	(28.0)	428.3	(20.1)
Households	91.9	(6.4)	89.0	(4.2)
Bureaus	337.0	(23.3)	288.8	(13.6)
Reconstruction/Repair	73.0	(5.1)	68.0	(3.2)
Purchased rice	96.8	(6.7)	95.0	(4.5)
Aid	146.5	(10.1)	183.7	(8.6)
Loans	127.7	(8.8)	80.8	(3.8)
Nikko costs	101.0	(7.0)	2.0	(0.1)
Main keep reconstruction			836.1	(39.3)
Others	66.5	(4.6)	57.5	(2.7)
Total	1445.4	(100)	2129.1	(100)

Oguchi, 'Finances of the Tokugawa Shogunate', 210.

Table 81 Expenditure structure of the Tokugawa Shogunate in 1730, 1843 and 1844, general and special accounts

		millions of *ryo*		
		1730	1843	1844
General account	Salaries of public servants	279.3	405.0	428.3
	Expenses of Shogunate House	60.4	91.9	89.0
	Civil services	149.5	337.0	288.8
	Public works	68.5	73.0	68.0
	Subsidies	12.1	146.5	183.7
	Expenses for Nikko visit	0.0	101.0	2.0
	Restoration of the Edo Castle	0.0	0.0	836.1
	Other expenditures	5.2	66.5	57.5
	Subtotal	593.0	1,220.9	1,953.4
Special accounts	Government purchase of rice	103.5	96.8	95.0
	Government lending	34.9	127.7	80.8
	Subtotal	138.4	224.5	175.5
Total		731.4	1,445.4	2,129.2

Nakabayashi, 'Rise of a Japanese fiscal state', 386. Based on Oguchi, 'Finances of the Tokugawa Shogunate', 195 and 210.

Infrastructural spending in terms of investment, e.g. in public works, was not very prominent. That is, if one does not want to consider expenditures such as rebuilding Edo Castle as such and if one ignores corvee, the impact of which, as far as I can see, has never been 'calculated' for the entire country or the Shogun's lands. The visit to Nikko referred to in Table 81 is a visit to Toshogu Shrine, the final resting place of Tokugawa Ieyasu in Nikko, apparently quite an expensive undertaking. This does not mean that government, i.e. Shogunate and *daimyo* would not have been directly or indirectly involved in creating infrastructure. They certainly played their part in urban building, in the creating and maintaining of road networks, the improvement and extension of rivers, canals and irrigation works, and the creation of new paddy fields.[69]

As Figure 8 and Table 82 show, the Shogunate as a rule managed to make ends meet and often had a surplus on its balance. I found no information that the Shogunate would have borrowed any money or incurred any public debts, in any case not in the second half of its rule, apart from at the very end of its existence. Domainal governments in contrast tended to be heavily indebted.[70]

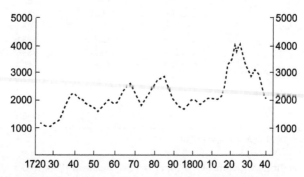

Figure 7 Annual expenditures of the Shogunate, 1720–1840, in 1000s of *ryo*.
Miyamoto, 'Prices and macroeconomic dynamics', 125.

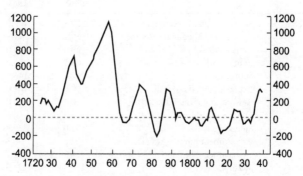

Figure 8 The budget balance of the Shogunate in moving five-year averages.
Miyamoto, 'Prices and macroeconomic dynamics', 125.

Table 82 Shogunate income and expenditure 1722–1844

Year or ten-year average	Produce (*koku*)		Money (*ryo*)	
	Income	Outgoings	Income	Outgoings
1722–1731	654,000	618,000	869,000	742,000
1742–1751	803,000	727,000	1,606,000	1,191,000
1793	488,000	452,000	1,115,000	1,066,000
1812–1821	566,000	574,000	2,153,000	2,228,000
1822–1832	522,000	539,000	3,057,000	3,029,000
1842	578,000	470,000	1,101,000	1,635,000
1844	609,000	657,000	4,580,000	3,970,000

Totman, *Politics in the Tokugawa Bakufu*, 288.

A state focusing on physical and institutional infrastructure

Modern economic growth requires an extensive and sophisticated material and institutional infrastructure. Industrializing Japan certainly was no exception to that rule. Carl Mosk even goes as far as to claim that its industrialization in the Meiji era was 'infrastructure driven' and that, which of course suits my approach very much, Japan's national and local governments played a crucial role in the creation of this infrastructure. Mosk emphasizes three aspects of investment in infrastructure: investment in physical infrastructure such as roads, electrical power grids and port facilities; investment meant to enhance human capital such as schools, public health measures and industrial research institutes, and investment in financial infrastructure.[71] But one could of course point at more examples. In the coming chapter I will try to do so.

As studies of the British Industrial Revolution have shown, the revolution in transport at the beginning of industrialization was not just striking and impressive *per se*, it also had a major impact on overall economic growth. Simon Ville in my view convincingly claims that changes in transport can be held responsible for almost one third of the total productivity growth in Britain during the period 1780–1860.[72] In 1851 the number of males working in transport in England and Wales was fifteen times as high as it had been in 1600. Only in mining, where the number was no less than almost fifty-seven times as high, was the increase bigger.[73] In industrializing Japan, things apparently were no different. According to William Lockwood: 'No single feature of Japan's industrial revolution was more striking than this factor of movement.'[74] Government heavily invested in transport (roads, rail and river improvement, docks, harbours, lighthouses and telegraph systems and, later, shipbuilding) and those investments indisputably reduced the costs of the movement of goods.[75] Apart from their strictly domestic effects, government policies in this respect also had the effect that they helped Japanese traders to get some grip on the country's foreign trade. In 1894, Japanese vessels carried only 7 per cent of the nation's exports and 8.7 per cent of its imports. Ten years later the figures were 40 and 34.4 per cent; in 1913, 51.9 and 46.6 per cent and in 1928, 72 and 63 per cent.[76] The Japanese tonnage of ships entering

Japanese ports increased substantially from 22 per cent in 1880 to 35 per cent in 1900. It too further increased afterwards.[77] In the beginning, (almost) all trade of Japan was handled by foreign middlemen who earned a lot of money in doing so. In 1880 only 11 per cent of overseas trade was done directly by Japanese; in 1890 19 per cent and in 1900 38 per cent. Government support, which included the provision of the financial infrastructure necessary for foreign trade on a substantial scale, played an important positive role here. By 1913, Japanese firms handled the bulk of overseas commerce. Japan became a major shipping nation in a couple of decades as shows in the numbers in Table 100 in appendix I. This change would not have been possible without an institutional innovation, or in any case a rather unique Japanese phenomenon that was a private but state-supported endeavour: the general trading companies that reduced risk, profited from all sorts of economies of scale and scope, and made efficient use of capital and skills.[78] It initially was quite problematic for Japanese firms to directly and on their own organize their exports. Such exports only amounted to 3.6 per cent of total exports in 1877. In 1887 that figure still was only 12.5 per cent. Direct imports were even lower, about one percentage point, for both years.[79] Over the years the general trading firms managed an increasing amount and an increasing share of Japan's foreign trade.

Shipping was a specific case and will therefore receive some extra attention.[80] World War One provided a golden opportunity for expansion. The merchant fleet almost doubled in size. The state gave subventions, built and purchased vessels, operated them itself, gave them away or leased them. It supported firms if they consolidated in big companies. Those then continued to get guarantees and subsidies. Since 1894, foreign shipping companies were barred from trade between principal Japanese ports. Since 1911, they were excluded form coastwise trade altogether, unless they were on a continuous voyage from a foreign country. Similar rulings were applied in the colonies. The Japanese had studied the rise of Great Britain to naval power and clearly understood the importance of the Navigation Acts. Operating subsidies in the form of postal contracts and navigation bounties were awarded annually to Japanese companies under laws enacted in 1896 and 1909. Navigation subsidies in shipping were restricted to ships of over a certain size, favouring newer and faster ships, especially when they were built in Japan. For big shipping companies with over 300,000 yen of capital government subsidies were the biggest source of net-earning. There were construction bounties for shipyards. According to Lockwood subsidies and other state encouragements were of fundamental importance: 'Without them the merchant marine could not possibly have doubled its tonnage every decade from 1880 to 1910, as it did.'[81] In the mid-1930s, a huge Japanese fleet carried almost all colonial trade and 70 per cent of all other foreign trade of Japan.[82] At that time Japan had acquired a strong competitive position with regard to Great Britain and the USA.

What in all probability stirred the imagination most was the development of Japan's railroad system and trains. In a recent paper on the importance of railroad transport for industrializing Japan, Junichi Yamasaki claims that 'railroad network construction was key to the modern economic growth in pre-First World War Japan'.[83] According to him, before the 1850s, the diffusion of Western technology was mostly blocked by the restrictive trade policy of the Tokugawa Shogunate. The new Meiji Government, more centralized than the Shogunate, was convinced that a strong and wealthy state needed a railway network. Constructing such a network required significant government spending, coordination, and a positive attitude towards Western technology. The provision of public goods such as transport – but also communication or the provision of energy – facilitated by the centralization and modernization of the government in 1868, certainly aided Japan's economic development.[84] I can only endorse his claims.

In the case of railways, government in principle opposed foreign ownership. It borrowed money to be able to start a railway system of its own that, however, till 1878 depended almost entirely on foreign engineers. One year later Japanese had fully replaced foreigners as locomotive engineers. When it comes to railroad machinery and equipment, it took till after 1900 before Japan could do without foreign supplies. In 1880, private entrepreneurs were allowed to run lines. In 1881, the first Japanese private firm did. In 1887, private lines were nearly double as long as state lines. The number of private firms increased quickly. In 1899, there were no fewer than forty-three of them. With the Railway Nationalization Act of 1906, a mixed system was created in which the state ran the trunk lines whereas local and commuter feeder transport was left to private enterprise. Private railroads from the early twentieth century clearly became the main transporter of passengers, whereas from 1907 onwards the bulk of freight was transported by the national railroads.[85]

The number of people working in the railway sector is impressive. In 1915 the state railways employed 115,000, people; in 1925 no fewer than 195,000. For the private railroads the figures are 30,000 and 65,000.[86] The growth in railroad track long was rather lethargic because of competition from sailing ships and steamships. With the exception of Kyoto, all major cities in Japan were near waterways.[87] It was not until 1912 that trains pulled ahead of boats for the conveyance of domestic freight.[88]

Development when it comes to roads initially also was less impressive, but that certainly does not mean it was less important.[89] The means of land transportation under early industrialization were not terribly different from what they were during the Tokugawa period.[90] The number of vehicles though and their motive power changed impressively. Under Tokugawa rule the use of horse-drawn wheeled vehicles had been prohibited and the role of animals in transport had been fairly marginal. Railways were non-existent, but on the other hand the government had – supported by several special payments and corvee labour by the population – taken care of the

Table 83 Length of operating railroads in kilometres

Year	National Railroads	Private Railroads	Total
1872	29.0		29.0
1882	274.9	(1883) 101.4	
1892	983.5	2,124.4	3,107.9
1902	2,071.5	4.843.1	6,914.6
1912	7,153.2	3,029.2	11,425.1
1922	11,274.6	5,965.3	17,239.9
1932	15,372.1	9,678,7	25,050.8
1942	18,581.4	8,999.8	27,501.2

Harada, 'Railroads' in: Yamamoto, *Technological innovation*, 57.

Table 84 The number of carts, motor vehicles, rickshaws, bicycles and motor-bicycles registered in Japan Proper, 1877–1937

	1877	1897	1917	1937
Horse carts	782	86,596	216,574	307,889
Oxcarts	1,786	16,430	35,362	111,146
Other goods-carts, human or animal drawn	158,240	1,225,923	1,936,406	1,519,334
Rickshaws	136,761	200,690	113,274	15,376
Bicycles			1,073,444	7,878,463
Motor vehicles			3,856	128,735

Lockwood, *Economic development*, 107. For figures for 1875 and 1903, see Rathgen, *Japaner und ihre wirtschaftliche Entwickelung*, 31.

organization of a network of roads, posthouses and provisioning centres for horses and bearers.[91] As compared to the situation in China roads were good.[92] Coastal and river transport by whatever means became more intense. For a general detailed overview, I refer to the literature.[93]

The development of means of communication is often overlooked in overviews of economic development. That is a mistake. In this sector too, there tended to be a central and often even monopolistic role for government. The Japanese authorities initiated a state-run postal service in 1871, and moved to a uniform rate regardless of distance in March 1873, the year in which a government monopoly over the carriage of post was instituted and private delivery services by couriers were made illegal.[94] The development of the Japanese postal service was extremely rapid. Already by the 1880s, it covered the nation almost as far as was practical. Government undertook systematic efforts to make postal services available for all Japanese in terms of geography, coverage and costs. Initially, transporting the mail was not easy because of a lack of trains and local postmasters. But these problems were overcome. Creating a national postal service was not only important in terms of intensifying communication, it also gave a further impulse to government policies of standardizing time, weights and measures, names of places and the development of maps.[95]

The post system retained a near monopoly on the transmission of virtually all non-urgent or strictly local information and the carrying of commodities. The number of items mailed per head of population between 1871 and 1938 grew from negligible, i.e. less than one, to some eighty at the end of the 1920s and the beginning of the 1930s, to then decline to sixty in 1937. That is an impressive growth although the number of letters per capita remained far lower than in the West.[96] In 1872, the new postal service carried 2.5 million items; in 1882 the number passed 100 million; in 1904, it was 1,000 million and in 1912 over 1,600 million.[97] Government clearly was convinced of the economic importance of the post service and took all sorts of measures to make it support the economy by facilitating cheap exchange of information and material for industry as well as agriculture. The postal service, for example, also delivered agricultural products, seeds and silkworm eggs. The available evidence suggests that the initial founding of the Japanese system was not a response to significant demand, except from the government itself. Sending newspapers was also part of the postal system. In 1877, it delivered over four million copies. By the end of the Meiji period, that number had increased to over 200 million annually. The postal money order system and the use of parcel post quickly boomed. With the underdevelopment of financial institutions sending money letters long remained popular. The parcel post system of 1892 was meant to give a boost to regional economies and small producers and businesses. The costs of sending things by mail became progressively lower. After the mid-1880s, the Postal Service moved from deficit to surplus. It came to be considered a service to the public as well as a revenue cow. Again, a comparison with the situation in China where the postal services developed much slower and with much less success throws an interesting light on the different structures and policies of the Japanese and the Chinese state.[98] In 1912, there were already 7,243 mail offices in Japan.[99] The number of people employed solely in post and telegraph offices, post offices, telephone exchange offices and postal money offices in 1907 amounted to over thirty-four thousand. If we include the number of carriers, telegraph and telephone workers and labourers, we would arrive at a total number of over seventy-four thousand.[100] In particular after World War One, the total number of mail items per person rose dramatically. But in this respect too, Japan at the end of the 1930s, still had the status of a developing country. When it comes to the extent of continuity with the Tokugawa period: there apparently was not much of it. The Tokugawa post system as a rule had struck Westerners as 'very primitive'.[101]

Government's role in telecommunication was also paramount. Here too central government operated as a monopolist. The number of telegrams, telephone calls and telephones increased quickly.[102] The national Japanese telephone system, it should be added, was entirely made by Japanese themselves. Telephone in 1900 had 20,000 subscribers; in 1915, the number had increased to 200,000; in 1940, it was a million.[103] What is striking, is that in Japan the development of a system of communications as well as of a railway network was already in a fairly advanced state *before* one can speak of substantial industrialization.

The development of mass media also promoted the exchange of information. Japan's new rulers began to publish an official government gazette in 1868. After a brief interruption from 1877 to 1883, when each ministry published its own newsletter, it appeared in the form of a daily publication containing news about official appointments, regulations and policies.[104] In the early 1880s, hundreds of newspaper companies printed more than sixty million copies. By 1890 circulation had increased to over 180 million copies.[105] The number of newspapers tripled between 1897 and 1911 when 236 papers were published in Tokyo and the provinces. The circulation of seven of the then existing dailies surpassed 100,000. Between 1905 and 1913, on average, annually some 27,000 book titles were published in Japan. Only Germany scored higher. In the USA only half so many titles were published. On top of that, during the same period of time, some 1500 to 2,000 magazines were produced. By 1923, the Osaka Asahi and the Osaka Mainichi, two dailies, were selling 800,000 and 920,000 copies daily. A year later, Japanese dailies had a circulation of 6.25 million.[106] One must of course be wary of assuming that more newspapers and a quickly increasing number of people with higher education working for the new mass media would mean more and better information. From the 1880s onwards newspapers turned increasingly towards sensationalism and patriotic agitation.[107] For some references to the newspaper tradition during the Tokugawa era, I refer to the literature.[108] Radio broadcasts were inaugurated in 1925. In 1929 there were 650,000 subscribing households; in 1936, 2.9 million.[109] Government leaders and business leaders greatly stimulated dissemination of information. It is on this foundation, that Christopher Howe claims that 'Japan was to become the most information-intensive society in the world'.[110]

By 1914, government had nationalized much of the railway network, managed all the main highways, and exercised direct control over post, telegraph and telephone systems. A centralized Ministry of Communications coordinated and managed transport and communications policies in what was deemed to be the national interest. There was not only massive government investment *in* but also and direct or indirect government subsidy *for* transportation (roads, railways, ports) and communication (telephone and telegraph). Japan's rulers saw to it that their country acquired a strong material infrastructure.

In this context, public utilities for the production of electricity, that became so important for Japan's economic development, deserve separate mention. The generating power of electricity utilities between 1905 and 1940 increased from thirty-nine thousand kWh to almost eight million kWh. These utilities often began in the form of a co-operation of the public and the private sector, of progressive government officials and pioneering engineers.[111] Demand for electricity did not just come from factories. Cities were also very important in this respect with their demand of energy for light and running machinery. City governments like that of Osaka were investors *in* and facilitators *of* private sector involvement in the creation of electrical power infrastructure. They also ran railroad companies. Building railroads and electrification overlapped.[112] The following figures give a good indication of how substantial government investment must have been: total gross capital stock of public works, railroads and electric utilities, in 1934–36 prices, increased from 804 million yen in 1880 to 2,348 million yen in 1900 and to 14,097 million yen in 1940.[113]

Considering the continued major importance of the agricultural sector, government spending on agriculture in any case before World War One may be considered low and clearly indicates that Japan's rulers were first and foremost interested in industrialization and strengthening the military. It, however, was not unimportant. It took the form of (help with) the spreading of knowledge, quality control, disease control, and other forms of support that need not necessarily cost much but did certainly make a difference. After World War One and in particular during the 1930s, government spent a lot of money supporting agriculture, in part in the form of simple money transfers or subsidies, but also in the form of investment in land improvement.[114]

Table 85 Investment in land improvement, in millions of yen

Early 1900s	20
1920	80
During the depression years	175

Francks, *Rural economic development*, 222.

According to Francks, government's share in this investment was 17 per cent in 1920, and 40 per cent in the late 1930s.[115]

Infrastructural investment and innovation were not confined to material infrastructure. Just as important, if not in some respects even more important, is the fact that Japan's new rulers instigated and implemented so much institutional innovation.[116] They did so in a process in which they, as in all their policies, selectively adopted and adapted examples from abroad which they then often liked to present as either actually already known to the Japanese for ages or as in principle 'universal'.[117] Table 86 gives an overview of the most important borrowings.

The impact of such 'institutional' and 'organizatorial' innovations on the functioning of the entire economy must have been enormous, and for me they are a major reason to think the state is of fundamental importance for economic development, although admittedly it would be hard if not impossible to measure their direct and indirect effects on efficiency and effectiveness and thus on GDP. In any case, I endorse the following quotes by Eleanor Westney (the first one) and Ian Inkster (the following two):

> in terms of development of organizations, the textile factories were not particularly important; their organization-sets were quite simple and their output did not directly stimulate the creation of new organizations. In contrast, the Meiji army epitomizes the strategic organization. Its complex organization-set, ranging from a universal school system to provide literate recruits to the industries that supplied its weapons and supplies, stimulated extensive organization-creation by the government in many sectors.[118]

> We may not divorce the telegraphs, railroads, roadways, ports and harbours, nor the schools, colleges, prisons and legal systems of the industrial drive (of the Meiji rulers P.V.) from the private entrepreneurship of the industrial revolution.[119]

Table 86 Major cases of organizational emulation in Japan

Source	Organization	Year initiated
Britain	Navy	1869
	Telegraph system	1869
	Postal system	1872
	Postal savings system	1875
France	Army	1869
	Primary school system	1872
	Judicial system	1872
	Tokyo police	1874
	Military police	1881
United States	National bank system (a)	1872
	Primary school system	1879
	Sapporo Agricultural College	1879
Germany	Army (a)	1878
Belgium	Bank of Japan	1882

a = Reorganization on a new model

Westney, *Imitation and innovation*, 13.

Furthermore, most of those historians who now minimise the role of government in Meiji industrialisation, restrict their analyses to rates of savings and capital accumulation and assume that the alternative to government action was a working market system. Such analyses seem to be predicated on the belief that the government *intruded* on an already established system for the production and distribution of goods, information and services, using modernised or westernised technologies and organisations. The same historians ignore social underpinnings of economic development and the economic impact of state action in the region of education, training, information dispersal, property rights, risk reduction and social control.[120]

I could also have quoted Carl Mosk, who claims that the most important policies developed by governments in Japan have not been those directly linked to industry but rather those involving investment in, and operation of infrastructure – financial, human capital-enhancing and physical – that have supported innovation and its diffusion in manufacturing.[121] But I do not think that is necessary. I am afraid that ignoring or even qualifying the importance of Japan's state for the economic development of the country in this respect is a matter of ideology and not of empirical scholarship.

When it comes to government investment in capital goods for production – i.e. not counting castle palaces and the like – the Tokugawa rulers overall do not seem to have been very engaged themselves *directly*, judging by their official expenditures, although they certainly did see to it that roads and rivers were maintained in a good condition via corvee services and encouraged the cultivation of new land, e.g. by all sorts of tax cuts. At the end of Tokugawa rule, productive investments of both the Shogunate and several domains in wharfs, factories and ships did increase. In that respect too, the last decades of Tokugawa rule can be seen as a 'preparation' for developments later on.[122] When it comes to *institutional* innovation, Tokugawa Japan had never been remarkable. In this respect, it overall certainly had been a conservative society.

An open *and* protective state

One very important contribution of the rulers of post-Restoration Japan to development and growth lay in the fact that they opened the country for the import of goods, capital, people, and ideas, while seeing to it that potential negative effects of those imports were minimized. Let us begin with the opening of the country for foreign goods – which of course initially was enforced rather than embraced – and the development of a new policy of actively promoting exports. This extension of the foreign market – that coincided with the extension of the domestic market thanks primarily to the country's unification and all the changes that went with it – after some serious initial disturbances and problems of adaptation in which certain regions 'gained' and others 'lost', certainly brought gains from trade.[123] How large these were, is a matter of debate: *not* that they existed. Especially for the period before the 1880s, when sufficient trustworthy data is lacking, the presented figures are estimates. Richard Huber, comparing the situation under autarky (1846–1853) with a period under free trade (1871–1879) comes up with an estimate that boils down to some 6–7 per cent of GNP.[124] Yasukichi Yasuba claims, on the basis of his estimates of Japan's terms of trade and its trade dependency, that Japan's gains from trade were 9.8 per cent of GNP in the period 1857 to 1875 and 9.5 per cent in the period 1875–95.[125] Daniel Bernhofen and John Brown, who made an estimate for the 1870s, think the direct addition due to trade to Japan's national income in that decade must have been 8 to 9 per cent.[126] David Flath, to give one last estimate, thinks that the figure for each year in the period 1885 to 1900 – the static gains of trade – will have been about 10–15 per cent of GDP.[127] It is evident that in principle a country can profit from opening its economy if at least it has something to offer on the international market. As Table 87 shows for the entire period under discussion in this book Japan's trade increased very fast. In the process, the balance of trade and the balance of payments did not evolve in parallel, with invisible trade at times having to compensate deficits in visible trade. However, even after three decades of open exchange, foreign trade per capita expressed in dollars still was comparatively tiny compared to major Western trade nations. The value of annual export per capita, for example, in 1897 for Japan amounted to 1.88$; for France to 18.43$; for Germany to 17.11$ and for the United Kingdom to 29.25$.[128] The overall increase of openness to trade is shown in the rising import and export and foreign trade ratios in Tables 87 and 88. The growth of trade is impressive in absolute terms, but much less so in relative terms. In that respect, I can only endorse Carl Mosk's comment that Japan's growth in the period discussed in this book was basically endogenous in the sense that it was largely shaped by domestic factors.[129]

Often, if not almost always, the opening up of an underdeveloped country to trade with more developed countries has quite *negative* effects for its manufacturing sector as existing manufacturing cannot compete with the more efficient foreign competitors. This was also the case in the long nineteenth century.[130] Japan's rulers considered opening the country to foreign trade a necessity in their effort to become a first-class nation and considered it a core ingredient of their policy of 'modernization'. But they knew they had to see to it that this opening up did not do damage to the country's vulnerable economy.

Table 87 Japan's balance of payments, 1890–1937, annual averages in millions of yen

	Exports	Imports	Merchandise balance	Current account balance	Long term capital	Basic balance
1890–1894	88	94	−6	−1	−1	−2
1895–1914	366	413	−47	−45	70	25
1915–1919	1,692	1,425	267	618	−347	271
1920–1931	2,118	2,513	−395	−190	−148	−338
1932–1936	2,779	2,857	−78	116	−335	−219

Howe, *Origins of Japanese trade supremacy*, 116.

Table 88 Foreign trade ratios of selected countries

Japan		Netherlands	
1878–1887	0.11	1900–1908	1.01
1898–1907	0.25	1929–1938	0.41
1928–1937	0.27		
France		**United States**	
1861–1870	0.31	1869–1878	0.14
1901–1910	0.33	1899–1908	0.12
1929–1938	0.24	1928–1938	0.08
United Kingdom			
1860, 1867, 1870	0.39		
1900–1909	0.41		
1930–1939	0.27		

Kuznets, *Six lectures on economic growth*, 101–103. The definition of foreign trade ratio used here is the sum of commodity exports and imports divided by the sum of national income and imports, all in current prices. This is the definition used by Rosovsky, in whose work I found the figures. See his *Capital formation*, 95, note 143. I added the Netherlands and the USA to show the ratios for a small and very open and a big and much more closed economy.

They were helped by the fact that, as indicated earlier, the period in which they set out to industrialize their country and turn it into a strong and modern country happened to be a period of unprecedented international free trade and free movement of people and ideas. Even though undeniably that openness, in particular considering the fact that Japan was *forced* to be open whereas the advanced Western economies could *afford* to be open, in certain respects provided a threat, the international setting of which Japan had become part with its opening in the 1850s, also offered opportunities. Everyone reading about the beginning industrialization of Japan can only be amazed about the ease with which the Japanese could borrow, adopt and adapt knowledge and technologies from abroad, very often even taught to them by foreigners.[131] Even when it comes to advanced military material and the expertise required to handle it, the Japanese could simply 'shop around' in the entire world. Which they certainly did.[132] In the decades before Japan's opening, Western economies had been more protectionist and they would again be, even more so, in the decade after 1929. At the time of the Great Depression of the 1930s, there was much more resistance to what now was considered the 'aggressive' economic expansion of Japan. What had mostly been regarded as industriousness and patriotism, was now increasingly considered 'unfair competition' and aggressive 'dumping'. Japan, which long had a low trade ratio anyhow, in any case does not seem to have become heavily and negatively dependent on global 'conjunctures'. It in this context is striking, for example, that it was already hit by a depression in 1927, when most of the world was still going through a boom, while having substantial economic growth from roughly 1932 onwards, when most of the world was going through a great depression.

On top of that, Japan could profit from the fact that countries that could have acted as serious competitors were hit by serious misfortune. China went through several severe crises in the second half of the nineteenth century. Those impacted negatively on its exports of silk and tea. As a colony, British India was not in a position to develop its own cotton industry. European silk production repeatedly suffered from the pebrine disease.[133] This created opportunities for Japanese producers. They grasped them with both hands, in particular when it comes to silk production. Silk exports increased at a very fast rate, not just in quantities but even more in terms of money, as the prices of silk, initially, thanks to the problems in Europe and China, rose quite steeply. Japan, moreover, had the luck that its potential competitors all were relatively poor and 'backward' countries. All this is of major importance: Silk production developed into Japan's biggest 'industry' with a fundamental role in the country's exports.[134] Later on, World War One proved an unmitigated disaster for the economies of many countries in the world. For Japan, that was not in in any significant sense involved, however, it gave an enormous boost to its economy and its status as a global player.[135] That, in a way, also was a 'lucky' circumstance.

This does not mean that all was well: Japan's trade balance was often negative and as such problematic. The situation, however, could have been much worse. Japan had the added good fortune that its terms of trade improved substantially in the fundamental first decades of its opening between the late 1850s and 1895.[136] That was in particular the case with raw silk (and for some time also eggs and cocoons), its main export product, the price of which, as indicated, increased very substantially. China, to again briefly refer to this other major East Asian economy, in that same period of time had the misfortune that the price it fetched on the international market for its main export products, tea, cotton and silk, decreased, whereas the price of opium, a product it massively imported, rose or at best fluctuated.[137]

One might add yet another lucky coincidence here: the fact that Japan *de facto* was on a silver standard since the beginning of Meiji rule till 1897. That happened to be a period in which silver tended to depreciate substantially. In any case, for exports and employment dependent on exports, this certainly had positive effects. For the Japanese economy, the falling value of silver had an effect similar to that of a 'protective tariff'. The effect was such that the Chambers of Commerce of Tokyo and Osaka in 1879 claimed that protective tariffs were unnecessary.[138] In 1897, Japan switched to a gold standard. This switch to a large extent was made possible thanks to the huge reparation payments by China after it had lost its war against Japan. Under the terms of the peace treaty at the end of the war in 1895, China had to pay an indemnity to the value of 200 million kuping taels. On top of that, it was convened that it would pay an equivalent of a further thirty million kuping taels for the retrocession by Japan to China of the southern portion of the Liaodong Peninsula. After intense negotiations, the Chinese government had to agree to pay the entire indemnity in London, using English currency. This meant it had to pay almost thirty-eight million pounds sterling that were directly convertible into gold.[139] In that way, Japan acquired a substantial gold-reserve to back its currency. From then on, being on the gold standard with its 'fixed' exchange rates made it easier to attract foreign loans or investment. Those were now less risky than under the silver standard under which Japan had a fluctuating, as a rule depreciating, currency. This meant that Japan could now more easily pay for the import of capital goods that it needed for its new, more capital-intense industries.[140] This is how Masayoshi Matsukata described the expectations in 1899:

> Since now that the capitalists of the gold standard countries have become assured that they will no longer be in constant danger of suffering unexpected losses from investments made in this country (i.e. Japan, P.V.) on account of the fluctuations in the price of silver, they seem to show a growing tendency to make such investments.[141]

It became easier for Japanese and the Japanese government to borrow abroad, and against lower interest rates.

The 'bad luck' of other countries was not the only 'fortunate coincidence' that spared Japan the havoc that many less developed countries suffered when they entered open competition with more developed manufacturing countries. The obvious way for such countries to protect their manufacturing sector against the negative impact of competition by industries in developed countries would be to set high import tariffs. But that strategy was not open to Japan as long as the unequal treaties applied. Government did come up with all sorts of measures to try and protect and support its own economy, but what in the end provided the best prop for domestic production was the continued preference of Japanese consumers for Japanese products.[142] The vast majority of the goods on which income – that overall rose – was spent, continued to be Japanese-style, traditional consumer goods. Japanese consumers continued to prefer Japanese products, not just when it came to rice, but also in case of soy sauce and sake, or the wood, ceramic, paper and lacquer goods, that constituted the furniture and fittings for Japanese-style housing, and very importantly, everyday clothing. The textiles' industry for many decades was the most important one in industrializing Japan. It did not lose its domestic market for 'traditional' silk and cotton cloth. The output of narrow-width Japanese-style cotton cloth, for example, even increased fourfold between 1885 and 1910. Narrow-width cloth for the home market, as a rule, was woven on handlooms or narrow power looms. As late as 1910, 87 per cent of all looms were still hand-powered and over half of them located in cottages. This means that this type of traditional production was also very important for employment. Even as late as the 1930s, there still were many of such looms for traditional production. Let me quote Penelope Francks:

> it soon became clear that the products of the new textile technology; mass-produced in the broad widths for which the machines were set up, were not suited to many uses within the Japanese clothing system, where quality, durability and distinctive design in narrow-width fabric were the keys to market success. Consequently, as the domestic textile market expanded, growing opportunities emerged for those who could produce fabrics that appealed to consumers, increasingly urban (or urban-influenced) and earning their incomes in new ways, but still for the most part dressed in Japanese style.[143]

It was stability in consumption patterns and lifestyles that kept traditional industries going. The fact that they still prevailed in the 1930s meant that the positive effects of the depreciation of the yen in 1931, were not erased by increasing costs of imports. The ordinary Japanese barely imported anything for their daily life. Depreciation thus barely changed their costs of living and therefore their bottom wage level. As late as 1955, about one half of total consumption expenditure was still on 'traditional' commodities.[144]

But Japan's trade successes of course were not all due to some form of luck. Government's trade policies also played their part. When it comes to influencing trade, the unequal treaties long set a quite low limit – not more than 5 per cent – to the tariffs Japan was allowed to charge on imports. Those treaties were only fully revoked in 1911. But tariff autonomy was established already in 1899 and tariffs from then on increased, initially fairly moderately and then with two general upward revisions in 1911 and 1926. Figure 9 gives an indication of their overall height.

Table 89 compares the level of import tariffs in Japan with those in four major developed countries and shows that it would be wrong to consider Japan a distinctly protectionist country. In any case when it comes to tariff rates, it actually behaved quite 'normal'.

In order to support certain of its industries and to minimize the import of finished, 'luxury' consumer goods, it did, however, become more protectionist. Rice production in the country itself became protected against imports from outside the realm. Policies with regard to rice imports from Korea and Taiwan, countries that were part of 'Greater

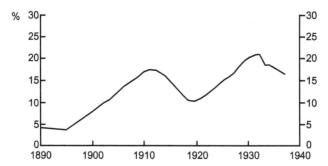

Figure 9 Tariff rates on taxable imports, 1890–1940, in seven-year moving averages.
Nakamura and Odaka, 'Inter-war period', 10.

Table 89 The average tariff on imported goods in Japan compared to several Western countries, 1875–1931

	Japan	France	Germany	UK	USA
1875	5	12.5–15	4–6	0	40–50
1913	19.8	20	13	0	44
1925	22.6	21	20	5	37
1931	23.8	30	21	n.a.	48

Amsden, *Rise of the 'rest'*, 45.

Japan', were more ambivalent and vacillating.[145] Government, moreover, as indicated before, had a policy of buying Japanese.

It would be naïve to suggest that protectionism always is a good thing. In case of the protection of Japanese infant industries during the period discussed in this book, I think, considering their growth and dynamism, it mostly was. Protecting rice production in Japan Proper from a strictly economic perspective does not seem to have been a very rational policy. But it is unclear, what in political terms might have been a realistic alternative. Overall, the policy of Japan's governments can best be described as an effort to mix openness, protectionism, emulation and import substitution. Those governments, in an effort that can be interpreted as yet another endeavour to acquire sovereignty, took successful efforts to bring international trade and banking – that at the time of 'the opening' of the country both depended almost entirely on foreigners – in Japanese hands as quickly and as completely as possible. They did so directly (by subsidizing shipbuilding and shipping, by selling ships to Japanese shipping lines cheaply and by creating port facilities) and indirectly (by their role in building roads, railroads and ports).

Whatever the exact size and characteristics of Japan's trade flows, Japan never found itself in the position of a dependent 'periphery' as defined in world-systems theory, economically, nor politically.[146] Its development was rather in the *opposite* direction. The country fairly quickly became the core region of its own empire, with all the positive *and* negative effects that usually implies for such a region. The extent to which Japan's economy depended on other countries was kept in check anyhow by the fact that its exports as well as imports continued to be diverse in character and were spread over many different countries.[147] Its trade with developed countries was different in nature from that with less-developed countries, with the contacts with the latter becoming increasingly important.[148] The competition among suppliers, mostly developed Western countries, moreover, gave the Japanese the opportunity to choose what suited their taste. All this of course had its impact but, again, it is important not to exaggerate: Japan's foreign trade was rather small as a percentage of GDP.

Nevertheless, time and again, and more than ever in the 1930s, people in Japan were expressing unease about the country's vulnerability because of its 'dangerous' dependency on imports and exports. There was a striking preoccupation with 'autarky'. The imperialist drive that was all but a constant, in particular in certain political and military circles, would be inexplicable without it. In particular in the 1930s a situation developed in which fears about 'dependency' may have been exaggerated, but considering the increasing political tensions and the very protectionist economic climate, certainly not just 'irrational'. The point of course is – and that has led to immense debates – *why* and *how* Japan had become more dependent on imports and exports and *why* Western powers had become increasingly reticent to allow Japan to build an empire and at the same time profit from a system of free trade as it had done *before* the 1930s. There can be no denying that Japan was imperialist and invested heavily in its empire (-building). But it would be hard to claim that it was *more* imperialist than France, German or the United Kingdom, or that it, as we already discussed, overall, as a percentage of its GDP, spent significantly more on its military.[149] Was the country's military aggression and colonial expansion just 'premature', as Freda

Utley puts it, i.e. was the country domestically not yet developed enough to do as Western capitalists tended to do?[150]

The Meiji Restoration also meant that in principle Japan would now be open to the inflow of foreign money. Actually, in this context too the policies of government overall were reticent and always cautious.

Japanese authorities were extremely wary of foreign capital and the effects of its penetration on the domestic economy during the Meiji era. Indeed, protectionists policies were enforced until the revision of the Commercial Law . . . in March 1899, and direct equity investment was not only discouraged, but also prohibited by law. Revision of the Commercial Law did, however, allow for foreign participation, particularly in the form of joint ventures.[151]

Government long tried to in principle avoid incurring foreign debt. In 1880, Iwakura Tomomi (1825–1883), the famous head of the Iwakura mission, rejected the suggestion to borrow fifty million yen in London by claiming: 'Rather than raise a foreign loan at the present time we would do better to sell Kyushu and Shikoku to a foreign country.'[152] According to Matsukata Masayoshi, at the time Japan's Minister of Finance, foreign debt would inevitably lead Japan to 'a disastrous scene that was presented by Turkey, Egypt and India'. In his view 'neither the government nor the people favoured foreign debts because, as the world's history shows, such obligations were liable to cause trouble politically between the two countries concerned.'[153] He feared foreign control over Japanese affairs if the country depended for capital on foreigners, who in his view, moreover, were superior in knowledge and financial power. References to the situation in countries that did become dependent on the West because of indebtedness were rife. Let me just add one more quote, this one by the very young Sakatani Yoshio (1863–1941), who would later serve as Japan's Minister of Finance and as Mayor of Tokyo, and in 1881 claimed that Japan should strive for independence, because, if it failed to repay one of its loans, it would have no alternative than to be like the 'Turks or Egyptians'.[154] Ironically to modern minds, proponents of using foreign capital cited India, Turkey and Egypt as examples of efficacious use of foreign investment.[155] They, however, failed to convince the government.

Strikingly enough no other than Ulysses Grant, President of the United States in the period 1869–1877, also advised Japan's rulers, in 1879, to avoid borrowing money from foreign nations.

There is nothing a nation should avoid as much as owing money abroad. . . . You are doubtless aware that some nations are very desirous to loan money to weaker nations whereby they might establish their supremacy and exercise undue influence over them. They lend money to gain political power. They are ever seeking the opportunity to loan. They would be glad, therefore, to see Japan and China, which are the only nations in Asia that are even partially free from foreign rule or dictation, at war with each other so that they might loan them on their own terms and dictate to them the internal policy which they should pursue.[156]

The Meiji Emperor was convinced that Grant was right in this claim and told Matsukata to avoid foreign lending at all costs.

Both the *Bakufu* and the Meiji government that superseded it, had been horrified by the opening of foreign banks in the port of Yokohama (which the *Bakufu* had chosen as the location for dealings with foreign merchants and the business of foreign exchange), regarding foreign banks as a threat to the government's grip on financial matters. The intrusion of foreign banking institutions had begun in 1863. Experiences with treacherous Western intermediaries instilled a deep distrust of openness and imperialist interference.[157] Ian Inkster, in my view with good reasons, argues that the decision to not depend on foreign capital in combination with the strategy of systematically employing foreign knowledge played a major role in determining the overall trajectory of Japan's economy throughout the Meiji period.[158] Japan till the 1890s basically financed its own industrialization. That is a feat of major importance.[159]

At the beginning of the Meiji period, government decided only twice to borrow relatively small amounts of money abroad, in 1869 and 1873. After that, it abstained from borrowing for more than two decades. Basically, it only started borrowing abroad again at the end of the nineteenth century. The sums borrowed were 'manageable' and borrowed on fairly good conditions. In total, the net inflow of capital was relatively high as compared to fixed domestic capital formation during the following three periods: from 1870 to the first half of the 1880s, during the period 1896–1898 and during the period 1905–1910, when it at times exceeded 40 per cent.[160] Issues of government bonds were especially important in times of emergency such as the Satsuma Rebellion, the Sino–Japanese War (52 per cent of the costs were met by the issue of securities) and the Russo–Japanese war (in this case 80 per cent of costs were met by government securities). But the country's central government didn't became heavily indebted abroad *before* World War One. During that war, Japan even turned into a creditor country.[161]

With the adoption of the gold standard and with the legal changes at the end of the nineteenth century, in principle foreign investment became less risky and one would expect it to increase. That indeed was the case. In total between then and World War Two, there was an inflow of some four billion yen in foreign capital into the country.[162] Simon Bytheway, who made an extensive study of the role of foreign capital in Japan between 1859 and 2011, claims that this inflow 'played a vital role in Japan's economic growth and development, particularly after Japan's adoption of the gold standard in 1897'.[163] I leave the decision to determine whether a specific sum of money would be 'vital' to an economy to the reader. I only want to point at the fact that Japan's Gross National Expenditure at market prices increased from roughly 2,400 million yen in 1900 to 31,000 million yen in 1939. In the light of these figures, the sum of 4,000 million yen in any case does not look very impressive.[164] That of course *a fortiori* goes for the amount of foreign direct investment, that was only a tiny fraction – 1.4 per cent – of foreign capital imported.[165]

Even though Bytheway is thus quite 'optimist' about the effects of foreign capital transfer for Japan's economic development in the period 1899–1939, he on the final page of the chapter in which he discusses it, very explicitly points out that Japan's government was always reluctant to give foreign investors free rein:

Throughout the history of foreign investment in Japan, the policies of the Japanese government were always critical to the success of foreign enterprises, and the Japanese government often took an interventionist stance – what has been described as the marginalization, or exclusion, of all non-Japanese enterprise in the Japanese economy – by limiting foreign investment in all but the strategically most important industries.[166]

On the other hand, it is clear that the country at times needed foreign money. What was crucial then was how to get it on good conditions. Japan's rulers correctly thought those conditions also depended on the international status of their country, not just in strictly financial and monetary terms but also in terms of its political and military

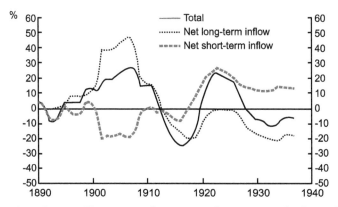

Figure 10 Contribution of foreign capital accounts to domestic gross fixed capital formation in seven-year moving averages. Capital accounts = capital imports minus capital exports.

Nakamura and Odaka, 'Inter-war period', 10.

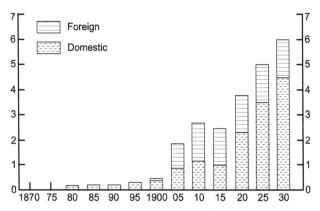

Figure 11 Central government bonds outstanding, in billion yen.

Japan Statistical Association, *Historical Statistics of Japan* (Tokyo 1988) 278–279.

strength. The deflationary policies of Matsukata, for example, were also a consequence of an effort to look financially trustworthy.[167] The decision to adopt the gold standard in 1897 too, was not just a strictly economic affair, as the following quote suggests:

> The civilisation of a country may be gauged in many ways and by many standards. But one of the surest ways of gauging it is by the standard of money. The passing from copper to silver marks one stage. The passing from silver to gold marks a more perfect stage in the progress of civilisation.[168]

'Great powers' with a stable, transparent financial system tended to be treated better than smaller ones that were financially 'volatile'. That 'rule' also applied to Japan. It's switch to the gold standard and then its victory over Russia in 1904–1905, meant cheaper loans and easier access to international finance.[169] After World War One, its position and status had greatly changed. Borrowing abroad became much more normal.

A clear break with the Tokugawa past

Here too, we will briefly discuss to what extent there was continuity between pre- and post- Restoration Japan. There is now a consensus that Tokugawa Japan, even during its period of *sakoku*, was not a fully closed country. It continued to trade with 'five entities', through 'four gateways', to put it in Kazui Tashiro's terms. In Nagasaki, private Chinese traders and traders of the Dutch East India Company were permitted to operate, indirectly but closely supervised by the *Bakufu*. Through the So *daimyo* of Tsushima, there were relations with Korea. Trade between Chinese and Japanese traders was also allowed on the Ryukyu Islands, a semi-independent kingdom for nearly all of the Edo period that was ruled by the Shimazu *daimyo* clan of Satsuma that also had a tribute relation with China. The Matsumae clan domain in southern Hokkaido (till 1869 usually called Ezo) traded with the Ainu people, and although not officially, also had exchanges with Russian traders.[170] I think though, that at least among economic historians, there is also a consensus that nevertheless, in particular from the end of the seventeenth century onwards, economic exchange with other countries was marginal and increasingly reduced to a small trickle. The Dutch–Japanese trade in Dejima Nagasaki, that has received so much attention, actually was tiny. In total 715 Dutch ships reached Japan in the period from 1621 to 1847.[171] According to Dutch historian Clé Lesger, at least about 4,000 ships entered the harbour of Amsterdam *annually* in the 1640s. In the peak years 1649 and 1650, the figure was above 5,000.[172] According to an estimate by Conrad Totman, the total value of foreign trade of Tokugawa Japan around 1700 would have been less than 1.5 per cent of its total domestic agricultural production.[173] All revisionism notwithstanding, I think one can only endorse the following conclusion by Hiroshi Shimbo and Akira Hasegawa:

> foreign imports to Nagasaki steadily declined, particularly in the eighteenth century. Moreover, trade with Korea via Tsushima dropped gradually from the end

of the seventeenth century. Since the Japanese economy itself was expanding, the relative importance of foreign trade was greatly reduced. By the early nineteenth century, conditions near to those of a closed economy had been established. Over the course of a hundred years Japan shifted, little by little, from an open to a closed economic system.[174]

Actually, a ban on building ocean going ships had been issued as part of the *sakoku* policies. It was only cancelled by the *Bakufu* three months after Perry's first visit in 1853. That ban had of course been bad for the development of shipbuilding and shipping. But it also left Tokugawa Japan without active trade networks, so that under Meiji rule long-distance overseas trade initially was almost entirely in the hands of foreigners.

The opening of Japan from the 1850s onwards, notwithstanding initial problems that in certain regions were quite substantial, has as a rule been considered as positive for the economic growth and development of the country. It will therefore not come as a surprise that many scholars considered the 'closure' of Japan under the Tokugawa a bad idea. Kazushi Ohkawa and Henry Rosovsky, to just give one example, wrote: 'A closed country meant a necessary condition of relative backwardness.'[175] We already referred to Fernand Braudel's claim that without long-distance trade no full-grown capitalism could develop in Japan. In his words: 'Unfortunately ... the necessary and crucial ingredient of a capitalist superstructure – foreign trade – was soon to be lost to Japan.'[176] He thinks that the bans and restrictions in force between 1638 and 1868, held back an economic development that once looked possible.[177]

There are, however, also more positive interpretations of the effects of the closed-country policies. Engelbrecht Kaempfer (1651–1716), the German physician and historian who spent many years in Japan and who was the first to talk about Tokugawa policies in terms of 'closing the country', concluded that on balance 'their country (the country of the Japanese P.V.) was never in a happier condition than it now is, governed by an arbitrary monarch, shut up, and kept from all commerce and communication with foreign nations'. He did so in an essay with the lengthy title 'An enquiry, whether it be conducive for the good of the Japanese Empire, to keep it shut up, as it is now and not to suffer its inhabitants to have any commerce with foreign nation, either at home or abroad', written in 1712.[178] Among modern scholars an adherent of dependency theory like Andre Gunder Frank, unsurprisingly, thought that Japan had managed to escape underdevelopment thanks to its 'closure'.[179] Some scholars go even further: Michio Morishima, for example, suggests that the *Bakufu* had, 'quite unconsciously', implemented a perfect protective trade policy'.[180] Mikiso Hane and Louis Perez in their overview of the pre-modern history of Japan, are also fairly positive about *sakoku*. According to them, it forced Japan 'to examine itself' and effectively 'channelled Japanese energies inwards'.[181] Penelope Francks, to give a final example, writes that Tokugawa's seclusion policy 'certainly acted to (and may have been adopted in part in order to) promote import substitution and restrict competition from overseas, in ways that ultimately favoured the rural economy'.[182] There certainly can have been positive effects of 'seclusion', but as such the policy of course had its limits, as, to argue along the lines of Adam Smith, the division of labour and thus the level of income that can be generated, is limited by the extent of the market.[183] It, moreover, could simply no longer be upheld against Western opposition. After Japan's opening, there clearly was much more foreign trade and more growth than during *sakoku*. In that respect, there was no continuity. One might construe a certain continuity though in the sense that after the country's opening a view persisted that 'dependency' on foreign countries was a necessary evil and that autarky, in the end, was preferable.

In this context, I can be extremely brief when it comes to discussing forms of continuity or discontinuity with the Tokugawa era. Apart from some minor exceptions in the Bakumatsu period (1853–1868), there were no examples of foreign investments or foreign loans during that era.

7

A State Promoting Knowledge
Transfer and Education

Seeking knowledge throughout the world

With the Meiji Restoration, Japan also became open in the sense that there now existed a central government that on a national level and over a broad range of topics set out to actively collect useful and reliable knowledge abroad. When it comes to collecting, diffusing and applying new knowledge, which is indispensable to sustain economic growth, the role of the state in post-Restoration Japan can hardly be exaggerated. As Inkster puts it, Japan's ruling classes were actively and selectively screening the world for the techniques and technicians they wanted, and *on their terms*.[1] They took article five of the Charter Oath of 1868 quite seriously. It read: 'Knowledge shall be sought throughout the world so as to strengthen the foundation of imperial rule.' For most of the Meiji era, government was the principal carrier and motor not just of institutional but also technical innovation in a process of creative searching, learning and adaptation.[2] It collected knowledge from abroad by sending out hundreds of people, many of them with high political positions, and by inviting hundreds of foreigners, the bulk of them 'experts'.

In this context, the Iwakura mission has become justly famous as it provides, as far as I know, an unprecedented example of a country that sends a substantial number of its rulers on a months-long mission to other continents to gather knowledge.[3] There had already been at least two official embassies to Europe and one to the USA before the Iwakura Mission and they had been well received. But they had been more modest. The Iwakura Mission was named after and headed by Iwakura Tomomi in the role of extraordinary and plenipotentiary ambassador, assisted by four vice-ambassadors, three of whom were also Ministers in the Japanese government. The historian Kume Kunitake (1939–1931), as private secretary to Iwakura Tomomi, wrote a log of the expedition that was published in 1878 in five volumes and provides a detailed account of Japanese observations in the United States and Europe. Also included in the mission were a number of administrators and scholars, totalling forty-eight people, and in addition to the mission staff, some fifty attendants and students, several of whom were left behind to complete their education in the foreign countries.[4]

The experts who were invited to come to Japan had a very broad range of expertise, ranging from textiles to mining, law or military affairs. Costs involved were high.

For the Ministry of Industry during the period 1870–1885, salaries for foreign experts amounted to on average 42 per cent of total expenditure.[5] Those salaries could be very high. Several foreign experts had a remuneration higher than Japan's Prime Minister.[6]

The foreign employees hired by government almost all came from advanced Western economies. In the period 1876–1895 their total number amounted to 3,916: 1,716 of them came from the United Kingdom, 625 from Germany, 583 from the USA and 360 from France.[7]

Table 91 provides information on Japanese who went abroad to 'seek knowledge'.

The number of students sent abroad by government in the period 1868–1881 was 415. During that same period of time, government sent 969 of its officials abroad. For the period 1882–1895, the numbers were 186 students and 2,814 officials.[8] Between 1868 and 1895, in total 125,000 Japanese went abroad to study and to engage in diplomacy and business.[9] It would be hard to overestimate the importance of borrowing,

Table 90 Foreign experts hired in Japan 1870–1900, figures in brackets are percentages hired by the public sector

	1870s	1880s	1890s	1870–1890
Science teaching	1,300	1,698	3,566	6,564
	(72.8)	(40.8)	(17.6)	(34.5)
Engineering	2,210	2,613	2,070	6,893
	(58.6)	(19.6)	(6.8)	(28.2)
Business	593	897	566	2,056
	(76.4)	(53.6)	(44.7)	(57.7)
Other	1,698	1,244	277	3,219
	(39.2)	(8)	(6.5)	(24.7)
Total	5,801	6,453	6,479	18,733
	(57.9)	(27.8)	(16)	(33.1)

Howe, *Origins of Japanese trade supremacy*, 258. Howe gives a total of 6,193 for all categories for the period 1870–1890. I guess that must be a mistake. For more details see Saito, 'Introduction of foreign technology'.

Table 91 Destinations of students and officials sent abroad and subjects studied, 1868–1895

	% of students	% of officials	Subjects studied	1881	1890
USA	24	7	Military	52	67
Britain	21	20	Language	15	0
Russia	4	4	Machinery/Ships	7	8
France	17	16	Law	5	2
Germany	18	2	Medicine	7	5
Total	601	3,783	Total	101	61

The 'military' category includes men sent either by ministries or by the army or the navy. It is important to point out that these students and officials also returned!

Howe, *Origins of Japanese trade supremacy*, 259.

imitating, adapting and improving 'foreign' knowledge, in the widest sense of the word for Japan's development. I here only refer to direct absorption of knowledge via persons but there also was an intense inflow of information via all sorts of publications.[10]

Government not only brought knowledge to Japan, it also saw to it that it was spread there. A well-known example is the so-called 'model factories'. By far the most famous or notorious example was the model factory for silk reeling in Tomioka. There, however, are more examples, like another silk reeling factory in Maebashi, but also factories for producing white tiles, cement, woollen web or sodium sulphate and bleaching powder.[11] We will later in the text briefly discuss to what extent these factories can be called an economic success as firms. I here only want to claim that they were quite helpful when it came to spreading knowledge as, for example, is evident in the case of the Tomioka factory, where about 5,000 people were trained during the period 1879–1893.[12] Under the heading of the spreading of knowledge by government one can also refer to the fairs and exhibitions that it – both central and local government – held; to the competitions it organized; to the information it spread and the training it gave; to the fact that it used successful farmers as teachers; to the fact that it organized quality control. Its role in this respect can be nicely illustrated in the hugely important silk industry. It took care of combatting diseases of silk worms and of trying to set up quality control when it comes to eggs as well as worms. It imported machinery and technology. It initiated a very successful policy focused on silkworm raising, improving the quality of silkworm eggs and spreading best practices. In 1911, it founded a national institute for improving the quality of silkworm eggs combined with a network of inspection stations, a schooling system and associations of producers.[13]

The importance of the state in quickly and systematically copying, adapting and spreading all sorts of knowledge and information also shows in the fact that public firms paid a lot of attention to skill formation and then passed over or 'lost' their personnel to the private sector. Sometimes government actually arranged such transfers. The big private firms often were closely connected to the state. Selling government enterprises to private entrepreneurs too could count as a form of promoting technology transfer. In the case of mining, the Meiji government took important steps to directly develop the industry itself. It first hired technical experts from Great Britain, the United States, France, and Germany and dispatched them to government-run mines, where they introduced advanced mining technology. Then, under the Mining Law of 1873, it nationalized all mineral resources. Although government allowed private enterprises to excavate mineral ores, mine development was placed off limits to foreign interests, a proscription that remained in effect for many years. These policies bore fruit, and up until the end of World War Two, copper and coal mining were among the mainstays of the Japanese economy. Overall, technological catch-up in Japan was extremely fast. The fact that we have focused here on the role of foreign knowledge and technology is not meant to suggest that these were simply borrowed and copied. Applying new knowledge and technology always implies adaptations. In the case of Japan, which we are discussing here, it must be emphasized that undoubtedly a lot of domestic ingenuity and dexterity was involved.[14]

Government clearly saw the artisanate as an impediment to modernization, and actively undermined its position as a corporate actor.[15] Government and government agencies virtually took the sole direction of the training of employees within the newly-founded factories, arsenals and offices. In the metalworking and engineering sectors, that were crucial to skill formation in industry, there was no relevant domestic knowledge available. Machinery as well as the skills to deal with it had to be imported. Throughout the entire Meiji era, these sectors happened to be dominated by public enterprises.[16] Those accounted for more workers than private firms throughout that entire period. In the 1880s, there was a certain take-off in the private sector, but a reversal of employment ratios only took place with World War One. In 1920, the employment in the private sector outweighed that in the public sector by a ratio of three to one.[17] As indicated, state enterprises were concentrated in certain capital-intensive, advanced sectors. In 1902, in the machinery industry, government factories had 83 per cent of the horsepower and 56 per cent of the workers.[18] By 1905, still more than two-thirds of the workforce employed in engineering works worked in the state sector.[19] For several decades, public firms that were large and modern required totally different skills from those required in traditional sectors. In 1877, engineering professor R.H. Smith claimed 'the only places where you can meet with labour-saving machinery is inside the new government workshops', adding 'and even there the most of it is destined to the manufacture of war materials'.[20] Spreading knowledge not only occurred in modern sectors of the economy. There are also many examples in agriculture where government for example used 'experienced farmers' who travelled the countryside to teach peasants how to improve their farming.

The success of technology transfer in Japan during take-off was striking in speed as well as in its broad outreach.[21] Technology transfers, especially from industrialized to non-industrialized nations, nearly always fail. They are not simply a matter of absorbing knowledge. They require willingness, adaptation and skills. Japan's rulers did play a major role in creating or at least facilitating them, but without a pre-existing openness to innovation and a reservoir of skills that enabled the workforce in all sectors of society to swiftly absorb new ideas and practices their work probably would have been to no avail. These again were a legacy of the Tokugawa legacy, or rather of the last decades of that era.[22]

But again, in knowledge transfer too, care was taken not to become *too* dependent on foreigners. Foreign experts never acquired a position of power and always only stayed as long as their hosts considered their presence absolutely necessary. Foreign knowledge was acquired from many different sources and places quite selectively, and then adapted and 'indigenized' in order to acquire or preserve autonomy. Government, moreover, separated knowledge imports from capital imports. Japan's rulers did not imitate/follow one specific model with all the potential risks involved but selectively borrowed what they considered useful from whatever country they thought had something to offer. When it came to building a navy, unsurprisingly, Great Britain functioned as example. For Japan's army that initially was France and then increasingly Germany. These two countries also provided inspiration for Japan's new state organization and laws. The country's central bank was set up in imitation of that of Belgium. In the field of education, one borrowed from France and later the USA. Even the Meiji Constitution was an idiosyncratic synthesis of elements borrowed from different countries.[23] But again: apart maybe from some over-enthusiastic modernizers in the very beginning, one did not just simply copy. There was a lot of adaptation, also some outright rejection and in several respects, but never technologically, a nationalistic backlash. It was clearly not the intention to fully Westernize and one did not have to in order to create a strong army and a rich country. Several core elements of the Western way of living and thinking like Christianity or individualism never found a welcoming reception.

Tokugawa legacies?

In the context of knowledge transfer and adaptation, the Meiji Restoration marked a clear break with the normal state of affairs during the Tokugawa era, at least until its last decades when the country, or rather several parts of it, became quite curious about Western knowledge and quite anxious to actually acquire it. Overall, the revisionist attempts to claim that also with respect to foreign knowledge, Tokugawa Japan would not have been a closed country – again with the clear exception of its final decades – to me aren't very convincing.[24] Revisionists as a rule refer to so-called 'rangaku' (Dutch learning) to support their claim that Tokugawa Japan was not closed to foreign knowledge. But that knowledge in my view, when it comes to economic development, in the end, was fairly irrelevant. Its actual importance tends to be exaggerated. To speak, as Terence Jackson does, about a 'Tokugawa information revolution' is voiding the word 'revolution' of any concrete meaning.[25] The fact that Tokugawa Yoshimune lifted the ban on the importation of foreign books that had been imposed at the time of adoption of the national seclusion policy will certainly have made a difference. As long as they did not deal with Christianity, books from China and the West could henceforth (from 1725) be brought into Japan through Nagasaki.

The effort to keep the country closed to foreign ideas was successful when it comes to containing and eradicating Christianity.[26] Christian preaching had made some inroads. Between 1563 and 1620, eighty-two *daimyo* were baptized, along with at least some 300,000 and maybe even some 700,000 Japanese.[27] Oda Nobunaga (1534–1582), the first of Japan's great unifiers in the sixteenth century, had actually encouraged foreign missionaries, probably because he wanted to keep in check the militant Buddhist sects that opposed him. Toyotomi Hideyoshi, who as indicated was in favour of stimulating trade contacts with the Europeans, increasingly came to view the missionary activities of the Portuguese and Spaniards in the wake of their trading as dangerous and subversive to his rule and to Japanese society. In 1587, he issued a decree ordering all foreign missionaries to leave the country. Although he did not actually enforce the decree, and the missionaries before long resumed their activities, his act foreshadowed a growing animosity on the part of Japan's leaders towards Christianity. In 1597, Toyotomi Hideyoshi proclaimed a more serious banning edict and executed twenty-six Christians. Intent on bringing Japan under complete control, the succeeding Tokugawa Shogunate further hardened the country's anti-Christian stance, accusing the religion of obstructing the authorities, anti-social behaviour and intolerance towards the established religions. In 1614, Christian missionary activities were banned. In the late 1630s, there was a rebellion on the Shimabara Peninsula that involved many Christians. Shogun Tokugawa Iemitsu mobilized more than 100,000 men to fight the rebels. Thousands of them were executed and a full ban on Christianity became strictly enforced.

Again, at the very end of the Tokugawa era there unmistakably already emerged important signs of an opening up in the form of increased contacts with e.g. the

Netherlands, France, Britain and the United States.[28] Pierre-François Souyri claims that before 1868 already some 300 Japanese had travelled to the West.[29] It of course is telling that a scholar should bring up this figure in support of a claim that a country of more than thirty million inhabitants was opening up.

Creating human capital: education, and some comments on health

Economic growth in general and modern economic growth in particular requires an increase in human capital. Japan's rulers were well aware of that. In 1871, a Ministry of Education was founded. Elementary school education was 'nationalized' and made compulsory, but not free, for four years from 1872 onwards. The initial idea had been to initiate a system in which pupils could take education over a period of eight years. But that turned out to be unrealistic. The intention then became to introduce four years of compulsory education. The objections against that rule were so intense that government soon had to decide to reduce them to sixteen months equally spread over four years. In 1885, it was decreed that three full years of education would be compulsory. One year later, there was a decree that raised the period to four, coming into effect in 1890. This means that the famous four years of compulsory education that were announced in 1872 took many years to materialize. In 1900, four years of compulsory education became free. But then already many pupils were taking five grades. From 1900, an extension of compulsory education from four to six years became in principle effective. It, however, was only successfully enforced in 1918.[30] The state took care that this basic education spread evenly over the entire country.

Table 92 Public expenditures on education as a percentage of national income

1885	1.8
1890	1.3
1895	1.2
1898	1.3
1903	2.3
1908	2.5
1915	2.1
1920	2.5
1925	3.4
1930	4.0
1935	3.3
1940	2.1

Kawada and Levine, *Human resources*, 82. As always there are also other figures. According to Howe, *Origins of Japanese trade supremacy*, 254, by 1935 government expenditure on education would have accounted for 2.7 per cent of GDP.

The relevant figures on expenditures can be found in Table 92. As indicated, the real extent of government expenditure on education can only be known by taking on board the amount spent by local government. During the fundamental period 1868–1912, central government devoted only between 1.5 and 2.5 per cent of its total expenditure to education but local government devoted between 24 and 34.6 per cent.[31]

These figures – for all the doubts one can always have about their exact meaning in terms of coverage and reliability – nevertheless in my view show beyond reasonable doubt that Japan, especially considering its poverty, invested substantially in education (although not necessarily in ordinary teachers). Their salaries were often notoriously low. Again, an international comparison, all complications notwithstanding, might be helpful. Japan's public expenditures on education as a share of GDP as compared to France, Germany and the United Kingdom, in the period 1870 to 1937, as far as we have trustworthy and comparable data, seem to have been quite high.[32]

From the outset, government itself focused on the universal, modern-type primary education that it had made compulsory. For decades, elementary education continued to absorb three-fourths of all public expenditures on education while secondary education, including its vocational training component, received barely 4–5 per cent. Even as late as the 1920s, elementary education still accounted for two-thirds of the total and by 1940 for more than half.[33] Without this broad educational base, it is unlikely that Japan would have succeeded in developing human talents for operating modern industries at an accelerating pace. Universal basic education would be needed whatever directions industrialization would take and in that sense, it was a safe and good investment, even if one may have one's doubts about the emphasis on nationalism. There was some private schooling. Its expenditures amounted to 2 per cent of total educational expenditures in 1902 and to 14 per cent in 1940.

Because of the crucial importance of human capital for modern economic growth in advanced economies many scholars have tended to exaggerate its importance for countries in their initial stages of industrialization. In that context it is telling that David Mitch claims that in Britain, as late as 1841, only 5 per cent of working men and 2 per cent of working women had a job that required them to really be 'literate'.[34] In those initial stages, overall there was even was some noticeable *deskilling* of the labour force, as machinery and factory discipline made many jobs simpler rather than more complicated.[35] There are many examples of such deskilling also during Japan's industrialization.[36] But with the passing of time the importance of formal education increased and from the very beginning at least certain key persons, who participated in the new mechanized production processes and in major factories, had to be skilled and trained and increasingly also formally schooled.

In discussing human capital some comments on general health are in order. In Japan, government's commitment to public health was exceptionally developed from the 1870s onwards. Considering how poor the country still was, life expectancy was quite high at the beginning of the twentieth century. It certainly helped that the country at the time was still predominantly agricultural and that industry was not yet very widespread. But government policies also played their part. Government, after the Meiji Restoration, gave its full support to the study, importation and adaptation of European medical and public health techniques, particularly vaccination and large-scale quarantine. In doing so it managed to prevent the spread of port-introduced diseases such as cholera and plague. It laid heavy emphasis on prevention and on cleanliness: the Japanese equivalent of 'spring cleaning' was required by law. Particularly striking were developments in military medicine. Louis Livingstone Seaman, an American officer, was convinced that by 1905 the Japanese practised the most advanced principles of military medicine in the world.[37] When it comes to managing the kind of endemic infectious diseases that Japan's quickly industrializing and urbanizing society was confronted with during the first four decades of the twentieth century, Japan's government clearly was less successful. According to Johansson and Mosk, from whom I take the information in this paragraph, the failure to further substantially raise life expectancy from the second decade of the century onwards would be due to the government's imperial ambitions, which made increasing military strength its priority. They claim that Japan was simply too poor to invest more in public health while simultaneously investing heavily in a major military build-up.[38]

The state in industrializing Japan did not do much to create a systematic vocation-oriented schooling beyond the elementary level. That was very probably a rational decision as it simply did not have the money to do everything at once and as there were good reasons to expect industry could not only take care of this itself but would do a better job. Therefore, vocational training for modern industry to a large extent was left to private initiative. When it comes to higher-level education, the efforts of government concentrated on creating an elite of highly motivated and deeply committed but also highly educated and well-trained policy makers, administrators, managers and technical personnel. Of course, not everything the state touched turned into gold and there were many successful private initiatives but as compared to what happened in other under-developed countries the efforts of Japan's government to improve education were impressive and successful.

Discussion about whether to teach skills or morals was always rife. At the local level, many people involved tended to emphasize practical skills; at the national level morality was considered of fundamental importance, in any case in general education. When it comes to higher education, practical subjects and approaches were preferred, because at that level of education, so at least many feared, there was a danger of over-education and of creating too many over-ambitious idlers who, on top of that, might have 'unhealthy thoughts'.[39] I will not go into detail here and only present some basic but impressive data and refer the reader for further information to the literature.[40]

In 1872 government established a three-tiered structure of primary schools, middle schools and universities. As compared to the most advanced Western European countries, its primary education did not 'score' badly. As compared to countries in the European periphery and certainly as compared to countries outside Europe, it scored very well.

Looking at the usual indicators, government policies were clearly successful. One may, of course, be sceptical about some of the actual results, as the following examples illustrate. In 1891 more than 60 per cent of all conscripts for the army were either completely or functionally illiterate. Only 14 per cent had graduated from a primary or higher school. In 1893, one third of the recruits in Osaka were illiterate while the majority of them could not distinguish left from right. But here too there definitely was

Table 93 Educational indicators, 1900–1940. School attainment levels of the population of working age (15–64)

	1900	1920	1940
% completed primary education	14.3	44.8	62.9
% completed post-primary education	0.2	2.9	4.5
% undertaken supplementary continuation of education	0	4.5	10.9
Absolute number of students in secondary and higher education specialising in science and education	3,021	48,089	148,515

Howe, *Origins of Japanese trade supremacy*, 255.

Table 94 Elementary school enrolment, share of six to twelve year olds, 1875–1920

Year	Male	Female
1875	50.8%	18.7%
1880	58.7%	21.9%
1885	65.8%	32.1%
1890	65.1%	31.1%
1895	76.7%	43.9%
1900	90.4%	71.7%
1905	97.7%	93.3%
1910	98.8%	97.4%
1915	98.9%	98.0%
1920	99.2%	98.8%

Alexander, 'Japan's economy in the twentieth century', Table 1. http://www.jei.org/Restricted/JEIR00/0003f.html

Table 95 Children enrolled in primary schools, per 1,000 children aged 5–14

	1900	1930	
Japan	507	609	
France	859	803	public and private
Germany	732	699	public only
UK	720	745	mostly public
Belgium	592	701	public and private
Denmark	717	674	
Italy	382	594	public and private
Netherlands	663	780	public and private
Portugal	194	300	only public
Russia	149		
Spain	475	717	
Sweden	689	779	public
Switzerland	727	701	only public
Outside Europe:			
British India	47	113	
Egypt	7	178	

Lindert, *Growing public*, 91–93. A blank space opposite a country name means that the source used does not indicate whether it includes private schools.

progress: in 1906, there was hardly anyone who was unable to write his name.[41] In 1900, actual illiteracy in the army as a whole had decreased to less than 17 per cent, though functional illiteracy still was more than 30 per cent.[42] In 1904, according to another source, one-third of the new recruits for the army still could not or hardly read and write. In 1907, the situation had improved: now it was 'only' one-fifth. By way of comparison: in 1909 in Germany of army recruits only 0.02 per cent and of navy recruits only 0.03 per cent were analphabetic. For France, these percentages were 7.1 per cent and 15.3 per cent.[43] In the 1920s, the illiteracy rate in Japan had become negligible, although as late as 1930 still almost 40 per cent of conscripts had not graduated from primary school.[44] In this respect too Freda Utley was quite underwhelmed. She claimed that in 1931 there were still about six million illiterates in Japan. Moreover, according to her, many of those who were set down as being literate only knew a few signs.[45]

The bulk of vocational training took place in factories.[46] The same goes for the training of managers.[47] It would be mistaken, however, to suggest that government neglected other forms of education than basic compulsory schooling. In that basic schooling and in normal schools, physical fitness, citizenship and character building continued to be important. But the fast economic and social changes made the extension of more Westernized curricula, especially from the 1880s onwards, unavoidable. Government also offered technical and vocational education, and in particular dedicated huge efforts to the training of teachers and future government officials (civilian and military). As a rule, around 2–3 per cent of central government expenditure went to higher education and training, less in times of general economic contraction, more when the economy expanded.

It would digress to try and discuss or even enumerate the most important initiatives here. The most famous of them was the University of Tokyo, but they also comprised agricultural and commercial schools, specific technical institutes and mechanical schools. Suffice to give some statistics. By the beginning of the twentieth century, some 1,600 institutions provided specialized technical instruction of some type, including over 1,000 agricultural technology courses attached to lower and normal schools as well as agricultural colleges. Around 100,000 students were in attendance. Between 1880 and 1940, there was a fortyfold increase in the number of students enrolled in higher scientific and technical education and an eightyfold increase in the number of students in further technical and commercial education. Between 1870 and 1920, the number of college and university students increased from almost negligible to 50,000 and the number of teachers (from *Kindergarten* through high school) from a little over 40,000 to more than 200,000.[48] When it comes to technical education, I refer to Ian Inkster, from whom I have taken most of the information in this paragraph and who claims: 'Attention to technical education in Meiji Japan was greater than could be found in most other industrializing nations.'[49] In 1877, a leading British engineer, Sir Norman Lockyer, observed that the Tokyo College of Engineering was becoming the largest institution of its kind in the world.[50] Henry Dyer, also an engineer, in this case from Scotland, with first-hand and extended knowledge of the situation in Japan, who described Japan in 1904 as 'a country ... which is now leading the way not only in education but also in many of the arts of peace and war', also made the following comment:

Not only are many journals and books written and published in Japan, but many of the best books of Europe and America are translated into Japanese, and the booksellers freely import books of all kinds; so that the Japanese have now every opportunity of making themselves acquainted with the latest developments in every department of thought and action. Japanese engineers and scientific men are often found better informed regarding the contents of British journals than are many in this country. (i.e. Britain P.V.)[51]

Japanese universities basically were institutes for applied sciences like agriculture but in particular engineering and medicine. Educating future officials was an important goal for them, but much less than is often thought. They focused on application rather than pure science or *Bildung*. Prior to 1920, the big majority of students graduated in other topics than law and when they entered government service, they did so as applied scientists. Those in charge of the universities realized how important applied science was for economic growth and they were keener on integrating existing knowledge in the Japanese system than on creating new knowledge.[52] It is not by accident that already in 1874 government founded the Institute of Technology, one of the first of such institutes in the world.[53]

It was not just in high-level technical and 'administrative' education that Japan caught up quickly. Referring to the situation at the end of the nineteenth and the beginning of the twentieth centuries, Chuhei Sugiyama writes: 'the time-lag between the more advanced countries and the late-starter Japan is unexpectedly small in the field of business education.'[54] To be fair, it has to be pointed out here, as I already indicated earlier on, that Meiji reformers inherited a (relatively) well-educated and literate population and many schools from Tokugawa times. In 1870, Japan already had 14,000 private schools.[55] So here too, we see a substantial amount of continuity between pre- and post-Restoration Japan.

8

Some Comments on What (Supposedly?) Went Wrong

Even the reader who is willing to see the positive effects of the government policies referred to above, may wonder whether there were not also downsides to the existence and policies of the Japanese state. The 'positive contributions' discussed in this text so far, at least in my view, are basically unproblematic. Who would want to deny that it is good for its economy when – to just refer to a couple of the factors I have discussed – a state is independent and strong, takes care of law and order, develops a material and institutional infrastructure, invests in the economy and supports the spread of knowledge and education? The *extent* to which all this is helpful and fundamental may be discussed but I assume it would be hard to claim all this was *bad*.

What about negative effects? When it comes to negative assessments of state activity the comment is repeatedly made that many government enterprises and projects, especially at the beginning of the Meiji era, did not make any profit, cost government money and in the end, were sold at very low prices.[1] The implication then evidently is that government in doing so wasted money. Let us first deal with that suggestion. Directly after the fall of the Shogunate, when it was impossible to generate much revenue via tariffs, efforts were indeed made by government to directly earn revenue by investing in, for example, railway building and mining. Not everyone, by the way, was in favour of these efforts. Saigo Takamori thought Westernizing projects like railway building were 'wasteful and mindless imitations'. With Okubo Toshimici, he thought the way to solve revenue problems was to reduce government expenditure by 'stopping the projects of railway and steam power' and eliminating 'redundant officials'. Okubo was impressed by the West and in favour of 'fostering industry and promoting enterprise', but he opposed heavy investment in railways and preferred less expensive, more labour-intensive projects aiming at import substitution.[2] But in the end, programmes to directly promote industry and enterprise by state firms or heavily subsidized endeavours were undertaken and in many instances, they indeed were quite unsuccessful, if we define success in terms of direct profit or viability. There can be no doubt about that.

One may of course ask whether government was actually to blame for that or whether we are dealing with *force majeure* or with bad luck that might just as well have hit private entrepreneurs. I do not think it would be fair to compare actual government enterprise with 'infallible', 'ideal' private enterprise. If we look at the concrete reasons for failure it is not always obvious to what extent government can be blamed.

Government's effort to build and operate two large blast furnaces in 1874, for example, was an utter failure. The reasons adduced, however, are that the furnaces lacked good ore, good coke and good personnel.[3] The famous model silk filature factory at Tomioka never turned out to be a success in terms of profitability. A major reason was the fact that it proved so hard to find and keep a good workforce.[4]

Cotton spinning also knew its experiments. A famous one was the Kagoshima Cotton Spinning Mill, completed in 1867 and associated with the Satsuma fief. It survived until 1897 but was simply too big and too sophisticated to be maintained in Japan 'with the primitive mechanical skill of the Japanese at the time'. It, moreover, quite quickly lost its English engineers in the upheavals of 1867–1868 and after the Satsuma Rebellion of 1877 its location had become rather peripheral.[5] Certainly not a very good start but can one blame it all on 'mistakes'? Admittedly many government-run or -supported cotton spinneries were unsuccessful. In the first half of the 1880s, seventeen cotton spinning mills, all utilizing equipment imported from Britain and mostly on a scale of 2,000 mule spindles, started up. Government had imported equipment for ten cotton spinning mills of 2,000 mule spindles and passed this on to private entrepreneurs, who also received various other forms of support. The results were miserable. Tetsuro Nakaoka gives three general reasons for failure of these large mills.[6] The private entrepreneurs running the mills lacked capital, government too became short of money and started retrenchment policies, and finally there was the incompetence of local engineers. Again, is that the government's fault? Could anyone have done better? Would it have been better to not invest at all in the cotton sector? According to Nakaoka failure also had more technical reasons: the scale of the firms and the use of steam. Smaller firms using water power fared better.[7] But, one may ask, would they have lasted long and did small firms using water show the way ahead? Problems in these factories also showed that modern factories had to be near skilled personnel and engineers. But what to do if there simply are not enough of them available? Most examples of failure refer to initiatives that dated from the 1870s and ended in the 1880s. There are also later examples though. The Yawata Imperial Iron and Steel Works – founded only in 1901 – only made a profit after a long period of problematic gestation.[8] A lot of rationalization and scientific management in the 1920s did not really work and the Ministry of Commerce and Industry could not push through all its plans.

One may not only wonder to what extent all this is government's fault or mistake, but, also and more importantly, ask whether in the end the outcome for Japan's economy would have been better if government had *not* taken these initiatives? Would modern private industries have spontaneously emerged in Japan without previous governments' experiments, cheap transfers from public to private enterprises and all sorts of public support? But that is running somewhat ahead of things. Let us first simply admit that government *failed* to make a profit. The question, then, is how relevant that is when it comes to determining the importance of the state and state policies to economic growth. To begin with one may wonder whether the primary or even sole goal of these government initiatives in the form of enterprises or subsidies actually was to make them profitable or 'successful' according to the same criteria one would apply to private firms. That is neither obvious nor evident. Okubo Toshimichi himself claimed: 'These industries (Japan's state-run factories, P.V) are absolutely necessary, even though they go against the laws of political economy.' In his view because, Japan was 'something different' and therefore needed 'different laws' to develop.[9] Even if one would not be convinced by such a claim, one should in my view in any case differentiate here between the micro- and the macro-level and between short-term and longer-term effects. Even if all these investments would have been 'unprofitable' for government from a direct balance sheet perspective, they could still be very useful from the perspective of society as a whole by directly or indirectly helping in the upgrading of production. An economy that only or primarily produces raw materials of semi-manufactured goods as a rule will have but a tiny chance to become wealthy. If private entrepreneurs, often for good, 'rational' reasons do not invest heavily in complex infrastructure or production, then that is up to the state that can better afford to make (initial) losses.

Besides, overall, those 'failed' investments were not destroyed and thus did not disappear. They were cheaply passed on to private enterprises that in turn could use them to their profit. Which they often did. That already indicates in what way time horizons can matter. It is not at all obvious that calculated over their entire life-span 'failed government investments' would indeed have to be considered 'failures' even from a simple book-keeper's point of view, let alone from a broader societal perspective. Inkster rightfully makes the following comments when it comes to the ratio of much government investment in Japan, in particular investment to introduce new knowledge and technology:

> Because the ultimate goals of the principal agent of transfer went well beyond commercial profits and into the defence of the nation, the transfer process (of technology and knowledge P.V.) was continued despite high costs and technical failures in the early years. In such a situation, the 'market' choice would have been to confine transfers to the importing of cost-reducing devices and to the final products of Western technologies rather than extend to the process-technology required for import substitution.[10]

In brief: catching up and building a competitive Japanese modern industry required policies like that of government. He suggests the selling of government firms in the 1880s could also be seen from that perspective. Their sale has often been regarded as indicating a transition to *laissez-faire* on the part of Japanese government. One may however wonder whether they really indicated a fundamental break and the beginning of a switch to 'laissez-faire' because previous policies had failed. I can again do no better than quote Ian Inkster:

> The relatively low rate of government investment and the 'selling up' of government enterprise to private interests in the early 1880s have often been taken as signs of failure. Clearly, they may be as readily viewed as signs of success – minimal expenditures yielded significant results and 'selling up' was part and parcel of the strategy of technology diffusion.[11]

Yet the evidence is far from clear: Government accelerated its economic interventions in the field of infrastructure and construction, education and training, technology applications and information dispersal, military contracting for industry and raw material supplies, as well as its indirect support for manufacturing through increased regulations relating to finance, quality control and the encouragement of manufacture exports. None of this reads like *laissez-faire* in any acceptable sense. The continuity of projects (e.g. the Hokkaido development project and railway and ship construction) across the divide and the low valuation of government assets during 'selling up', suggests that the movement away from direct investment in manufacturing was part and parcel of an overall strategy of multi-fold interventions, the timing of which was certainly influenced by the need to cut expenditure wherever possible and reduce inflation.[12]

Government investments indeed were often simply passed on to private enterprise which makes sense as a developmental strategy. An overall withdrawal by the state from the economy starting in the 1880s has never occurred. None of the relevant indicators (e.g. tax revenue, government expenditures and investment, development of the bureaucracy), analysed for the entire period from the 1880s till the eve of the Pacific War points in that direction. In the early 1880s, government turned towards more indirect forms of encouraging industry and transport (although this included new loans and subsidies) and retained direct interests primarily in strategic or military areas of the economy. The shedding of foreign experts from government employment in the 1880s actually often meant a redeployment of Westerners from the public to the private sector.[13]

All this of course does not mean that government in Japan or wherever in the world never really wasted money and always had a clear strategy that it successfully implemented. That would be absurd. It only means that one has to be careful and precise in concluding government investments were failures. If non profitable investments by government – from a strictly bookkeeping perspective – are a sufficient reason to be against government investment per se – would that not mean that non-profitable investments by private entrepreneurs are a sufficient reason to be against private investment? Why are proponents of the market economy so upset by governments 'wasting' money when the history of the market economy is a history littered with hundreds of thousands of non-profitable investments that not just harm the investor but cause enormous societal damage? As compared to *which countries* and *which alternatives* can Japan's government policies be said to have *failed* and *how* exactly? I would like to remind the reader of the fact that the rate of growth in Japan's manufacturing in the period discussed was higher than in any major economy in the world and that its overall growth rates also were quite impressive.

That brings to a previous comment: The fundamental question is what would have happened when government had *not* made these investments. Would Japan's GDP then have turned out to be higher, or lower? My guess would be lower, because if government had not made these investments – plus the many others in infrastructure and the like – my claim would be that no one for quite some time would have done so, which would have left Japan with fewer modern firms and thus less income later on.[14] The state invested in sectors with major macro-economic importance where others did *not*, or *not yet* invest. I would like to remind the reader of the quote by Landes that I used earlier on in this text and where he claims that many government activities and investments occurred in the period of time in between those in which industrializing follower countries 'perceived the necessity and opportunity of an industrial revolution and the time when human and material resources and the institutional structure made such a revolution feasible'.[15] Penelope Francks made a similar comment:

> the sale of the government enterprises had important long-term consequences for the state's role in Japans' development. It meant . . . that the state had, in some cases, borne the risks and supplied the initial investment required to establish a number of new enterprises until such time as the private sector was able to operate them.[16]

I would suggest that we indeed, like Ian Inkster, also look at government investments from the perspective, that Alexander Gerschenkron sketches in his analysis of the role of the state in the catching-up process of relatively backward economies.[17] Actually, so Inkster argues, the activities of Japan's state were to be expected in a situation of industrialization under conditions of relative backwardness. In such a situation, the presence of a strong strategic elite is of the utmost importance. That means that the relation between market and technology transfer is different than mainstream economists tend to claim and that there is a different role for the state than in advanced industrialized economies.[18] The fact that Japan's rulers wanted to keep development in their own hands, made their strategic role even more important:

> The exclusion by law of foreign capital (and particularly of foreign companies entering Japan) meant that a prime role of government was to substitute for the key functions played by these advanced external sources in the case of late development.[19]

John Tang has made an analysis of government investment under the Meiji that underpins a 'Gerschenkronian' interpretation of Japan's government policies, at least in the Meiji era. In his opinion 'the government sought to encourage private enterprise by leading entry into targeted sectors with its pilot factories, acquiring and demonstrating new technologies, and supporting the opening of new markets'.[20] He describes government policies in this respect in terms of '(providing) a model of investment for the private sector to imitate', 'absorbing unavailable (sic! P.V.) initial costs and losses that private entrepreneurs could hardly be expected to bear', and '(helping) overcome certain technological difficulties that previously had been considered insurmountable'.[21] On the basis of what, in my view, is solid evidence, he comes to the following conclusion:

> government was more likely to invest in capital-intensive industries than the private sector, which may indicate capital market failure for large-scale investments early in the Meiji Period. Nor did the government ignore light industries with those that it pioneered becoming major contributors to economic growth. Since these sectors did not require substantial financing, it may be that private entrepreneurs had risk aversion, and the government's initiative did much to allay doubts about the viability of foreign technology and market potential. Finally, the government also succeeded in spreading the effects of industrialization across the country to more sparsely populated and remote areas.[22]

The interest of the government ostensibly was in long-term national strength and wealth, not short-term profit maximization. It therefore made substantial investments in strategic industries, first and foremost transport and communications; metal and coal mining; metal processing and manufacture; shipbuilding and machinery; armaments and chemicals. It seems that what in the end mattered for Meiji investors was effectiveness rather than efficiency.[23] Tang is very positive about government investment policies, actually too positive, at least in the way he wants to illustrate his point.[24] Government in its investment policies clearly had and continued to have a 'bias' towards capital-intensive and large-scale endeavours. In its initial plans to develop agriculture on Hokkaido it had a similar 'bias' and wanted to create American-style large farms, i.e. large, mechanized, 'capitalist' enterprises. Those plans came to naught and were given up.[25] To all intents and purposes its strategy here, for the agricultural sector, can be described as a failure, also if we would look at it from a longer-term perspective.

The kind of industries Meiji governments primarily focused upon required lots of capital and resources, both of which Japan was not really well endowed with. One might therefore claim, as Yasukichi Yasuba indeed does, that it was not a good idea to try and create capital-intensive, heavy industry in Japan, at least before World War Two. The more so, in his view as this industry was part of an effort at empire building. He considers this bad allocation of scarce resources and suggests that in order to increase incomes for the ordinary Japanese it would have been better to focus on sectors of production in which the country had a comparative advantage.[26] That brings us to the second critique that has often been ushered with regard to the role of Japan's state in the country's economic development. Whether it was a wise decision to focus so much on heavy industries that should primarily serve the military, of course is a completely different and in my view undecidable matter, but to just stick to those sectors in which the country traditionally had a comparative advantage in my view, as I already suggested earlier, would have been unwise. For an economy as large as that of Japan, reaching Western levels of income – and development – in the end was only possible when it upgraded at least part of its production to high-added value goods and services. The production of such goods and services at the time tended to require economies of scale and scope and a high capital, energy and technology intensity. Even if it may have been counter to Japan's comparative advantage in the short run to invest in heavy industry and the production of capital goods, e.g. machinery, it nevertheless made sense. Otherwise it would have continued to be fully dependent on other countries for high added value products, for the simple reason that it lacked the means to produce them itself.[27]

9

A Brief Summary

The summary of this text can be brief. My goal was to figure out how important the state was for Japan's economic take-off in the period 1868–1937. My method was to describe and where possible 'measure' the functioning and policies of that state and compare them with states and state policies in economically successful countries (primarily the United Kingdom, France and Germany) and in countries that economically speaking were much less successful.

I began my analysis by determining how wealthy and developed Japan was at the eve of the Meiji Restoration that has long been considered a fundamental break in the economic history of Japan. My conclusion was that Tokugawa Japan indeed, as many revisionists have been claiming, was more dynamic and more developed than has long been assumed but that on the other hand it still was rather poor as compared to the wealthiest parts of North-western Europe, *before* as well as *during* their take-off. Then I set out to determine how wealthy and developed Japan was at the end of the 1930s, to figure out what exactly had changed in the country's economy that was in need of explanation. The outcome was twofold. In terms of real GDP or real income per capita, but also in terms of level of development and industrialization, Japan indeed had made very impressive progress. But, on the other hand, it showed that nevertheless at the end of the 1930s, it was still far from having really caught up with the United Kingdom, Germany, and France and other highly developed Western economies. Then I set out to chart – always in a systematically comparative way – those characteristics of Japan's state and its policies that might have contributed to its impressive economic rise. When looked at from a global comparative perspective, Japan's state and its policies had a unique configuration of characteristics – i.e. for a country that was semi-developed at best when the process that I study started – that in my view contributed in decisive ways to the country's take-off and without which that take off would have been impossible.

The first and literally fundamental fact that has to be pointed out is that Japan in the period under discussion to all intents and purposes continued to be an independent and sovereign country with a government that was only too aware that power and wealth are as a rule mutually reinforcing and that thus tried to make its state stronger. It did so successfully. The country never became a colony, on the contrary. It won its wars and created an empire. The country's international position thereby was strengthened, also in economic terms. Had Tokugawa Japan continued to exist in its unreformed version, it would in all probability have been dismantled or in any case have ended up in a position with far less room to manoeuvre. The development of Japan in the age of high, formal and informal, imperialism was a unique one.

Starting with the Meiji Restoration Japan quickly became a modern state. That not only means that it became more efficient and effective as a polity. The 'rationalization' and 'professionalization' of the administration that characterize such a state have positive effects on the economy of the country involved. This also was the case in post-Restoration Japan, which was a fundamentally different polity from that over which the Shoguns had ruled. In this context, it is important to add that Japan not only became a modern state in theory but also in practice. It actually functioned like one. Mainstream economists are in a habit of taking the existence of modern functioning states for granted whereas they actually have always been very exceptional.

Unsurprisingly, the modernization of Japan's state after Restoration entailed a drastic centralization and integration of the country as a political entity. These political processes in turn facilitated, promoted and often even required centralization and integration of the country's economy which clearly had their positive economic spin-offs. I fail to see how Tokugawa Japan with its over 250 different domains – next to the Shogun's land – might have been able to generate and sustain a level of economic growth and development similar to that of post-Restoration Japan. Here too, apart from certain continuities, I see a fundamental discontinuity. The new Japan certainly had the additional luck of not being *too* big and *too* diverse.

For a state to be able to facilitate or actively promote economic development and growth it must be powerful, i.e. it must have the capability to get things done. An analysis of the strength of Japan's post-Restoration state focusing on its political, ideological, economic and military-bureaucratic power showed that it was quite powerful in all these respects. Japan at the eve of the Restoration still lacked much of the necessary infrastructure for a modern national economy, materially as well as institutionally. Only a state with power can eliminate vested interests and push through the major changes that the creating of such infrastructure might require. When it comes to state power, the new rulers of Japan could certainly build on a Tokugawa legacy. Under the Shogunate, the effective rulers, i.e. the Shogun primarily in his own lands – and to a certain extent also for entire Japan – and the *daimyo* in their domains, had been quite powerful, in particular when it came to political and economic power. Their governments certainly were no small governments. But after the Restoration state power was strengthened in the sense of more centralized, streamlined and codified, and more professionalized, which e.g. meant the supplanting of many amateur officeholders and warriors by professionals. My findings for the case of Japan in the period 1868–1937 clearly have wider implications when it comes to certain cherished ideas in the social sciences about relations between state formation and economic development and growth. They flatly contradict claims by Daron Acemoglu and James Robinson about the economic effects of exclusive and extractive institutions and at the very least modify existing ideas about the relationships between the emergence of a strong fiscal state and public debt on the one hand and political representation and warfare on the other.

All the characteristics summed up so far of course are of little avail and could easily have become a *dis*advantage when that modern centralized, integrated and powerful state that began to emerge with the Restoration, would not have been interested in development and growth. The post-Restoration state, however, was. It was 'developmental', which in this case also meant that it in principle not just condoned but often actually enforced capitalist logics and rules, even though it did not hesitate to suspend them whenever it saw fit. When it comes to developmental policies there certainly were precedents in the Tokugawa era, but again the scale then was smaller and the intensity certainly in the lands of the Shogun lower. In practice, many things may have happened in Tokugawa Japan that conferred the impression it was capitalist, but its entire legal and institutional structure clearly was *not*. In that sense, the Restoration was a decisive break with the Tokugawa past. Now capitalism was officially accepted and even promoted. Japan's new rulers actually *created* and *supported* the institutional infrastructure without which a capitalist economy cannot function. Japan's state between 1868 and 1937 was friendly to big business and unfriendly to labour. In the first stage of industrialisation that is not an unusual policy or rather the only one I know of. In macro-economic terms, it probably was helpful to create growth. In this respect, there was not much difference with the Tokugawa era when government also tended to be rather harsh towards its working subjects.

Being the government of a fairly poor and semi-developed state, Japan's post-Restoration governments spent a substantial amount of its substantial resources on buying (Japanese) goods and services and on investment, even in comparison to many advanced economies. Its social spending was negligible. In its material investments, it focused on investment in infrastructure, in particular transport and communication. These are of fundamental importance for development, but individuals, 'the market' or even 'society' at large as a rule do not tend to take care of such public goods spontaneously. Its investment in creating new institutional arrangements like, to name but a few, a new army, navy and police force, a new bureaucracy, new legal, monetary, financial, fiscal or educational systems, also was substantial. The importance of these investments and accompanying innovations for growth and development can hardly be over-estimated. When it comes to infrastructural and certainly institutional innovation, the overall assessment of the Tokugawa regime can only be that it was fairly conservative and not as prominently present.

The men who took over Japan from the Tokugawa, whatever their deepest convictions, decided to not oppose and in many respects enthusiastically support the 'opening' of Japan. Every introductory textbook into mainstream economics can come up with numerous arguments why that would be a good idea. And it certainly was for Japan after 1868. But Japan's rulers did not make the mistake to think that such an opening only had advantages and must be unconditional. They knew certain protective mechanisms were necessary and as much and as soon as possible took care of them. It would certainly be seriously incorrect to give them all the credit for that, but Japan's manufacturing was not wiped out by foreign competition, its government and business community did not become dependent on foreign capital, foreign experts or expertise, and foreign investment did not really penetrate the Japanese economy. All revisionism notwithstanding, Tokugawa Japan in comparison was a far more closed economy and society. That certainly may have had its advantages, whereas the disadvantages were still rather small as there relatively speaking was not yet much that the Japanese missed in their isolation. With industrialization in the West this changed completely and the price of isolation became much higher.

The long-term motor of modern growth is sustained innovation. Such innovation, which can also consist in adopting or adapting as yet unknown ways of doing things from elsewhere, feeds on knowledge. Japan's government systematically and massively supported the transfer of knowledge from abroad and its subsequent dissemination at home. It, moreover, spent large amounts of money – also when compared to highly developed Western countries – on education. In both respects government during the Tokugawa era was much less active, although admittedly the country had a relatively high level of education, literacy and numeracy.

Adding all these things up, it in my view is clear beyond any reasonable doubt that the importance of Japan's state as an institution and as an agent was fundamental for the country's economic development. Without it the growth rates and the level of development that were realized would simply have been unthinkable. I am afraid that all those critics who qualify or even deny its fundamental importance do not realize how exceptional it was for a state of a non-developed country in the period studied here to even have just a couple of the characteristics of Japan's state. I would claim that *no* other non-Western country had them all. Those critics seem to compare Japan's state at the time to what they consider to be a perfect state in a highly developed economy instead of to a 'normal' state of a fairly poor country.[1] As such I think it did strikingly well. Those scholars who like to emphasize continuities with the preceding era in Japanese history in my view ignore the major institutional changes that started with the Meiji Restoration and that turned Japan into a very different and much more growth-facilitating and growth-promoting polity.

Of course, Japan's state was not 'perfectly' arranged, whatever that may mean. Its rulers weren't omniscient foreseers of the future, who flawlessly implemented a consistent set of policies. They certainly weren't always successful. Many of their successes in a way were unintended and many intentions never materialized. Often, they were not even aiming for growth, let alone the well-being of the population. Of course, the state is not the only variable explaining Japan's growth and development; without the private sector, it would have been impossible. But is there any scholar who points at its fundamental importance who would deny that? I in any case do not. And of course, its rulers made mistakes, but is the market flawless?

I have not discussed private well-being, full well realizing that behind the often-impressive growth figures there was often extremely hard toil. I have not discussed inequality, full well realizing that it increased. I only referred to the fact that for the bulk of the population political freedoms and rights for most of the period I discussed were quite restricted. I did not dwell on the moral side of militarization and empire building that did play a part in growth. All these topics are highly relevant and interesting and they certainly deserve close attention. But they were not subject of this book. This book was about the role of the state for macro-economic development and growth. Its conclusion can only be that this role was fundamental, indispensable and major.

Appendix I

All the references to countries are to contemporary borders.

Table 96 Output of coal, 1870–1953, in million metric tons

	Japan	France	Germany	United Kingdom
1870	0.2	13.3	32.0	112.1
1913	21.3	40.8	277.3	292.0
1929	34.4	55.0	337.9	262.0
1951	44.7	55.0	358.3	225.8

Millward, *State and business*, 248.

Table 97 Output of iron ore and pig iron 1870–1951, in '000 metric tons

		Japan	France	Germany	United Kingdom
1870	iron ore	n.a	2,614	2,918	14,602
	pig iron	n.a	1,178	1,261	6,059
1913	iron ore	17	21,918	26,608	16,254
	pig iron	243	5,207	16,761	10,425
1929	iron ore	88	50,728	6,374	13,427
	pig iron	1,112	10,300	13,240	7,711
1951	iron ore	600	35,207	12,923	15,014
	pig iron	3,227	8,750	11,039	9,824

Millward, *State and business*, 248.

Table 98 Electricity supply in net gigawatt hours, 1913–1951

	Japan	France	Germany	United Kingdom
1913	1.14	1.80	8.0	2.5
1929	15.12	15.60	30.66	16.98
1951	47.86	38.15	75.19	69.37

Millward, *State and business*, 253.

Appendix I

Table 99 Electricity supply and population, net kilowatt hours per 100 population in net gigawatt hours

	Japan	France	Germany	United Kingdom
1913	2	5	12	6
1929	24	38	47	37
1951	57	90	109	137

Millward, *State and business*, 253.

Table 100 Merchant fleets, 1870–1951, net registered weight in '000 metric tons

	Japan	France	Germany	United Kingdom
1870	16	1,072	939	5,691
1913	1,528	1,582	3,320	12,120
1929	3,862	2,007	2,402	11,369
1951	2,182	3,367	1,099	10,955

Millward, *State and business*, 254.

Table 101 Length of open railway track, in miles

	Japan	France	Germany	United Kingdom
1870	18	9658	11,728	13,395
1913	6,568	25,332	39,380	20,270
1929	12,840	26,283	36,152	20,281
1951	17,124	25,600	30,955	19,356

Millward, *State and business*, 254.

Table 102 Railway track spread, rail track miles per 1000 square miles of territory

	Japan	France	Germany	United Kingdom
1870	0.1	45	59	149
1913	41	122	193	226
1929	79	123	209	226
1951	94	121	226	216

Millward, *State and business*, 255.

Table 103 Density of telecommunication, 1870–1951, telegrams per 100 population and telephones in use per 100 population

		Japan	France	Germany	United Kingdom
1870	Telegrams	0.03	14.9	22.1	27.4
1913	Telegrams	63.6	131.2	78.1	191.0
	Telephones	0.5	0.78	2.1	n.a.
1929	Telegrams	102.5	117.5	47.8	155.4
	Telephones	1.0	2.5	4.9	n.a.
1951	Telegrams	117.8	58.7	49.1	122.5
	Telephones	2.1	6.0	4.5	11.3

Millward, *State and business*, 257.

Appendix II

Table 104 Government revenues in millions of yen over the period 1871–1937

Fiscal Year	Total Revenue	New Debt Issue	Total Current Revenue	Total Tax Revenue	Government Enterprise Surplus	Non-Tax Revenue
1868						
1869						
1870					0.1	2.0
1871	15.5		15.5	12.8	0.7	2.0
1872	47.2	23.2	24.0	21.8	1.1	1.1
1873	80.6	12.6	68.0	65.0	2.5	0.5
1874	76.3	6.3	70.0	65.3	3.9	0.8
1875	73.2	8.9	64.3	59.4	4.0	0.9
1876	55.5	−1.9	57.4	52.0	3.9	1.5
1877	235.8	184.3	51.5	48.2	2.0	1.3
1878	68.7	14.2	54.5	51.8	1.9	0.8
1879	82.3	−2.2	84.5	79.9	2.1	2.5
1880	87.3	−0.9	88.2	82.6	2.4	3.2
1881	98.2	−3.2	101.4	95.1	2.3	4.0
1882	102.8	−5.6	108.4	103.3	2.0	3.1
1883	93.7	−12.8	106.5	103.8	1.8	0.9
1884	122.9	14.2	108.7	101.2	2.4	5.1
1885	93.6	4.8	88.8	81.5	2.5	4.8
1886	111.3	3.2	108.1	97.1	1.7	9.3
1887	117.0	6.1	110.9	97.6	2.2	11.1
1888	111.0	1.1	109.9	96.1	2.9	10.9
1889	119.4	3.0	116.4	102.6	3.3	10.5
1890	127.1	15.2	111.9	100.2	5.6	6.1
1891	113.4	0.8	112.6	98.3	5.3	9.0
1892	127.7	5.5	122.2	103.5	5.5	13.2
1893	124.4	−5.3	130.0	108.6	7.7	13.7
1894	194.4	59.3	135.1	111.7	10.2	13.2
1895	229.2	83.7	145.5	122.8	12.0	10.7
1896	161.0	0.9	162.1	135.8	11.9	12.4
1897	196.4	16.7	179.7	165.2	11.6	2.9
1898	214.8	−0.9	215.7	175.2	15.8	24.7
1899	314.7	101.3	263.4	221.1	16.3	25.0
1900	312.1	23.5	288.6	243.3	17.8	27.5
1901	372.0	58.3	317.3	264.4	22.6	26.7
1902	361.1	26.0	335.1	286.1	23.5	25.5
1903	376.7	38.7	338.3	286.3	28.0	24.0
1904	847.9	459.4	388.5	327.2	38.4	22.9
1905	1,522.5	1,032.4	490.1	408.5	44.1	37.5
1906	794.8	228.5	566.3	457.9	48.5	59.9
1907	641.1	−10.3	656.4	509.5	79.3	67.6

Table 104 *Continued*

Fiscal Year	Total Revenue	New Debt Issue	Total Current Revenue	Total Tax Revenue	Government Enterprise Surplus	Non-Tax Revenue
1908	680.7	−1.6	682.3	557.3	73.5	51.5
1909	1,099.3	421.5	117.8	576.7	52.7	48.4
1910	859.2	134.6	724.6	576.9	88.4	59.3
1911	890.2	88.8	801.4	604.4	65.3	131.7
1912	822.3	19.5	802.8	650.3	64.6	87.9
1913	759.5	−54.2	813.7	659.5	74.3	79.9
1914	755.2	−26.8	782.0	617.2	83.9	80.9
1915	785.2	18.0	767.2	601.2	84.6	81.4
1916	902.9	8.0	893.9	652.1	141.5	100.3
1917	1,365.8	247.9	1,117.9	787.1	202.1	128.7
1918	1,752.8	394.6	1,358.2	956.1	223.4	178.7
1919	2,133.2	269.5	1,863.7	1,249.7	254.8	359.2
1920	2,653.0	666.7	1,901.3	1,477.7	169.9	253.7
1921	2,572.8	409.3	2,163.5	1,633.8	227.3	302.4
1922	2,895.0	405.2	2,498.8	1,817.3	276.4	599.6
1923	2,840.1	583.9	2,856.2	1,013.8	247.3	359.1
1924	2,773.2	308.4	2,464.8	1,756.4	283.5	424.9
1925	2,947.9	418.6	2,534.3	1,763.7	301.8	448.8
1926	2,970.7	444.7	2,526.0	1,801.1	266.6	458.3
1927	3,304.5	689.2	2,615.3	1,790.2	309.4	515.7
1928	3,421.4	117.9	2,753.5	1,848.3	334.2	571.0
1929	3,020.5	299.7	2,720.8	1,827.7	302.3	590.8
1930	2,540.6	419.6	2,121.0	1,751.1	165.0	240.9
1931	2,416.5	371.5	2,045.0	1,521.7	181.0	340.3
1932	3,127.7	1,050.7	2,077.0	1,402.1	231.0	383.9
1933	3,443.6	1,234.6	2,309.0	1,559.9	281.0	368.1
1934	3,581.2	1,038.2	2,543.0	1,709.7	399.0	434.3
1935	3,700.3	985.3	2,715.0	1,836.7	419.0	459.3
1936	4,021.3	1,043.3	2,979.0	2,032.8	438.0	507.2
1937	6,505.9	2,219.9	4,286.0	2,441.3	1,259.0	585.7

Ohkawa, Shinohara and Meissner, *Patterns of Japanese economic development*, 376–377.

Notes

Introduction

1 See Pomeranz, *Great Divergence*, Part One. For the many fundamental differences between early modern Great Britain and China see my *Escaping poverty*, 401–409. For an extensive analysis of the numerous and fundamental differences between the British and the Chinese state when it comes to their functioning and policies see my *State, economy, and the Great Divergence*.

2 For an overview of recent additions to the debate, see Vries, 'What we do and do not know'.

3 In 2016 Penelope Francks published a concise and very knowledgeable survey of the current state of the art – *Japan and the Great Divergence* – that I would recommend to the interested reader. However, it only deals with the Tokugawa period, whereas in my text the focus clearly is on later periods. What in my view needs to be explained is how Japan could catch up, not why it wasn't the first country to leap forward. I rate the chance that that would have occurred at zero.

4 See pages 30–31 for an explanation of these concepts.

5 Takekoshi, *Self-portrayal of Japan*, 5.

6 Umesao, *Ecological view*, 166.

7 See e.g. Table 11 and Appendix I.

8 After the 'China Incident' of 1937, even official Japanese sources referred to the country's economy as a 'war economy'.

9 I paraphrase Abramovitz, 'Catching up, forging ahead, and falling behind'.

10 Popper, *Conjectures and refutations*.

11 See my publications in the bibliography.

12 I was strengthened in this conviction when comparing the role of the state in my previous book on Great Britain and Qing China. I encountered a striking number of wild claims and lots of ideology but rather few systematically contextualized and compared data.

13 See for examples and references, pages 87–88.

14 In 1930, for example, John Orchard wrote: 'The part played by the government cannot be overemphasized. Japanese industry of the present day owes its state of development primarily to the efforts of a highly paternalist central government.' Orchard and Orchard, *Japan's economic position*, 90. Harold Moulton, one year later, claimed: 'In view of the conditions prevailing at the beginning of the Meiji era, it is doubtful if, without the stimulus and general coordination which resulted from government policies, any considerable industrial and commercial expansion would have occurred prior to the World War.' Moulton and Ko, *Japan*, 341. In 1935, Gilbert Hubbard wrote: 'The characteristic partnership existing in Japan between the state and private enterprise deserves special attention since it constitutes one of the main sources of her competitive strength' and he calls Japan's government the 'chief repository of economic power and initiative', that is 'presiding over the whole industrial hierarchy'. Hubbard,

Eastern industrialization, 66, 67 and 93. Guenther Stein in that same year, also stressed the guiding and positive role of the state in Japan's economic modernization since the Restoration. See e.g. Stein, *Made in Japan*, chapter 7.

15 Just some quotes, the first two from 1946, the third one from 1955: Norman, *Origins of the modern Japanese state*, 47: 'The *speed* with which Japan had simultaneously to establish a modern state, to build an up-to-date defence force in order to ward off the dangers of invasion (which the favourable balance of world forces and the barrier of China could not forever postpone), to create an industry on which to base this armed force, to fashion an educational system suitable to an industrial modernized nation, dictated that these important changes be accomplished by a group of autocratic bureaucrats rather than by the mass of the people working through democratic organs of representation.'; Allen, *Short economic history*, 36: 'there was scarcely any important Japanese industry of the Western type during the latter decades of the nineteenth century which did not owe its establishment to state initiative'; Smith, *Political change*, 63: 'It seems clear that without government help . . ., private capital would have been no more successful in developing machine cotton spinning in the decade after 1880 than it had been in the decade before; in short in this field as in all others except silk reeling, the government was responsible for overcoming the initial difficulties of industrialization.'

16 See Johnson, 'Developmental state', 37. In this article Johnson synthesized the thesis *of* and the debates *about* his *MITI and the Japanese miracle*. Personally, as will be apparent in this book, I consider Japan a developmental state already from the Meiji Restoration onwards. For analysis and discussion of the developmental state see, besides the publications by Johnson himself in the bibliography: Amsden, *Rise of 'the Rest'*, even though she does not use the concept as such; Wade, *Governing the market* and Woo-Cummings, *Developmental state*.

17 Crawcour for example claims: 'government intervention and manipulation were an important positive factor in Japan's economic development up to 1920 . . . they did not on the whole counteract the underlying economic conditions and in fact enabled a fuller realization of the economy's development potential than would have been achieved without them.' See Crawcour, 'Industrialization and technological change', 450. Howe thinks it was omnipresent in trade affairs and undertook many initiatives when it came to the textiles industry, in particular in the silk industry where its role can scarcely be overestimated. Howe, *Origins of Japanese trade supremacy*, 97, 138, 179 and 182. Ian Inkster describes government's infrastructural investment, and institutional interventions as 'crucially important in mobilising the "response" of the Japanese economic system to the new external and internal political systems'. In his view: 'The rise of private enterprise was on the back of government infrastructural and service investment and technological diffusion policies, training and educational schemes and a social engineering which successfully kept opposition at bay.' Inkster, *Japanese industrialisation*, 39, 37 and 35.

18 For Akamatsu and his ideas, see Akamatsu, 'Theory of unbalanced growth' and idem, 'Historical pattern of economic growth'. For a discussion of them, see e.g. Kojima, 'The "flying geese" model'; Oizumi and Muñoz, 'Kaname Akamatsu'; Schroeppel and Nakajima, 'Changing interpretation'. For those who read German, Bachinger and Matis, *Entwicklungsdimensionen*, 283–326, provides a very helpful analysis of Akamatsu's ideas and further references.

19 Sheridan, *Governing the Japanese economy*, 3.

20 Yoshihara, *Japan's economic development*, 50.

21 Tsuzuki, *Pursuit of power*, 71–72 and 74.

22 Flath, *Japanese economy,* 39–40.
23 Flath, *Japanese economy,* 40.
24 Flath, *Japanese economy,* 211.
25 Flath, *Japanese economy,* 2.
26 Tipton, 'Government policy'.
27 All this may be true, but is the amount of added value at a certain moment in time the best measure of the relevance of economic activities in the longer run? The modern sector indeed started small, but does that mean it was 'irrelevant'? Does everything new not start small?
28 Powell, 'How entrepreneurs created the great boom'. My synthesis of his ideas is basically a paraphrase.
29 Oshima, 'Meiji fiscal policy', 353–357. The quote is on page 354.
30 Minami, *Economic development,* 121 and 264.
31 Yasuba, 'Natural resources'.
32 Fukao and Settsu, 'Japan. Modern economic growth'. They are not only positive. They also refer to 'inappropriate macro-economic policies'.
33 See, for example, Yamamura, 'Success ill-gotten' or Rosovsky, *Capital formation,* chapter II.
34 Lockwood, *Economic development,* 588.
35 Lockwood, *Economic development,* 574.
36 Lockwood, *Economic development,* 575.
37 Rosovsky, *Capital formation,* 21–22.
38 Rosovsky, *Capital formation,* 13. On page 34 of that book, he added: 'it seems safe to make the generalization that in industrialization occurring before World War II in non-Communist countries, government investment had relatively less importance than it had in Japan.'
39 Landes, 'Japan and Europe', 101–102, 105 and 106.
40 In the index of his *Japanese economic development* there is not one reference to (developmental) 'state' or 'government' (policies).
41 Morris-Suzuki, *Technological transformation,* 85.
42 Hunter, *Women and the labour market,* 33.
43 Hunter, *Emergence of modern Japan,* chapter 6. The quote is on page 113.
44 Brown, *Britain and Japan,* 14–15.
45 Francks, *Japanese economic development,* 14 and 57. When it comes to the cotton industry, I think Francks belittles the importance of large-scale investments and factories.
46 I paraphrase Agov, 'Meiji Japan'.
47 See e.g. Hane, *Modern Japan,* 105–109. The quote is on page 107.
48 Minami, *Economic development,* 121 and 264. He admits that the state may have played a substantial role in the early industrialization of Japan but then comments that it did so too in other countries – which in my view is not exactly a refutation of the thesis that it would be important – and adds that government changed its policies after the early Meiji period and – most importantly – that without private response industrialization would not have been successful anyhow. Minami, *Economic development,* 120–121.
49 Hashino and Saito, 'Tradition and interactions'.
50 Nakaoka, 'Role of domestic technical innovation'; Nakaoka, 'On technological leaps'; Nakaoka, 'Transfer of cotton manufacturing technology'.
51 Ohno, *Economic development,* 56. In his most recent book, he argues along similar lines: 'The tentative conclusion of this book based on a large number of facts and cases, is that

private dynamism was the primary engine but policy also played a useful role in the post-war high-growth period. This conclusion is basically the same as for the Meiji industrialization much earlier.' See Ohno, *History of Japanese economic development*, 141.

52 Hayami, *Japan's industrious revolution*, 107.
53 Hayami, *Japan's industrious revolution*, 107.
54 See e.g. Hayami, *Japan's industrious revolution*, 126: 'the state has always been interventionist in the industrialization process since the early Meiji years until today. Even when the private sector was the driving force of economic progress, the government tended to act in the interests of the business corporations.'
55 Morris-Suzuki, *Technological transformation of Japan*, 85.
56 See Francks, *Japanese economic development*; Morris-Suzuki, *Technological transformation*, 88–104; Takeuchi, *Role of labour-intensive sectors*; Tanimoto, *Role of tradition*. Federico, in his *Economic history*, makes this same point confining himself to the production and sale of silk.
57 Morris-Suzuki, *Technological transformation*, 85.
58 Brown, *Britain and Japan*, 14.
59 Brown, *Britain and Japan*, 14–15. I would claim the state did far more than just creating 'an appropriate infrastructure'.
60 Francks, *Japanese economic development*, 5 and 56. See also *ibid.*, 68 and 71: 'the story of the development of Japanese shipping in the nineteenth century is not one of the pursuit of a clear and predetermined state policy or of the dominant role of state leadership.' and 'Japanese bureaucrats did not always operate with long-term strategic plans to control or supersede the market, . . . they did not always get everything right.'
61 Miwa, *Japan's economic planning*, Preface, X–XII, 'Myth of the competent state'. On page X there is this quote: 'That the government planned for the war incompetently casts doubt on the accounts of the decades before the war as well . . . . if – with vastly more authority and power than at any time before or since – it could not coherently prepare for war, then perhaps it did not plan much for peace either.'
62 Saito, 'Japan', 179.
63 Johnson, 'The developmental state', 34.
64 See e.g. his 'Comparative capitalism', chapter three in *Japan: Who governs* and his 'Developmental state: Odyssey of a concept', 32.
65 In chapter 5 I will discuss what I mean by 'capitalist' and refer to recent literature discussing the concept.
66 The book will also be published by Bloomsbury Publishing. I hope that will happen in 2020.
67 For Gerschenkron's ideas about catching up by late-comers and the role in it of the state see his *Economic backwardness*. I am *not* claiming that Japan's industrialization would perfectly fit Gerschenkron's ideas about late developers. In several fundamental respects, it certainly did *not*.
68 Studwell, *How Asia works*, 134–135.
69 See for this 'three-pronged' investment, Amsden, *Rise of the 'rest'*, chapter 1.
70 Reinert, *How rich countries got rich*, chapters 4 and 5.
71 See note 18 of this chapter.
72 Inkster, *Japanese industrial economy*, 61.
73 For examples see Tanimoto, *Role of tradition*.
74 Johnson, *MITI*, 18–24.
75 Saito, 'Was modern Japan a developmental state?'.

76 He, *Paths toward the modern fiscal state*, 79.

77 For a helpful brief overview of the main economic plans and policies in the period 1868–1990, see Sheridan, *Governing the Japanese economy*, 8–17. Table I.1.

78 I found this expression in He, *Paths toward the modern fiscal state*, 231.

79 For these controversies, I refer to overviews of Japanese political history at the time, e.g. by Banno or Tsuzuki.

80 See for this difference e.g. Crawcour, 'Kogyo iken'; Metzler, 'Cosmopolitanism of national economics' and Smethurst, 'Takahashi Korekiyo's economic policies'.

81 See e.g. Sheridan, *Governing the Japanese economy*, 29–31.

82 See for such controversies during the inter-war period Masato, 'Japanese economy'.

83 I have taken this information from He, *Paths toward the modern fiscal state*, 37–38 and 98.

84 For the transition from a silver standard to a gold standard in 1897, see Bytheway, 'Japan's adoption of the gold standard' and more extensively Bytheway, *Investing Japan*. For an overview of changes in Japan's monetary system in the period 1897–1931, see e.g. Goldsmith, *Financial history*.

1 Continuities and Changes

1   For this consensus, I refer to the work of the two scholars who did most to demolish it: Hanley and Yamamura, *Economic and demographic change*, chapters 1 and 2.

2   Ohkawa and Rosovsky, *Japanese economic growth*, 4. At least for the first half of the Tokugawa era.

3   This is exactly the same position that would later on be defended by Ryoshin Minami in his *Economic development of Japan*, 29–31.

4   Ohkawa and Rosovsky, 'Century of economic growth', 58.

5   Halliday, *Political history*, 4–18. For the quotations see page 4.

6   Hane, *Japan. A historical survey*, 227. Hane has continued to be quite pessimistic about the plight of the ordinary people under Tokugawa rule, as shows in his later books dealing with that period.

7   Goldsmith, *Financial history*, chapter 2.

8   Nafziger, *Learning from the Japanese*, 11.

9   Orchard, *Japan's economic position*, 71.

10 Utley, *Japan's feet of clay*, 218.

11 The exact size of the population of Tokugawa Japan has been the subject of fierce controversy, in particular estimates for the seventeenth century. In this book, I will use the figures presented on page 25. With regard to population figures of Meiji Japan there is hardly any debate. All the authors I consulted think it grew from around thirty-three million in 1872 to around fifty million at the end of the reign of the Meiji Emperor and some seventy million in the late 1930s.

12 For a discussion of the meaning of the word 'Malthusian' in this context, see my *Escaping poverty*, 66–80.

13 Totman, *Early modern Japan*, 235–242.

14 Roberts, *Mercantilism in a domain*, under 'famine'.

15 Hane, *Modern Japan*, 56. For further details see e.g. Drixler, *Mabiki*.

16 See e.g. his *History of Japan*, where he describes the period from 1700 to 1850 as one of stasis and decay; chapters twelve and thirteen of his *Early modern Japan*, and chapter

six of his *Environmental history of Japan*. His interpretation, in which Tokugawa Japan entered a kind of ecological and demographical high-level equilibrium trap in the eighteenth century, finds a clear echo in Richards, *Unending frontier*, chapter five, and Parker, *Global crisis*, chapter sixteen. The focus in the work of Totman and in the references to it in the work of Parker and Richards is on the strategies of intensification and resource-saving that were developed to deal with ecological constraints.

17 Bix, *Peasant protests in Japan*; Borton, *Peasant uprisings*; Burton, 'Peasant struggle in Japan'; Paik, Steele, and Tanaka, 'Rebellion and taxation'; Vlastos, *Peasant protests*; Walthall, *Peasant uprisings*; White, *Ikki*.

18 Howell, *Capitalism from within*, 6.

19 For the position of Hanley and Yamamura see especially Hanley and Yamamura, *Economic and demographic change* and Hanley, *Everyday things*. For an up-to-date synthesis of the revisionist position in its current form see Hayami and Kito, 'Demography and living standards' and Francks, *Japan and the Great Divergence*.

20 See for a general analysis of the (absence of a) connection between poverty, hunger, disease and death, Livi-Bacci, *Population and nutrition*.

21 For fires in Japan see for example Jones, *Growth recurring*, 163.

22 Hanley and Yamamura, *Economic and demographic change*, 75.

23 Hanley, 'High standard of living in nineteenth-century Japan', 183. Although this view has become mainstream, it is not shared by all scholars in the field. For doubt and criticism with regard to Hanley's statement on the standard of living in late Tokugawa Japan see Yasuba, 'Standard of living'. Hanley reacts in her, 'Standard of living'. For other more critical and more recent comments see note 27 of this chapter. When it comes to life expectancy and health, the optimism of Hanley and Yamamura was shared by Alan Macfarlane in his *Savage wars of peace*.

24 See, for example, Spencer, 'Japan's pre-Perry preparation' and Pauer, 'Ten lost years'.

25 See for the concept 'advanced organic economy', Wrigley, *Continuity, chance and change* and for the concept 'Smithian growth', Kelly, 'Dynamics of Smithian growth'.

26 See for example his contribution to Austin and Sugihara, *Labour-intensive industrialization*.

27 I refer the reader in particular to chapter 5 of that book. For a very optimistic interpretation of the economy of Tokugawa Japan, see Brown, 'Meiji Japan'. As I wrote before, more negative interpretations have not entirely disappeared. See e.g. Hane and Perez, *Pre-modern Japan*; Kumon, 'How equality created poverty' and Kwon, *State formation*.

28 Jones, *European miracle*, 158–159. I here refer to the pages in the second edition of the book of 1987. The book by Jacobs that Jones is referring to with approval is Jacobs, *Origin of modern capitalism*.

29 Jones, *Growth recurring*, 151. For claims by Jones that Japan could and would have done it on its own, see for example Jones, *Growth recurring*, 37–39, 152–153, 166–167 and 191–192; idem, 'Capitalism: one origin or two?' and idem, 'Missing out'.

30 Jones, 'Missing out'.

31 Jones, *Growth recurring*, and 'Missing out'.

32 Powelson, *Centuries of economic endeavour*, passim, 2.

33 Sanderson, *Social transformations*, chapter five.

34 Landes, *Wealth and poverty*, 360 and 368.

35 Zöllner, *Geschichte Japans*, 223. The translation is mine.

36 Alexander, *Arc of Japan's economic development*, 24.

37 Bernier, *Capitalisme, société et culture*, 382–383. The original reads: 'Pour résumer: rien ne nous permet de dire que Japon serait devenue une puissance industrielle selon ses propres tendances sans l'intervention occidentale.' See also, 389–393.
38 Hayami, *Japan's industrious revolution*, 98, 124 and 128.
39 Howe, *Origins of Japanese trade supremacy*, 71.
40 Inkster, *Japanese industrial economy*, 6. See also Inkster, *Japanese industrialization*, 11 and 27.
41 Macfarlane, *Japan through the looking glass*, 74.
42 See page 6–7.
43 Hunter, 'Roots of divergence', 85.
44 See e.g. Lockwood, *Economic development*, 11, where he writes that when it comes to Japan's industrialization: 'Its tempo reflected the release of indigenous forces long latent in Japan' or Morris-Suzuki, *Technological transformation*, 34–36.
45 Mosk, *Japanese economic development*, 93. See also page 53 of that text.
46 For a thorough critique of the construction, use, and interpretation of data with regard to pre-industrial, often pre-statistical and only partially 'marketized' and monetized economies, and of the assumptions underlying these constructs, see Deng and O'Brien, 'Establishing statistical foundations' and idem, 'How well did facts travel'. I am very sceptical even when it comes to the information for the nineteenth and twentieth centuries that one can distil from often-used 'data sets' like the book by Tanzi and Schuknecht, *Public spending* or Max Roser, *Our world in data*. I found much of the information in them 'unverifiable', and a lot of it highly improbable and not suited as data for serious comparative analysis.
47 See Saito, 'Japan', 173 for these figures and a reference to how he and Takashima calculated it.
48 Kumon, 'How inequality created poverty'.
49 Francks, *Japanese consumer*; idem, 'Simple pleasures; idem, *Japan and the Great Divergence*; Francks and Hunter, *Historical consumer*; Hanley, *Everyday things*; Macfarlane, *Savage wars of peace*.
50 Hanley, *Everyday things*, chapter six.
51 Hanley, *Everyday things*, 135 and 137.
52 See pages 68–69.
53 Crawcour, 'Tokugawa heritage', 41.
54 Crawcour, 'Tokugawa heritage', 41.
55 Goldsmith, *Financial development of Japan*, 5. It is not clear to me how exactly Goldsmith comes to this estimate.
56 Compare, however, Ohkawa and Rosovsky, 'Century of Japanese economic growth', 57, where the authors come up with a much lower level of marketization, claiming: 'The statement that Japanese agriculture by the 1860s had become basically commercial is not rare but it is almost certainly wrong. At present (1963) slightly over sixty per cent of agricultural output reaches the market. In the 1860s, before the land tax, the ratio probably stood at the level of about twenty per cent.' In a footnote, they make this very important qualification: 'In our assessment of agricultural output reaching the market we *exclude* (Italics, P.V.) the rice tax sold by the *bushi* class because the real point is the extent to which the farmer was practicing commercial agriculture.'
57 Francks, *Rural economic development*, 51 and 126.
58 Dore, *Education*, 31, 291 and 317–322. Interestingly enough Dore himself wrote a few years later: 'I found it hard to follow the logic of the reasoning which led to this guess.'

See the collection of his texts edited by D. Hugh Wittaker, *Social evolution, economic development and culture* (Cheltenham 2001) 194.

59 Passin, *Society and education*, 57. For some further information in particular with regard to schooling during the Tokugawa era, see Inkster, *Japanese industrialisation*, 48–51; Kawada and Levine, *Human resources*, 38–47.

60 I found this quote in Saito, 'Japan', 177–178.

61 As far as this can be deduced from information about schooling.

62 See for that comment Rubinger, 'From "Dark Corners" into "The Light"', 608. I could not consult this text myself but found the reference in Alexander, *Arc of Japanese development*, 22. For general information on literacy in the Tokugawa and the Meiji era see Rubinger, *Popular literacy*.

63 Lindert, *Growing public*, 91–93.

64 For further general information on Tokugawa literacy and schooling see Amano, *Education and examination*; Dore, *Education in Tokugawa Japan*; Passin, *Society and education in Japan*, and Tsujimoto and Yamasaki, *History of education in Japan*, the relevant parts. For the later period, in particular the Meiji era, see Duke, *History of modern Japanese education*; Platt, *School, community and state integration*; Platt, *Burning and building*, and Tsujimoto and Yamasaki, *History of education in Japan*, the relevant parts. For some comparative data with regard to years of education, see Van Leeuwen and Van Leeuwen-Li, 'Education since 1820', 96.

65 Ma, 'China', 190.

66 See for further explanation of this concept Wrigley, *Continuity, chance and change*, chapter 2. Akira Hayami and Hiroshi Kito in their 'Demography and living standards', 245 explicitly refer to Tokugawa Japan as such.

67 Rostow, *Stages of economic growth*, chapter four.

68 Hobsbawm, *Age of revolution*, 45.

69 Kuznets, *Prize lecture*.

70 The tendency to do so can be quite misleading, as I discuss in my *Escaping poverty* 17–79, but it is undeniable that often industrialization did play a major role. The concept and the emphasis will not go away so I guess it is better to, prudently, keep using it.

71 Landes, *Wealth and poverty*, 186.

72 Wrigley, *Continuity, chance and change*.

73 Fukao and Settsu, 'Japan: modern economic growth'.

74 Maddison, *Contours of the world economy*, 383 and 380.

75 Mokyr, *Enlightened economy*, 261. Total net investment will have been an estimated two to four per cent lower. There are other estimates, but they are not fundamentally different. See e.g. Crafts, *British economic growth*, 73.

76 Fukao and Settsu, 'Japan: Modern economic growth'.

77 Utley, *Feet of clay*, chapters I and II.

78 Allen, *Global economic history*, 126.

79 See for example Hobsbawm, *Nations and nationalism*, 66.

80 Ravina, *To stand with the nations of the world*, 106 and 107.

81 Ravina, *To stand with the nations of the world*, 119.

82 Ravina, *To stand with the nations of the world*, 123 and 86 and https://en.wikipedia.org/wiki/Tokugawa_Yoshinobu Wikipedia.

83 There are no trustworthy precise figures for Japan's GDP for this period. For an estimate that it would have amounted to some 300 million yen in the '1860s', see Goldsmith, *Financial history*, 4.

84　He, *Paths toward the modern fiscal state*, 92–93.

85　He, *Paths toward the modern fiscal state*, 84.

86　Souyri, *Moderne sans être occidental*, 56–57.

87　Ravina, *To stand with the nations of the world*, 56.

88　Ravina, *To stand with the nations of the world*, 83. For a similar view see Beasley, *Modern history*, 36. For a different one, see e.g. Thomas Huber, who writes about 'a domestic affair, in which the western challenge figured only as a convenient instrumentality'. Huber, *Revolutionary origins*, 3.

89　For the concepts 'modern' and 'national state' see chapter 2.

2　A Sovereign and Modern State

1　For a brief overview of contacts between Western imperialist powers and Tokugawa Japan from the late eighteenth century onwards, see Ravina, *To stand with the nations of the world*, chapter 2.

2　See e.g. Beasley, *Japanese imperialism*, 20–22.

3　Inkster, *Japanese industrialisation*, 44.

4　Macpherson, *Economic development*, 1.

5　Marx, *Capital*, Vol. I, 878. This part of *Capital* was published in 1867.

6　I found this quote in Morris-Suzuki, *Technological transformation*, 13.

7　Moulder, *Japan, China and the modern world economy*, 2.

8　I found this quote in Allen, *Short economic history*, 48.

9　See e.g. Ravina, *To stand with the nations of the world*, 139.

10　I found this comment in Hattori, *Foreign commerce*, 44 who refers for its original to the lemma 'Japan' in the *Encyclopaedia Britannica*, new vol., 29.

11　A typical opinion was that of a French observer, published in 1905: « En somme il faut dire que l'industrie japonaise semble incapable d'entrer en concurrence sérieuse, sur les marchés européens, avec nos usines . . . il (le Japon P.V.) ne doit guère songer à lutter avec les nations européennes en ce qui concerne les manufacturés même avec les avantages de main d'œuvre à bon marché dont il jouit. Au point de vue industriel, il ne fera toujours que de mauvaises contrefaçons des produits européens, dignes au plus, par leur bas prix, d'approvisionner les marchés d'Extrême-Asie. » I found this quote in Allen, *Short economic history*, 98–99.

12　Such ideas may have been popular but they were never shared by all foreigners. See for changing images of Japan, e.g. Lehmann, *Image of Japan* and Miyoshi and Harootunian, *Japan in the world*.

13　See pages 87–88.

14　Japan, moreover, profited from setbacks that hit competing economies and from the fact that its effort to catch up took place in a period in which goods, people and ideas could move freely around the globe. See for further comments pages 190–202.

15　For the extent to which Western powers ruled the world in the period discussed in this book see Etemad, *Possessing the world*.

16　Moulder, *Japan, China, and the modern world economy*.

17　See for scholars who also point at less negative effects of these treaties, pages 46–47.

18　See e.g. Beasley, *Japanese imperialism*, 17 and 25.

19　See e.g. Auslin, *Negotiating with imperialism*.

20　For the text of the most important 'model' treaty, the Treaty of Amity and Commerce of July 1858 between the USA and Japan, see Walthall and Steel, *Politics and society*, 59–65.

21 For background information see Perez, 'Revision'.
22 For the thesis that they were not really harmful see e.g. Nafziger, *Learning from the Japanese*, 29, and Sugiyama, *Japan's industrialization*, 53–54, 67–68 and 74–76.
23 See e.g. Allen, *Short economic history*, 10 and 170; Hattori, *Foreign commerce*, 15; Nakamura and Odaka, 'Inter-war period', 7; Powell, 'How entrepreneurs created the great boom'.
24 Mosk, *Japanese industrial history*, 65. See for an analysis of life in those treaty ports, Phipps, *Empires on the waterfront*.
25 Westney, *Imitation and innovation*, 22.
26 Inkster, *Technology transfer*, 184.
27 Inkster, *Japanese industrial economy*, 31–32.
28 See, for example, Hellyer, *Defining engagement*, in the Index, under 'Choson, Kingdom, proposed Japanese invasions of'; Ravina, *To stand with the nations of the world*, 162, notes 78 and 81. For imperialist ideas that predated the Meiji Restoration, see e.g. Tsuzuki, *Pursuit of power*, 27–36.
29 Ohno, *Economic development of Japan*, 86.
30 The quote is from *The New York Times*, 6 December 1874. I found it in Ravina, *To stand with the nations of the world*, 169.
31 The quote is from the *Pall Mall Gazette*, 20 March 1876. I found it in Ravina, *To stand with the nations of the world*, 170.
32 For reactions to this conflict in the West, see Paine, *Sino-Japanese War*. The quote is from this book, page 295.
33 Lone, *Army, empire and politics*, 100–105.
34 See e.g. Lehmann, *Image of Japan*, chapter 6.
35 For a list of humiliating experiences see Stein, *Made in Japan*, 121–122.
36 I took this information from Inkster, *Japanese industrialisation*, 57–59; Nafziger, *Learning from the Japanese*, 43; Norman, *Japan's emergence*, 116–117.
37 For Sino-Japanese 'political' relations during the Tokugawa era, see Kang, *East Asia before the West*.
38 For the concept 'tozama daimyo' see the index.
39 I distinguish between the Portuguese and Spaniards and their respective religious orders as they in practice pursued different policies even though their two countries were effectively under one ruler from 1580 to 1640.
40 For the current view on *sakoku*, see Arano, 'Foreign relations'; Innes, *Door ajar*; Tashiro, 'Foreign relations': Toby, *State and diplomacy*.
41 For the concept 'modern state' see Vries, 'States'.
42 The various elements of the definition will all be discussed extensively at suitable places in my analysis. Here I confine myself to the general claim that after the Meiji Restoration Japan became a modern state and to some specific comments.
43 I here refer to the Ryukyu Islands, the Bonin or Osagawara Islands, and Ezo, or, as it came to be called, 'Hokkaido'. The relationship between Japan and China when it came to Korea and Taiwan also was 'unclear' from the perspective of Western international law. Here too the Japanese enforced their solution.
44 I refer for further information to Ravina, *To stand with the nations of the world*, under the relevant references in the index.
45 For information on the 'colonization' of Hokkaido, I refer to Seaton, 'Japanese empire in Hokkaido'.
46 See Sakata, 'Transformation of Hokkaido'. *Gaichi*, or outer territories, was the designation of the regions that were *not yet* included in the mainland: Taiwan, Korea,

Karafuto, Kwantung Leased Territory and the South Sea Islands. In principle, they would be incorporated into mainland Japan once they had been fully assimilated.

47 See e.g. Shosuke, 'Hokkaido and its progress'.

48 Zöllner, *Geschichte Japans*, 201.

49 See for these figures http://www.ainu-museum.or.jp/en/study/eng01.html. Paul Mayet estimated the island's total population at 124,000 in 1871 and at 163,000 in 1880. See Mayet, *Agricultural insurance*, 190. Over time an increasing number of Ainu intermarried with Japanese.

50 Ravina, *To stand with the nations of the world*, the Index, under 'Ryukyu, as part of the Meiji state'.

51 Rabson, 'Meiji assimilation policy', 642.

52 https://apjjf.org/2013/11/41/Steve-Rabson/4008/article.html

53 This had consequences for the implementation of the freedom of worship that Meiji Japan officially had declared. In the Meiji Constitution, Article 28 reads 'Japanese subjects shall, within limits not prejudicial to peace and order and not antagonistic to their duties as subjects, enjoy the freedom of religious belief.' The Constitution as such did not adopt the principle of separation of religion from the state. In particular radical Shintoists could be very anti-Christian.

54 I found this phrase in Souyri, *Moderne sans être occidental,* 227 and 296. The claim as such that the *Tenno* of Japan was Emperor and Pope at the same time is made frequently in the literature.

55 For further information about the relation between state and nation in Japan see Doak, *History of nationalism*; Gluck, *Japan's modern myths*; Souyri, *Moderne sans être occidental.*

56 Longford, *Evolution of new Japan*, 62.

57 See the next note.

58 McCormack, *Japan's outcaste abolition.*

59 See e.g. for concrete examples Yoshimi, *Grassroots fascism*, chapter 2, the part about 'ranking the people'.

60 See e.g. Gluck, *Japan's modern myths*; Oguma, *Genealogy of Japanese self-images*; idem, *Boundaries of 'the Japanese',* the volumes of 2014 and 2017.

61 Doak, *History of nationalism*, 148.

62 Taiwan, Korea and Karafuto, in the end, were meant to be integrated culturally and politically into Japan. See Beasley, *Japanese imperialism*, 143.

63 Ravina, *To stand with the nations of the world*, 216.

64 I took this information from Totman, *Politics in the Tokugawa Bakufu*, chapter X.

65 For information on the different kinds of *daimyo*, their functions and status see pages 56–59.

66 Totman, *Politics in the Tokugawa Bakufu*, 62–63.

67 Totman, *Politics in the Tokugawa Bakufu*, 62–63.

68 Ikegami, *Taming of the samurai*, 159.

69 These so-called 'five-men groups' were only abolished in 1888. See Samson, *History of Japan*, 103.

70 Westney, *Imitation and innovation*, 35–37.

71 See for further information Ravina, *To stand with the nations of the world*, 26–37.

72 We will expand on that on pages 64–70. The reference to provinces indicates that Tokugawa Japan was not only split up in a large number of fiefs or *han* but also still knew the traditional division in provinces.

73 And not as the expression suggests already from the Peace of Westphalia of 1648 onwards.

74 See again Ravina, *To stand with the nations of the world* and, for more detailed information, Kang, *East Asia before the West*.

75 Totman, *Politics in the Tokugawa Bakufu*, 131.

76 I am rather imprecise here because in almost every text I consulted I found a different figure for their exact number at the time when the system was abolished. All the figures I found, however, lay between 250 and 300. For the purposes of my analysis that is 'precise' enough.

77 Koyama, Moriguchi and Sng, 'Geopolitics and Asia's Little Divergence', 9.

78 This is not the place to dwell on what different rights and obligations belonging to a specific estate entailed. For such information, I refer to e.g. Hall and McClain, *Cambridge History of Japan. Volume 4*, chapters 3–5. Here I only want to emphasize that Tokugawa Japan, much more than post-Restoration Japan, was a society of estates.

79 Again, we find quite differing estimates. See e.g. Ramming, 'Wirtschaftliche Lage', 5–6.

80 Hane and Perez, *Premodern Japan*, 195ff; Samson, *History of Japan*, 32 and Vande Walle, *Geschiedenis van Japan*, 179.

81 See for these estimates Hane, *Modern Japan*, 36 and 98. In *Japan Encyclopaedia* the number of *eta* at the end of the Tokugawa era is given as 280,000 and that of *hinin* as 2,350. According to Zöllner, *Geschichte Japans*, 198, the number of *eta* in 1870 would have been 443,000 and that of *hinin* 77,000.

82 Groemer, 'Creation of the Edo outcast order'; Hane, *Peasants, rebels, women, and outcastes*, 138–171; McCormack, *Japan's outcaste abolition* and Vaporis, *Voices of early modern Japan*, 158–162.

83 I want to emphasize (again) that pointing at the importance of the centralization of Japan from the Meiji era onwards, does not imply that local and regional government would become irrelevant.

84 Mosk, *Japanese industrial history*, 70.

85 Scott, *Seeing like a state*, 2. I already discussed legibility in my *State, economy and the Great Divergence*, chapter 8 and therefore will not repeat myself extensively here.

86 See e.g. Foucault and Sennellart, *Security, territory, population*.

87 This is a, not entirely correct, short-hand. For the exact way in which the land tax was assessed see page 116.

88 See e.g. Wigen, Sugimoto and Karacas, *Cartographic Japan*. Although the book is more about maps than about the discipline and organization of cartography, it is certainly helpful and provides many references for further reading. For the Tokugawa period Berry, *Japan in print* also provides interesting information.

89 For some general information see www.soumu.go.jp/main_content/000439906.pdf. For a timeline of the development of statistics in Japan see www.nstac.go.jp/en/about/timeline.html. For the *Dajokan* see Frédéric, *Japan Encyclopaedia* and Ravina, *To stand with the nations of the world*, the Index, under 'Council of State'.

90 Ravina, *To stand with the nations of the world*, 155. For the comment on salary payment see footnote 46 of that page.

91 For written Japanese see Twine, 'Standardizing written Japanese'.

92 He, *Paths toward the modern fiscal state*, 95.

93 The value of the yen as such of course could change as could its backing in gold or silver. I only want to indicate here that it became the national currency of Japan.

94 He, *Paths toward the modern fiscal state*, 232.

95 Masaki, 'Formation and evolution', 29.

96   For further information see Shizume and Tsurumi, 'Modernizing the financial system'. For an overview of the financial history of Japan at the time see Goldsmith, *Financial development of Japan*.

97   Tamaki, *Japanese banking*. Part Two: 'Monetary confusion and banking experiments, 1868–1881'.

98   Mosk, *Japanese industrial history*, 68 and 211.

99   Patrick, 'Japan, 1868–1914'. For more information about the banking system see e.g. various authors in Tolliday, *Economic development of modern Japan*, Volume II, Part One, 1–131.

100 Patrick, 'Japan 1868–1914', 284 and 288, and Sheridan, *Governing the Japanese economy*, 38, 54, and 78–79.

101 Patrick, 'Japan 1868–1914', 289 and Masaki, 'Formation and evolution', 32.

102 Mosk, *Japanese industrial history*, 92.

103 Masaki, 'Formation and evolution', 32.

104 He, *Paths toward the modern fiscal state*, 4–5.

105 He, *Paths toward the modern fiscal state*, 108.

106 He, *Paths toward the modern fiscal state*, 128.

107 He, *Paths toward the modern fiscal state*, 105, 109 and 111.

108 See for details Bassino, Fukao and Settsu, 'Economic geography'.

109 Mosk, *Japanese industrial history*, 78–79.

110 Epstein, *Freedom and growth*, 69.

111 Toby, 'Rescuing the nation'.

112 Totman, *Politics in the Tokugawa Bakufu*, 251.

113 For the debate on how to designate the Tokugawa polity, see e.g. Eisenstadt, *Japanese civilization*, passim and Ravina, 'State-building and political economy'. For the claim that Tokugawa Japan would have been a 'compound' state see Ravina, *To stand with the nations of the world*, 37.

114 Hane and Perez, *Premodern Japan*, 265.

115 Bytheway, *Investing Japan*, 9 and 14.

116 The classic text is Roberts, *Mercantilism in a Japanese domain*. See for further examples Gramlich-Oka and Smits, *Economic thought*, in particular 89–177.

117 Morris-Suzuki, 'Sericulture', 106.

118 Roberts, *Mercantilism in a Japanese domain*, 140 and 190.

119 Landes, *Wealth and poverty*, 360 and 363.

120 Hayami, *Japan's industrious revolution*, 62–65 and 107–110.

121 See Tsukahira, *Feudal control* and Vaporis, *Tour of duty*.

122 Roberts, *Mercantilism in a domain*, 18.

123 Tsukahira, *Feudal control*, 88–102.

124 Ravina, *To stand with the nations of the world*, 44. He does so referring to a text by Maruyama Yasunari from 2007.

125 Taxes in principle were assessed in terms of rice or rice equivalents and based on the (estimated) yield of different types (paddy, dry and built), and qualities (above average, average, below) of land. Originally, at least in those regions where rice was grown, tax primarily had to be paid in kind. Overall, however, the importance of payments in money increased steadily. See for further details pages 125–135.

126 Mosk, *Japanese industrial history*, 34–35.

127 Tsukahira, *Feudal control* and Hall, 'Castle town'.

128 See for further discussion Rozman, *Urban networks* and Rozman, 'East Asian urbanization'.

129 The figures in this paragraph are from Totman, *Japan. An environmental history*, 162, and Vaporis, *Voices of early modern Japan*, XXVI.
130 See e.g. Smith, 'Pre-modern economic growth'.
131 Smith, 'Pre-modern economic growth', 129.
132 Malanima, *Pre-modern European economy*, 242–243.
133 Miyamoto, 'Quantitative aspects', 81.
134 Miyamoto, 'Quantitative aspects', in particular 74–82, and Shimbo and Hasegawa, 'Dynamics of market economy and production'.
135 Saito and Settsu, 'Money, credit and Smithian growth', 13.
136 I am paraphrasing Mosk, *Competition and cooperation*, 27–33.
137 For a quote in which a younger son of a local samurai in 1765 explicitly refers to this goal, see Roberts, *Mercantilism in a domain*, 157.

3 A Powerful State: Politics, Ideology, the Military and the Bureaucracy

1 For these definitions see Mann, 'Autonomous power', 113.
2 Morris, *Why the West rules for now*, 24.
3 Mann, 'Autonomous power', 113.
4 Mann provides an extensive explanation of the meaning of these four sources, without, however, coming up with a brief definition that I can use as a 'shortcut'. I therefore refer to his *Sources of social power*. Volume I, 22–33.
5 Besley and Persson, *Pillars of prosperity*, 6.
6 Johnson and Koyama, 'States and economic growth', 'Introduction'.
7 Johnson and Koyama, 'States and economic growth', 'Introduction'. I do not endorse the claim that the eighteenth-century British state had high state capacity *even though it played a very limited role in the economy* (italics P.V.). I think that I showed in my *State, economy and the Great Divergence* that this role was substantial.
8 See for comparative analyses with a focus on economic and in particular financial resources and dealing with countries and periods relevant for the analysis of this book: Cardoso and Lains, *Paying for the liberal state*; Dincecco, *Political transformations and public finances*; Gupta, Ma and Roy, 'States and development'; He, *Paths toward the modern fiscal state*; Johnson and Koyama, 'States and economic growth'; Koyama, Moriguchi and Sng, 'Geopolitics and Asia's Little Divergence'; Ma, 'State capacity and Great Divergence'; Sng and Moriguchi, 'Asia's little divergence'; Vries, *State, economy and the Great Divergence*; Yun-Casalilla, O'Brien and Comín-Comín, *Rise of fiscal states*.
9 As is claimed by Caplan in his 'State capacity'.
10 Perkins, 'Government as an obstacle'.
11 Caplan, 'State capacity'.
12 Caplan, 'State capacity'.
13 See for the number of people involved and of fatalities page 93.
14 Hane, *Modern Japan*, 126; Hane, *Peasants, rebels, & outcasts*, 21–27; Inkster, *Japanese industrialisation*, 74.
15 Inkster, *Japanese industrialisation*, 76.
16 Inkster, *Japanese industrialisation*, 76.
17 Najita and Koschmann, *Conflict in modern Japanese history*.
18 See Gordon, *Labour and imperial democracy*, 3 and 33.

19 I took this information from Lewis, *Rioters and citizens.*
20 See for a positive interpretation of the 1920s in Japan's history, Dickinson, *World War I.*
21 For further information see Banno, *Japan's modern history*, 195–231.
22 Garon, *Beyond our means*, 147.
23 For that mission see page 203.
24 This oath opens with the sentence: 'By this oath, we set up as our aim the establishment of the national wealth on a broad basis and the framing of a constitution and laws.' Its first article reads: 'Deliberative assemblies shall be widely established and all matters decided by open discussion.' The second one reads: 'All classes, high and low, shall be united in vigorously carrying out the administration of affairs of state.'
25 I paraphrase Doak, *History of nationalism*, 91.
26 I refer the reader who thinks this is exaggerated to Hane, *Modern Japan*, which extensively shows how limited the rights of the Japanese as subjects of the Emperor and the ruling cliques were at the time.
27 See chapter 5.
28 In writing these paragraphs, I based myself primarily on Banno, *Japan's modern history*; Hane, *Modern Japan* and Tsuzuki, *Pursuit of power.*
29 A revised electoral law of 1900 also applied to Hokkaido and Okinawa. See Tsuzuki, *Pursuit of power*, 111. The inhabitants of European and US ancestry of the Bonin Islands were granted Japanese nationality in 1882.
30 See for its text www.ndl.go.jp/constitution/e/etc/c02.html
31 Gluck, *Japan's modern myths*, 49.
32 Gluck, *Japan's modern myths*, 132–135 and Souyri, *Moderne sans être occidental*, 305–323.
33 He, *Paths toward the modern fiscal state*, 91.
34 Ienaga, *Pacific War*, 35.
35 For further explanation see Ienaga, *Pacific War*, chapter 3.
36 Beasley, *Japanese imperialism*, 145. Taiwan, Korea, and South Sakhalin are here considered as *de facto* Japan's colonies. In the Kwantung leased territory in China where the South Manchuria Railway Company had its concession, the role of the military also was quite prominent. For basic information, I refer to https://en.wikipedia.org/wiki/Kwantung_Leased_Territory. When the puppet state of Manchukuo was created, it too effectively was administered by the Japanese military.
37 See for a brief overview Banno, *Japan's modern history*, 195–231.
38 Tamanoi, *Under the shadow of nationalism*, 43 and Nolte and Hasting, 'Meiji's state policy', 154–155.
39 In this paragraph I paraphrase Gluck, *Japan's modern myths*, 48–59.
40 Dickinson, *World War I.*
41 See for the change of climate, Dickinson, *World War I*, chapter 5, 'Disarmament', where on pages 116–121 there is even talk of 'armed services as pariahs', and Peattie, *Ishiwara Kanji*, chapter I.
42 Drea, *Japan's imperial army*, 181. See for a description and analysis of terrorism Byas, *Government by assassination* and Skya, *Japan's holy war*, chapter 8.
43 See for that text De Bary, Gluck and Tiedemann, *Sources of Japanese tradition, Volume Two, part two*, 277–284.
44 See for these laws https://en.wikipedia.org/wiki/Peace_Preservation_Law. For the general political climate, I can refer to the many surveys of Japan's political history in the period discussed, e.g. Banno, *Japan's modern history*. For the way in which labour and 'socialist' organizations more generally were treated, see Garon, *State and labor*;

idem, *Molding Japanese minds*; idem, *Evolution of labour relations*; idem, *Labor and imperial democracy*; Large, *Yuaikai*; Marsland, *Birth of the Japanese labour movement*. For the history of the press see Coyne, *Censorship of publishing*; Kasza, *State and the mass media*; Mitchell, *Censorship*. According to the Constitution, there was freedom of the press, but only 'within the limits of the law'. Freedom of the press only became a fundamental right after 1945.

45 Gluck, *Japan's modern myths*, 175–176.
46 See chapter 5.
47 Hane, *Modern Japan*, 203.
48 See for this quote Ravina, *To stand with the nations of the world*, 167. Banno in this context also makes comparisons with what he calls the 'development dictatorship' of several Asian countries after World War Two. See his *Japan's modern history*, 75.
49 As we will see later, it was *also* strong in terms of infrastructural power.
50 Acemoglu and Robinson, *Why nations fail*.
51 Acemoglu and Robinson, *Why nations fail*, 119.
52 Acemoglu and Robinson, *Why nations fail*, 297.
53 Acemoglu and Robinson, *Why nations fail*, 366.
54 Acemoglu and Robinson, *Why nations fail*, 429–430. See for several other, always slightly varying, descriptions, the Index, under 'extractive institutions' and 'inclusive institutions'.
55 For general information, I refer to the many general introductions to the (political) history of Japan at the time. See, for example, Banno, *Japan's modern history*.
56 I will discuss that extensively in my next book.
57 See e.g. Engerman and Sokoloff, *Economic development*, 159; Fukuyama, *Political order and political decay*, 412–426. The link between economic growth and representation, so dear to many institutionalist economists, in any case for the initial stages of industrialization, is all but absent, 'even' for the case of Great Britain. See my *State, economy and the Great Divergence*.
58 I am very critical of their book. See my 'Does wealth entirely depend on inclusive institutions and pluralist politics'.
59 For the quotes see Ward, 'Authoritarianism', 479 and 483.
60 For their claims, the texts where they make them, *and* the reasons why in my view they are incorrect, see my *State, economy and the Great Divergence*, the Index, under their names.
61 See for that claim and the literature in which it is made, the many references to Tilly and Brewer in my *State, economy and the Great Divergence*.
62 He, *Paths toward the modern fiscal state*, 19–20.
63 I found this quote in Westney, *Imitation and innovation*, 35.
64 Longford, *Evolution of new Japan*, 9, 11 and 12.
65 Norman, *Japan's emergence as a modern state*, 12.
66 Vande Walle, *Geschiedenis van Japan*, 166.
67 See e.g. Hane and Perez, *Premodern Japan*, in which the authors speak about the Tokugawa regime in terms such as 'rigorous', 'harsh', or 'discriminating'.
68 See, for examples, Vaporis, *Voices of early modern Japan* and Nakane and Oishi, *Tokugawa Japan*.
69 Vaporis, *Voices of early modern Japan*, 68–73.
70 See pages 109–110.
71 Vaporis, *Voices of early modern Japan*, 74–78.

72 See for the self-governing of villages, chapters 6 and 7 of *Cambridge History of Japan. Volume Four*. For a concrete example of such strict and elaborate rules, in this case for one village in 1640, see Vaporis, *Voices of early modern Japan*, 86–87. For their high degree of autonomy, see for example Aratake, 'Samurai and peasants'.

73 For an introductory overview, see Nabuhiko, 'Commercial change' and Vaporis, *Voices of early modern Japan*, 89–97.

74 See, for example, Botsman, *Punishment and power*.

75 Hane, *Modern Japan*, 57–60.

76 Bendix, *Kings or people*, 440.

77 See for further information: Hane and Perez, *Premodern Japan*; Nakane and Oishi, *Tokugawa Japan*; Totman, *Early modern Japan*; Vaporis, *Voices of early modern Japan*, and *Cambridge History of Japan. Volume 4*.

78 Totman, *Politics in the Tokugawa Bakufu*, 242.

79 Mann, *Sources of social power*, I, 22–24.

80 Rostow, *Stages of economic growth*, 7.

81 Rostow, *Stages of economic growth*, 120. Marshall uses exactly the same expression for the case of Meiji Japan, see his *Capitalism and nationalism* 13.

82 Rostow, *Stages of economic growth*, 34.

83 See Gerschenkron, *Economic backwardness*, 22–26, and Lewis, *Theory of economic growth*, 376–377.

84 For exact references and further explanation, I refer to my *State, economy and the Great Divergence*, chapter 8.

85 See for example Sheridan, *Governing the Japanese economy*, chapter 2. It would be a digression to expand on that here, but in this respect too Japan's post-Restoration rulers could build on Tokugawa legacies in the form, e.g. of a labour force that had been disciplined into working hard.

86 Dyer, *Dai Nippon*, 32.

87 Dyer, *Dai Nippon*, 33, 48 and 49.

88 Stead, *Great Japan*, 2, 5, 17 and 163–164. For further information on this fascination in Great Britain with Japanese national efficiency at the beginning of the twentieth century, see Searle, *Quest for national efficiency*, 57–59 and Tonooka, 'Reverse emulation'.

89 Pearse, *Cotton industry*, 14.

90 Gluck, *Japan's modern myths*, chapter I.

91 Gluck, *Japan's modern myths*, 39. See also *ibid.*, 16.

92 See Skya, *Japan's holy war*, passim.

93 Gluck, *Japan's modern myths*, chapter II.

94 Gluck, *Japan's modern myths*, 115. The term 'kokutai' refers to the 'national essence' or 'national identity' of Japan.

95 Gluck, *Japan's modern myths*, 118–119. Chapter V of this book deals in its entirety with 'civil morality'.

96 Thus it reads in a document produced by a meeting of prefectural governors in 1890. See Gluck, *Japan's modern myths*, 117.

97 I refer the reader who wants to read it to De Bary, Gluck and Tiedemann, *Sources of Japanese tradition 1600 to 2000, Volume Two, Part Two*, 108–110. There are also several versions of it on the internet under 'Imperial Rescript on education'.

98 Inkster, *Japanese industrialisation*, 91.

99 Gluck, *Japan's modern myths*, 147.

100 We must overall be wary of making too tight a connection between education and schooling on the one hand and the building of human capital that can be made

relevant for economic development on the other. In the first phases of industrialization, in Japan as elsewhere, skill requirements, especially for skills learned in formal education, as a rule were not high and, what is more, they often across the board tended to *decrease* instead of increase. See note 35, chapter 7.

101 Garon, *Molding Japanese minds*. The book also covers several decades after World War Two.

102 The text of this Rescript is too long to reproduce here. I refer the reader to the internet. I used www.facstaff.bucknell.edu/jamesorr/impressoldsailors1882web.htm.

103 Gluck, *Japan's modern myths*, 147.

104 Drea, *Japan's imperial army*, 154.

105 For further information on state ideology in Japan I refer to Doak, *History of nationalism*; Gluck, *Japan's modern myths*; Skya, *Japan's holy war* and Souyri, *Moderne sans être occidental*.

106 See Hardacre, *Shinto and the state* and, in particular, Skya, *Japan's holy war*.

107 See for this phenomenon Mosse, *Nationalization of the masses*.

108 Doak, *History of nationalism*, chapter two. For more details see Burns, *Before the nation*.

109 Ravina, *To stand with the nations of the world*, 180.

110 Drea, *Japan's imperial army*, 29, 31, 51 55 and 154.

111 Drea, *Japan's imperial army*, 31.

112 Drea, *Japan's imperial army*, 188 and 199.

113 Drea, *Japan's imperial army*, 30, 77, 93, 95, 135 and 160.

114 Drea, *Japan's imperial army*, 67.

115 France and the United Kingdom also had a substantial military in their colonies. One has to be careful in interpreting such numbers, as it is hard to determine who should count as military and who shouldn't. Just think of people in training, reservists, etc. The only thing I want to indicate here is that it is far from obvious that Japan in terms of sheer numbers would have been extraordinarily 'militarized'.

116 Alexander, *Arc of Japan's economic development*, 58.

117 All figures in this paragraph are, unless indicated otherwise, from Drea, *Japan's imperial army*, 40, 45, 81, 84, 86, 91, 108, 116, 119, 137, 143 and 197.

118 Ienaga, *Pacific war*, 152.

119 As in many other sectors one tried not to be *dependent* on foreigners and their expertise and technology. Between 1882 and 1918 for example, the Imperial Japanese Navy did not rely on any foreign instructors.

120 The United States and Britain were each allocated 525,000 tons of capital ships, Japan 315,000 tons, whereas France and Italy were restricted to 175,000 tons each. Also agreed to was a ten-year moratorium on battleship construction. The replacement of battleships was allowed after they had reached twenty years of service. However, the battleships could not be bigger than 35,000 tons or carry guns larger than sixteen inches. Carriers were also restricted with the same 5:5:3 ratio.

121 See my *State, economy and the Great Divergence*, 300, in particular notes 24 and 26.

122 Smethurst, 'Creation of the Imperial Military Reserve Association'.

123 Bolito, 'The han', 220 and Totman, *Politics in the Tokugawa Bakufu*, 43.

124 Gat, *War in human civilization*, 364.

125 See for some figures Ramming, *Wirtschaftliche Lage*, 12–14.

126 Dowdy, *Japanese bureaucracy*, 44.

127 Ravina, *To stand with the nations of the world*, 39.

128 See pages 125–135. For a concise presentation see Tanimoto, 'From feudal lords to local notables', 20, Table 1.
129 The information in this paragraph is from Westney, *Imitation and innovation*, chapter 2.
130 Harootunian, 'Progress of Japan', 260–261.
131 See for further information pages 107–109.
132 For this definition *à la Weber*, see Mann, *Sources of social power, II*, 444–445.
133 See Silberman, *Cages of reason*; Fulger, 'Bureaucratisation of the state'; Kawada and Levine, *Human resources*; Koh, *Japan's administrative elite*, which is almost entirely about the period *after* 1945.
134 For the quotes by Johnson in this paragraph, see Johnson, *MITI*, 18–19, 21 and 317.
135 Muehlhoff, 'Economic costs'.
136 Emi, *Government fiscal activity*, 53.
137 Allen, *Short economic history*, 131.
138 At least not when compared to most other countries at the time.
139 See, for more details, pages 107–109.
140 See for the question in what respects and to what extent samurai might be considered officials or bureaucrats, Dowdy, *Japanese bureaucracy*, passim; Ikegami, *Taming of the samurai*, under 'bureaucracy', and Totman, *Politics in the Tokugawa Bakufu*, passim.
141 Totman, *Politics in the Tokugawa Bakufu*, 40 and Appendix B. For further information see also Dowdy, *Japanese bureaucracy* and Sng and Moriguchi, 'Asia's little divergence', chapters 2.2 and 2.3, that contain a comparison with Qing China and again show that also in terms of administration and monitoring Tokugawa Japan had more state capacity than the Qing Empire. See also Lieberman, *Strange parallels*, 442, note 207.
142 Dowdy, *Japanese bureaucracy*, 51, 129 and 133.
143 See my *State, economy and the Great Divergence*, 267–270.
144 I am actually quoting Ikegami, *Taming of the samurai*, 162.
145 Totman, *Politics in the Tokugawa Bakufu*, 45.
146 Totman, *Politics in the Tokugawa Bakufu*, 142.
147 Ikegami, *Taming of the samurai*, 162. The term *ie* can best be translated as 'household' including its 'entourage' and domestics.
148 Ikegami, *Taming of the samurai*, 267.
149 Ikegami, *Taming of the samurai*, 269–276.
150 Totman, *Politics in the Tokugawa Bakufu*, 151.
151 Totman, *Politics in the Tokugawa Bakufu*, 246.
152 Totman, *Politics in the Tokugawa Bakufu*, 147.
153 Dowdy, *Japanese bureaucracy*, XIII–XIV.
154 Totman, *Politics in the Bakufu*, chapter IX, 'The vertical clique'.
155 Dowdy, *Japanese bureaucracy*, chapters four and five. Berry, *Japan in print*, Chapter 4 also provides interesting insights.
156 Souyri, *Moderne sans être occidental*, 103 and 182.
157 Inkster, *Japanese industrialisation*, 77 and 97.
158 Sonoda, 'Decline of the Japanese warrior class', 103. For an analysis of the low level of social mobility in Japan after the Restoration, see also Clark and Ishii, 'Social mobility'.
159 Souyri, *Moderne sans être occidental*, 182.
160 Ikegami, *Taming of the samurai*, 363.
161 Multiple offices and job rotation were so popular because both created employment.

4 A Powerful State: The Economy

1   See the literature under note 8, chapter 3.
2   I took these figures from Yamawaki, *Japan in the beginning of the twentieth century*, 95–97. Rein in his *Industries of Japan*, 12 comes up with a similar figure for the percentage arable of all land. He claims that 12 per cent of total land of Japan was used for the cultivation of field products.
3   Vande Walle, *Geschiedenis van Japan*, 242.
4   I take these figures from Yamawaki, *Japan in the beginning of the twentieth century*, 95–97. Hiroshi Uchida claims that state-owned land comprised 67.5 per cent of all the land in Japan in 1883. That percentage then decreased to 51.4 per cent in 1924, due to the fact that state-owned land was sold off to Japanese nationals, businesses and the Meiji Emperors. Uchida, 'Marx's theory of history', 46. I found it impossible to check these figures but what counts in my analysis are useful and reliable approximations. The ones I found, all point at substantial landownership by the state.
5   Lockwood, *Economic development*, 554–555.
6   Yamawaki, *Japan in the beginning of the twentieth century*, 226–229.
7   For land as a percentage of total wealth in Japan and several other countries see page 107 and the literature referred to there.
8   For land owned by China's government see Huang, *Peasant economy and social change*, 87. Pomeranz, *Great Divergence*, 71, refers to this publication and concludes that crown land under the Qing never amounted to more than 3 per cent of total arable land. For public lands, see also Chen, *System of taxation*, 47–51.
9   The extension mainly took place in the 1880s. According to Mikiso Hane, between 1001 and 1890 'imperial land' increased from 634 *cho* to 3,654,000 *cho*. Hane, *Modern Japan*, 138. See also Halliday, *Political history of Japanese capitalism*, 11.
10 Hane, *Modern Japan*, 138.
11 Uchida, 'Marx's theory of history', 46.
12 Brown, *Cultivating commons*, 179–187.
13 Howell, *Capitalism from within*, 183.
14 Sheridan, *Governing the Japanese economy*, 260–261. For the value of land as a percentage of total wealth see also Shiomi, 'On Japan's national wealth and income', 31, and Hattori, 'Foreign trade', 11. Hattori there refers to an estimate for the end of the nineteenth century when land would have amounted to more than 60 per cent of Japan's national wealth, which seems rather high. We find a similarly high estimate though for the same period in time in Dyer, *Dai Nippon*, 307. In the calculations by Shiomi, covering the period 1905 to 1924, the percentage hovers between roughly thirty and forty-three. Lockwood, in his *Economic development*, 239, comes up with a calculation for 1930 in which land amounted to 37.4 per cent of national wealth and trees to 6.1 per cent.
15 I collected the information for this paragraph from Kawada and Levine, *Human resources*, 151–152, 155, 176, 242, 243, 246, 259–260.
16 Emi, *Government fiscal activity*, 10.
17 Ando, 'Formation of heavy industry', 455
18 Allen, 'Japanese industry', 610.
19 Hall, '*Bakuhan* system', 150–152. Philip Brown claims that from 1601 to 1760 there were 551 cases of peaceful fief transfers and 234 confiscations. See Brown, *Central authority*, 24.
20 See Sakudo, 'Domain paper currencies' and Totman, *Early modern Japan*, 328–332.
21 He, *Paths toward the modern fiscal state*, 210, note 88.

22 Vaporis, *Breaking barriers*, 28–31.

23 He, *Paths toward the modern fiscal state*, 107.

24 See for such measures chapters 2 and 3 of He, *Pathways toward the modern fiscal state*.

25 Sheridan, *Governing the Japanese economy*, 35–36.

26 See e.g. Table 47, page 125.

27 For total tax revenue see Piketty, *Capital in the twenty-first century*, 475; for total government revenue see Cardoso and Lains, 'Introduction', 18.

28 Spoerer, 'Evolution of public finances', 105 and 119.

29 Again, it is important to point out that we are only discussing tax revenue here. As we will see later, Japan's government also, and to an increasing extent, had other sources of revenue.

30 See Piketty, *Capital in the twenty-first century*, 475, for information on France and the United Kingdom and Spoerer, 'Öffentliche Finanzen', 106 and 110 for information on Germany. Please note, just like in the case of Japan, total government revenue in the other countries referred to in this text need not be identical to government's total tax revenue. Here more in-depth research would be welcome. Suffice it to say that in the German case for which I found information, total government revenue in the period 1913–1932 was about one-third higher than tax revenue, and in 1938 more than 50 per cent. See Spoerer, 'Öffentliche Finanzen', 106.

31 See for comments and estimates the literature dealing with China under note 8, chapter 3; Von Glahn, *Economic history*, 380–382, and my *State, economy and the Great Divergence*, chapter one, passim, in particular pages 101–103.

32 Yeh-chien Wang estimated, that total tax revenue of the Qing government in 1908 amounted to only 2.4 per cent of net national product. Wang, *Land taxation in China*, 133.

33 Pamuk, 'Evolution of fiscal institutions', 325.

34 Gatrell, 'Russian fiscal state', 207.

35 See for these figures, Roy, *Economic history*.

36 Frankema, 'Colonial taxation'.

37 Frankema, 'Raising revenue', 466.

38 Cogneau, Dupraz, and Mesplé-Somps, 'Fiscal capacity', 19, Figure 2. Provincial and departmental revenues are included but not municipal revenues.

39 Colonial subjects on top of tax payments often also had to provide corvée labour. See Waijenburg, 'Financing the African colonial state'. This was also the case in Tokugawa Japan, though no longer in Meiji Japan. For the situation in Tokugawa Japan see pages 132–133.

40 All this information is from Cogneau, Dupraz and Mesplé-Somps, 'Fiscal capacity and dualism', 35. The calculations are made in French Francs of 1937.

41 Emi, *Government fiscal activity*, 91.

42 For more information see He, *Paths toward the modern fiscal state*: the Index, under 'alcohol taxes, in Japan'. Strikingly enough, taxes on alcohol had also been very prominent in total tax revenue of the state in Great Britain during its 'take off'. See my *State, economy and the Great Divergence*, 175–176.

43 Francks, *Rural economic development*, 137.

44 Ike, 'Taxation and landownership', 164.

45 Francks, *Rural economic development*, passim.

46 These are the figures for the average land tax revenue of all levels of government, in million yen: 1894–1898, 59.2; 1879–1883, 60.7; 1899–1903, 84.9; 1904–1908, 114.7; 1909–1911, 126.2. See Oshima, 'Meiji fiscal policy', 359.

47 Rosovsky, *Capital formation*, 85.

48 Mayet, *Agricultural insurance*, 229.

49 Mayet, *Agricultural insurance*, 230.

50 Liebscher, *Japan's landwirthschaftliche und allgemeinwirthschaftliche Verhältnisse*, 105.

51 Wang, *Land taxation*, 128.

52 Metzler, 'Policy space', 227.

53 Oshima, 'Meiji fiscal policy', 354.

54 Oshima, 'Meiji fiscal policy', 380–381.

55 For the crisis of the countryside and the rise of fascism, see e.g. Francks, *Rural economic development*, chapter 10; Havens, *Farm and nation*; Smith, *Time of crisis*; Vlastos, 'Agrarianism without tradition'.

56 For a general synthesis see Francks, *Rural economic development*.

57 Francks, *Rural economic development*, 143.

58 Francks, *Rural economic development*, 115–116.

59 Francks, *Rural economic development*, 28–29, 142 and 221.

60 Francks, *Rural economic development*, 221.

61 Francks, *Rural economic development*, 141.

62 See Francks, *Rural economic development*, 145. Francks here refers to Brandt, 'Inter-war Japanese agriculture', 270, and Napier, 'Transformation', 364.

63 See e.g. Hayami and Godo, *Development economics*, 167.

64 Francks, *Rural economic development*, 102.

65 Francks, *Rural economic development*, 193.

66 Francks, *Rural economic development*, 212.

67 Francks, *Rural economic development*, 257, plus pages 188–189 of this text.

68 Moriguchi and Saez, 'Evolution of income concentration'. The authors claim that such an income tax was only instituted in 1891 in Prussia; in 1909 in the United Kingdom; in 1913 in the United States; and in 1914 in France. It is not clear to me on what grounds they make their claim for the United Kingdom.

69 For an overview of the history of the income tax in Britain till 1914, see Daunton, *Trusting Leviathan*, under 'income tax'.

70 I took this information from the articles dealing with these countries in Cardoso and Lains, *Paying for the liberal state*, 75, 116 and 96.

71 Stein, *Made in Japan*, 128.

72 See for some calculations Minami, *Economic development*, 258.

73 My analysis is based on information provided by Garon, *Beyond our means*, chapters 4, 5 and 8.

74 According to Garon, sumptuary regulations still mushroomed in Japan during the eighteenth and the first half of the nineteenth centuries. See Garon, *Beyond our means*, 127. See for sumptuary laws in Tokugawa Japan: Hirano, 'Regulating excess'; Shively, 'Sumptuary regulation'; Totman, *Early modern Japan*, the Index under 'sumptuary regulation', and my references to reform on pages 135–137. For an example of the heavy emphasis on frugality, in this case in an ordinance by the Shogunate of 1841–1842, see Walthall and Steel, *Politics and society*, 42–48.

75 For the ideas underlying the *Hokotu* movement and its activities see Najita, *Ordinary economies*, in the Index under '*Hokotu*, movement'.

76 Here, as in my entire discussion of saving in Japan, I strongly paraphrase, and quote, Garon, *Beyond our means*. The quote is from page 149 of his book.

77 Sheridan, *Governing the Japanese economy*, 78.

78 Den, 'Japanese communications', 416.

79 Den, 'Japanese communications', 416. Which apparently was never the case in the period discussed here.
80 At least according to Kawamura Takeji, an official of the Home Ministry, in a book published in 1906. See Garon, *Beyond our means*, 155.
81 Ferber, 'Run the state'. For the figures see Westney, *Imitation and innovation*, 137.
82 See for that quote Garon, *Beyond our means*, 162. See further chapter 8 of that book.
83 Garon, *Beyond our means*, 163 and 93.
84 Garon, *Beyond our means*, 238.
85 See for these quotes Furushima, 'Village and agriculture'. For more examples of peasant oppression by taxation, see Hane and Perez, *Premodern Japan*, passim.
86 Hane and Perez, *Premodern Japan*, 203 and 204.
87 For literature that does so, see under note 17, chapter 1.
88 Or rather an estimate on the basis of the assumed quality of the land that was being taxed.
89 See for some concrete examples, Honjo, 'Finance of the Tokugawa government'.
90 Totman, *Politics in the Tokugawa Bakufu*, 78.
91 Totman, *Politics in the Tokugawa Bakufu*, 80.
92 See e.g. Brown, *Central authority*.
93 See Verschuer, *Rice, agriculture, and food supply*.
94 This was not just an advantage. It could force peasants to time and again negotiate with the tax inspectors, which could imply expensive bribes.
95 See e.g. Paik, Steele and Tanaka, 'Rebellion and taxation'.
96 For some further analysis see Smith, 'Land tax'.
97 For some comments on corruption, in particular in relation to tax collection, that was substantial in Japan but certainly much less than in Qing China see Sng and Moriguchi, 'Asia's little divergence', chapter 4.1., 'Corruption'.
98 See pages 129–132.
99 Totman, *Early modern Japan*, 306. In his *Politics in the Tokugawa Bakufu*, 287, he gives figures for the land tax rate in *Bakufu* land over the period 1716 to 1841: the lowest rate, at the end of the period, being 31.66 per cent and the highest 37.63 per cent.
100 White, *Ikki*, 76. It is not entirely clear to me what exactly White means by 'real land tax rate'.
101 Francks, *Rural economic development*, 46. She bases her claim on an estimate by Matao Miyamoto in a publication from 1989.
102 Miyamoto, 'Prices and macroeconomic dynamics', 124.
103 Oguchi, 'Finances of the Tokugawa Shogunate', 199 and Metzler, 'Policy space', 226–227.
104 Nakabayashi, 'Rise of a Japanese fiscal state', 380–384 and 395–398. The estimate by Miyamoto he refers to is in Myamoto, 'Quantitative aspects of the Tokugawa economy', 38.
105 See Kwon, *State formation*, 46; Nakabayashi, 'Rise of a Japanese fiscal state', 383; Metzler, 'Policy space', 226, and Sng and Moriguchi, 'Asia's Little Divergence', chapter 4.2.
106 For further details and explanation of the working of the monetary system during the late Tokugawa era, see Crawcour and Yamamura, 'Tokugawa monetary system'.
107 See Sng and Moriguchi, 'Asia's Little Divergence', Figure 7.
108 See also Totman, *Politics in the Bakufu*, 87–88: 'In 1841, forty-eight per cent of the *Bakufu* income came from other sources than agriculture, and half of this was direct merchant levies. Three years later fifty-four per cent of the *Bakufu* income was from 'abnormal' sources.'

109 Honjo, 'On the finance of the Tokugawa government' gives a succinct, handsome overview of Tokugawa finances that shows that people in cities paid much less tax overall than peasants.

110 He, *Paths toward the modern fiscal state*, 30.

111 For some general comments, see Totman, *Early modern Japan*, under 'corvee labour'.

112 Kalland, *Fishing villages*, 220. Chapter 13 of Kalland's book deals extensively with all sorts of corvee labour duties that could be very heavy – and specific for them – in coastal villages. The term *kako* stands for persons having to perform corvee duties.

113 For examples, see Dowdy, *Japanese bureaucracy*, chapter 4 and Samson, *History of Japan*, 210–218.

114 For a general overview with some case studies, see Nishikawa and Amano, 'Domains and their economic policies'. The article, surprisingly enough, does not refer to the work of Roberts, *Mercantilism in a domain*. For some comments, see also Francks, *Japanese economic development*, 35–39.

115 For examples of import substitution in Tokugawa Japan, see Hellyer, *Defining engagement*, chapter 6, and Roberts, *Mercantilism in a domain*, chapter 8.

116 He, *Paths toward the modern fiscal state*, 80 and 88.

117 See for some comparisons my 'Governing growth' and more recently Yun-Casalilla, O'Brien and Comín-Comín, *Rise of fiscal states*. I have put the term 'GDP' in parentheses as I think it is rather anachronistic in this context.

118 Crawcour in his 'Industrialization and technological change' claimed that central and local authorities collected some 20 per cent of national output at the end of Tokugawa rule. In an earlier text, he had written it would have been 25–27 per cent. See his 'Tokugawa heritage', 31. I also found a very recent estimate of the effective tax rate as a percentage of GDP in the shogunal lands of thirty per cent for the mid-seventeenth century and of sixteen to seventeen per cent for the mid-nineteenth century. See Sakai, 'Outsourcing the lord's finance', 71 for these figures and their source.

119 See e.g. Smith, 'Premodern economic growth', 155.

120 Metzler, 'Policy space', 227.

121 For all the following estimates and the literature from which I have distilled them, see my *State, economy and the Great Divergence*, 100–102. In that book, the reader can also find figures with regard to government expenditure in the countries discussed. That expenditure as a rule was substantially higher than revenue.

122 It has to be pointed out here that in Great Britain after the Napoleonic Wars there existed a consensus that tax pressure and public debt had become too high. For the rest of the long nineteenth century, Great Britain's government became much less of a spendthrift.

123 I compare tax revenue to different entities here like national income or GDP because these are the comparisons as I found them in the literature.

124 Sng and Moriguchi, 'Asia's Little Divergence', Figure 1. Land tax income was only *one*, and on top of that only a *shrinking* part of the total income of the Shogunate. See pages 129–132.

125 See for a general overview; Crawcour, 'Economic change'; Jansen, 'Japan in the early nineteenth century' and Tsuji, 'Politics in the eighteenth century'.

126 Totman, *Politics in the Tokugawa Bakufu*, 82–88.

127 This is the closing sentence of Sng and Moriguchi, 'Asia's little divergence'.

128 Ravina, *To stand with the nations of the world*, 48–55 and Tsuji, 'Politics in the eighteenth century', 441–456.

129 Tsuji, 'Politics in the eighteenth century', 467–477.

130 Jansen, *Cambridge History of Japan*, *Volume five*, the Index under 'Tempo reforms'.

5 A Capitalist State, Friendly to Employers but Much Less so to Workers

1   There are numerous definitions of capitalism with many different emphases, but these in my view are their common denominators. See for differences and explanations, my *Escaping poverty*, 332–350. Since I finished that book several publications on (the history of) capitalism have appeared. I only refer to Kocka, *Capitalism*; Kocka and Van der Linden, *Capitalism*; Marks, *Information nexus* and Neal and Williamson, *Cambridge History of Capitalism*.

2   Eric Jones and Kozo Yamamura would be examples of scholars who claim that in this sense Tokugawa Japan and Western Europe both developed their own 'capitalism'. For Jones see under notes 28–30 of chapter 7; for Yamamura see Yamamura, 'Agricultural and commercial revolution', 104.

3   See e.g. Saito, 'Proto-industrialization'. I consider the expression unfortunate because quite often this proto-industry was *not* a first stage of industrialization.

4   I paraphrase Howell, *Capitalism from within*, 5: 'only when capitalist relations of production predominate can a society as a whole be characterized as capitalist'. In practice, it is hard to determine when exactly that would be the case.

5   See e.g. Howell, *Capitalism from within*. For the way in which Japanese Marxists debated the (non-)development of capitalism in Japan, see Hoston, *Marxism and the crisis*.

6   It would lead too far to enter into detail here. For further explanation see my 'Europe and the rest'.

7   See e.g. Braudel, *Civilization & capitalism. Volume II,* 585-594.

8   Braudel, *Civilization & capitalism. Volume II,* 580–581.

9   Braudel, *Civilization & capitalism. Volume II,* 592–593. See for a discussion of this so-called *sakoku* policy pages 200–202.

10 The existence in Tokugawa Japan of large-scale and sophisticated trade and finance has been proved beyond any reasonable doubt. See for a recent overview, with relevant references, Francks, *Japan and the Great Divergence*, chapters 6, 7 and 10. As compared to in particular Great Britain and the Dutch Republic, though, Japan's capitalism *à la Braudel* under the Tokugawa remained rather 'stunted'.

11 As we will see in the following pages, rulers during the Tokugawa era often simply did not manage to stop the emergence and spread of market transactions.

12 See for further information my *Escaping poverty*, 332–350.

13 According to Ravina, retainers remained in the countryside in some capacity only in some 20 per cent of the domains, which constituted approximately 50 per cent of the territory of Japan. Ravina, *Land and lordship*, 64.

14 For this and further information see McKean, 'Defining and dividing'; McKean, 'Management of traditional common lands' and Wigen, 'Common losses'.

15 Brown, *Cultivating the commons,* 1.

16 Brown, *Cultivating the commons,* 1.

17 For land in cities, there were no such restrictions.

18 For legislation against fragmentation of land and how it was circumvented, see Ooms, *Tokugawa village practice*, 234–240.

19 Kwon, *State formation*, 72.

20 Saitô, 'Land, labour and market forces'.

21 See the abstract of Kumon, 'How inequality created poverty'.

22 De Vries, 'Industrious peasants', 112.

23 See pages 106–107.

24 According to Margareth McKean only some 2.5 million ha of land were still managed as commons in the 1980s. See her 'Defining and dividing', 1.

25 Saito, 'Land, labour and market forces'.

26 Overton, *Agricultural Revolution*, 178, and Lindert and Williamson, 'Revising England's social tables'.

27 De Moor and Van Zanden, 'Girl power', in particular pages 11–16. For the claim with regard to the percentage of servants or apprentices, see page 11, note 16. It in this respect is striking that Leupp claims "By 1700 Japan was one of the most urban of non-western societies. In the towns and cities, one-fifth to one-third of the population typically consisted of hired servants, shophands and manual laborers. Few other societies embarked upon the road to industrialization with so large and experienced an urban proletariat at hand." Leupp, *Servants, shophands, and laborers*, page 176 for the quote and chapter 5 for further information. Much of course depends on the exact definition of 'proletarian'.

28 For the expression 'realm of great peace' see e.g. Vaporis, *Voices of early modern Japan*, XVII.

29 Hane and Perez, *Premodern Japan*, 268.

30 See note 74, chapter 4.

31 Ravina, *To stand with the nations of the world*, 41–48.

32 Ikegami, *Taming of the samurai*, 176 and 362.

33 Howell, *Capitalism from within*, 11.

34 Howell, *Capitalism from within*, 177.

35 Howell, *Capitalism from within*, 14–15.

36 A comparison with China at the time shows that scarcity is a relative concept. When the output of the Qing mints peaked between 1756 and 1765, national production reached 3,640 million pieces annually, or fifteen copper coins per head. By comparison, the Shogunate produced 1,096 million copper coins annually between 1764 and 1788, or thirty-five pieces per head. See Sng and Moriguchi, 'Asia's little divergence', chapter 4.4.1.

37 I refer the reader for concrete figures to the tables and figures in Saito and Settsu, 'Money, credit and Smithian growth'.

38 See pages 67–70.

39 Howell, *Capitalism from within*, 3.

40 Howell, *Capitalism from within*, 5 and 23.

41 Howell, *Capitalism from within*, 179.

42 Howell, *Capitalism from within*, 180 and 183–184.

43 For further explanation see, Dore, *British factory, Japanese factory*; Gordon, 'Invention of Japanese-style labor management', and Harada, *Labour conditions*.

44 For an introductory discussion of the dual structure of Japan's economy, in particular in its manufacturing sector, see note 82 of this chapter.

45 He, *Paths toward the modern fiscal state*, 226.

46 For further explanation of the concept 'monetary sovereignty', see Helleiner, *Making of national money*.

47 Yamamura, 'From coins to rice'.

48 For Alexander's endorsement, see Alexander, *Arc of Japan's economic development*, 19.

49 Howell, *Capitalism from within*, 178–179.

50 For the rate of land tax to total tax revenue of central government, see Table 44 on page 117. For some comments on the pros and cons of taxing land versus taxing goods, see my *State, economy and the Great Divergence*, 145–150.

51 See e.g. Marshall, *Capitalism and nationalism* and Sagers, *Confucian capitalism*. It is
    striking though that the big merchants from the late Tokugawa era played only a
    marginal role in Japan's industrialization as it began under Meiji rule.

52 For examples see Garon, *State and labor*, 19; Lockwood, *Economic development*, 563,
    and Tsuzuki, *Pursuit of power*, 149–151.

53 See e.g. Utley, *Japan's feet of clay*, the Index under 'corruption'.

54 Stein, *Made in Japan*, 134.

55 Johnson, *MITI*, 19.

56 I mean 'in general'. In specific cases and when it comes to specific circumstances there
    of course could be – and at times indeed *were* – differences of opinion and even
    conflicts.

57 For literature see the following notes.

58 For an introduction in the history of the *zaibatsu*, see Morikawa, *Zaibatsu*; Part Three
    of Volume One of Tolliday, *Economic development of modern Japan* and Yonekura and
    Shimuzu, 'Entrepreneurship in pre-World War II Japan'. For an analysis of their
    functioning till the beginning of the 1920s, see Schenkein, *Japan, the great power*. For a
    case study I refer to Roberts, *Mitsui*.

59 Lockwood, *Economic development*, 217 and 220. See further Lockwood, *Economic
    development*, the Index under '*zaibatsu*'. More about their wealth can be found in that
    book on pages 278–280 and 284-285.

60 Yamamura, 'Japanese economy, 1911–1930', 312.

61 Yamamura, 'Japanese economy, 1911–1930', 314.

62 See for many examples for the period till 1922, Schenkein, *Japan, the great power*.

63 Schenkein, *Japan, the great power*.

64 For a list of the major cartels in effect during the Taisho period (1912–1926), see
    Yamamura, 'Japanese economy, 1911–1930', 313.

65 Nakamura and Odaka, 'Inter-war period', 37–38.

66 See e.g. Yamamura, 'General trading companies'.

67 See for example Hashimoto, 'Rise of big business'.

68 Nakamura and Odaka, 'Inter-war period', 39. For further information I refer to the
    volume in which the article by Nakamura and Odaka is published.

69 I here base myself on Stein, *Made in Japan*. The quote is from that book, page 132.

70 Stein, *Made in Japan*, 133.

71 Stein, *Made in Japan*, 134–136. The quote is on page 136.

72 Stein, *Made in Japan*, 122.

73 The phrase *in the specific setting of Japan at the time* is essential, as I would not want to
    turn my claim about the positive effects of scale and scope in this context into a
    universally valid statement. One may already have doubts about its validity for Japan
    in the 1920s and 1930s, in economic but certainly in social terms.

74 Mosk, *Japanese industrial history*, 67.

75 Federico, *Economic history*, 21–24. The reference to Katakura is on page 22.

76 Allen, 'Japanese industry', 596–624. The information in the rest of this paragraph also
    comes from this text.

77 It has to be pointed out that, e.g. in the cotton textiles industry, bigger did not
    necessarily mean more productive. See for a counterargument and figures, e.g. Clark,
    Conditions of economic progress, chapter VI, 'The productivity of manufacturing
    industry'.

78 Schenkein, *Japan, the great power*.

79 See e.g. Schenkein, *Japan, the great power*, Graph 9.

80 For a balanced assessment see Lockwood, *Economic development*, 60–61, 192 and 228.

81 For their contribution to technological innovation see, for example, Nicholas, 'Origins of Japanese technological modernization'.

82 It, moreover, would be misleading to fully separate large and small firms and place them in two different 'worlds'. Industrializing Japan indeed developed a dual economy, but its progress, again in the words of Lockwood, 'owes much to her comparative success in combining large and small enterprise in intricate patterns of co-operation'. See Lockwood, *Economic development*, 193. For Japan's dual economy see e.g. Odaka, 'The dual structure of the Japanese economy' and Shinohara, 'Formation and transition'.

83 For child labour see Saito, 'Children's work, industrialism and the family economy'.

84 See Table 56. As indicated in the text, those small workshops were inspected though, when they had a mechanical power source.

85 Stein, *Japan as number one*, 50.

86 Garon, *State and labor*, Appendix VI.

87 Rosovsky, *Capital formation*, 104.

88 For this quote see Tsurumi, *Factory girls*, 182. Ito was prime minister of Japan several times.

89 Francks, *Rural economic development*, 129.

90 Botsman, *Punishment and power*, chapter 7 and 'Conclusion'; Jolliffe, *Gefängnisse und Zwangsarbeit,* especially for the situation on Hokkaido, and Sakata, 'Japan in the eighteenth and nineteenth centuries'.

91 Botsman, *Punishment and power*, 180.

92 Botsman, *Punishment and power*, 188.

93 Botsman, *Punishment and power*, 188.

94 Botsman, *Punishment and power*, 189.

95 For some general information see Hane, *Peasants, rebels & outcasts*, the chapter on coal miners and, in particular for female miners, Burton, *Coal-mining women*.

96 Burton, *Coal-mining women*, 13.

97 See, for example, for the plight of Korean mineworkers in Japan, Hane, *Peasants, rebels & outcastes*, 236–242 and 245.

98 See for general comments Hane, *Peasants, rebels & outcastes* and Hane, *Modern Japan*. For a more institutional history of the relation between state and labour, see the literature referred to under note 44, chapter 3. For the concepts 'industrious revolution' and 'labour-intensive industrialization', see Austin and Sugihara, *Labour-intensive industrialization* and Hayami, *Japan's industrious revolution*.

6 A Developmental State

1 See e.g. Samuels, *Rich nation, strong army*.

2 See for his definition Johnson, *MITI*: idem, *Japan: Who governs*; idem, 'Developmental state'.

3 See for some comments, pages 14–15.

4 Henley, *Asia-Africa development divergence*. The subtitle of the book *is A question of intent*. For the quotes, see the announcement of the book by Chicago University Press.

5 For these policies see Allen, 'Japanese industry', 741–786; Hashimoto, 'Rise of big business'; Johnson, *MITI,* chapters three and four; Mass and Miyajima, 'Organization

of the developmental state' and Tsutsui, *Manufacturing ideology*, chapters 1 and 2, dealing with the efficiency and rationalization movements and so-called 'scientific management' in the period 1911 to 1937.

6   Howe, *Origins of Japanese trade supremacy*, 261–267.
7   See for the period of the late Qing, Vries, 'Economic reasons of state'. The period from 1911, the end of Qing rule, till 1937, the beginning of a new full-blown war with Japan, was one of warlordism and anarchy.
8   Scholars hold quite differing opinions when it comes to the success of this movement. Richard von Glahn is not impressed, as shows in this quote: 'The immediate objective was to modernize the Qing military by building arsenals and shipyards utilizing Western technologies. The results were dismal.' See Von Glahn, *Economic history*, 378. See for further comments, 374–399. Benjamin Elman comes up with a more positive assessment and for example writes: 'China's Jiangnan Arsenal and the Fuzhou Shipyard, for example, were generally acknowledged by contemporary Europeans and Japanese to be more advanced than their chief competitor in Meiji Japan, the Yokosuka Dockyard, until the 1880s'. See Elman, *Science in China,* 202. Tonio Andrade too is more positive. See Andrade, *Gunpowder age,* chapter 18, where the reader can also find a good overview of literature on the movement. The fact that the Chinese military lost the war against Japan according to many scholars was not a matter of 'material' but of 'men'. Experts at the time were convinced that Japan would lose that war. See for the ideas behind the Self-Strengthening Movement and more in general behind efforts to modernize China, Schell and Delury, *Wealth and power*.
9   For a brief introduction see Zürcher, *Turkey*, chapters 4–7.
10 See e.g. Greenfeld, *Spirit of capitalism*, Part III; Metzler, 'Cosmopolitanism of national economics'; Morris-Suzuki, *History of Japanese economic thought*; Sagers, 'Origins of Japan's economic philosophy'; Sugiyama, *Origins of economic thought* and Wolfe, 'Hamilton's ghost'.
11 Landes, *Wealth and poverty*, 376.
12 Sugiyama, *Origins*, 54, 56 and 58.
13 Sugiyama, *Origins*, 55 and 52.
14 Sheridan, *Governing the Japanese economy*, 23.
15 For the promotion of saving and frugality see pages 123–125.
16 See e.g. Najita, *Visions of virtue*; Ramseyer, 'Thrift and diligence' and Sheldon, *Rise of the merchant class*. For a recent synthesis see Francks, *Japan and the Great Divergence*, chapters 9 and 10.
17 One can find such discussions in the many publications of Akira Hayami about Japan's industrious revolution. For Japan's Protestant ethic see Bellah, *Tokugawa religion* and Landes, *Wealth and poverty*, 360, 363 and 383. Landes uses the phrase on page 383. For him, industriousness clearly provides a key to explain Japan's economic development in the early modern and modern era.
18 See e.g. pages 65–67.
19 Emi, *Government fiscal activity*, 82–83.
20 Emi, *Government fiscal activity*, 86.
21 Emi, *Government fiscal activity*, 21–22.
22 See for information on Great Britain as well as France, Cardoso and Lains, 'Introduction', 19.
23 Burhop, *Wirtschaftsgeschichte des Kaiserreichs*, 84. The figures presented here are estimates. For the year 1913-1914, we also have an estimate of 14.2 per cent. See Spoerer, 'Evolution of public finances', 114.

24 Facchini and Melki, 'Optimal government size', Figure 4.

25 See Knortz, *Wirtschaftsgeschichte der Weimarer Republik*, 166, for the higher estimate, and Spoerer, 'Öffentliche Finanzen', 104, for the lower one.

26 Daunton, *Wealth and welfare*, 475.

27 I here refer to Sheridan, *Governing the Japanese economy*, 179–189 for further details.

28 Ravina, *To stand with the nations of the world*, 182.

29 Mosk, *Japanese industrial history*, 181.

30 Emi, *Government fiscal activity*, 99.

31 Daunton, 'Creating legitimacy', 46.

32 Spoerer, 'Evolution of public finances', 119.

33 Knortz, *Wirtschaftsgeschichte der Weimarer Republik*, 166.

34 Bonney, 'Apogee and fall', 83.

35 Inkster, *Japanese industrialisation*, 34.

36 See pages 208–209.

37 Emi, *Government fiscal activity*, 43.

38 Emi, *Government fiscal activity*, 43.

39 Emi, *Government fiscal activity*, 38.

40 Sheridan, *Governing the Japanese economy*, 51.

41 Francks, *Japanese economic development*, 67. See for a similar figure Nafziger, *Learning from the Japanese*, 31. For the importance of government support for the development of shipping in Japan see also, for example, the history of Mitsubishi and its shipping battle with Mitsui in the 1880s.

42 Kawada and Levine, *Human resources*, 156 and 173.

43 Emi, *Government fiscal activity*, 29 and 33.

44 Rosovsky, *Capital formation*, 15, 25 and 27.

45 See Fukao and Settsu, 'Japan. Modern economic growth in Asia', Table I, and Sugihara, 'Japan's industrial recovery', 160.

46 Eloranta, 'Military spending patterns in history', Table 2.

47 I strictly confine myself to macro-economic considerations here.

48 Max Roser, https://ourworldindata.org/military-spending, the graph 'UK spending as a percentage of GDP, 1692–2004'.

49 Rosovsky, *Capital formation*, 23.

50 Ohkawa and Rosovsky, *Japanese economic growth*, 17.

51 Flath, *Japanese economy*, 192.

52 Nakabayashi, 'Rise of a Japanese fiscal state', 405–407, Table 16.5

53 Nakamura and Odaka, 'Inter-war period', 16.

54 Mosk, *Japanese economic development*, 138

55 For an extensive overview of the government's major role in capital formation in Japan, in her analysis of the situation during the period 1901–1936, I refer to Sheridan, *Governing the Japanese economy*, chapter 3.

56 Sheridan, *Governing the Japanese economy*, 60 and 64.

57 Nakamura and Odaka, 'Inter-war period', 15.

58 Nakamura and Odaka, 'Inter-war period', 15.

59 Macdonald, *Free nation deep in debt*, 355.

60 Cardoso and Lains, 'Introduction', 20.

61 Spoerer, 'Evolution of public finances', 125.

62 Goldsmith, *Financial development*, 127.

63 Moulton and Ko, *Japan*, 208.

64 See e.g. Minami, *Economic development*, 159–160.

65 Nakamura and Odaka, 'Inter-war period', 40.

66 Smethurst, *From foot soldier to finance minister*.

67 Inkster, *Japanese industrialisation*, 80. For further information see Ericson, '"Matsukata deflation" reconsidered' and Listwa, 'Japanese deflation'.

68 Those will be discussed here together for the pragmatic reason that there is not much to be said about debts.

69 See e.g. Mosk, *Japanese industrial history*, chapter 2.

70 See for this claim about Tokugawa finances also Metzler, 'Policy space', 228 and Totman, *Politics in the Tokugawa Bakufu*, chapter four. For some examples of domains in debt see Dowdy, *Japanese bureaucracy*, 101–105 and Samson, *History of Japan*, 210–221.

71 This is the main gist of his *Japanese industrial history*. See for example pages 5–6, 8, 66 and 87.

72 Ville, 'Transport', 323.

73 These figures come from a presentation by Sebastian Keibek and Leigh Shaw-Taylor, 'The regional foundations on which the world's first industrial nation was built', Workshop Economic Geography of Long-Run Industrialization, Amsterdam 22 & 23 March 2018. I have permission to use them.

74 Lockwood, *Economic development*, 109. For some general figures about the developments in transportation, I can refer to *ibid.*, 105–109 and Yamamoto, *Technological innovation*.

75 Inkster, *Japanese industrialisation*, 31.

76 Moulton and Ko, *Japan*, 83.

77 Hattori, *Foreign commerce*, 28–30 and Nafziger, *Learning from the Japanese*, 137.

78 I refer the reader to the literature – see next note – for their precise structure and functioning and here confine myself to referring to their impact.

79 Yamamura, 'General trading companies', 169. On page 179 of that same chapter the reader can find an overview of the proportions of international trade by foreign and by Japanese traders in the period 1880–1911. The share of Japanese traders grew quickly. For further information on the activities of 'normal' trade association see Omori, 'How local trade associations and manufacturer's associations worked'.

80 I paraphrase Lockwood, *Economic development*, 539ff in this paragraph. For more detailed information with case studies, see e.g. Fukasaku, *Technology and industrial development* and Wray, *Mitsubishi and the NYK*.

81 Lockwood, *Economic development*, 548.

82 Totman, *Japan. An environmental history*, 210.

83 Yamasaki, 'Railroads'.

84 See the conclusion of Yamasaki, 'Railroads'. For further information see Ericson, *Sound of the whistle*.

85 Harada, 'Policy' in: Yamamoto, *Technological innovation*, 168–169.

86 I took the information in this paragraph from Kawada and Levine, *Human resources*, 191–197.

87 Mosk, *Japanese industrial history*, 137.

88 Ericson, *Sound of the whistle*, 375–377.

89 See e.g. Lockwood, *Economic development*, 105–109.

90 Mosk, *Japanese industrial history*, 86.

91 Alexander, *Arc of Japan's economic development*, 17.

92 Sng and Moriguchi, 'Asia's Little Divergence', chapter 4.4.2. and Vaporis, *Breaking barriers*.

93 See Yamamoto, *Technological innovation*.

94   All the information in this paragraph, unless otherwise indicated, is from Hunter, 'People and post offices' and Maclachlan, *People's Post Office*.

95   Westney, *Imitation and innovation*, 142.

96   www.cirje.e.u-tokyo.ac.jp/research/dp/2005/2005cf344.pdf, Figure seven.

97   See for these, and other, figures Lockwood, *Economic development*, 106, note 31, and Hunter, 'People and post offices'.

98   Westney, *Imitation and innovation*, 138–141.

99   Westney, *Imitation and innovation*, 145.

100 Den, 'Japanese communications', 410–411.

101 Westney, *Innovation and imitation*, 103–106.

102 Millward, *State and business*, 256.

103 Kawada and Levine, *Human resources*, 182.

104 Westney, *Imitation and innovation*, 156.

105 Ravina, *To stand with the nations of the world*, 190.

106 Gluck, *Japan's modern myths*, 12, 171 and 232–233; Dickinson, *World War I*, 52.

107 Westney, *Imitation and innovation*, 214 and 207. For further information see Huffman, *Creating a public*.

108 See e.g. Berry, *Japan in print*, passim and Westney, *Imitation and innovation*, 151–153.

109 Nakamura and Odaka, 'Inter-war period', 45.

110 Howe, *Origins of Japanese trade supremacy*, 257. For information with regard to the print media and the new media in the period 1919–1930, I refer to Dickinson, *World War I*, 50–58.

111 For information on electric utilities see Minami, *Power revolution*, 149–162. The figures are on page 153. For private investment in electricity, see e.g. Rosovsky, *Capital formation*, 302–303 and Nakamura and Odaka, 'Inter-war period', 33. For the history of the electric power industry see Kikkawa, 'History of Japan's electric power industry'.

112 Mosk, *Japanese industrial history*, 137–157.

113 Minami, *Power revolution*, 360.

114 See for those money transfers and subsidies Emi, *Government fiscal activity*, 26, reproduced on page 171.

115 Francks, *Rural economic development*, 222.

116 I fully endorse this claim by Ian Inkster: 'capital formation may have been of far less importance in dictating the economic dynamics of Meiji Japan than was institutional innovation, a process led by government and influenced from afar.' Inkster, *Japanese industrialisation*, 39.

117 Ravina, *To stand up to the nations of the world*, 9, here refers to a critical tension that was present in Tokugawa and, I would think even stronger, in Meiji thought, i.e. the tension between radical nostalgia and cosmopolitan chauvinism. I refer to his text for further explanation.

118 Westney, *Imitation and innovation*, 31–32.

119 Inkster, *Japanese industrialisation*, 39.

120 Inkster, *Japanese industrialisation*, 73.

121 Mosk, *Japanese industrial history*, 181.

122 See for some examples, under note 28, chapter 7.

123 See for details Bassino, Fukao and Settsu, 'Economic geography'.

124 Huber, 'Effects on price'.

125 Yasuba, 'Natural resources', chapter 2.

126 Bernhofen and Brown, 'Empirical assessment'.

127 Flath, *Japanese economy*, 35 and 160–161.
128 Hattori, *Foreign commerce*, 10.
129 Mosk, *Japanese industrial history*, passim. See e.g. 253.
130 See for a general analysis Williamson, *Trade and poverty*.
131 See e.g. this hypothesis by Kozo Yamamura, which as the context shows the author believes confirmed: 'the major reason for the success of Japanese industrialization needs to be stated as follows: Japan industrialized rapidly because it was able to borrow and imitate the heart of the necessary technology, quickly and effectively by taking maximum advantage of the willing and wide-ranging assistance provided by the most technologically advanced Western firms.' Yamamura, 'Japan's deus ex machina', 93.
132 A fascinating and curious example would be the so-called Sempill Mission, a semi-official British mission led by Captain the Master of Sempill and sent to Japan in September 1921, with the objective of helping the Imperial Japanese Navy develop its aero-naval forces. The mission consisted of a group of twenty-nine instructors, and stayed in Japan for eighteen months. They trained Japanese colleagues on several new aircraft and taught them several new techniques, such as torpedo bombing and flight control.
133 The fact that Japan itself by and large was safeguarded from pebrine was not a matter of luck but due to specific techniques used by the Japanese in their sericulture. See Morris-Suzuki, 'Sericulture', 117–119.
134 See for further information Howe, *Origins of Japanese trade supremacy*, chapter 5.
135 For a very concise synthesis of its economic effects when it comes to exports, see e.g. Dickinson, *World War I*, 21, and when it comes to production in general Hubbard, *Eastern industrialization*, 51.
136 According to Yasuba, it improved with 395 per cent between 1857 and 1875 and with another 38 per cent between 1875 and 1895. Yasuba, 'Natural resources', chapter 2.
137 Williamson, *Trade and poverty*, 34.
138 He, *Paths toward the modern fiscal state*, 113.
139 A kuping tael was the equivalent of 37.57 grams of silver. The thirty-eight million pounds sterling were the equivalent at the time of 365 million yen. GDP of Japan in 1895 was an estimated 1,500 million yen.
140 For further explanation see Bytheway, *Investing Japan*, chapter 3.
141 I found this quote in Bytheway, *Investing Japan*, 54.
142 See Francks, *Rural economic development*, in particular 119–120 and 131; Francks, *Japanese consumer*; Francks and Hunter, *Historical consumer*. In the coming two paragraphs, I strongly paraphrase Francks, *Rural economic development*. The country's geographical distance from production centers in the West may also have helped somewhat.
143 Francks, *Japanese economic development*, 148.
144 Macpherson, *Economic development*, 44. I could not consult the original reference.
145 For an analysis of the role of the state in protecting/supporting Japan's agriculture in the period 1868–1937, see the relevant chapters in Francks, *Rural economic development*. For a discussion of protective policies with regard to rice production in Japan and its empire in terms of tariffs and trade intervention see Francks, *ibidem*, in particular, 168–183.
146 Moulder, *Japan, China, and the modern world economy*. The country did, however, increasingly import raw materials and in that respect, certainly in the 1930s, could indeed feel 'dependent' on other countries.

147 For the diversification of its exports in terms of commodities and for the composition of its imports and exports when it comes to trade partners, see e.g., in alphabetical order: Francks, *Japanese economic development*, 183; Meissner and Tang, 'Upstart industrialization and exports'; Nafziger, *Learning from the Japanese*, 143; Ohno, *Economic development*, 61. (For the situation till 1910.)

148 See e.g. Howe, *Origins of Japanese trade supremacy*, 132.

149 See pages 173–175.

150 Utley, *Japan's feet of clay*, 214.

151 Bytheway, *Investing Japan*, 151. It is interesting that Bytheway, immediately after the text just quoted, continues with the following comment: 'Nevertheless, there are only a few examples of foreign firms taking an active interest in the new market created by these legislative changes, and foreign investment in Japan accounted for a small fraction of total foreign investment in Asia.' Apparently, for whatever reason, foreign capital was not very interested in Japan.

152 I found that quote in Smith, *Political change*, 97–98.

153 I found these quotes in Sohn, *Japanese industrial governance*, 26, and Matsugata (sic!), 'Japan's finance', 375.

154 Cited in Metzler, *Lever of empire*, 24. For similar remarks see Mitchener et al, 'Why did countries adopt the gold standard', 45.

155 Inkster, *Japanese industrialization*, 78.

156 I found this quote in Keen, *Emperor of Japan*, 316.

157 Schiltz, *Money doctors*, 39.

158 Inkster, *Japanese industrialization*, 79.

159 Ian Inkster goes as far as to claim: 'Perhaps the most important role played by the Meiji government lay in its successful resistance to foreign capital into the 1890s.' Inkster, *Japanese industrial economy*, 9. See also *ibidem*, 34.

160 Nakamura and Odaka, 'Inter-war period', 10,

161 Sussman and Yafeh, 'Institutions, reforms, and country risk' and Goldsmith, *Financial development*, chapter 4.

162 See Bytheway, *Investing Japan*, 142–143 for an overview of total loan issues and direct foreign investment, over the period 1870–1939.

163 Bytheway, *Investing Japan*, 89.

164 For these figures see Ohkawa, Shinohara and Meissner, *Patterns of Japanese economic development*, 251–253.

165 Here too Bytheway emphasizes the importance of foreign capital: 'While a cursory glance at the sum total of the capital involved suggests that direct foreign investment in the Japanese economy was insignificant in comparison with other forms of indirect lending, the effects of direct investment were often disproportionate to the size of the actual investment. It is also important to remember that foreign capital was overwhelmingly directed toward the top end of the technology market in the heavy industries, often taking the form of patent technology itself. Moreover, monetary values alone cannot fully express the socioeconomic significance of the technologies introduced ...' Bytheway, *Investing Japan*, 179. I find that argumentation unconvincing.

166 Bytheway, *Investing Japan*, 180.

167 Ericson, '"Matsukata deflation" reconsidered' and Listwa, 'Japanese deflation'.

168 I found this statement by a contemporary, made during the debate in 1897 about the introduction of the gold standard, in Howe, *Origins of Japanese trade supremacy*, 147.

169 Sussman and Yafeh, 'Institutions, reforms, and country risk'.
170 Tashiro, 'Foreign relations'.
171 Jansen, 'Japan in the early nineteenth century', 89.
172 Lesger, *Rise of the Amsterdam market*, 91–92.
173 Totman, *Early modern Japan*, 148.
174 Shimbo and Hasegawa, 'Market economy', 167–168. See for further comments Cullen, 'Nagasaki trade'; Tashiro, 'Foreign trade', and the publications by Chaiklin and Goodman in note 25, chapter 7.
175 Ohkawa and Rosovsky, *Japanese economic growth*, 6. The phrasing is not very clear but I guess the meaning is. Rosovsky does not seem to be of one mind. He also makes positive comments on Japan's policy of seclusion as it would have allowed Japan to, slowly and peacefully, reach a base point from which it could leap into industrialization. See e.g. Rosovsky, *Capital formation*, 86.
176 Braudel, *Civilization & capitalism. Volume II*, 593.
177 The fact that after its opening Japan could catch up so quickly in his view was due to its 'long-standing merchant capitalism, which it had patiently built by its own efforts'. Borrowing an image from a book written in 1930 by Yosaburo Takekoshi, he too thinks that 'The grain was growing under the snow'. Braudel, *Civilization & capitalism. Volume II*, 593–594.
178 That essay was part of a publication by him with the abbreviated title *Amoenitatum exoticarum*, that was translated in 1801 by Shizuki Tadao (1760–1806), a *rangaku* (Dutch learning) scholar, as 'Sakokuron' or 'Essay on the closed country', which was the first instance of Tokugawa Japan actually being described in terms of *sakoku*. For Kaempfer's main work, that has become known as his 'History of Japan', see Bodart–Bailey, *Kaempfer's Japan*. For Dutch learning see note 25, chapter 7.
179 Frank, *Dependent accumulation*, 154. See also Moulder, *Japan, China, and the modern world-economy*.
180 Morishima, *Why has Japan 'succeeded'*, 59–60. The quote is on page 60.
181 Hane and Perez, *Premodern Japan*, 291.
182 Francks, *Rural economic development*, 103.
183 See for this claim Smith, *Inquiry*, Book 1, Chapter III.

7 A State Promoting Knowledge Transfer and Education

1 Inkster, *Japanese industrialisation*, 51–56.
2 Inkster, *Japanese industrialisation*, 27 and 35.
3 The mission left Japan in December 1871 and returned there in September 1873. The main *other* goal of the mission was trying to negotiate an end to the unequal treaties.
4 I took the raw data from Wikipedia. A good selection of the observations made can be found in Kume, *Japan rising*.
5 Emi, *Government fiscal activity*, 116.
6 See, for further examples, e.g. Amsden, *Rise of the 'Rest'*, 55; Inkster, *Japanese industrialisation,* 63; Kiyokawa, 'Transplantation', 29 and Ohno, *Economic development*, 63.
7 Emi, *Government fiscal activity*, 117.
8 Emi, *Government fiscal activity*, 122.
9 Broadbridge, 'Aspects of economic and social policy', 1118.

10 See pages 187–188.

11 Allen, *Short economic history*, 35.

12 Kiyokawa, 'Transplantation'; McCallion, 'Trial and error'. See also Federico, *Economic history*, 181, and Kawada and Levine, *Human resources*, 225.

13 Federico, *Economic history*, chapter 9.

14 Nicholas, 'Origins of Japanese technological modernization'.

15 For further information, I refer to Levine and Kawada, *Human resources*, the Index under 'patron-client system'; Thelen, *How institutions evolve*, 148–177, and Weiss, 'War, state and origins'.

16 Thelen, *How institutions evolve*, 150–152.

17 Taira, 'Factory labour', 263.

18 Inkster, *Japanese industrialisation*, 64.

19 Weiss, 'War, state and origins', 333.

20 Inkster, *Japanese industrialisation*, 64.

21 See for many examples Kiyokawa, 'Entrepreneurship and innovation'.

22 Inkster, *Japanese industrialisation*, 56–68 and 96. It is also surprising how little evidence there is of 'Luddite-like' resistance against technological innovation.

23 Colley, 'Writing constitutions', 173–175.

24 I am only referring here to Western knowledge but do so assuming that knowledge from other parts of the world, with which there was not much enthusiastic exchange either, will not have contributed much to heightening the potential for *modern* economic growth, whatever other positive effects it may have had.

25 For *rangaku* see e.g. Chaiklin, *Cultural commerce*; Goodman, *Japan. The Dutch experience*; idem, *Japan and the Dutch*; Jackson, *Network of knowledge*. For the claim that the importance of *rangaku* was marginal for the economic development of Japan, a claim that I endorse, see Inkster, *Japanese industrial economy*, 99–100.

26 Elisonas, 'Christianity and the *daimyo*'

27 For the estimate of 300,000, referring to the moment when Tokugawa Ieyasu proclaimed his ban in 1614, see Vaporis, *Voices of early modern Japan*, 209, and Hane and Perez, *Premodern Japan*, 172, who indicate there are also estimates as high as 700,000, a figure one, for example, finds in Landes, *Wealth and poverty*, 355; Ravina, *To stand with the nations of the world*, 34, and Vande Walle, *Geschiedenis van Japan*, 174.

28 For the exchange with the West of people, ideas, machines and techniques during the final decades of Tokugawa rule, see Hellyer, *Defining engagement*, passim; Morris-Suzuki, *Technological transformation*, 55–67, and Sagers, *Origins*, passim.

29 Souyri, *Moderne sans être occidental*, 39.

30 Kawada and Levine, *Human resources*, 48–51.

31 Emi, *Government fiscal activity*, 128 and 129.

32 See e.g. Roser, *Our world in data*, under 'Financing education'.

33 Kawada and Levine, *Human resources*, 95.

34 Mitch, *Rise of popular literacy*, 14–15.

35 See for this so-called 'deskilling hypothesis', De Pleijt and Weisdorf, 'Human capital formation'.

36 I will deal with this de-skilling extensively in my forthcoming book on Japan's labour-intensive industrialization.

37 Seaman, *Real triumph of Japan*.

38 Considering the fact that Japan's GDP and the budget of government structurally increased over the first four decades of the twentieth century, whereas the country's

military spending went through ups and downs, I am not convinced that this explanation holds water.

39 See e.g. Gluck, *Japan's modern myths*, 167–169.
40 See e.g. Howe, *Origins of Japanese trade supremacy*, 253–260; Inkster, *Japanese industrialization*, chapter 5; Kawada and Levine, *Human resources*; Mosk, *Japanese economic development*, 159–164.
41 Gluck, *Japan's modern myths*, 172.
42 Drea, *Japan's imperial army*, 73.
43 Heber, *Japanische Industriearbeit*, 213.
44 Drea, *Japan's imperial army*, 73.
45 Utley, *Lancashire and the Far East*, 154. For comments on the literacy of factory labour I refer to Taira, 'Education and literacy', 382–387. In his conclusion, Koji Taira indicates that he at least at the moment did not see any clear-cut answer to the question how exactly education and literacy impacted on economic efficiency and social progress. See ibidem, 393–394.
46 I here refer to Kawada and Levine, *Human resources*, chapters 4 to 8, and to Thelen, *How institutions evolve*, 148–177.
47 I here, for examples in the textiles industry, refer to Kiyokawa, 'Entrepreneurship and innovations'.
48 Alexander, *Arc of Japan's economic development*, 29.
49 Inkster, *Japanese industrialisation*, 84. The information I used in this paragraph is from the same book, 81–85. For institutes of higher education, I also refer to Howe, *Origins of Japanese trade supremacy*, 253–258.
50 Howe, *Origins of Japanese trade supremacy*, 255.
51 Dyer, *Dai Nippon*, 176. For the claim about Japan leading the way, see page 2 of that book.
52 Bartholomew, 'Japanese modernization'.
53 Nakagawa, 'Business management', 32.
54 Sugiyama, *Origins of economic thought*, 75. See for another example of praise, in this case of commercial education in a special report from the British Foreign Office in 1899, Howe, *Origins of Japanese trade supremacy*, 255.
55 Dowdy, *Japanese bureaucracy*, 120.

8 Some Comments on What (Supposedly?) Went Wrong

1 Powell, 'How entrepreneurs created the great boom'.
2 He, *Paths toward the modern fiscal state*, 88–89, 92 and 98. The quotes are on page 92.
3 Yamamura, 'Success ill-gotten', 115.
4 McCallion, 'Trial and error', and idem, *Silk reeling in Meiji Japan*, an extensive analysis that I could not consult myself.
5 See for this analysis Nakaoka, 'Transfer of cotton manufacturing technology'. The quote is on page 183.
6 See Nakaoka, 'Transfer of cotton manufacturing technology', where the author refers to Naosuke Takamura, *An introduction to the history of Japanese cotton spinning industry* (Tokyo 1971).
7 See Nakaoka's article referred to in the previous note and Fletcher, 'Japan Spinners Association', 54–55.

8 Powell in his 'How entrepreneurs created the great boom' gives an 'impressive' or, if you like, 'depressive' enumeration of examples.
9 I found this quote in Pyle, *Making of modern Japan*, 100. See for further quotes Marshall, *Capitalism and nationalism*, chapter 2.
10 Inkster, *Japanese industrialisation*, 68.
11 Inkster, *Japanese industrialisation*, 73.
12 Inkster, *Japanese industrialisation*, 87.
13 Inkster, *Japanese industrialisation*, 69.
14 This counterfactual, like all counterfactuals, cannot be proven. It can only be supported by reasonable assumptions and knowledge of what has actually taken place. Both strongly suggest that without government support and guidance Japan's economy would simply have continued to produce those products in which it had a comparative advantage but, I would claim, little future.
15 See page 8.
16 Francks, *Japanese economic development*, 56.
17 Inkster, 'Politicising the Gerschenkron schema'.
18 Inkster, *Japanese industrial economy*, 21.
19 Inkster, *Japanese industrial economy*, 9.
20 Tang, 'Public- versus private-led industrialization'. See also Tang, 'Technological leadership' and Tang, 'Fukoku Kyohei'.
21 Tang, 'Public- versus private-led industrialization', 7. He does so in a reference to a failed government initiative.
22 Tang, 'Public- versus private-led industrialization', 17.
23 For that distinction see Johnson, *MITI*, 21–22.
24 He claims: 'Whatever the metric, its broad-based policies (i.e. that of Meiji government P.V.) paid off with per capita GDP increasing 5.1 per cent annually between 1875 and 1912, over twice the rate of the United States in the same period.' Tang, 'Public- versus private-led industrialization', 17. That figure cannot be correct. Compare pages 31–32.
25 See e.g. Francks, *Rural economic development*, 85 and 162 and her references to 'big-farm theory'; Ogura, *Can Japanese agriculture survive*, 6–29; Havens, *Farm and nation*, 38. Several experts at the time were not enthusiast. George Liebscher, the German expert to whom we referred earlier, thought that introducing modern, large-scale agriculture in Japan would be „das denkbar unrichtigste Mittel zum Fortschritt" (the most unlikely means to achieve progress). See his *Japan's landwirthschaftliche und allgemeinwirthschaftliche Verhältnisse*, 114–115. Johannes Rein in his *Industries of Japan*, 18–21, comments extensively on the failure of introducing 'American agriculture' on Hokkaido. Compare, however, Paul Mayet, who had fairly high expectations of it. See his *Agricultural insurance*, chapter II, even though it might be necessary to 'conscript' Japanese peasants to go there.
26 Yasuba, 'Did Japan ever suffer' and Yasuba, 'Natural resources'.
27 Sheridan, *Governing the Japanese economy*, 77.

9 A Brief Summary

1 Which basically means they argue completely a-historically.

Bibliography

Abramovitz, Moses, 'Catching up, forging ahead, and falling behind', *The Journal of Economic History*, 46, 2 (1986) 385–406.

Acemoglu, Daron and James A. Robinson, *Why nations fail. The origins of power, prosperity and poverty* (London 2012).

Agov, Avram, 'Meiji Japan, 1868–1911. Government's role in economic growth and the rise of Mitsui zaibatsu', http://mediatimesreview.com/february05/meiji2.php

Akamatsu, Kaname, 'A theory of unbalanced growth in the world economy', *Weltwirtschaftliches Archiv. Zeitschrift des Instituts für Weltwirtschaft an der Universität Kiel* 86, 1 (1961) 196–217.

Akamatsu, Kaname, 'A historical pattern of economic growth in developing countries', *The Developing Economies. The Journal of the Institute of Economics* 1 (1962) 3–25.

Akita, Shigeru, '"Gentlemanly capitalism", intra-Asian trade and Japanese industrialisation at the turn of the last century', *Japan Forum* 8, 1 (1996) 51–65.

Alexander, Arthur J., 'Japan's economy in the twentieth century', *Japan Economic Institute Report* 3, January 21, 2000.

Alexander, Arthur J., *The arc of Japan's economic development* (London and New York 2008).

Allen, George C., 'Japanese industry. Its organization and development to 1937' in: Schumpeter, *Industrialization of Japan and Manchukuo*, 477–786.

Allen, George C., *A short economic history of modern Japan* (fourth edition; London 1981).

Allen, Robert C., 'The Great Divergence in European wages and prices from the Middle Ages to the First World War', *Explorations in Economic History* 38, 4 (2001) 411–447.

Allen, Robert C., *Global economic history. A very short introduction* (Oxford and New York 2011).

Allen, Robert C., Jean-Pascal Bassino, Debin Ma, Christine Moll-Murata and Jan Luiten van Zanden, 'Wages, prices, and living standards in China, 1738–1925: in comparison with Europe, Japan and India', *The Economic History Review* 64, 1 (2011) 8–38.

Amano, Ikuo, *Education and examination in modern Japan* (Tokyo 1990).

Amsden, Alice H., *The rise of the "rest". Challenges to the West from late-industrializing economies* (Oxford 2001).

Anchordoguy, M., 'Nippon Telegraph and Telephone Company (NTT) and the building of a telecommunications industry in Japan', *Business History Review* 75, 3 (2001) 507–541.

Ando, Yoshio, 'The formation of heavy industry. One of the processes of industrial development in the Meiji period', *The Developing Economies*, 3, 4 (1965) 450–470.

Arano, Yasunori, 'Foreign relations in early modern Japan: Exploding the myth of national seclusion', www.nippon.com/en/features/c00104/

Aratake, Kenichiro, 'Samurai and peasants in civil administration of early modern Japan' in: Tanimoto and Wong, *Public goods provision*, 38–56.

Arnason, Johann P., *The peripheral centre. Essays on Japanese history and civilization* (Melbourne 2002).

Asada, Keiichi and Giichi Ono, *Expenditures of the Sino-Japanese War* (New York 1922).

Ashworth, William J., *The industrial revolution. The state, knowledge and global trade* (London 2017).

Auslin, Michael R., *Negotiating with imperialism. The unequal treaties and the culture of Japanese diplomacy* (Cambridge Mass. 2009).

Austin, Gareth and Kaoru Sugihara, eds., *Labour-intensive industrialization in global history* (Abingdon Oxon and New York 2013).

Bachinger, Karl and Herbert Matis, *Entwicklungsdimensionen des Kapitalismus. Klassische sozioökonomische Konzeptionen und Analysen* (Vienna, Cologne, Weimar 2009).

Banno, Junji, *Japan's modern history, 1857–1937: A new political narrative* (London 2014).

Bartholomew, James R., 'Japanese modernization and the imperial universities', *Journal of Asian Studies* 37, 2 (1978) 251–271.

Bary, Wm. Theodore de, Donald Keene, George Tanabe and Paul Varley, eds., *Sources of Japanese tradition. Volume One. From earliest times to 1600* (second edition; New York 2001).

Bary, Wm. Theodore de, Carol Gluck and Arthur E. Tiedemann, eds., *Sources of Japanese tradition. Volume Two. Part One. From 1600 to 1868* (second abridged edition; New York 2006).

Bary, Wm. Theodore de, Donald Keene, George Tanabe and Paul Varley, eds., *Sources of Japanese tradition. Volume Two. Part Two. 1868 to 2000* (second abridged edition; New York 2006).

Bassino, Jean-Pascal and Debin Ma, 'Japanese unskilled wages in international perspective, 1741–1913' in: Alexander J. Field, Gregory Clark, William A. Sundstrom, eds., *Research in Economic History* 23 (2005) 229–248.

Bassino, Jean-Pascal, Kyoji Fukao and Tokihiko Settsu, 'The economic geography of Japanese industrialization (1800–2010). Paper presented at the International Workshop on The Economic Geography of Long-Run Industrialization (ca. 1800–2010) International Institute of Social History, Amsterdam, 22–23 March 2018.

Bassino, Jean-Pascal, Stephen Broadberry, Kyoji Fukao, Bishnupriya Gupta, Masanori Takashima, 'Japan and the Great Divergence, 725–1874', www.lse.ac.uk/economicHistory/pdf/Broadberry/JapanGreatDivergence6c.pdf. Forthcoming in *Explorations in Economic History*

Baten, Joerg, ed., *A history of the global economy, 1500 to the present* (Cambridge 2016).

Batten, Bruce L., *To the ends of Japan. Premodern frontiers, boundaries, and interactions* (Honolulu 2003).

Beasley, William G., *Great Britain and the opening of Japan, 1834–1858* (London 1951).

Beasley, William G., 'Feudal revenue at the time of the Meiji Restoration', *The Journal of Asian Studies* 19, 3 (1960) 255–271.

Beasley, William G., *The Meiji Restoration* (Stanford 1972).

Beasley, William G., *The modern history of Japan* (London 1981).

Beasley, William G., *Japanese imperialism, 1894–1945* (Oxford 1987).

Beasley, William G., 'The foreign threat and the opening of the ports' in: *Cambridge History of Japan*, Vol. 5, 259–307.

Beasley, William G., 'Meiji political institutions' in: *Cambridge History of Japan*, Vol. 5, 618–673.

Beasley, William G., *Japan encounters the barbarian. Japanese travellers in America and Europe* (New Haven and London 1995).

Beasley, William G., *The rise of modern Japan. Political, economic and social change since 1850* (second edition; London 1995).

Beauchamp, Edward R., and Akira Iriye, eds., *Foreign employees in nineteenth-century Japan* (Boulder 1990).

Befu, Harumi, 'Village autonomy and articulation with the state. The case of Tokugawa Japan', *Journal of Asian Studies* 25, 1 (1963) 19–32.

Bellah, Robert N., *Tokugawa religion. The values of pre-industrial Japan* (Boston 1957).

Bendix, Reinhard, *Kings or people. Power and the mandate to rule* (Berkeley 1978).

Benson, John and Takao Matsumura, *Japan 1868–1945. From isolation to occupation* (Harlow 2001).

Bernhofen, Daniel M. and John C. Brown, 'An empirical assessment of the comparative advantage gains from trade: Evidence from Japan', *American Economic Review* 95, 1 (2005) 208–225.

Bernhofen, Daniel M. and John C. Brown, "Understanding the gains from trade through the window of Japan during the nineteenth-century globalization. Analysis of a counterfactual', http://eh.net/eha/wp-content/uploads/2016/08/ BernhofenBrown.pdf.

Bernier, Bernhard, *Capitalisme, société et culture au Japon. Aux origines de l'industrialisation* (Montréal 1988).

Bernstein, Gail L., ed., *Recreating Japanese women, 1600–1945* (Berkeley 1991).

Berry, Mary E., 'Was early modern Japan culturally integrated?', *Modern Asian Studies* 31, 3 (1997) 547–581.

Berry, Mary E., *Japan in print. Information and nation in the early modern period* (Berkeley 2006).

Besley, Timothy and Torsten Persson, *Pillars of prosperity: the political economics of development clusters* (Princeton 2011).

Bird, Richard M., 'Land taxation and economic development. The model of Meiji Japan', *Journal of Development Studies* 13, 2 (1977) 162–174.

Bix, Herbert P., *Peasant protests in Japan, 1590–1884* (New Haven 1986).

Bolitho, Harold, *Treasures among men. The fudai daimyo in Tokugawa Japan* (New Haven 1974).

Bolitho, Harold, 'The Tempo crisis' in: *Cambridge History of Japan*, Vol. 5, 116–167.

Bolitho, Harold, 'The han' in: *Cambridge History of Japan*, Vol. 4, 183–234.

Bonney, Richard, 'The apogee and fall of the French rentier regime, 1801–1914' in: Cardoso and Lains, *Paying for the liberal state*, 81–102.

Botsman, Daniel V., *Punishment and power in the making of modern Japan* (Princeton 2005).

Borton, Hugh, *Peasant uprisings in Japan of the Tokugawa period* (New York 1968). Originally published in 1938 in the *Transactions of the Asiatic Society of Japan*, second series.

Brandt, L., 'Inter-war Japanese agriculture: Revisionist views on the impact of the colonial rice policy and the labor-surplus hypothesis', *Explorations in Economic History* 30 (1993) 259–293.

Braudel, Fernand, *Civilization & capitalism. Volume II. The wheels of commerce* (London 1982; originally Paris 1979).

Bray, Francesca, Peter A. Coclanis, Edda L. Fields-Black and Dagmar Schäfer, eds., *Rice. Global networks and new histories* (New York 2015).

Broadbridge, Seymour A., 'Shipbuilding and the state in Japan since the 1850s', *Modern Asian Studies* 11, 4 (1977) 601–613.

Broadbridge, Seymour A., 'Aspects of economic and social policy in Japan, 1868–1945' in: Peter Mathias and Sidney Pollard, eds., *The Cambridge Economic History of Europe, Volume VIII* (Cambridge 1989) 1106–1145.

Brown, Alexander, 'Meiji Japan. A unique technological experience?' *Student Economic Review*, 19 (2005) 71–83. www.tcd.ie/Economics/assets/pdf/SER/2005/Alexander_David_Brown.pdf.

Brown, Kenneth D., *Britain and Japan. A comparative economic and social history since 1900* (Manchester 1998).

Brown, Philip C., 'The mismeasure of land. Land surveying in the Tokugawa period', *Monumenta Nipponica* 42, 2 (1987) 115–155.

Brown, Philip C., 'Practical constraints on early Tokugawa land taxation. Annual versus fixed assessments in Kaga Domain', *Journal of Japanese Studies* 14, 2 (1988) 369–401.

Brown, Philip C., *Central authority and local autonomy in the formation of early modern Japan. The case of Kaga domain* (Stanford 1993).

Brown, Philip C., 'State, cultivator, land. Determination of land tenures in early modern Japan reconsidered', *The Journal of Asian Studies* 56, 2 (1997) 421–444.

Brown, Philip C., *Cultivating the commons. Joint ownership of arable land in early modern Japan* (Honolulu 2011).

Brown, Sidney D., 'Okubo Toshimichi. His political and economic policies in early Meiji Japan', *The Journal of Asian Studies* 21, 2 (1962) 183–197.

Burhop, Carsten, *Wirtschaftsgeschichte des Kaiserreichs, 1871–1918* (Göttingen 2011).

Burns, Susan L., *Before the nation. Kokugaku and the imagining of community in early modern Japan* (Durham 2003).

Burton, W. Donald, 'Peasant struggle in Japan, 1590–1760', *Journal of Peasant Studies* 5, 2 (1978) 135–171.

Burton, W. Donald, *Coal-mining women in Japan. Heavy burdens* (London and New York 2014).

Byas, Hugh, *Government by assassination* (New York 1942).

Bytheway, Simon, 'Japan's adoption of the gold standard: financial and monetary reform in the Meiji period' in: P.B. Bertola, J. McGuire and P.D. Reeves, eds., *Evolution of the world economy* (New Delhi 2001) 79–96.

Bytheway, Simon, *Investing Japan. Foreign capital, monetary standards and economic development, 1859–2011* (Cambridge Mass. 2014).

Calman, Donald, *The nature and origins of Japanese imperialism. A reinterpretation of the great crisis of 1873* (London 1992).

The Cambridge History of Japan, general editors John W. Hall, Marius B. Jansen, Madoka Kanai and Denis Twitchett, Vol. 6, *The twentieth century*, edited by Peter Duus (Cambridge 1988).

The Cambridge History of Japan, general editors John W. Hall, Marius B. Jansen, Madoka Kanai and Denis Twitchett, Vol. 5, *The nineteenth century*, edited by Marius B. Jansen (Cambridge 1989).

The Cambridge History of Japan, general editors John W. Hall, Marius B. Jansen, Madoka Kanai and Denis Twitchett Vol. 4, *Early modern Japan*, edited by John W. Hall and James L. McClain, assistant editor (Cambridge 1991).

Caplan, Bryan, 'State capacity is sleight of hand'. http://econlog.econlib.org/archives/2018/06/state_capacity.html.

Cardoso, José Luís and Pedro Lains, eds., *Paying for the liberal state. The rise of public finance in nineteenth-century Europe* (Cambridge 2010).

Cardoso, José Luís and Pedro Lains, eds., 'Introduction' in: Cardoso and Lains, *Paying for the liberal state*, 1–26.

Cha, Myung Soo, 'Did Takahashi Korekiyo rescue Japan from the Great Depression?', *The Journal of Economic History* 63, 1 (2003) 127–144.

Chaiklin, Martha, *Cultural commerce and Dutch commercial culture* (Leiden 2003).

Chandler, Alfred, with the assistance of Takashi Hikino, *Scale and scope. The dynamics of industrial capitalism.* (Cambridge Mass. and London 1990).

Chang, Ha-Joon, *Kicking away the ladder. Development strategy in historical perspective* (London 2002).

Chen, Shao-Kwan, *The system of taxation in China in the Tsing Dynasty, 1644–1911* (London 1914).

Clark, Colin, *The conditions of economic progress* (third edition, largely rewritten: London and New York 1957).

Clark, Gregory, *A farewell to alms. A brief economic history of the world* (Princeton and Oxford 2007).

Clark, Gregory and Tatsuya Ishii, 'Social mobility in Japan, 1868–2012. The surprising persistence of the samurai', http://old.econ.ucdavis.edu/faculty/gclark/papers/ Japan%202012.pdf.

Cogneau, Denis, Yannick Dupraz, Sandrine Mesplé-Somps, 'Fiscal capacity and dualism in colonial states: The French Empire 1830–1962', PSE Working Papers n°2018-27. 2018. https://halshs.archives-ouvertes.fr/halshs-01818700/document.

Cole, Robert E., and Ken'ichi Tominaga, 'Japan's changing occupational structure and its significance' in: Patrick, *Japanese industrialization*, 53–96.

Colley, Linda, 'Writing constitutions and writing world history' in: James Belich a.o., eds., *The prospect of global history* (Oxford 2016) 160–177.

Conrad, Sebastian, 'The opened and the closed country. Conflicting views of Japan's position in the world' in: Benedict Stuchtey and Eckhardt Fuchs, eds., *Writing world history, 1800–2000* (Oxford 2003) 327–351.

Coyne, Fumiko Hoshida, *Censorship of publishing in Japan, 1868–1945* (Chicago 1967), microfilm.

Crafts, Nicholas, *British economic growth during the Industrial Revolution* (Oxford 1985).

Craig, Albert M., *Choshu in the Meiji Restoration* (Cambridge Mass. 1961).

Craig, Albert M., ed., *Japan. A comparative view* (Princeton 1979).

Crawcour, E. Sydney, 'The Tokugawa heritage' in: Lockwood, *State and economic enterprise*, 17–46.

Crawcour, E. Sydney, 'The Tokugawa period and Japan's preparation for modern economic growth', *Journal of Japanese Studies* 1, 1 (1974) 113–125.

Crawcour, E. Sydney, 'Industrialization and technological change, 1885–1920' in: *Cambridge History of Japan, Vol. 6*, 385–450.

Crawcour, E. Sydney, 'Economic change in the nineteenth century' in: *Cambridge History of Japan, Vol. 5*, 569–617.

Crawcour, E. Sydney, 'Kogyo iken. Maeda Masana and his view of Meiji economic development', *Journal of Japanese Studies* 23, 1 (1997) 69–104.

Crawcour, E. Sydney and Kozo Yamamura, 'The Tokugawa monetary system 1787–1868', *Economic Development and Cultural Change* 18, 4 (1970) 489–518.

Cullen, Louis M., *A history of Japan, 1582–1941. Internal and external worlds* (Cambridge 2003).

Cullen, Louis M., 'The Nagasaki trade of the Tokugawa era. Archives, statistics and management', *Japan Review* 31 (2017) 69–104.

Daunton, Martin, *Trusting Leviathan. The politics of taxation in Britain, 1799–1914* (Cambridge 2001).

Daunton, Martin, 'Creating legitimacy. Administering taxation in Britain, 1815–1914' in: Cardoso and Lains, *Paying for the liberal state*, 27–56.

Daunton, Martin, *Wealth and welfare. An economic and social history of Britain, 1851–1951* (Oxford 2007).

Deane, Phyllis, 'Capital formation in Britain before the railway age', *Economic Development and Cultural Change* 9, 3 (1961) 352–368.

Den, Kenjiro, 'Japanese communications: the post, telegraph and telephone' in: Okuma, *Fifty years of new Japan*, Volume I, 408–424.

Deng, Kent and Patrick O'Brien, 'Establishing statistical foundations of a chronology for the Great Divergence: a survey and critique of the primary sources for the construction of relative wage levels for Ming–Qing China', *The Economic History Review* 69, 4 (2016) 1057–1082.

Deng, Kent and Patrick O'Brien, 'How well did facts travel to support protracted debate on the history of the Great Divergence between Western Europe and Imperial China?', Economic History Working Papers, 257/2017. London School of Economics and Political Science, Economic History Department, London, UK.

Dickinson, Frederick, *World War I and the triumph of a new Japan, 1919–1930* (Cambridge 2013).

Dincecco, Mark, *Political transformations and public finances, Europe, 1650–1913* (Cambridge 2011).

Doak, Kevin M., *A history of nationalism in modern Japan. Placing the people* (Leiden and Boston 2012).

Dore, Ronald P., 'Agricultural improvement in Japan, 1870–1900', *Economic Development and Cultural Change* 9, 1, part 2 (1960) 69–91.

Dore, Ronald P., 'Talent and social order in Tokugawa Japan', *Past & Present* 21 (1962) 60–72.

Dore, Ronald P., *Education in Tokugawa Japan* (Berkeley and Los Angeles 1965).

Dore, Ronald P., 'The modernizer as a special case. Japanese factory legislation, 1882–1911', *Comparative Studies in Society and History* 11, 4 (1969) 433–450.

Dore, Ronald P., *British factory Japanese factory. The origins of national diversity in industrial relations* (Berkeley 1973).

Dore, Ronald P., *Land reform in Japan* (London 1984, with a new preface; originally 1959).

Dowdy, Edwin, *Japanese bureaucracy. Its development and modernization* (Melbourne 1972).

Drea, Edward J., *Japan's imperial army. Its rise and fall, 1853–1945* (Lawrence 2009).

Drixler, Fabian, *Mabiki. Infanticide and population growth in Eastern Japan, 1660–1950* (Berkeley 2013).

Duke, Benjamin C., *The history of modern Japanese education. Constructing the national school system, 1872–1890* (New Brunswick 2009).

Dunn, Charles J., *Everyday life in traditional Japan* (Boston 1972).

Duus, Peter, 'Economic dimensions of Meiji imperialism. The case of Korea, 1895–1910' in: Myers and Peattie, *Japanese colonial empire*, 128–171.

Duus, Peter, 'Introduction' in: *Cambridge History of Japan. Vol. 6*, 1–54.

Duus, Peter, 'Socialism, liberalism and Marxism', *Cambridge History of Japan. Vol. 6*, 654–710.

Duus, Peter, *Modern Japan* (Boston and New York 1998).

Duus, Peter, Ramon H. Myers and Mark R. Peattie, eds., *The Japanese informal empire in China* (Princeton 1989).

Duus, Peter, Ramon H. Myers and Mark R. Peattie, eds., *The Japanese wartime empire 1931–1945* (Princeton 1996).

Dyer, Henry, *Dai Nippon. The Britain of the East. A study in national evolution* (London 1904).

Earle, E.M., 'Adam Smith, Alexander Hamilton, Friedrich List. The economic foundations of military power' in: Peter Paret, ed., *Makers of modern strategy. From Machiavelli to the nuclear age* (Princeton 1986) 117–154.

Edmonds, Richard L., *Northern frontiers of Qing China and Tokugawa Japan. A comparative study of frontier policy* (Chicago 1985).

Eiji, Takemura, *The perception of work in Tokugawa Japan. A study of Ishida Baigan and Ninomiya Sontoku* (Lanham and Oxford 1997).

Eisenstadt, Shmuel N., *Japanese civilization. A comparative view* (Chicago and London 1996).

Elisonas, Jurgis, 'Christianity and the daimyo' in: *Cambridge History of Japan, Volume 4,* 301–371.

Elman, Benjamin, *Science in China, 1500–1800. Essays by Benjamin A. Elman* (Princeton 2015).

Eloranta, Jari, 'Military spending patterns in history', http://eh.net/encyclopedia/military-spending-patterns-in-history.

Eloranta, Jari and Mark Harrison, 'War and disintegration, 1914–1950' in: Stephen Broadberry and Kevin H. O'Rourke, eds., *The Cambridge Economic History of Modern Europe. Volume 2: 1870 to the present* (Cambridge 2010) 133–155.

Emi, Koichi, *Government fiscal activity and economic growth in Japan, 1868–1960* (Tokyo 1963).

Engerman, Stanley and Kenneth L. Sokoloff, *Economic development in the Americas since 1500. Endowments and institutions* (Cambridge 2012).

Epstein, S.R., *Freedom and growth: The rise of states and markets in Europe, 1300–1750* (London and New York 2000).

Ericson, Steven J., *The sound of the whistle. Railroads and the state in Meiji Japan* (Cambridge Mass. and London 1996).

Ericson, Steven J., 'Importing locomotives in Meiji Japan. International business and technology transfer in the railroad industry' in: Low, *Beyond Joseph Needham*, 129–153.

Ericson, Steven J., 'The 'Matsukata deflation' reconsidered. Financial stabilization and Japanese exports in a global depression, 1881–1885', *Journal of Japanese Studies* 40, 1 (2014) 1–28.

Etemad, Bouda, *Possessing the world. Taking the measurements of colonisation from the eighteenth to the twentieth century* (New York 2007).

Evans, David C, and Mark R. Peattie, *Kaigun: strategy, tactics, and technology in the Imperial Japanese Navy, 1887–1941* (Annapolis, Maryland 1997).

Facchini, François and Mickaël Melki, 'Optimal government size and economic growth in France (1871–2008). An explanation by the State and market failures', *Documents de travail du Centre d'Economie de la Sorbonne* https://halshs.archives-ouvertes.fr/halshs-00654363/document

Ferber, Katalin, "Run the state like a business". The origins of the deposit fund in Meiji Japan', *Japanese Studies* 22, 2 (2002) 131–151.

Ferguson, Niall, *The cash nexus. Money and power in the modern world, 1700–2000* (London 2001).

Flath, David, *The Japanese economy* (second edition; Oxford 2005).

Fletcher, W. Miles III., 'The Japanese Spinners Association. Creating industrial policy in Meiji Japan', *Journal of Japanese Studies* 22, 1 (1996) 49–75.

Flora, Peter, Franz Kraus and Winfried Pfennig, *State, economy and society in Western Europe, 1815–1975.* (Chicago 1983 and 1987). Two volumes.

Floud, Roderick and Paul Johnson, eds., *Cambridge Economic History of Modern Britain. Volume I Industrialisation, 1700–1860* (Cambridge 2004).

Flynn, Dennis O., Arturo Giráldez and Richard von Glahn, eds., *Global connections and monetary history, 1470–1800* (Aldershot and Burlington 2003)

Fogel, Joshua, A., *The teleology of the modern nation-state. Japan and China* (Philadelphia 2005).

Fogel, Joshua, A., ed., *Late Qing China and Meiji Japan. Political and cultural aspects* (Norwalk 2004).

Foucault, Michel, and Michel Sennellart, *Security, territory, population. Lectures at the College de France* (New York 2010).

Francks, Penelope, *Technology and agricultural development in pre-war Japan* (New Haven and London 1984).

Francks, Penelope, 'Japan and an East Asian model of agriculture's role in industrialisation', *Japan Forum* 12, 1 (2000) 43–52.

Francks, Penelope, 'Rural industry, growth linkages, and economic development in nineteenth-century Japan', *The Journal of Asian Studies* 61, 1 (2002) 33–55.

Francks, Penelope, 'Rice for the masses. Food policy and the adoption of imperial self-sufficiency in early twentieth-century Japan', *Japan Forum* 15 (2003) 125–146.

Francks, Penelope, *Rural economic development in Japan. From the nineteenth century to the Pacific War* (London and New York 2006).

Francks, Penelope, *The Japanese consumer. An alternative economic history of modern Japan* (Cambridge 2009).

Francks, Penelope, 'Simple pleasures: food consumption in Japan and the global comparison of living standards', *Journal of Global History* 8, 1 (2013) 96–116.

Francks, Penelope, 'Rice and the path of economic development in Japan' in: Bray, Coclanis, Fields Black and Schäfer, *Rice*, 318–334.

Francks, Penelope, *Japanese economic development. Theory and practice* (fully revised and updated third edition; London and New York 2015). Originally published in 1992.

Francks, Penelope, *Japan and the Great Divergence. A short guide* (London 2016).

Francks, Penelope, Johanna Boestel, and Choo Hyop Kim, *Agriculture and economic development in East Asia. From growth to protectionism in Japan, Korea and Taiwan* (London 1999).

Francks, Penelope and Janet Hunter, eds., *The historical consumer. Consumption and everyday life in Japan, 1850–2000* (Basingstoke and New York 2012).

Frank, Andre Gunder, *Dependent accumulation and underdevelopment* (London 1978).

Frankema, Ewout, 'Raising revenue in the British empire, 1870–1940: how 'extractive' were colonial taxes?', *Journal of Global History* 5, 3 (2010) 447–477.

Frankema, Ewout, 'Colonial taxation and government spending in British Africa, 1880–1940. Maximizing revenue or minimizing effort?', *Explorations in Economic History* 48, 1 (2011) 136–149.

Frédéric, Louis, *La vie quotidienne au Japon au début de l'ère moderne (1868–1912)* (Paris 1984).

Frédéric, Louis, *Japan Encyclopedia* (Cambridge Mass. and London 2002). Originally in French 1996.

Friday, Karl F., ed., *Japan emerging. Premodern history to 1850* (Boulder 2012).

Fukao, Kyoji and Tokihiko Settsu, 'Japan. Modern economic growth in Asia'. In: *Cambridge Economic History of the Modern World, Volume Two*. Chapter 4. Forthcoming

Fukasaku, Yukiko, *Technology and industrial development in pre-war Japan. The Mitsubishi-Nagasaki shipyard 1884–1934* (London 1992).

Fukuyama, Francis, *Political order and political decay. From the Industrial Revolution to the globalisation of democracy* (London 2014).

Fukuzawa, Yukichi, *An outline of a theory of civilization* (Tokyo 1973). Translated by David A. Dilworth and G. Cameron Hurst III, with an introduction by Takenori Inoki.

Fukuzawa, Yukichi, *The autobiography of Yukichi Fukuzawa* (New York 2007). Reprinted with a revised translation by Eiikchi Kiyooka and a Foreword and Afterword by Albert M. Craig.

Fulger, James, 'The bureaucratisation of the state and the rise of Japan', *British Journal of Sociology* 39, 2 (1988) 228–254.

Furushima, Toshio, 'The village and agriculture during the Edo period' in: *Cambridge History of Japan. Vol. 4*, 478–518.

Garon, Sheldon, *The state and labor in modern Japan* (Berkeley 1987).

Garon, Sheldon, *Molding Japanese minds. The state in everyday life* (Princeton 1997).

Garon, Sheldon, *Beyond our means. Why America spends while the world saves* (Princeton 2011).

Gasteren L.A. van, H.J. Moeshart, H.C. Toussaint and P.A. de Wilde, eds., *In een Japanse stroomversnelling. Berichten van Nederlandse watermannen, - rijswerkers, ingenieurs, werkbazen 1872 –1903* (Zutphen 2000).

Gat, Azar, *War in human civilization* (Oxford and New York 2006).

Gatrell, Peter, 'The Russian fiscal state, 1600–1914' in: Yun-Casalilla, O'Brien, and Comín-Comín, *Rise of fiscal states*, 191–212.

Gerschenkron, Alexander, *Economic backwardness in historical perspective. A book of essays* (Cambridge Mass. 1962).

Glahn, Richard von, *The economic history of China. From Antiquity to the nineteenth century* (Cambridge 2016).

Gluck, Carol, *Japan's modern myths. Ideology in the late Meiji period* (Princeton 1985).

Goldsmith, Raymond W., *The financial development of Japan, 1868–1977* (New Haven and London 1983).

Gooday, Graeme J.N., and Morris F. Low, 'Technology transfer and cultural exchange. Western scientists and engineers encounter Late Tokugawa and Meiji Japan' in: Low, *Beyond Joseph Needham*, 99–128.

Goodman, Grant K., *Japan. The Dutch experience* (London 1986).

Goodman, Grant K., *Japan and the Dutch* (Richmond 2000).

Gordon, Andrew, *The evolution of labor relations in Japan. Heavy industry, 1853–1955* (Cambridge Mass. 1985).

Gordon, Andrew, *Labor and imperial democracy in pre-war Japan* (Berkeley 1993).

Gordon, Andrew, 'The invention of Japanese-style labor management' in: Vlastos, *Mirror of modernity*, 19–36.

Gordon, Andrew, *A modern history of Japan. From Tokugawa times to the present* (Oxford 2013).

Gordon, M.S., 'Japan's balance of international payments, 1904–1931' in: Schumpeter, *Industrialization of Japan and Manchukuo*, 865–925.

Gouk, Penelope, ed., *Wellsprings of achievement. Cultural and economic dynamics in early modern England and Japan* (Farnham and Burlington 1995).

Grad, Andrew J., *Land and peasant in Japan* (New York 1952).

Gramlich-Oka, Bettina and Gregory Smits, eds., *Economic thought in early modern Japan* (Leiden and Boston 2010).

Greenfeld, Liah, *The spirit of capitalism. Nationalism and economic growth* (Cambridge Mass. 2001).

Groemer, Gerald, 'The creation of the Edo outcast order', *Journal of Japanese Studies* 27, 2 (2001) 263–293.

Gupta, Bishnupriya, Debin Ma and Tirthankar Roy, 'States and development. Early modern India, China, and the Great Divergence' in: Jari Eloranta, and others, eds., *Economic history of warfare and state formation* (Singapore 2016) 51–73.

Hackett, Roger F., *Yamagata Aritomo in the rise of modern Japan, 1838–1922* (Cambridge Mass. 1971).

Hall, John A., 'States and economic development: reflections on Adam Smith' in: idem, *States in history*, 154–176.

Hall, John A., ed., *States in history* (Oxford and Cambridge Mass. 1986).

Hall, John W., *Tanuma Okitsugu. Forerunner of modern Japan* (Cambridge 1955).

Hall, John W., 'The castle town and Japan's modern urbanization', *Journal of Asian Studies* 15, 1 (1955) 37–56.

Hall, John W., 'E.H. Norman on Tokugawa Japan', *Journal of Japanese Studies* 3, 2 (1977) 365–374.

Hall, John W., 'The *bakuhan* system' in: *Cambridge History of Japan. Vol. 4*, 128–182.

Hall, John W., and Marius B. Jansen, eds., with an introduction by Joseph R. Strayer, *Studies in the institutional history of early modern Japan* (Princeton 1968).

Halliday, Jon, *A political history of Japanese capitalism* (New York 1975).

Hane, Mikiso, *Peasants, rebels & outcastes. The underside of modern Japan* (New York 1982).

Hane, Mikiso, *Modern Japan. A historical survey* (third edition; Boulder 2001).

Hane, Mikiso and Louis G. Perez, *Premodern Japan. A historical survey* (Boulder 2014).

Hanley, Susan B., 'A high standard of living in nineteenth-century Japan: fact or fantasy?', *Journal of Economic History* 43, 1 (1983) 183–192.

Hanley, Susan B., 'Standard of living in nineteenth-century Japan. Reply to Yasuba', *Journal of Economic History* 46, 1 (1986) 225–226.

Hanley, Susan B., 'Tokugawa society: material culture, standard of living, and life-styles' in: *Cambridge History of Japan. Vol. 4*, 660–705.

Hanley, Susan B., *Everyday things in premodern Japan. The hidden legacy of material culture* (Berkeley and London 1997).

Hanley, Susan B., and Kozo Yamamura, 'Quiet transformation in Tokugawa economic history', *The Journal of Asian Studies* 30, 2 (1970–1971) 373–384.

Hanley, Susan B., and Kozo Yamamura, *Economic and demographic change in preindustrial Japan, 1600–1868* (Princeton 1977).

Harada, Shuichi, *Labour conditions in Japan* (1928, repr. New York, 1979).

Hardacre, Helen, *Shinto and the state, 1868–1988* (Princeton 1991).

Harootunian, Harry D., 'The progress of Japan and the samurai class, 1868–1882', *Pacific Historical Review* 28, 3 (1959) 255–266.

Harootunian, Harry D., 'The economic rehabilitation of the samurai in the early Meiji period', *The Journal of Asian Studies* 19, 4 (1960) 433–444.

Harootunian, Harry D., *Toward restoration. The growth of political consciousness in Tokugawa Japan* (Berkeley, Los Angeles, Oxford 1970).

Yamawaki, Haruki, *Japan in the beginning of the twentieth century.* Published by the Imperial Commission to the Louisiana Purchase Exposition (Tokyo 1904).

Harrison, John A., 'The Capron mission and the colonization of Hokkaido, 1868–1875', *Agricultural History* 25, 3 (1951) 135–142.

Harrison, John A., *Japan's northern frontier* (Gainesville 1953).

Harrison, Mark, "The economics of World War II. An overview' in: Mark Harrison, ed., *The economics of World War II. Six great powers in international comparison* (Cambridge 1988) 1–42.

Hashimoto, Juro, 'The rise of big business' in: Nakamura and Odaka, *Economic History of Japan, 1914–1955*, 190–222.

Hashino, Tomoko and Osamu Saito, 'Tradition and interactions. Research trends in modern Japanese industrial history', *Australian Economic History Review* 44, 3 (2004) 241–258.

Hattori, Yukimasa, *The foreign commerce of Japan since the Restoration. 1869–1900. Volume 22* (Baltimore 1904).

Havens, Thomas R., *Farm and nation in modern Japan. Agrarian nationalism, 1870–1940* (Princeton and London 1974).

Hayami, Akira, 'Introduction. The emergence of economic society' in: Hayami, Saito and Toby, *Emergence of economic society*, 1–35.

Hayami, Akira, *Japan's industrious revolution. Economic and social transformations in the early modern period* (Tokyo 2015).

Hayami, Akira and Hiroshi Kito, 'Demography and living standards' in: Hayami, Saito and Toby, *Emergence of economic society*, 213–246.

Hayami, Akira, Osamu Saito and Ronald P. Toby, eds., *Emergence of economic society in Japan, 1600–1859* (Oxford 2004). Volume One of *The Economic History of Japan, 1600–1990*.

Hayami, Yujiro and Yoshihisha Godo, *Development economics. From the poverty to the wealth of nations* (third edition; New York 2005).

Hazama, Hiroshi, *The history of labour management in Japan* (Basingstoke and New York 1997; originally 1964).

He, Wenkai, *Paths toward the modern fiscal state. England, Japan, and China* (Cambridge Mass. 2013).

Heber, E. A., *Die japanische Industriearbeit. Eine wirtschaftswissenschaftliche und kulturhistorische Studie* (Jena and Zürich 1912).

Helleiner, Eric, *The making of national money. Territorial currencies in historical perspective* (Ithaca 2003).

Hellyer, Robert, *Defining engagement. Japan and global contexts, 1640–1868* (Cambridge Mass. 2009).

Hellyer, Robert, 'Poor but not pirates. The Tsushima Domain and foreign relations in early modern Japan' in: Robert Antony, ed., *Elusive pirates, pervasive smugglers. Violence and clandestine trade in the Greater China Seas* (Hong Kong 2010) 115–126.

Hellyer, Robert, 'The West, the East and the insular middle. Trading systems, demand, and labour in the integration of the Pacific, 1750–1875', *Journal of Global History* 8, 3 (2013) 391–413.

Henley, David, *Asia-Africa development. A question of intent* (Chicago 2015).

Henshall, Kenneth G., *A history of Japan. From Stone Age to superpower* (Houndmills and London 1999).

Hentschel, Volker, *Wirtschaftsgeschichte des modernen Japans* (Wiesbaden 1986). Two volumes.

Herail, Francine a.o., *Histoire du Japon* (Le Coteau 1990).

Hidetoshi, K., 'The significance of the period of national seclusion reconsidered', *Journal of Japanese Studies* 7, 1 (1981) 85–109.

Hillsborough, Romulus, *Samurai revolution. The dawn of modern Japan seen through the eyes of the Shogun's last samurai* (Tokyo, Rutland, Singapore 2014).

Hirano, Katsuya, 'Regulating excess. The cultural politics of consumption in Tokugawa Japan' in: Giorgio Riello and Ulinka Rublack, eds., *The right to dress. Sumptuary laws in a global perspective c. 1200–1800* (Cambridge 2019) 435–460.

Hirobumi, Ito, 'Some reminiscences of the grant of the new constitution' in: Okuma, *Fifty years of New Japan*, Volume I, 122–132.

Hiroshi, Mitami, *Escape from impasse. The decision to open Japan* (Tokyo 2006).

Hirschmeier, Johannes and Tsunehiko Yui, *The development of Japanese business, 1600–1973* (Cambridge Mass. 1975).

Hobsbawm, Eric J., *The age of revolution* (London 1962).

Hobsbawm, Eric J., *Nations and nationalism since 1870. Program, myth, reality* (Cambridge 1990).

Honjo, Eijiro, *The social and economic history of Japan* (Kyoto 1935).

Honjo, Eijiro, 'On the finance of the Tokugawa government', *Kyoto University Economic Review* 6, 2 (1931) 16–33.

Hoston, Germaine A., *The state, identity and the national question in China and Japan* (Princeton 1984).

Hoston, Germaine A., *Marxism and the crisis of development in pre-war Japan* (Princeton 1986).

Hoston, Germaine A., 'Conceptualizing bourgeois revolution: The pre-war Japanese left and the Meiji Restoration', *Comparative Studies in Society and History 33*, 3 (1991) 539–581.

Hoston, Germaine A., 'The state, modernity and the fate of liberalism in pre-war Japan', *The Journal of Asian Studies* 51, 2 (1992) 287–316.

Howe, Christopher, *The origins of Japanese trade supremacy. Development and technology in Asia from 1540 to the Pacific War* (London 1996).

Howell, David L., *Capitalism from within: economy, society, and the state in a Japanese fishery* (Berkeley 1995).

Howell, David L., *Geographies of identity in nineteenth-century Japan* (Berkeley 2005).

Howland, Douglass R., 'Samurai status, class and bureaucracy. A historiographical essay', *The Journal of Asian Studies* 60, 2 (2001) 353–380.

Hubbard, Gilbert Ernest, assisted by Denzil Baring, *Eastern industrialization and its effect on the West, with special reference to Great Britain and Japan* (Oxford and London 1935).

Huber, J. Richard, 'Effects on price of Japan's entry into world commerce after 1858', *Journal of Political Economy* 79, 3 (1971) 614–629.

Huber, Thomas M., *The revolutionary origins of modern Japan* (Stanford 1981).

Huffman, James L., *Creating a public. People and press in Meiji Japan* (Honolulu 1997).

Huffman, James L., *Modern Japan. A history in documents* (second edition; Oxford 2010).

Huffman, James L., *Japan in world history* (Oxford 2010).

Hunter, Janet E., *The emergence of modern Japan. An introductory history since 1853* (London 1989).

Hunter, Janet E., 'Roots of divergence? Some comments on Japan in the "Axial Age", 1750–1850', *Itinerario. European Journal of Overseas History* 24, 3/4 (2000) 75–88.

Hunter, Janet E., *Women and the labour market in Japan's industrialising economy. The textile industry before the Pacific War* (London and New York 2003).

Hunter, Janet E., 'Understanding the economic history of postal services. Some preliminary observations from the case of Meiji Japan', Economic History Department London School of Economics and Political Science, 2005.

Hunter, Janet E., 'People and post offices: consumption and postal services in Japan from the 1870s to the 1970s' in: Francks and Hunter, *The historical consumer*, 235–283.

Ienaga, Saburo, *The Pacific War. 1931–1945. A critical perspective on Japan's role in World War II* (New York 1978; originally 1968).

Ike, Nobutaka, 'Taxation and landownership in the westernization of Japan', *The Journal of Economic History* 7, 2 (1947) 160–182.

Ikegami, Eiko, *The taming of the samurai. Honorific individualism and the making of modern Japan* (Cambridge 1995).

Ikegami, Eiko, *Bonds of civility* (Cambridge 2005).

Inkster Ian, 'Meiji economic development in perspective. Revisionists comments upon the Industrial Revolution in Japan', *The Developing Economies* 17, 1 (1979) 45–68.

Inkster Ian, *Japan as a developmental model. Relative backwardness and technological transfer* (Bochum 1980).

Inkster Ian, 'Prometheus bound: technology and industrialization in Japan, China and India prior to 1914 – a political economy approach', *Annals of Science* 45, 4 (1988) 329–426.

Inkster Ian, 'Science, technology and economic development – Japanese historical experience in context', *Annals of Science* 48, 6 (1991) 545–563.

Inkster Ian, 'Culture, action, and institutions: on exploring the historical economic successes of England and Japan' in: Gouk, *Wellsprings of achievement*, 239–267.

Inkster Ian, 'Technology transfer and industrial transformation. An interpretation of the pattern of economic development circa 1870–1914' in: Robert Fox, ed., *Technological change. Methods and themes in the history of technology* (Abingdon, Oxon and New York 1996) 177–200.

Inkster Ian, 'Motivation and achievement. Technological change and creative response in comparative industrial history', *The Journal of European Economic History* 27, 1 (1998) 29–66.

Inkster Ian, *Japanese industrialisation. Historical and cultural perspectives* (London 2001).

Inkster Ian, *The Japanese industrial economy. Late development and cultural causation* (London and New York 2001).

Inkster Ian, 'Politicising the Gerschenkron schema. Technology transfer, late development and the state in historical perspective', *Journal of European Economic History* 31, 1 (2002) 45–88.

Innes, Robert L., *The door ajar. Japan's foreign trade in the seventeenth century* (Ann Arbor 1980). Two volumes.

Irie, Hiroshi, 'Apprenticeship training in Tokugawa Japan', *Acta Asiatica* 54 (1988) 1–23.

Iriye, Akira, 'Japan's drive to great-power status' in: *Cambridge History of Japan. Vol. 5*, 721–782.

Ishii, Kanji, 'The mercantile response in the Meiji period: capital accumulation by merchants and the government's rejection of foreign capital', *Social Science Japan Journal* 12, 2 (2009) 211–225.

Iwahashi, Masaru, 'The institutional framework of the Tokugawa economy' in: Hayami, Saito and Toby, *Emergence of economic society*, 85–104.

Iwata, Masakazu, *Okubo Toshimichi. The Bismarck of Japan* (Berkeley and Los Angeles 1964).

Jackson, Terrence, *Network of knowledge. Western science and the Tokugawa information revolution* (Honolulu 2016).

Jacob, Frank, *Tsushima 1905. Ostasiens Trafalgar* (Paderborn 2017).

Jacobs, Norman, *The origin of modern capitalism and Eastern Asia* (Hong Kong 1958).

Jansen, Marius B., 'Rangaku and Westernization', *Modern Asian Studies* 18, 4 (1984) 541–553.

Jansen, Marius B., 'Introduction' in: *Cambridge History of Japan. Vol. 5*, 1–49.

Jansen, Marius B, 'Japan in the early nineteenth century' in: *Cambridge History of Japan. Vol. 5*, 50–115.

Jansen, Marius B., 'The Meiji Restoration' in: *Cambridge History of Japan. Vol. 5*, 308–366.

Jansen, Marius B., *The making of modern Japan* (Cambridge Mass. 2000).

Jansen, Marius B., ed., *Changing Japanese attitudes toward modernization* (Princeton 1965).

Jansen, Marius B., and Gilbert Rozman, eds., *Japan in transition. From Tokugawa to Meiji* (Princeton 1986).

Jaundrill, D. Colin, *Samurai to soldier. Remaking military service in nineteenth-century Japan* (Ithaca 2016).

Johansson, S. Ryan, and Carl Mosk, 'Exposure, resistance and life expectancy: disease and death during the economic development of Japan, 1900–1960', *Population Studies* 41 (1987) 207–235.

Johnson, Chalmers, *MITI and the Japanese miracle. The growth of industrial policy, 1925–1975* (Stanford 1982).

Johnson, Chalmers, *Japan: Who governs? The rise of the developmental state* (New York and London 1995).

Johnson, Chalmers, 'The developmental state. Odyssey of a concept' in: Woo-Cummings, *Developmental state*, 32–60.

Johnson, Noel D. and Mark Koyama, 'States and economic growth: capacity and constraints', *Explorations in Economic History* 64, 3 (2017) 1–20.

Jolliffe, Pia, *Gefängnisse und Zwangsarbeit auf der japanischen Nordinsel Hokkaido* (2016 Vienna).

Jones, Eric L., *Growth recurring. Economic change in world history* (Cambridge 1988).

Jones, Eric L., 'Capitalism: one origin or two?', *Journal of Early Modern History* 1, 1 (1997) 71–76.

Jones, Eric L., *The European miracle. Environments, economies and geopolitics in the history of Europe* (third edition; Cambridge 2003).

Jones, Eric L., 'Missing out on industrial revolution', *World Economics* 9, 4 (2008) 101–128.

Kaempfer, Engelbert, *Kaempfer's Japan. Tokugawa culture observed*. Edited, translated and annotated by Beatrice M. Bodart-Bailey (Honolulu 1999).

Kalland, Arne, *Fishing villages in Tokugawa Japan* (Honolulu 1995).

Kang, David C., *East Asia before the West. Five centuries of trade and tribute* (New York 2012).

Kasza, Gregory J., *The state and the mass media in Japan, 1918–1945* (Berkeley, Los Angeles. London 1993).

Kawada, Hisashi and Solomon B. Levine, *Human resources in Japanese industrial development* (Princeton 1980).

Keene, Donald, *The Japanese discovery of Europe, 1720–1830* (Stanford 1969; revised edition, originally 1952).

Keene, Donald, *Emperor of Japan. Meiji and his world, 1852–1912* (New York 2002).

Kelley, William W., *Water control in Tokugawa Japan. Irrigation organization in a Japanese river basin, 1600–1870* (Ithaca 1962).

Kelley, William W., *Deference and defiance in nineteenth-century Japan* (Princeton 1985).

Kelly, Morgan, 'The dynamics of Smithian growth', *The Quarterly Journal of Economics* 112, 3 (1997) 939–964.

Kikkawa, Takeo, 'The history of Japan's electric power industry before World War II', *Hitotsubashi Journal of Commerce and Management* 46 (2012) 1–16.

Kim, Hyung-Ki, Michio Muramatsu, T.J. Pempel and Kozo Yamamura, eds., *The Japanese civil service and economic development. Catalysts of change* (Oxford 1995).

Kim, Key-Hiuk, *The last phase of the East Asian world order. Korea, Japan, and the Chinese empire, 1860–1882* (Berkeley 1980).

Kim, Kyu Hyun, *The age of visions and arguments: Parliamentarianism and the national public sphere in early Meiji Japan* (Cambridge, Mass. 2008).

Knortz, Heike, *Wirtschaftsgeschichte der Weimarer Republik* (Göttingen 2010).

Kocka, Jürgen, *Capitalism. A short history* (Princeton and Oxford 2016).

Kocka, Jürgen and Marcel van der Linden, eds., *Capitalism. The re-emergence of a historical concept* (London 2016).

Koh, Byung C., *Japan's administrative elite* (Berkeley and Oxford 1989).

Kojima, Kiyoshi, 'The 'flying geese' model of Asian economic development: origin, theoretical extensions, and regional policy implications', *Journal of Asian Economics* 11, 4 (2000) 375–401.

Kornicki, Peter F., ed., *Meiji Japan: political, economic and social history 1868–1912. Volume I Meiji Japan. The emergence of the Meiji state* (London 1998).

Koschmann, J. Victor, *The Mito ideology* (Berkeley and Los Angeles 1987).

Kowner, Rotem, *Historical Dictionary of the Russo-Japanese War* (Lanham 2017).

Koyama, Mark, Chiaki Moriguchi and Tuan-Hwee Sng, 'Geopolitics and Asia's Little Divergence: A comparative analysis of state building in China and Japan after 1850 (October 28, 2015). GMU Working Paper in Economics No. 15–54. Available at SSRN: https://ssrn.com/abstract=2682702 or http://dx.doi.org/10.2139/ssrn.2682702.

Kreiner, Josef, *Geschichte Japans* (third edition: Stuttgart 2016).

Kume, Kunitake, *Japan rising. The Iwakura Embassy to the USA and Europe, 1871–1873* (Cambridge 2009). The book is edited by Chushichi Tsuzuki and R. Jules Young, and has an introduction by Ian Nish.

Kumon, Yuzuru, 'How equality created poverty. Japanese wealth distribution and living standards 1600–1870', http://yuzurukumon.com/Kumon HowEqualityCreatedPoverty. pdf

Kuznets, Simon, *Six lectures on economic growth* (Glencoe 1959).

Kuznets, Simon, *Economic growth of nations. Total output and production structure* (Cambridge Mass. 1971).

Kuznets, Simon, *Prize Lecture. Lecture to the memory of Alfred Nobel*, December 11, 1971.

Kwon, Grace H., *State formation, property relations, and the development of the Tokugawa economy (1600–1868)* (New York and London 2002).

Landes, David S., 'Japan and Europe: contrasts in industrialization' in: Lockwood, *State and economic enterprise*, 93–182.

Landes, David S., *The wealth and poverty of nations. Why are some so rich and others so poor?* (London 1998).

Landes, David S., *The unbound Prometheus. Technological change and industrial development in Western Europe from 1750 to the present* (second edition: Cambridge 2003).

Large, Stephen S., *The Yuaikai 1912–1919. The rise of labour in Japan* (Tokyo 1972).

Lee, John, 'Trade and economy in preindustrial East Asia, c. 1500–c. 1800: East Asia in the age of global integration', *The Journal of Asian Studies* 58, 1 (1999) 2–26.

Leeuwen, Bas van, and Jieli van Leeuwen-Li, 'Education since 1820' in: Van Zanden, *How was life*, 88–100.

Lehmann, Jean-Pierre, *The image of Japan. From feudal isolation to world power, 1850–1905* (London 1978).

Lehmann, Jean-Pierre, *The roots of modern Japan* (London and Basingstoke 1982).

Lensen, George A., *The Russian push toward Japan. Russo-Japanese relations 1697–1875* (Princeton 1959).

Lesger, Clé, *The rise of the Amsterdam market and information exchange. Merchants, commercial expansion and the change in the spatial economy of the Low Countries c. 1550–1630* (Abingdon, Oxon and New York 2016; originally 2006).

Leupp, Gary P., *Servants, shophands and laborers in the cities of Tokugawa Japan* (Princeton 1992).

Lewis, Michael, *Rioters and citizens. Mass protest in Imperial Japan* (Berkeley, Los Angeles, Oxford 1990).

Lewis, William Arthur, *The theory of economic growth* (London 1955).

Lieberman, Victor, *Strange parallels. Southeast Asia in global context, c. 800–1830.* Volume Two (Cambridge 2009).

Liebscher, G., *Japan's landwirthschaftliche und allgemeinwirthschaftliche Verhältnisse. Nach eignen Beobachtungen dargestellt* (Jena 1882).

Lindert, Peter H., *Growing public. Social spending and economic growth since the eighteenth century* (Cambridge 2004).

Lindert, Peter H. and Jeffrey Williamson, 'Revising England's social tables, 1688–1812', *Explorations in Economic History* 19, 4 (1982) 385-408.

Listwa, Daniel, 'Japanese deflation: Matsukata and reform', *Columbia Economics Review* June 9 2014 http://columbiaeconreview.com/2014/06/09/japandeflation/

Liu, David, *Japan: A documentary history Vol. 1: The dawn of history to the late eighteenth century* (Abingdon, Oxon and New York 2015; originally 2005).

Liu, David, *Japan: A documentary history Vol. 2: The late Tokugawa period to the present* (Abingdon, Oxon and New York 2015; originally 1997).

Livi-Bacci, Massimo, *Population and nutrition. An essay on European demographic history* (Cambridge 1991; originally Milan 1987).

Livi-Bacci, Massimo, *Population of Europe* (Oxford 2000, originally 1998).

Livingston, Jon, Joe Moore and Felicia Oldfather, eds., *Imperial Japan, 1800–1945* (New York 1973).

Lockwood, William W., *The economic development of Japan. Growth and structural change.* (Expanded edition: Princeton 1968; originally 1954).

Lockwood, William W., ed., *The state and economic enterprise in Japan. Essays in the political economy of growth* (Princeton 1965).

Lone, Stewart, *Provincial life and the military in Imperial Japan. The phantom samurai* (London 2009).

Longford, Joseph, *The evolution of new Japan* (Cambridge 1913).

Low, Morris F., ed., 'Beyond Joseph Needham. Science, technology and medicine in East and Southeast Asia', *Osiris* second series, issue 13 (Ithaca 1998).

Lu, Sidney Xu, 'Colonizing Hokkaido and the origins of Japanese transpacific expansion, 1869–1894', *Japanese Studies* 36, 2 (2016) 251–274.

Ma, Debin, 'State capacity and great divergence, the case of Qing China (1644–1911)', *Eurasian Geography and Economics* 54, 5/6 (2014) 484–499.

Ma, Debin, 'China' in: Baten, *History of the global economy*, 188–203.

MacCormack, Gavan and Yoshio Sugimento, eds., *The Japanese trajectory. Modernization and beyond* (Cambridge Mass. 1988).

Macdonald, James, *A free nation deep in debt. The financial roots of democracy* (Princeton and Oxford 2003).

Macé, François and Mieko Macé, *Le Japon d'Edo* (Paris 2006).

Macfarlane, Alan, *The savage wars of peace. England, Japan and the Malthusian trap* (Oxford 1997).

Macfarlane, Alan, '"Japan" in an English mirror', *Modern Asian Studies* 31, 4 (1997) 763–806.

Macfarlane, Alan, *The making of the modern world. Visions from the West and East* (Houndmills Basingstoke and New York 2002).

Macfarlane, Alan, *Japan through the looking glass* (London 2007).

Maclachlan, Patricia, *The people's post office. The history and politics of the Japanese postal system, 1871–2010* (Cambridge 2012).

Macpherson, William J., *The economic development of Japan, c. 1868–1941* (Cambridge 1995; originally 1987).

Maddison, Angus, *The world economy. A millennial perspective* (Paris 2001).

Maddison, Angus, *Contours of the world economy, 1-2030 AD. Essays in macro-economic history* (Oxford 2007).

Malanima, Paolo, *Premodern European economy. One thousand years (10th–19th centuries)* (Leiden and Boston 2009).

Mann, Michael, 'The autonomous power of the state: its origins, mechanisms and results' in: Hall, *States in history*, 109–136.

Mann, Michael, *The sources of social power. Volume I. A history of power from the beginning to A.D. 1760* (Cambridge 1986).

Mann, Michael, *State, war and capitalism. Studies in political sociology* (Oxford 1988).

Mann, Michael, *The sources of social power. Volume II. The rise of classes and nation states, 1760–1914* (Cambridge 1993).

Mann, Michael, *The sources of social power. Volume III. Global empires and revolution, 1890–1945* (Cambridge 2012).

Marks, Steven G., *The information nexus. Global capitalism from the Renaissance to the present* (Cambridge 2016).

Marshall, Byron K., *Capitalism and nationalism in pre-war Japan. The ideology of the business elite, 1868–1941* (Stanford 1967).

Marsland, Stephen E., *The birth of the Japanese labour movement* (Honolulu 1989).

Marx, Karl, *Capital. A critique of political economy. The Pelican Marx Library.* (Harmondsworth 1976). Three Volumes.

Masaki, Hisashi, 'The formation and evolution of the corporate business systems in Japan', *Japanese Yearbook on Business History* 3 (1986) 26–51.

Masamichi, Inoki, 'Civil bureaucracy' in: Robert E. Ward and Dankwart A. Rustow, eds., *Modernization in Japan and Turkey* (Princeton 1970) 283–300.

Masaru, Iwahashi, 'The institutional framework of the Tokugawa economy' in: Hayami, Saito and Toby, *Emergence of economic society*, 85–104.

Masato, Shizume, 'The Japanese economy during the Interwar Period: Instability in the financial system and the impact of the world depression', *Bank of Japan Review* May 2009.

Mason, Michele M., *Dominant narratives of colonial Hokkaido and imperial Japan* (New York 2012).

Mass, Jeffrey P., and William B. Hauser, eds., *The Bakufu in Japanese history* (Stanford 1985).

Mathias, Regine, 'Japan in the seventeenth century. Labour relations and work ethics', *International Review of Social History* 56, special issue (2011) 217–243.

Matsugata, Marquis Masayoshi, 'Japan's finance' in: Okuma, *Fifty years of new Japan.* Vol. One, 359–389.

Mayet, Paul, *Agricultural insurance, in organic connection with savings-banks, land-credit and the commutation of debts* (London 1893; translated from German).

Mazzucato, Mariana, *The entrepreneurial state. Debunking public versus private sector myths* (London 2013).

McCallion, Stephen William, 'Trial and error. The model filature at Tomioka' in: William D. Wray, ed., *Managing industrial enterprise. Cases from Japan's pre-war experience* (Cambridge and London 1989) 87–120.

McClain, James L., *Japan. A modern history* (New York and London 2002).

McClain, James L., and Osamu Wakita, eds., *Osaka. The merchant's capital of early modern Japan* (Ithaca 1999).

McClain, James L., John Merriman and Kaoru Ugawa, eds., *Edo and Paris. Urban life & the state in the early modern era* (Ithaca and London 1994).

McCormack, Noah Y., *Japan's outcaste abolition. The struggle for national inclusion and the making of the modern state* (Abingdon Oxon and New York 2012).

McKean, Margaret A., 'Defining and dividing property rights in the Japanese commons' http://dlc.dlib.indiana.edu/dlc/bitstream/handle/10535/917/Defining_and_Dividing_Property_Rights_in_the_Japanese_Commons.pdf?sequence=1

McKean, Margaret A., 'Management of traditional common lands (*iriaichi*) in Japan' in: Daniel Bromley, ed., *Making the commons work. Theory, practice, and policy* (San Francisco 1992) 63–98.

McVeigh, Brian J., *Nationalisms of Japan. Managing and mystifying identity* (New York 2004).

Meissner, Christopher M., and John P. Tang, Upstart industrialization and exports, Japan 1880–1910 NBER Working Paper No. 23481 Issued in June 2017 http://sydney.edu.au/arts/economics/downloads/documents/pdf/cliometrics_workshop/Meissner.pdf

Menton, Linda K., Noren W. Lush, Eileen H. Tamura and Chance I. Gosukuma, *The rise of modern Japan* (Honolulu 2003).

Metzler, Mark, 'The cosmopolitanism of national economics: Friedrich List in a Japanese mirror' in: A.G. Hopkins, ed., *Global history, Interactions between the universal and the local* (Basingstoke 2006) 98–130.

Metzler, Mark, *Lever of Empire. The international gold standard and the crisis of liberalism in pre-war Japan* (Oakland 2006).

Metzler, Mark, 'Policy space, polarities, and regimes' in: Gramlich-Oka and Smits, *Economic thought in early modern Japan*, 217–250.

Millward, Robert, *The state and business in the major powers. An economic history, 1815–1939* (Abingdon, Oxon and New York 2014).

Mitchener, Kris, James, Masato Shizume, Marc D. Weidenmier, 'Why did countries adopt the gold standard? Lessons from Japan', NBER Working Paper No. 15195 2009 https://www.nber.org/papers/w15195.

Minami, Ryoshin, *The turning point in economic development. Japan's experience* (Tokyo 1973).

Minami, Ryoshin, *Power revolution in the industrialization of Japan, 1885–1940* (Tokyo 1987).

Minami, Ryoshin, *The economic development of Japan. A quantitative study* (second edition; New York 1994).

Mitani, Hiroshi, *Escape from impasse. The decision to open Japan* (Tokyo 2006).

Mitch, David, *The rise of popular literacy in Victorian England. The influence of private choice and public policy* (Pennsylvania 1992).

Mitchell, B.R., *British historical statistics* (Cambridge 1988).

Mitchell, Richard H., *Censorship in imperial Japan* (Princeton 1983).

Mitchell, Richard H., *Janus-faced justice. Political criminals in imperial Japan* (Honolulu 1992).

Miwa, Yoshiro, *Japan's economic planning and mobilization in wartime, 1930–1940s. The competence of the state* (Cambridge 2015).

Miwa, Yoshiro and J. Mark Ramseyer, 'Japanese industrial finance at the close of the nineteenth century. Trade credit and financial intermediation', *Explorations in Economic History* 43, 1 (2006) 94–118.

Miyamoto, Matao, 'Quantitative aspects of Tokugawa economy' in: Hayami, Saito and Toby, *Emergence of economic society*, 36–84.

Miyamoto, Matao, 'Prices and macroeconomic dynamics' in: Hayami, Saito and Toby, *Emergence of economic society*, 119–158.

Miyamoto, Matao and Yoshiaki Shikano, 'The emergence of the Tokugawa monetary system in East Asian international perspective' in: Flynn, Giráldez and Von Glahn, *Global connections and monetary history*, 169–186.

Miyamoto, Mataji, Yotaro Sakudo and Yasukichi Yasuba, 'Economic development in pre-industrial Japan', *The Journal of Economic History* 25, 4 (1965) 541–564.

Miyoshi, Masao and Harry Harootunian, eds., *Japan in the world* (Durham NC and London 1993).

Mizuno, Noritho, 'Early Meiji policies towards the Ryukyus and the Taiwanese aboriginal territories', *Modern Asian Studies* 43, 23 (2009) 683–739.

Mokyr, Joel, *The enlightened economy. An economic history of Britain, 1700–1850* (New Haven and London 2009).

Moore, Barrington Jr., *Social origins of dictatorship and democracy. Lord and peasant in the making of the modern world* (Boston 1966).

Moore, Stephen, *Constructing East Asia. Technology, ideology, and empire in Japan's wartime era, 1931–1945* (Stanford 2015).

Moriguchi, Chiaki and Emmanuel Saez, 'The evolution of income concentration in Japan, 1885–2002: Evidence from income tax statistics'. http://eml.berkeley.edu//~saez/moriguchi-saez05japan.pdf

Morikawa, Hidemasa, *Zaibatsu. The rise and fall of family enterprise groups in Japan* (Tokyo 1992).

Morimoto, Kokichi, *The standard of living in Japan* (Baltimore 1918).

Morishima, Michio, *Why has Japan 'succeeded'? Western technology and the Japanese ethos* (Cambridge 1982).

Morris, Ian, *Why the West rules – for now. The patterns of history and what they reveal about the future* (London 2010).

Morris-Suzuki, Tessa, *A history of Japanese economic thought* (London and Oxford 1989).

Morris-Suzuki, Tessa, 'Sericulture and the origins of Japanese industrialization', *Technology and Culture* 33, 1 (1992) 101–121.

Morris-Suzuki, Tessa, *The technological transformation of Japan. From the seventeenth to the twenty-first century* (Cambridge 1994).

Mosk, Carl, *Competition and cooperation in Japanese labour markets* (Basingstoke and London 1995).

Mosk, Carl, *Making health work. Human growth in modern Japan* (Berkeley, Los Angeles and London 1996).

Mosk, Carl, *Japanese industrial history. Technology, urbanization and economic growth* (New York and London 2001).

Mosk, Carl, *Japanese economic development. Markets, norms, structures* (London and New York 2008).

Mosk, Carl, *Traps embraced or escaped. Elites in the economic development of modern Japan and China* (Singapore 2011).

Mosk, Carl, *Nationalism and economic development in modern Eurasia* (Abingdon, Oxon and New York 2013).

Mosse, George, *The nationalization of the masses: Political symbolism and mass movements in Germany, from the Napoleonic Wars through the Third Reich* (New York 1975).

Moulder, Frances V., *Japan, China, and the modern world economy. Toward a reinterpretation of East Asian development (ca. 1600 to ca. 1918)* (Cambridge 1977).

Moulton, Harold G., with collaboration of Junichi Ko, *Japan. An economic and financial appraisal* (Washington 1931).

Muehlhoff, Katharina, 'The economic costs of sleaze or how replacing samurai with bureaucrats boosted regional growth in Meiji Japan', *Cliometrica* 8, 2 (2014) 201–239.

Myers, Raymond H. and Mark R. Peattie, eds., *The Japanese colonial empire, 1895–1945* (Princeton 1984).

Myers, Ramon H. and Yamada Saburo, 'Agricultural development in the Empire' in: Myers and Peattie, *Japanese colonial empire*, 420–454.

Nafziger, E. Wayne, *Learning from the Japanese. Japan's pre-war development and the Third World* (London and New York 1995).

Nagata, Mary L., *Labor contracts and labor relations in early modern Central Japan* (London and New York 2005).

Najita, Tetsuo, 'Political economism in the thought of Dazai Shundai (1680–1747)', *Journal of Asian Studies* 31, 4 (1972) 821–839.

Najita, Tetsuo, *Visions of virtue in Tokugawa Japan. The Kaitokudo Merchant Academy of Osaka* (Chicago 1987).

Najita, Tetsuo, *Ordinary economies in Japan. A historical perspective, 1750–1950* (Berkeley, Los Angeles, London 2009).

Najita, Tetsuo and J. Victor Koschmann, eds., *Conflict in modern Japanese history. The neglected tradition* (Princeton 1982).

Nakabayashi, Masaki, 'The rise of a Japanese fiscal state' in: Yun-Casalilla, O'Brien, and Comín-Comín, *Rise of fiscal states*, 378–409.

Nakai, Nabuhiko and James L. McClain, 'Commercial change and urban growth in early modern Japan' in: *Cambridge History of Japan. Vol. 4*, 519–595.

Nakamura, James I., 'Growth of Japanese agriculture, 1875–1920' in: Lockwood, *State and economic enterprise in Japan*, 249–324.

Nakamura, James I., *Agricultural production and the economic development of Japan 1873–1922* (Princeton 1966).

Nakamura, James I., 'Human capital accumulation in premodern rural Japan', *Journal of Economic History* 41, 2 (1981) 263–281.

Nakamura, Takafusa, *Economic growth in pre-war Japan* (New Haven 1983).

Nakamura, Takafusa, Depression, recovery and war, 1920–1945' in: *Cambridge History of Japan. Vol. 6*, 451–493.

Nakamura, Takafusa and Konosuke Odaka, 'The inter-war period, 1914–1937. An overview' in: iidem, *Economic History of Japan, 1914–1955*, 1–54.

Nakamura, Takafusa and Konosuke Odaka, eds., *Economic History of Japan, 1914–1955* (Oxford 2003). Volume 3 of *The Economic History of Japan 1600–1990*.

Nakane, Chie and Shinzaburo Oishi, eds., *Tokugawa Japan. The social and economic antecedents of modern Japan* (Tokyo 1990).

Nakaoka, Tetsuro, 'The role of domestic technical innovation in foreign technology transfer', *Osaka City University Economic Review* 18 (1982) 45–62.

Nakaoka, Tetsuro, 'On technological leaps of Japan as a developing country', *Osaka City University Economic Review* 22 (1987) 1–25.

Nakaoka, Tetsuro, 'The transfer of cotton manufacturing technology from Britain to Japan' in: David Jeremey ed., *International technology transfer. Europe, Japan and the USA, 1700-1914* (Aldershot 1991) 181-198.

Nanto, Dick K. and Shinji Takagi, 'Korekiyo Takahashi and Japan's recovery from the Great Depression', *American Economic Review* 75, 2 (1985) 369-374.

Napier, Ron, 'The transformation of the Japanese labor market, 1894-1937' in: Najita and Koschmann, *Conflict in modern Japanese history*, 342-365.

Neal, Larry and Jeffrey G. Williamson, eds., *The Cambridge History of Capitalism* (Cambridge 2014). Two Volumes.

Nicholas, Tom, 'The origins of Japanese technological modernization', *Explorations in Economic History* 48 (2011) 272-291.

Nish, Ian H., ed., *The Iwakura mission in America and Europe. A new assessment* (Richmond 1998).

Nishikawa, Shunsaku and Masatoshi Amano, 'Domains and their economic policies' in: Hayami, Saito and Toby, *Emergence of economic society*, 246-267.

Nobutaka, Ike, 'War and modernization' in: Robert E. Ward, ed., *Political development in modern Japan* (Princeton 1968) 189-211.

Nolte, Sharon H., and Sally A. Hastings, 'The Meiji state's policy towards women, 1890-1910' in: Bernstein, *Recreating Japanese women*, 151-174.

Norman, E.H., *Soldier and peasant in Japan* (New York 1943).

Norman, E.H., *Origins of the modern Japanese state. Political and economic problems of the Meiji Period* (New York 1946).

Notehelfer, F.G., 'Meiji in the rear-view mirror. Top-down versus bottom-up history', *Monumenta Nipponica* 45, 2 (1990) 207-228.

Odaka, Konosuke, 'The dual structure of the Japanese economy' in: Nakamura and Odaka, *Economic History of Japan 1914-1955*, 111-136.

Oguchi, Yujiro, 'The finances of the Tokugawa Shogunate' in: Hayami, Saito and Toby, *Emergence of economic society*, 192-212.

Oguma, Eiji, *A genealogy of Japanese self-images* (Transpacific Press 2002).

Oguma, Eiji, *The boundaries of "the Japanese". Okinawa, 1818-1972. Inclusion and exclusion.* (Transpacific Press 2014).

Oguma, Eiji, *The boundaries of "the Japanese". Korea, Taiwan and the Ainu, 1868-1945* (Transpacific Press 2017).

Ogura, Takekazu, *Can Japanese agriculture survive?* (Tokyo 1979).

Oguro, Kazumasa, 'Seventy years after the defeat in World War II, can Japan avoid another defeat by showing a path to fiscal reconstruction?', *Priorities for the Japanese Economy in 2015* (January 2015) A publication of Research Institute of Economy, Trade and Industry.

Ohkawa, Kazushi and Henry Rosovsky, 'A century of Japanese economic growth' in: Lockwood, *State and economic enterprise*, 47-92.

Ohkawa, Kazushi and Henry Rosovsky, *Japanese economic growth. Trend acceleration in the twentieth century* (Stanford 1973).

Ohkawa, Kazushi and Henry Rosovsky, 'Capital formation in Japan' in: Yamamura, *Economic emergence of modern Japan*, 203-238.

Ohkawa, Kazushi, Bruce F. Johnston and Hiromitsu Kaneda, eds., *Agriculture and economic growth. Japan's experience* (Princeton and Tokyo 1970).

Ohkawa, Kazushi, Miyohei Shinohara and Larry Meissner, eds., *Patterns of Japanese economic development. A quantitative appraisal* (New Haven and London 1979).

Ohno, Kenichi, *The economic development of Japan. The path travelled by Japan as a developing country* (Tokyo 2006; originally 2005).

Ohno, Kenichi, *The history of Japanese economic development. Origins of private dynamism and policy competence* (Abingdon Oxon 2017).

Oizumi, Yoichi and Felix-Fernando Muñoz, 'Kaname Akamatsu and the Japanese industrial development model', *Revista de Económia Mundial*, January 2014.

Okuma, S. ed., *Fifty years of New Japan* (London 1909). Two Volumes.

Okura, Takehiko and Hiroshi Shimbo, 'The Tokugawa monetary policy in the eighteenth and nineteenth centuries', *Explorations in Economic History* 15, 1 (1978) 84–100.

Omori, Kazuhiro, 'How local trade associations and manufacturer's associations worked in pre-war Japan' in: Tanimoto, *Role of tradition*, 157–180.

Ono, Akira and Tsunehiko Watanabe, 'Changes in income inequality in the Japanese economy' in: Patrick, *Japanese industrialization*, 363–390.

Ono, Giichi and Hyoye Ouchi, *War and armament expenditures of Japan* (New York 1922).

Ooms, Herman, *Tokugawa ideology* (Princeton 1985).

Ooms, Herman, *Tokugawa village practice. Class, status, power, law* (Berkeley, Los Angeles 1996).

Orchard, John E., with collaboration of Dorothy J. Orchard, *Japan's economic position. The progress of industrialization* (New York 1930).

Oshima, Harry T., 'Meiji fiscal policy and economic progress' in: Lockwood, *State and economic enterprise*, 353–390.

Overton, Mark, *Agricultural Revolution in England. The transformation of the agrarian economy 1500–1850* (Cambridge 1996).

Paik, Christopher, Abbey Steele, Seiki Tanaka, 'Rebellion and taxation: Evidence from early modern Japan', http://privatewww.essex.ac.uk/~ksg/esrcjsps/Tanaka.pdf

Paine, S.C.M., *The Sino-Japanese War of 1894–1895. Perceptions, power, and primacy* (Cambridge 2003).

Paine, S.C.M., *The Japanese Empire. Grand strategy from the Meiji Restoration to the Pacific War* (Cambridge 2017).

Pamuk, Sevket, 'Institutional change and the longevity of the Ottoman empire, 1500–1800', *Journal of Interdisciplinary History* 35 (2004) 225–247

Pamuk, Sevket, 'The evolution of fiscal institutions in the Ottoman Empire' in: Yun-Casalilla, O'Brien, and Comín-Comín, *Rise of fiscal states*, 304–325.

Parker, Geoffrey, *Global crisis. War, climate change and catastrophe in the seventeenth century* (New Haven and London 2013).

Passin, Herbert, *Society and education in Japan* (New York 1965)

Patrick, Hugh, 'Japan, 1868–1914' in: Rondo Cameron, a.o. eds., *Banking in the early stages of industrialization* (London 1967) 239–289.

Patrick, Hugh, 'An introductory overview' in: idem, *Japanese industrialization and its social consequences*, 1–19.

Patrick, Hugh, ed., with the assistance of Larry Meissner, *Japanese industrialization and its social consequences* (Berkeley, Los Angeles, London 1976).

Pauer, Erich, 'Japanischer Geist – westliche Technik. Zur Rezeption westlicher Technologie in Japan', *Saeculum* 38, 1 (1987) 19–51.

Pauer, Erich, 'Traditional technology and its impact on Japan's industry during the early period of the Industrial Revolution', *The Economic Studies Quarterly* 38, 4 (1987) 354–371.

Pauer, Erich, 'The years economic historians lost. Japan, 1850–1890', *Japan Forum* 3, 1 (1991) 1–9.

Pearse, Arno J., *The cotton industry of Japan and China* (Manchester 1929; originally 1926).

Peattie, Mark R., *Ishiwara Kanji and Japan's confrontation with the West* (Princeton 1975).

Peattie, Mark R., 'The Japanese colonial empire, 1895–1945' in: *Cambridge History of Japan. Vol. 6*, 217–270.

Penrose, E.F., *Population theories and their application, with special reference to Japan* (Stanford 1934).

Penrose, E.F., 'Japan, 1920–1936' in: Schumpeter, *Industrialization of Japan and Manchukuo*, 80–270.

Perez, Louis G., 'Revision of the unequal treaties and abolition of extraterritoriality' in: Helen Hardacre and Adam Kern, eds., *New directions in the study of Meiji Japan* (Leiden 1997) 320–335.

Perez, Louis G., *Daily life in early modern Japan* (Westport 2002).

Perkins, Dwight H., 'Government as an obstacle to industrialization: the case of nineteenth-century China', *The Journal of Economic History* 27 (1967) 478–492.

Phipps, Catherine L. *Empires on the waterfront: Japan's ports and power, 1858–1899* (Cambridge Mass. 2015).

Piketty, Thomas, *Capital in the twenty-first century* (Cambridge Mass. and London 2014; originally Paris 2013).

Pilat, Dirk, *The economics of rapid growth. The experience of Japan and Korea* (Aldershot 1994).

Platt, Brian W., *School, community and state integration in nineteenth-century Japan* (Urbana Champaign Illinois 1998).

Platt, Brian W., *Burning and building. Schooling and state formation in Japan, 1750–1890* (Cambridge Mass. 2004).

Pleijt, Alexandra M. de & Jacob L. Weisdorf, 'Human capital formation from occupations: the 'deskilling hypothesis' revisited', *Cliometrica. Journal of Historical Economics and Econometric History* 11,1 (2017) 1–30.

Pomeranz, Kenneth, *The Great Divergence. China, Europe, and the making of the modern world economy* (Princeton 2000).

Popper, Karl, R., *Conjectures and refutations. The growth of scientific knowledge* (London and New York 1962).

Powell, Jim, 'How entrepreneurs created the great boom that made modern Japan', www.cato.org/publications/commentary/how-entrepreneurs-created-great-boom-made-modern-japan also published in *Forbes*, March 2012.

Powelson, John P., *Centuries of economic endeavor. Parallel paths in Japan and Europe and their contrast with the Third World* (Ann Arbor 1994).

Pratt, Edward, *Japan's proto-industrial elite. The economic foundations of the Gono* (Cambridge 1999).

Pseudoerasmus, 'Labour repression and the Indo-Japanese divergence. A blog about global economic history and economic development', posted 02-10-2017, https://pseudoerasmus.com/2017/10/02/ijd/

Pyle, Kenneth B., *The new generation in Meiji Japan. Problems of cultural identity, 1885–1895* (Stanford 1969).

Pyle, Kenneth B., 'The technology of Japanese nationalism. The local improvement movement, 1900–1918', *The Journal of Asian Studies* 33, 1 (1973/1974) 51–65.

Pyle, Kenneth B., 'Advantages of followership. German economics and Japanese bureaucrats, 1890–1925', *Journal of Japanese Studies* 1, 1 (1974) 127–164.

Pyle, Kenneth B., 'Meiji conservatism' in: *Cambridge History of Japan. Vol. 5*, 674–720.

Pyle, Kenneth B., *The making of modern Japan* (second edition; Lexington Mass. and Toronto 1996).

Ramming, Martin, 'Die wirtschaftliche Lage der Samurai am Ende der Tokugawa Periode', *Mitteilungen der Deutschen Gesellschaft für Natur – und Völkerkunde Ostasiens, Band XXII, Teil A* (Tokyo 1928) 1–47.

Ramseyer, Mark, 'Thrift and diligence. House codes of Tokugawa merchant families', *Monumenta Nipponica* 34, 2 (1979) 221–226.

Ramseyer, Mark, and Frances M. Rosenbluth, *The politics of oligarchy. Institutional choice in Imperial Japan* (Cambridge 1966).

Ranis, Gustav, 'The financing of Japanese economic development', *Economic History Review* 11, 3 (1959) 440–454.

Ransome, Stafford, *Japan in transition. A comparative study of the progress, policy, and methods of the Japanese since their war with China* (New York and London 1899).

Ravina, Mark, 'State-building and political economy in early modern Japan', *The Journal of Asian Studies* 54, 4 (1995) 997–1022.

Ravina, Mark, *Land and lordship in early modern Japan* (Stanford 1999).

Ravina, Mark, *To stand with the nations of the world. Japan's Meiji Restoration in world history* (Oxford 2017).

Rein, J.J., *The industries of Japan: Together with an account of its agriculture, forestry, arts and commerce. From travels and researches undertaken at the costs of the Prussian government* (London 1899).

Reinert, Erik S., *How rich countries got rich . . . and why poor countries stay poor* (New York 2007).

Richards, John F., *The unending frontier. An environmental history of the early modern world* (Berkeley, Los Angeles, London 2003).

Roberts, John G., *Mitsui. Three centuries of Japanese business* (New York 1973).

Roberts, Luke S., *Mercantilism in a Japanese domain. The merchant origins of economic nationalism in eighteenth-century Tosa* (Cambridge 1998).

Roser, Max, *Our world in data*, https://ourworldindata.org.

Rosovsky, Henry, *Capital formation in Japan, 1868–1940* (New York 1961).

Rosovsky, Henry, 'Japan's transition to modern economic growth 1868–1885' in: Henry Rosovsky, ed., *Industrialization in two systems. Essays in honour of Alexander Gerschenkron* (New York 1966) 91–139.

Rosovsky, Henry, 'Rumbles in the rice fields', *The Journal of Asian Studies* 27, 2 (1969) 347–360.

Rostow, Walt W., *The stages of economic growth. A non-communist manifesto* (London 1960).

Roy, Tirthankar, *Economic history of India, 1857–1947* (Delhi 2012).

Rozman, Gilbert, *Urban networks in Ch'ing China and Tokugawa Japan* (Princeton 1973).

Rozman, Gilbert, 'Social change' in: *Cambridge History of Japan. Vol. 5*, 499–568.

Rozman, Gilbert, 'East Asian urbanization in the nineteenth century. Comparisons with Europe' in: Ad van der Woude, Jan de Vries and Akira Hayami, eds., *Urbanization in history. A process of dynamic interactions* (Oxford 1996) 61–73.

Rubinger, Richard, 'From "Dark Corners" into "The Light". Literacy studies in modern Japan', *History of Education Quarterly* (1990) 601–612.

Rubinger, Richard, *Popular literacy in early modern Japan* (Honolulu 2007).

Sagers, John, 'The origins of Japan's economic philosophy', *Japan Policy Research Institute Critique* VII, 9 October (2000).

Sagers, John, *Origins of Japanese wealth and power. Reconciling Confucianism and capitalism, 1830–1885* (London and New York 2006).

Sagers, John, *Confucian capitalism. Shibusawa Eiichi. Business ethics and economic development in Japan* (London 2018).

Saito, Masaru, 'Introduction of foreign technology in the industrialization process. Japanese experience since the Meiji Restoration (1868)', *The Developing Economies* 13, 2 (1975) 168–186.

Saito, Osamu, 'The labor market in Tokugawa Japan. Wage differentials and the real wage level, 1727–1830', *Explorations in Economic History* 15, 1 (1978) 84–100.

Saito, Osamu, 'Population and the peasant family economy in proto-industrial Japan', *Journal of Family History* 8, 1 (1983) 30–54.

Saito, Osamu, 'The rural economy. Commercial agriculture, by-employment, and wage work' in: Jansen and Rozman, *Japan in transition*, 400–420.

Saito, Osamu, 'Scenes of Japan's economic development and the 'longue durée'', *Bonner Zeitschrift für Japanologie* 8 (1986) 15–27.

Saito, Osamu, 'Children's work, industrialism and the family economy in Japan, 1872–1926' in: Hugh Cunningham and Pier Paolo Viazzo, eds., *Child labour in historical perspective, 1800–1985. Case studies from Europe, Japan and Colombia* (Florence 1996) 73–90.

Saito, Osamu, 'The context of everyday things', *Monumenta Nipponica* 53, 2 (1998) 257–263. Review of Hanley, *Everyday things in premodern Japan*.

Saito, Osamu, 'The frequency of famines as demographic correctives in the Japanese past' in: Tim Dyson and Cormac Ó Gráda, eds., *Famine demography. Perspectives from the past and present* (Oxford 2002) 218–239.

Saito, Osamu, 'Wages, inequality and pre-industrial growth in Japan, 1727–1894' in: Robert C. Allen, Tommy Bengtsson and Martin Dribe, *Living standards in the past. New perspectives on well-being in Asia and Europe* (Oxford 2005) 77–97.

Saito, Osamu, 'Premodern economic growth revisited. Japan and the West', Working Papers of the Global Economic History Network (GEHN), 16/05, 2005. Department of Economic History, London School of Economics and Political Science.

Saito, Osamu, 'The economic history of the Restoration Period, 1853–1885' http://gcoe.ier. hit-u.ac.jp/english/research/discussion/2008/pdf/gd10-163.pdf

Saito, Osamu, 'Early Meiji Japan. A developmental state?' http://gcoe.ier.hit-u.ac.jp/ research/discussion/2008/pdf/gd10-163.pdf

Saito, Osamu, 'Land, labour and market forces in Tokugawa Japan', *Continuity and Change* 24, 1 (2009) 169–196.

Saito, Osamu, 'Forest history and the Great Divergence. China, Japan and the West compared', *Journal of Global History* 4, 3 (2009) 379–404.

Saito, Osamu, 'An industrious revolution in an East Asian market economy? Tokugawa Japan and the implications for the Great Divergence', *Australian Economic History Review* 50, 3 (2010) 240–261.

Saito, Osamu, 'Proto-industrialization and labour-intensive industrialization. Reflections on Smithian growth and the role of skill intensity' in: Austin and Sugihara, *Labour-intensive industrialization*, 85–106.

Saito, Osamu, 'Was modern Japan a developmental state?' in: Keijiro Otsuka and Takashi Shiraishi, eds., *State building and development* (Oxford 2014) 23–45.

Saito, Osamu, 'Growth and inequality in the Great and Little Divergence debate: a Japanese perspective', *Economic History Review* 68, 2 (2015) 399–419.

Saito, Osamu, 'Japan' in: Baten, *History of the global economy*, 167–184.

Saito, Osamu and Tokihiko Settsu, 'Money, credit and Smithian growth in Tokugawa Japan', Hitotsubashi University Repository Discussion Paper Series 139, 2006-02 https://hermes-ir.lib.hit-u.ac.jp/rs/bitstream/10086/13705/1/D05-139.pdf

Saito, Osamu and Masayuki Tanimoto, 'The transformation of traditional industries' in: Hayami, Saito and Toby, *Emergence of economic society*, 268–300.

Sakai, Kazuho, 'Outsourcing the lord's finance. An origin of local public finance in early modern Japan' in: Tanimoto and Wong, *Public goods provision*, 57–72.

Sakai, Robert K., 'The Satsuma-Ryukyu trade and the Tokugawa seclusion policy', *The Journal of Asian Studies* 23, 3 (1964) 391–403.

Sakata, Minako, 'Japan in the eighteenth and nineteenth centuries' in: Clare Anderson, ed., *A global history of convicts and penal colonies* (London 2018) 307–336.

Sakudo, Yotaro, 'Domain paper currencies and money merchants in the Tokugawa period', *Acta Asiatica* 39 (1980) 61–77.

Samson, George, *A history of Japan, 1615–1867* (Stanford 1963).

Samuels, Richard J., *Rich nation, strong army. National security and technological transformation of Japan* (Ithaca 1994).

Sanderson, Stephen K., *Social transformations. A general theory of historical development* (Oxford and Cambridge Mass. 1995).

Schell, Orville and John Delury, *Wealth and power. China's long march to the twenty-first century* (New York 2013).

Schencking, J. Charles, *Making waves: Politics, propaganda, and the emergence of the Imperial Japanese Navy, 1868–1922* (Stanford 2005).

Schenkein, Josh, *Japan, the great power. Industrialization through the lens of Zaibatsu firm characteristics*, kindle ebook 2014, originally 2012.

Scherer, Anke, *Japanese emigration to Manchuria. Local activists and the making of the village-division campaign* (Bochum 2006).

Schiltz, Michael, 'Money on the road to empire. Japan's adoption of gold monometallism, 1873–1897', *Journal of Economic History* 65, 3 (2012) 1147–1169.

Schiltz, Michael, *The money doctors from Japan. Finance, imperialism, and the building of the yen bloc, 1895–1937* (Cambridge Mass. and London 2012).

Schroeppel, Christian and Mariko Nakajima, 'The changing interpretation of the flying geese model of economic development', *German Institute for Japanese Studies / Japanstudien*, 14, 1 (2002) 203–236.

Schumpeter, E.B., 'Government policy and recovery' in: Schumpeter, *Industrialization of Japan and Manchukuo*, 3–40.

Schumpeter, E.B., 'The population of the Japanese Empire' in: Schumpeter, *Industrialization of Japan and Manchukuo*, 41–79.

Schumpeter, E.B., 'Japan, Korea and Manchukuo, 1936–1940' in: Schumpeter, *Industrialization of Japan and Manchukuo*, 271–476.

Schumpeter, E.B., 'Industrial development and government policy, 1936–1940' in: Schumpeter, *Industrialization of Japan and Manchukuo*, 789–864.

Schumpeter, E.B., ed., with G.C. Allen, M.S. Gordon and E.F. Penrose, *The industrialization of Japan and Manchukuo, 1930–1940. Population, raw materials and industry* (New York 1940).

Schwartz, Herman M., *States versus markets. The emergence of a global economy* (second edition; Houndmills Basingstoke 2000).

Scott, James C., *Seeing like a state. How certain schemes to improve the human condition have failed* (New Haven and London 1998).

Searle, G.R., *The quest for national efficiency. A study in British politics and political thought, 1899–1914* (Berkeley 1971).

Seaton, Philip, 'Japanese empire in Hokkaido', http://asianhistory.oxfordre.com/view/10.1093/acrefore/9780190277727.001.0001/acrefore-9780190277727-e-76

Seaman, Louis Livingston, *The real triumph of Japan. The conquest of the silent foe* (New York 1908).

Senghaas, Dieter, 'Friedrich List and the basic problems of modern development', *Review of the Fernand Braudel Center* 14, 3 (1991) 451–467.

Sheldon, Charles D., *The rise of the merchant class in Tokugawa Japan, 1600–1800. An introductory survey* (New York 1958).

Sheridan, Kyoko, *Governing the Japanese economy* (Cambridge 1993).

Shibagaki, Kazuo, 'The early history of zaibatsu', *The Developing Economies. Journal of the Institute of Developing Economies* 4, 4 (1996) 535–566.

Shimada, Ryuto, *The intra-Asian trade in Japanese copper by the Dutch East India Company during the eighteenth century* (Leiden and Boston 2006).

Shimbo, Hiroshi and Akira Hasegawa, 'The dynamics of market economy and production' in: Hayami, Saitô and Toby, *Emergence of economic society*, 159–191.

Shimbo, Hiroshi and Osamu Saito, 'The economy on the eve of industrialization' in: Hayami, Saito and Toby, *Emergence of economic society*, 337–368.

Shin, Jang-Sup, *The economics of the latecomers: Catching up, technology transfer and institutions in Germany, Japan and South Korea* (London and New York 1996).

Shinohara, Miyohei, 'Formation and transition of the dual economy in Japan', *Hitotsubashi Journal of Economics* 8, 2 (1968) 1–38. http://hermes-ir.lib.hit-u.ac.jp/rs/bitstream/10086/8055/1/HJeco0080200010.pdf

Shively, Donald H., 'Sumptuary regulation and status in early Tokugawa Japan', *Harvard Journal of Asiatic Studies* 25 (1964–1965) 23–64.

Shively, Donald H., ed., *Tradition and modernization in Japanese culture* (Princeton 1971).

Shizume, Masato and Masayoshi Tsurumi, 'Modernizing the financial system in Japan during the 19th century: National Banks in Japan in the Context of Free Banking', WINPEC Working Paper Series No. E1607 September 2016.

Shosuke, Sato, 'Hokkaido and its progress in fifty years' in Okuma, *Fifty years of New Japan*, Vol. 2, 513–530.

Silberman, Bernhard S., *Cages of reason. The rise of the rational state in France, Japan, the United States and Great Britain* (Chicago 1993).

Sippel, Patricia, 'Abandoned fields: negotiating taxes in the Bakufu domain', *Monumenta Nipponica* 53, 2 (1998) 197–223.

Skya, Walter, *Japan's holy war. The ideology of radical Shinto ultranationalism* (Durham 2009).

Smethurst, Richard J., 'The creation of the Imperial Military Reserve Association in Japan', *The Journal of Asian Studies* 3, 4 (1971) 815–828.

Smethurst, Richard J., *A social basis for pre-war Japanese militarism: The army and the rural community* (Berkeley, Los Angeles and London 1974).

Smethurst, Richard J., *Agricultural development and tenancy disputes in Japan, 1870–1940* (Princeton 1986).

Smethurst, Richard J., *From foot soldier to finance minister: Takahashi Korekiyo, Japan's Keynes* (Cambridge 2007).

Smith, Adam, *An inquiry into the nature and causes of the wealth of nations* (London 1776). I use the edition by R.H. Campbell and A.S. Skinner that was published by Liberty Fund in Indianapolis in 1981.

Smith, K., *A time of crisis. Japan, the Great Depression and rural revitalization* (Cambridge Mass. 2001).

Smith, Thomas C., 'The introduction of Western industry during the last years of the Tokugawa period', *Harvard Journal of Asiatic Studies* 11, 1 and 2 (1948) 130–152.

Smith, Thomas C., *Political change and industrial development in Japan. Government enterprise, 1868–1880* (Stanford 1955).

Smith, Thomas C., 'The land tax in the Tokugawa period', *The Journal of Asian Studies* 18, 1 (1958) 3–19.

Smith, Thomas C., *The agrarian origins of modern Japan* (Stanford 1959).

Smith, Thomas C., '"Merit" as ideology in the Tokugawa period' in R.P. Dore, ed., *Aspects of social change in modern Japan* (Princeton 1967) 71–90.

Smith, Thomas C., 'Pre-modern growth: Japan and the West', *Past and Present* 60 (1973) 127–160.

Smith, Thomas C., 'The right to benevolence. Dignity and Japanese workers, 1890–1920', *Comparative Studies in Society and History* 26, 4 (1984) 587–613.

Smith, Thomas C., 'Peasant time and factory time in Japan', *Past and Present* 111 (1986) 165–197.

Smith, Thomas C., *Native sources of Japanese industrialization, 1750–1920* (Berkeley 1988).

Smitka, Michael, ed., *The Japanese economy in the Tokugawa era, 1600–1868* (New York and London 1998). Volume 6 of *Japanese economic history 1600–1960*.

Smits, Gregory J., *Visions of Ryukyu. Identity and ideology in early modern thought and politics* (Honolulu 1999).

Sng, Tuan-Hwee and Chiaki Moriguchi, 'Asia's Little Divergence. State capacity in China and Japan before 1850', *Journal of Economic Growth* 19, 4 (2014) 439–470. Also available at https://link.springer.com/article/10.1007/s10887-014-9108-6. I refer to the internet version.

Sohn, Yul, *Japanese industrial governance. Protectionism and the licensing state* (Abingdon Oxon 2005).

Sonoda, Hidehiro, 'The decline of the Japanese warrior class, 1840–1880', *Japan Review* 1 (1990) 73–111.

Souyri, Pierre-François, *Moderne sans être occidental. Aux origines du Japon d'aujourd'hui* (Paris 2016).

Spaulding, Robert M., *Imperial Japan's higher civil service examinations* (Princeton 1967).

Spencer, Daniel L., 'Japan's pre-Perry preparation for economic growth', *American Journal of Economics and Sociology* 17, 2 (1958) 195–216.

Spoerer, Mark, 'The evolution of public finances in nineteenth-century Germany' in: Cardoso and Lains, *Paying for the liberal state*, 103–131.

Spoerer, Mark, 'Öffentliche Finanzen' in: Thomas Ralhf, ed., *Deutschland in Daten. Zeitreihen der historischen Statistik* (Bonn 2015) 102–112.

Stead, Alfred, *Great Japan. A study in national efficiency* (London 1906).

Stein, Guenther, *Made in Japan* (London 1935).

Stephan, John J., *Ezo under the Tokugawa Bakufu, 1799–1821. An aspect of Japan's frontier history* (London 1969).

Streeck, Wolfgang, and Kozo Yamamura, eds., *The origins of nonliberal capitalism. Germany and Japan in comparison* (Ithaca and London 2001).

Studwell, Joe, *How Asia works. Success and failure in the world's most dynamic region* (London 2013).

Sugihara, Kaoru, 'Japan's industrial recovery, 1931–1936' in: Ian Brown, ed., *The economies of Africa and Asia in the interwar depression* (London 1989) 152–169.

Sugihara, Kaoru, 'The economic motivations behind Japanese aggression in the late 1930s: Perspectives of Freda Utley and Nawa Toichi', *Journal of Contemporary History* 32, 2 (1997) 259–280.

Sugihara, Kaoru, 'The state and the industrious revolution in Tokugawa Japan', www.lse.ac.uk/economic History/Research/GEHN/GEHNPDF/WorkingPaper02KS.pdf, February 2004.

Sugiyama, Chuhei, *Origins of economic thought in modern Japan* (Abingdon Oxon 2013; originally 1994).

Sugiyama, Chuhei and Hiroshi Mizuta, *Enlightenment and beyond. Political economy comes to Japan* (Tokyo 1988).

Sugiyama, Shinya, *Japan's industrialization in the world economy, 1859–1899. Export trade and overseas competition* (London 2013).

Sukehiro, Hirakawa, 'Japan's turn to the West' in: *Cambridge History of Japan. Vol. 5*, 432–498.

Sussman, Nathan and Yishay Yafeh, 'Institutions, reforms, and country risk. Lessons from Japanese government debt in the Meiji Era', *The Journal of Economic History*, 60, 2 (2000) 442–467.

Swale, Alistair, *The Meiji Restoration: Monarchism, mass communication and conservative revolution* (Basingstoke 2009).

Taira, Koji, 'Factory legislation and management modernization during Japan's industrialization, 1886–1916', *Business History Review* 44, 1 (1970) 84–109.

Taira, Koji, *Economic development and the labor market in Japan* (New York 1970).

Taira, Koji, 'Education and literacy in Meiji Japan', *Explorations in Economic History* 8, 4 (1971) 371–394.

Taira, Koji, 'Factory labour and the industrial revolution in Japan' in: Yamamura, *Economic emergence of modern Japan*, 239–292.

Taira, Koji, 'Economic development, labour markets, and industrial relation in Japan, 1905–1955' in: *Cambridge History of Japan*, Vol. 6, 606–653.

Takekoshi, Yosaburo, *Economic aspects of the civilization of Japan* (London 1930).

Takekoshi, Yosaburo, *Self-portrayal of Japan* (Tokyo 1939).

Takeuchi, Johzen, *The role of labour-intensive sectors in Japanese industrialization* (Tokyo 1991).

Takii, Kazuhiro, *The Meiji Constitution. The Japanese experience of the West and the shaping of the modern state* (Tokyo 2007).

Tamaki, Norio, *Japanese banking. A history, 1859–1959* (Cambridge 1995).

Tamaki, Toshiaki, 'Comparative perspectives on the 'fiscal-military state' in Europe and Japan' in: Rafael Torres Sánchez, ed., *War, state and development. Fiscal-military states in the eighteenth century* (Pamplona 2007) 409–435.

Tamaki, Toshiaki, 'A fiscal-military state without wars. The relations between the military regime and economic development in Tokugawa Japan' in: Stephen Conway and Rafael Torres Sánchez, eds., *The spending of states. Military expenditure during the long eighteenth century. Patterns, organisation, and consequences, 1650–1815* (Berlin 2011) 155–179.

Tamaki, Toshiaki, 'The transformation of the Tokugawa military regime in the first half of the eighteenth century in Japan, with special reference to Yoshimune's Reformation' in: Richard Harding and Sergio Solbes, eds., *The contractor state and its implications, 1659–1815* (Las Palmas 2012) 287–308.

Tamanoi, Mariko Asano, *Under the shadow of nationalism. Politics and poetics of rural Japanese women* (Honolulu 1998).

Tang, John P., 'Financial intermediation and late development: the case of Meiji Japan 1868 to 1912', *US Census Bureau. Center for Economic Studies. Paper* No. CES-08-01, 2008.

Tang, John P., 'Public- versus private-led industrialization in Meiji Japan, 1868–1912', U.S. Census Bureau Center for Economic Studies 2008 http://eml.berkeley.edu/~webfac/cromer/e211_sp08/tang.pdf

Tang, John P., 'Technological leadership and late development. Evidence from Meiji Japan, 1868–1912', *Economic History Review* 64, 1 (2011) 99–116. http://www8.gsb.columbia.edu/rtfiles/japan/WP%20278.pdf

Tang, John P., 'Entrepreneurship and Japanese industrialisation in historical perspective', *US Census Bureau, Center for Economic Studies. Discussion Paper 09-30* 2012.

Tang, John P., 'Fukoku Kyohei. Evaluating the impact of public investment in Meiji Japan, 1869–1912', 2011 http://eh.net/eha/wp-content/uploads/2013/11/Tang.pdf

Tang, John P., 'Financial intermediation and late development in Meiji Japan, 1868–1912', *Financial History Review* 20, 2 (2013) 111–135.

Tang, John P., 'Railroad expansion and industrialization: Evidence from Meiji Japan', *The Journal of Economic History* 74, 3 /2014, 863–886.

Tanimoto, Masayuki, 'From 'feudal' lords to local notables. The role of regional society in public goods provision from early modern to modern Japan' in: Tanimoto and Wong, *Public goods provision*, 17–37.

Tanimoto, Masayuki, ed., *The role of tradition in Japan's industrialization. Another path to industrialization* (Oxford 2006).

Tanimoto, Masayuki and R. Bin Wong, eds., *Public goods provision in the early modern economy. Comparative perspectives from Japan, China and Europe* (Oakland 2019).

Tanzi, Vito, and Ludger Schuknecht, *Public spending in the 20th Century: A global perspective* (Cambridge 2000).

Tashiro, Kazui. 'Foreign relations during the Edo period: *sakoku* re-examined', *Journal of Japanese Studies* 8, 2 (1982) 283–306.

Tashiro, Kazui. 'Foreign trade in the Tokugawa period, particularly with Korea' in: Hayami, Saito and Toby, *Emergence of economic society*, 105–118.

Thelen, Kathleen, *How institutions evolve. The political economy of skills in Germany, Britain, the United States and, Japan* (Cambridge 2004).

Thomas, J.E., *Modern Japan. A social history since 1868* (London 1996).

Tipton, F,,, *Modern Japan. A social and political history* (second edition; Abingdon Oxon and New York 2008).

Tipton, Frank B. Jr., 'Government policy and economic development in Germany and Japan. A skeptical re-evaluation', *The Journal of Economic History* 41, 1 (1981) 139–150.

Toby, Ronald P., *State and diplomacy in early modern Japan. Asia in the development of the Tokugawa Bakufu* (Princeton 1984).

Toby, Ronald P., 'Rescuing the nation from history. The state of the state in early modern Japan', *Monumenta Nipponica* 56, 2 (2001) 197–237. A review of Ravina, *Land and lordship* and Roberts, *Mercantilism in a Japanese domain.*

Tokugawa, Tsunenari, *The Edo inheritance* (Tokyo 2009).

Tolliday, Steven, ed., *The economic development of modern Japan, 1868–1945. From the Meiji Restoration to the Second World War.* (Cheltenham etc. 2001). Two Volumes.

Tomlinson, B.R., 'Rural society and agricultural development in Japan, 1870–1920. An overview', *Rural History* 6, 1 (1995) 47–65.

Tonooka, Chika, 'Reverse emulation and the cult of the Japanese efficiency in Edwardian Britain', *Historical Journal*, 60, 1 (2017) 95–119.

Totman, Conrad D., *Politics in the Tokugawa Bakufu, 1600–1843* (Cambridge Mass. 1967).

Totman, Conrad D., *The collapse of the Tokugawa Bakufu, 1862–1868* (Honolulu 1980).

Totman, Conrad D., 'From *sakoku* to *kaikoku*. The transformation of foreign-policy attitudes, 1853–1868', *Monumenta Nipponica* 35, 1 (1980) 1–19.

Totman, Conrad D., *Japan before Perry. A short history* (Berkeley 1981).

Totman, Conrad D., 'Tokugawa peasants: Win, lose, or draw?', *Monumenta Nipponica* 41, 4 (1986) 457–476.

Totman, Conrad D., *The green archipelago. Forestry in preindustrial Japan* (Berkeley 1989).

Totman, Conrad D., *Early modern Japan* (Cambridge 1993).

Totman, Conrad D., *A history of Japan* (Malden and Oxford 2000).

Totman, Conrad D., *Japan. An environmental history* (London 2014).

Trimberger, Ellen K., *Revolution from above. Military bureaucrats and development in Japan, Turkey, Egypt and Peru* (New Brunswick 1988).

Tsuji, Tatsuya, 'Politics in the eighteenth century' in: *Cambridge History of Japan. Vol. 4*, 425–477.

Tsujimoto, Masashi and Yoko Yamasaki, eds., *The history of education in Japan (1600–2000)* (New York 2017).

Tsukahira, Toshio G., *Feudal control in Tokugawa Japan. The sankin kotai system* (Cambridge 1966).

Tsurumi, E. Patricia., *Factory girls. Women in the thread mills of Meiji Japan* (Princeton 1990).

Tsutsui, William M., *Manufacturing ideology. Scientific management in twentieth-century Japan* (Princeton 1998).

Tsutsui, William M., ed., *A companion to Japanese history* (Chichester 2009).

Tsuzuki, Chushichi, *The pursuit of power in modern Japan* (Oxford 2000).

Uchida, Hiroshi, 'Marx's theory of history reappraised' in: Hiroshi Uchida, ed., *Marx for the 21st century* (London and New York 2006) 39–52.

Umegaki, Michio, 'From domain to prefecture' in: Jansen and Rozman, *Japan in transition*, 91–110.

Umegaki, Michio, *After the restoration. The beginning of Japan's modern state* (New York 1988).

Umesao, Tadao, *An ecological view of history: Japanese civilization in the world context* (Melbourne 2003).

Utley, Freda, *Lancashire and the Far East* (London 1931).

Utley, Freda, *Japan's feet of clay* (London 1937).

Vande Walle, Willy, *Een geschiedenis van Japan. Van samurai tot soft power* (Leuven 2007).

Vaporis, Constanine N., 'Post station and assisting villages. Corvée labor and peasant contention', *Monumenta Nipponica* 41, 4 (1986) 377–414.

Vaporis, Constanine N., *Breaking barriers. Travel and the state in early modern Japan* (Cambridge 1994).

Vaporis, Constanine N., *Tour of duty. Samurai, military service in Edo, and the culture of early modern Japan* (Honolulu 2008).

Vaporis, Constanine N., *Voices of early modern Japan. Contemporary accounts of daily life during the age of the Shoguns* (Santa Barbara 2012).

Verschuer, Charlotte von, *Rice, agriculture and the food supply of premodern Japan* (Abingdon, Oxon 2016).

Ville, Simon, 'Transport' in: Floud and Johnson, *Cambridge Economic History of Modern Britain. Volume I*, 295–331.

Vlastos, Stephen, *Peasant protests and uprisings in Tokugawa Japan* (Berkeley and Los Angeles 1986).

Vlastos, Stephen, 'Opposition movements in early Meiji, 1868–1885' in: *Cambridge History of Japan. Vol. 5*, 367–431.

Vlastos, Stephen, 'Tradition past/ present. Culture and modern Japanese history' in: Vlastos, *Mirror of modernity*, 1–16.

Vlastos, Stephen, 'Agrarianism without tradition. The radical critique of pre-war Japanese modernity' in: Vlastos, *Mirror of modernity*, 79–74.

Vlastos, Stephen, ed., *Mirror of modernity. Invented traditions of modern Japan* (Berkeley 1998).

Vogel, Steven K., *Marketcraft. How governments make markets work* (Oxford 2018).

Vries, Jan de, 'Industrious peasants in East and West. Markets, technology and family structure in Japanese and Western European agriculture', *Australian Economic History Review* 51, 2 (2011) 107–119.

Vries, Jan de, 'The industrious revolutions in East and West' in: Austin and Sugihara, *Labour-intensive industrialization*, 65–84.

Vries, Peer, 'Governing growth. A comparative analysis of the role of the state in the rise of the West', *Journal of World History* 13, 1 (2002) 67–138.

Vries, Peer, 'Europe and the rest: Braudel on capitalism' in: Guillaume Garner and Matthias Middell, eds., *Aufbruch in die Weltwirtschaft. Braudel wiedergelesen* (Leipzig 2012) 81–144.

Vries, Peer, 'Does wealth entirely depend on inclusive institutions and pluralist politics? A review of Daron Acemoglu and James A. Robinson, *Why nations fail. The origins of power, prosperity and poverty*', *Tijdschrift voor Sociale en Economische Geschiedenis* 9, 3 (2012) 74–93.

Vries, Peer, *Escaping poverty. The origins of modern economic growth* (Vienna and Göttingen 2013).

Vries, Peer, *State, economy and the Great Divergence. Great Britain and China, 1680s to 1850s* (London 2015).

Vries, Peer, 'States: a subject in global history' in: Catía Antunes and Karwan Fatah-Black, eds., *Explorations in globalization and history* (Abingdon, Oxon and New York 2016) 155–176.

Vries, Peer, 'Economic reasons of state in Qing China: a brief comparative overview' in: Philipp Rössner, ed., *Economic growth and the origins of modern political economy: Economic reasons of state, 1500-2000* (Abingdon Oxon and New York 2016) 204–220.

Vries, Peer, 'What we do and do not know about the Great Divergence at the beginning of 2016', *Historische Mitteilungen der Ranke Gesellschaft*, 28 (2016) 249–297.

Wade, Robert, *Governing the market. Economic theory and the role of government in industrialization. With a new introduction by the author* (Princeton and Oxford 2004; originally 1990).

Wakabayashi, Bob Tadashi, *Anti-foreignism and western learning in early modern Japan. The New Theses of 1825* (Cambridge Mass. 1986).

Wakabayashi, Bob Tadashi, 'In name only. Imperial sovereignty in early modern Japan', *Journal of Japanese Studies* 17, 1 (1991) 25–57.

Wakabayashi, Bob Tadashi, 'Opium, expulsion, sovereignty. China's lessons for Bakumatsu Japan', *Monumenta Nipponica* 47, 1 (1992) 1–25.

Walker, Brett L., *The conquest of Ainu lands. Ecology and culture in Japanese expansion, 1590-1800* (Berkeley 2006).

Walker, Brett L., *A concise history of Japan* (Cambridge 2015).

Walthall, Anne, *Peasant uprisings in Japan. A critical anthology of peasant histories* (Chicago 1991).

Walthall, Anne, *Japan. A cultural, social and political history* (Boston 2006).

Walthall, Anne, and M. William Steele, *Politics and society in Japan's Meiji Restoration* (Boston 2017).

Wang, Yeh-chien, *Land taxation in China, 1750-1911* (Cambridge Mass. 1973).

Ward, R.E., 'Authoritarianism as a factor in Japanese modernization' in: Jason L. Finkle and Richard W. Gable, eds., *Political development and social change* (New York 1968) 478–484.

Ward, R.E., ed., *Political development in modern Japan. Studies in the modernization of Japan* (Princeton 1968).

Waswo, Ann, *Japanese landlords. The decline of a rural elite* (Berkeley and Los Angeles 1977).

Waswo, Ann, 'The transformation of rural society, 1900–1950' in: *Cambridge History of Japan. Vol. 6,* 541–605.

Waswo, Ann, *Modern Japanese society* (Oxford 1996).

Waijenburg, Marlous van, 'Financing the African colonial state. The revenue imperative and forced labour', *Journal of Economic History* 78, 1 (2018) 40–80.

Weiss, Linda, 'War, the state and the origins of the Japanese employment system', *Politics and Society* 21, 3 (1993) 325–354.

Weiss, Linda, and John M. Hobson, *States and economic development. A comparative historical analysis* (Oxford and Cambridge 1995).

Westney, D. Eleanor, *Imitation and innovation. The transfer of Western organizational patterns to Meiji Japan* (Cambridge 1987).

Wigen-Lewis, Kären, *Common losses. Transformations of common land and peasant livelihood in Tokugawa Japan, 1603–1868* (MA Thesis University of California, Berkeley 1985).

Wigen-Lewis, Kären, *The making of a Japanese periphery, 1750–1920* (Berkeley 1995).

Wigen, Kären, Sugimoto Fumiko and Cary Karacas, eds., *Cartographic Japan. A history in maps* (Chicago and London 2016).

Williamson, Jeffrey G., *Trade and poverty. When the Third World fell behind* (Cambridge Mass. and London 2011).

Wilson, Sandra, 'The 'New Paradise': Japanese emigration to Manchuria in the 1930s and 1940s', *The International History Review* 17, 2 (1995) 249–286.

Wilson, Sandra, *The Manchurian crisis and Japanese society* (London 2002).

Wilson, Sandra, 'The discourse of national greatness in Japan, 1890–1919', *Journal of Japanese Studies* 25, 1 (2005) 35–51.

White, James W., *Ikki. Social conflict and political protest in early modern Japan* (Ithaca 1995).

Wittner, David G., *Technology and the culture of progress in Meiji Japan* (Abingdon Oxon 2008).

Wittner, David G., 'From public to private. Technology transfer in Meiji Japan's silk reeling industry', www.worldbhc.org/files/full%20program/A5_B5_WittnerFromPublictoPrivate.pdf

Wolfe, Kathy, 'Hamilton's ghost haunts Washington from Tokyo -- Excerpts from the leaders of the Meiji Restoration', *Executive Intelligence Review,* January, 1992 http://members.tripod.com/american_almanac/mejei.htm.

Woo-Cummings, Meredith, ed., *The developmental state* (Ithaca and London 1999).

Wray, Harry and Hilary Conroy, eds., *Japan examined. Perspectives on modern Japanese history* (Honolulu 1983).

Wray, William D., *Mitsubishi and the NYK, 1870–1914. Business strategy in the Japanese shipping industry* (Cambridge Mass. 1985).

Wrigley, E. A., *Continuity, chance and change. The character of the industrial revolution in England* (Cambridge 1988).

Yamamoto, Hirofumi, ed., *Technological innovation and the development of transportation in Japan* (Tokyo 1993).

Yamamoto, Yuzo, 'Japanese empire and colonial management' in: Nakamura and Odaka, *Economic History of Japan, 1914–1955,* 223–246.

Yamamura, Kozo, 'The increasing poverty of the Samurai in Tokugawa Japan, 1600–1868', *The Journal of Economic History* 31, 2 (1971) 378–406.

Yamamura, Kozo, 'Japan, 1868–1930. A revised view' in: Rondo Cameron, ed., *Banking and economic development* (New York 1972) 168–198.

Yamamura, Kozo, *A study of samurai income and entrepreneurship. Quantitative analyses of economic and social aspects of the samurai in Tokugawa and Meiji Japan* (Cambridge Mass. 1974).

Yamamura, Kozo, 'The Japanese economy, 1911–1930. Concentration, conflicts and crises' in: B.S. Silberman and H.D. Harootunian, eds., *Japan in crisis. Essays in Taisho democracy* (Princeton 1974) 299–328.

Yamamura, Kozo, 'General trading companies in Japan – their origins and growth' in: Patrick, *Japanese industrialization and its social consequences*, 160–199.

Yamamura, Kozo, 'Success ill-gotten? The role of Meiji militarism in Japan's technological progress', *The Journal of Economic History* 37, 1 (1977) 113–135.

Yamamura, Kozo, 'Entrepreneurship, ownership, and management in Japan' in P. Mathias and M.M. Postan, eds., *The Cambridge Economic History of Europe*, Volume 7, 2 chapter 5 (Cambridge 1978) 215–264.

Yamamura, Kozo, 'The Meiji land tax reform and its effects' in: Jansen and Rozman, *Japan in transition*, 382–400.

Yamamura, Kozo, 'From coins to rice. Hypotheses on the Kandaka and Kokudaka systems', *Journal of Japanese Studies* 14, 2 (1988) 341–367.

Yamamura, Kozo, ed., *The economic emergence of Japan* (Cambridge 1997).

Yamasaki, Junichi, 'Railroads, technology adoption and modern economic development. Evidence from Japan'. http://www.iser.osaka-u.ac.jp/library/dp/2017/DP1000.pdf

Yasuba, Yasukichi, 'Anatomy of the debate on Japanese capitalism', *The Journal of Japanese Studies* 2, 1 (1975) 63–82.

Yasuba, Yasukichi, 'Standard of living in Japan before industrialization. From what level did Japan begin? A comment', *The Journal of Economic History* 46, 1 (1986) 217–224.

Yasuba, Yasukichi, 'The Tokugawa legacy. A survey', *The Economic Studies Quarterly* 38, 4 (1987) 290–307.

Yasuba, Yasukichi, 'Did Japan ever suffer from a shortage of natural resources before World War II?', *The Journal of Economic History* 56, 3 (1996) 543–560.

Yasuba, Yasukichi, 'Natural resources in Japanese economic history, 1800–1940'. Website of The Cliometric Society 2010.

Yoda, Yoshiie and Kurt Radtke, *The foundations of Japan's modernization. A comparison with China's path towards modernization* (Leiden 1997).

Yonekura, Seiichiro and Hiroshi Shimuzu, 'Entrepreneurship in pre-World War II Japan: The role and logic of the Zaibatsu' in: David S. Landes, Joel Mokyr and William J. Baumol, eds., *The invention of enterprise. Entrepreneurship from ancient Mesopotamia to modern times* (Princeton 2010) 501–526.

Yoshihara, Kunio, *Japan's economic development* (third edition; Oxford 1994).

Yoshimi, Yoshiaki, *Grassroots fascism. The war experience of the Japanese people* (New York 2015).

Yun-Casalilla, Bartolomé, and Patrick K. O'Brien, with Francisco Comín-Comín, eds., *The rise of fiscal states. A global history, 1500–1914* (Cambridge 2012).

Yuzo, Yamamoto, 'Japanese empire and colonial management' in: Nakamura and Odaka, *The economic history of Japan, 1600–1990. Volume 3, 1914–1955*, 223–246.

Zanden, Jan Luiten van, and others, eds., *How was life? Global well-being since 1820* (OECD Publishing 2014).

Zöllner, Reinhard, *Geschichte Japans. Von 1800 bis zur Gegenwart* (Paderborn 2006).

Index

Page numbers in *italics* refer to figures and tables

Lightning Source UK Ltd.
Milton Keynes UK
UKHW021133270821
389561UK00004B/111